W9-AED-567

WITHDRAWN

THOREAU

as World Traveler

THE ROWSE PORTRAIT OF HENRY DAVID THOREAU
AT THE AGE OF THIRTY-SEVEN, 1854

THOREAU
as World Traveler

JOHN ALDRICH CHRISTIE

Published by
COLUMBIA UNIVERSITY PRESS
with the cooperation of the
AMERICAN GEOGRAPHICAL SOCIETY
New York and London

SALEM COLLEGE LIBRARY
WINSTON-SALEM, N. C

PS
3056
C4

John Aldrich Christie is Professor of English at Vassar College.

This book also appears as Special Publication Number 37 of the American Geographical Society.

Copyright © 1965 Columbia University Press

First printing 1965
Second printing 1966

Library of Congress Catalog Card Number: 65-24586
Printed in the United States of America

Preface

I have tried to introduce the reader to the subject of this book in much the same way that I was introduced to it: through the discovery in the writings of a man who boasted of staying at home all the signs of a global traveler. The discovery came over ten years ago, when I was a considerably younger teacher taking his inevitable sojourn in graduate work, and the first exploration produced a doctoral dissertation. But like those early voyages of "perpetual expectation" the accounts of which Thoreau found so exhilarating, this venture of mine continued to push into new latitudes and longitudes so long as the wind held, and the gusty years between that temporary harboring and this port suggest that the voyage may be only begun.

However uncompleted the route through any writer's reading experience, in this instance the one I took brought me once full circle round, suggesting that the portion of Thoreau's world in which I sailed at least had sphericity and wholeness to it. As the manner and extent of Thoreau's travel reading unfolded, it offered a literal paradox to parallel that figurative one with which Thoreau described his aim in life: to "live at home like a traveler." If my exploration has proved the relationship between these two paradoxes to have been a necessary one for Thoreau and his art, then a study which has these last years seemed at times a delightfully prolonged indulgence may claim for itself some scholarly finish and value. Through a reminder of Thoreau's attitude toward travel, seen for

the first time against the background of the wide-ranging routes
which he traveled and the peculiarly rich resources which they
furnished him, the reader may be able to shift by a bit his vantage
point for viewing this controversial author, the better to appreciate
the convictions which constituted the core of his life and his writings.

Aware as I am of the amorphous term "travel literature," I have
let Thoreau's own demands of the genre define the works to which
I have limited my concern: namely, those narratives whose authors
were travelers in the regions they describe, not simply students or
historians of them. The presence of the traveler and a route have
been requisite. The bibliography of Thoreau's reading in the genre
would have been considerably longer had I included such "texts" of
scientific study as Samuel Morse's *Universal Geography* or Alexander
von Humboldt's *Aspects of Nature*; such "histories" as Thomas
Jefferson's *Notes on the State of Virginia* or Thomas Raffles' *History
of Java*. Relevant as these funds of information were to Thoreau's
knowledge of geography, their contribution differed in kind as well
as in degree from that with which this book is primarily concerned,
as I hope the chapters which follow will make clear. Excluded also
from direct consideration are those numerous accounts of travel
exclusively within the boundaries of New England, accounts which,
it turned out, while modifying none of the conclusions to which my
study came, served less effectively to illustrate them than the narratives which represented Thoreau's vicarious travels in areas where
he never set foot.

Both the subject matter and its durability have brought me into
long and varied indebtednesses. They begin with that to Professor
Clarence Gohdes of Duke University, who in guiding a doctoral
dissertation set a standard for scholarly accuracy which made me as
impatient with careless scholarship as it now makes me tremble for
the shortcomings of my own attempts to do better by Thoreau. No
scholar ever made an error for which someone did not pay the price.
I have tried to keep such costs as low as possible in this book.

Much of my research has depended upon specific editions of
travel books long out of print, and I have been indebted to libraries
and librarians too numerous to include here who have offered me
courteous access to rare or special collections in their custodianship.

I profited from continual use of the special resources of the Sterling Memorial Library of Yale University. But my greatest debt in this area has been to the Librarian and staff of the Vassar College Library, and most particularly to Dorothy Plum, the Bibliographer, for whom no rare edition was too difficult to locate. I was also dependent in my study upon a vast array of unpublished primary material by or relating to Thoreau, manuscripts and books scattered among many libraries. I have been grateful for the opportunity to study Thoreau materials in the Concord Free Public Library, the Abernathy Library of Middlebury College, the Baker Library of Dartmouth College, the Henry E. Huntington Library in California, and the Library of Congress. For extended opportunities to study and for permission to quote from unpublished Thoreau holograph manuscripts I am especially indebted to the Librarian of the New York Public Library and to John D. Gordon, Curator of the Berg Collection, for material in the Henry W. and Albert A. Berg Collection; to the Harvard College Library and to E. L. Nicholes, Curator of the Widener Memorial Rooms, for material in the Harry Elkins Widener Collection, and to W. H. Bond, Librarian of the Houghton Library, for material in that library; to Frederick B. Adams, Jr., Director of the Pierpont Morgan Library, for materials in that collection. Walter Harding and Robert O. Dougan, Librarian of the Huntington Library, have kindly permitted me to quote directly from certain holograph manuscripts in that library when the original has varied from previously published versions.

To Charles B. Hitchcock, Director of the American Geographical Society, I am indebted for making possible a collaboration from which this book has richly benefited. Douglas Waugh, Chief Cartographer of the Society, gave generous attention to the maps for the book. To David Lowenthal, Research Associate of the Society, I owe more than a single debt. Not only did he edit the manuscript for correction of an amateur geographer's errors; he was the first to read an early version of this study some years ago, and has since brought gentle but persistent pressure upon its author to bring it to publication. His continuing interest in its progress, his constructive criticism of its changing shape and expression, and his practical initiative in behalf of its present appearance give me the warmest assurance of the fraternity of the arts and sciences as well as that of seasoned colleagues in the liberal arts. To the editors of the Columbia University Press, and particularly to William Bernhardt, I express my appreciation for a splendid collaboration which at every stage has offered me generous and competent assistance.

Vassar College granted me two leaves of absence, a Faculty Fellowship, and a special summer financial grant, for pursuing my interest in this subject. A number of able and invaluable Vassar students have given me help at one time or another over the last ten years. One in particular, Barbara Culliton, my Academic Assistant at Vassar, contributed unnumbered hours in assisting with the final stages of text and documentation. She well knows how inequitably an expression of thanks weighs in the scale of help she gave me.

To trace thirty-eight years of Thoreau's reading, even in part, meant traveling his routes in one-fourth the time. It has been my family who have paid the cost of my averted interest, and my wife, underwriter and wisest guide, who has taken the whole trip with me, carrying more than her share on every portage. It is my hope that she too was sustained in this case by a faith Thoreau once expressed in the rewards to be derived from imaginative ways:

> If with fancy unfurled
>   You leave your abode,
> You may go round the world
>   By the Old Marlborough Road.

J.A.C.

Vassar College
August, 1965

Contents

Part IV.   The Reward

Illustrations

Maps

PART I

The Paradox

This world is but canvass to our imaginations. I see men with infinite pains endeavoring to realize with their bodies, what I, with at least equal pains, would realize to my imagination.

Thoreau, *A Week on the Concord and Merrimack Rivers*, 1849

᪲ CHAPTER I ᪲

Departure and Return

Methinks I should be content to sit at the backdoor in Concord, under
the poplar tree, henceforth forever.

Thoreau to his mother, August 1, 1843

It is too easy to see Henry David Thoreau "all of a piece." He lends
himself to simplification and caricature, to tag and license, with such
apparent ease that it is difficult to resist the labeling for the product.
We are quite right in expecting no deceit from this writer. But
neither can we presume for long upon his honesty if we read him carefully, for the clichés which wrap like comforters about our critical
gestures are only fair-weather protection. With Thoreau the literal is
but trap for the analogous, the direct for the implied, the simple for
the complex, the fact for the truth. While one need not read round
this man's words, one must certainly read through them; and Thoreau did not make it easy for his readers or his listeners to receive him
fully.

This book is all about one such example of Thoreau's challenge to
his readers. The subject is travel, Thoreau's view and practice of it. It
would seem to be a subject holding scant room for conjecture or correction. Is it a matter of recording Thoreau's own judgment of it?
"Staying at home is the heavenly way." The statement has a simple,
straightforward ring to it—if one misses the overtones of a "stay"
that is at once a "way," or the reverberations of a "home" that is
"heavenly." Does one wish to turn to his own succinct summary of
the traveling he does? "I have traveled a good deal in Concord."
Who would doubt it? And how little does such travel really have to
do with geographical space—if one underestimates the kinds of
"travel" one can do in Concord.

Which is what we have done, of course. There is no gainsaying the
ready help Thoreau himself has given us for taking the most limiting
view of his travels. Few American authors have turned out literary
products which appear more congenial to a provincial reputation. His
capacity for dramatizing his conflict with the prevailing temper of his
day would seem splendidly illustrated by the legacy of a literary canon
intent upon celebrating the regional and insular in a period of unprecedented expansion and universality. Even his conspicuous exploitation of his day's most popular literary genre, the travel book,
appears only a deceitful façade when his "travel" writings are placed
beside those of his contemporaries, where they offer a fascinating
counterpoint to the far-flung ventures which characterized the global
travels of his time.

While Richard Henry Dana, Jr. prepared for publication an account of his voyage on a merchantman around Cape Horn, Thoreau
gathered subject matter for his first travel book by taking a thirteen-
day trip in a homemade dory on the Concord and Merrimack rivers.
Emerson published his travel book on England the same year Thoreau published his account of two years spent on Emerson's woodlot.
Of the remaining pieces published before his death, most of them
"travel" accounts, only one work of Thoreau's records a trip outside
of New England. And the same year that Thoreau spent his week in
Canada with William Ellery Channing, gathering the experiences
and observations which were to be the subject of his "Excursion to
Canada," Commodore M. C. Perry was making a daring voyage to
Japan which was to furnish him material for a five-hundred-page best
seller, and all American eyes were on the Grinnell expedition heading
for the Arctic in search of a lost English explorer. While world travelers pushed as far northwest and southeast as skill could take them,
Thoreau pushed on to Montreal. The year that saw the publication
of Francis Parkman's *The Oregon Trail* found Thoreau making the
first of five trips to Cape Cod, the total mileage of which, if stretched
westward, would have taken him halfway to Oregon but which in
actuality never carried him farther than one hundred and forty miles
from Concord. Thoreau's first trip to the Maine woods appeared in
the *Union Magazine* on the very heels of Melville's two most popular
books, travel tales of adventures in the Marquesas Islands and Tahiti.
The account of Thoreau's second trip was printed in the *Atlantic*

Monthly the same year that an excited reading public was following David Livingstone's voluminous travels in South Africa. Even Thoreau's lectures suggested rambles rather than travels: "A Walk to Wachusett," "A Winter Walk," "Concord River," "Walden," "Walking." In February, 1859, while Melville was lecturing on "The South Seas," Thoreau was lecturing on autumnal tints in New England.

Put as bluntly and as persistently as possible, Thoreau's own affirmations and remonstrances spring out at us from every corner of his writings as if to confirm his provincial predilections. "Why avoid my friends and live among strangers? Why not reside in my native country?" he asks rhetorically in his Journal.[1] To read "of things distant" is to slight those at home. "I would rather watch the motions of the cows in the Concord pasture, than wander to Europe or Asia and watch other motions there, for it is only ourselves we report in either case." [2] Sometimes he put it more fully:

> I am afraid to travel much or to famous places, lest it might completely dissipate my mind. Then I am sure that what we observe at home, if we observe anything, is of more importance than what we observe abroad. The far-fetched is of the least value. What we observe in traveling are to some extent the accidents of the body, but what we observe when sitting at home are, in the same proportion, phenomena of the mind itself.[3]

Scribbled on a single-page fragment among some miscellaneous notes in Thoreau's hand now in the Berg Collection of the New York Public Library is a comment even more rife with excuses:

> A man can hardly travel without diminishing self-respect and independence. . . . He comes home from this excursion too often contented to sit still in any sense for the remainder of his life—instead of seeking and doing—his private and priceless energies all paralyzed and becalmed as it were in the memory of the sights he has seen. Much travel is apt to take all the youth out of one and make his afterlife pathetic. Above all, it requires more money—implying the sacrifice of many years if he has inherited only his manhood.

And again and again we find him congratulating himself upon the possession of those physical features which have limited his travels:

> I cannot but regard it as a kindness in those who have the steering of me that, by the want of pecuniary wealth, I have been nailed down to

this my native region so long and so steadily, and made to study and love this spot of earth more and more. What would signify in comparison a thin and diffused love and knowledge of the whole earth instead, got by wandering? The traveler's lot is but a barren and comfortless condition.[4]

It will pay us to keep in mind the plethora of arguments which Thoreau here marshals for his case, against the time when we shall have occasion to examine more closely his motives for using them. For the moment they may stand as suggestions of a contentment stubborn enough to defy the faith of the most confirmed cosmopolitan.

It is small wonder that Thoreau, viewed in the light which he so assiduously threw on himself, came to be regarded as an archetype of the provincial author. The brief drama of the Walden episode was not the only basis for the popular view of him as Concord's "hermit." For fifty years after his death critics tried to place him in the history of American literature, and a glance at their views shows that they only succeeded in placing him in Concord. "Instead of engineering for all America, he was the captain of a huckleberry party," declared Emerson at his funeral.[5] His strong admirer and champion Thomas Wentworth Higginson wrote: "He is a man of vast digestive power, who, prizing the flavor of whortleberries and wild apples, insists on making these almost his only food. It is amazing to see what nutriment he extracts from them; yet would not, after all, an ampler bill of fare have done better?" [6] Even the *Atlantic Monthly*, loyal to its sons, conceded that Thoreau "has been accused, indeed, of treating Nature herself 'as if she had been brought up in Concord,'—and perhaps there was something narrowing in the persistence with which he clung to the flat plains, swampy meadows, and low hills of the Musketaquid valley." [7] John Burroughs tagged him "the lamb of New England fields and woods," and found that one source of Gilbert White's charm shared by Thoreau's *Walden* was that "these men stayed at home; they made their nests, and took time to brood and hatch." [8] The posthumously published extracts from Thoreau's Journal in the seventies were seen by the *Nation* as having "prime value as the field-notes of a naturalist in the latitude of Concord," [9] while Henry James declared that Thoreau "was worse than provincial—he was parochial." [10] Readers of Thoreau's books in the eighties were reminded that an excellent map of Concord was an indispensable adjunct to his works.[11] And his biographer summed up the century's appraisal in the *Atlantic Monthly* in December, 1900, by announcing, "Thoreau for his part . . . has become the proprietor of the Concord landscape. . . . It is now visited for Thoreau's sake." [12]

Indeed, Concord is still visited for Thoreau's sake. Only the local Recreational Development Commission and the commercial interests have appeared immune to the sacred character of Walden Pond, and Thoreau had some views of his own about the latter. "This village is his monument, covered with suitable inscriptions, by himself," affirmed a friend after his death.[13] It remains his unique monument. Other writers, such as Yeats, have been provoked by Thoreau into celebrating particular spots of earth dear to them; but by comparison with Walden, their plots of sacred ground float off detached and ethereal into realms of the fancy and the heart having little to do with geography. While Thoreau and Walden remain inseparable, the latter for most people as securely rooted in topography as in ideology, it is scarcely surprising that Thoreau is known for having lived and died in Concord.

The biographical facts are not in question. Indeed, inspected more specifically they would seem to confirm posterity's emphasis. During the nineteen years between 1843 and his death in 1862, when Thoreau did almost all his literal "traveling," his travels or "excursions" as he called them, systematically undertaken during the summers or early falls, took him out of New England only three times: once to the Catskills in July and August, 1844, once to Quebec in September of 1850, and once to Minnesota, the last a vain effort to restore his health in 1862 and although of all his excursions the most removed from Concord, one of his least rewarding.[14] Other departures from Concord were frequent, to be sure, but they did not take him far. His lectures took him only spasmodically and briefly away from home, seldom for longer than overnight.[15] Such other trips as he made outside of Massachusetts, for business or sociability, can be counted on the fingers of both hands and are represented by such extremes as Walpole, New Hampshire, and Perth Amboy, New Jersey. By no stretch of concession to the day or the culture can it be claimed that Thoreau saw either his geographical world or indeed his own country at firsthand. In comparison with the travels of such relatively provincial American authors as Bryant and Whittier, or with those of such fellow Concord residents as Channing, Emerson, Alcott, and Hawthorne, the radius of Thoreau's firsthand travel is microscopic. In contrast with a Cooper or an Irving or a Melville, he can scarcely be said to have left home at all. Even though Whitman's "Passage to India" was but a metaphysical trip, Whitman himself was a well-traveled man by contrast with Thoreau.

It would pay us to look even more closely and fully at a representative segment of Thoreau's biography for a moment, to take more careful measure of attitude and motivation as they worked their alchemy upon the facts of a young man's departure and return. For depart from Concord Henry Thoreau did, at one crucial moment in his life with a seriousness of intent inevitably muted by the later record of such consistent local preference. Moreover, this early experience offers an essential preface to that familiar pattern of life which all literary history of Thoreau has accentuated.

On Saturday, May 6, 1843, a twenty-five-year-old Thoreau left home and Concord to seek his fortunes elsewhere. His preparations had been conspicuously lengthy and definitive. His destination, the home of Emerson's brother on Staten Island, had been contrived by his friends to provide a temporary steppingstone for his stride into the greater world. Ahead lay prospects of professional literary fulfillment and reward, the cultural resources of the worldly milieu of a great city, with its museums and galleries, its lectures and public events, for the fresh adventurer and writer, new friends, new contexts, at once a new window on the world.

Twice before in his young life Thoreau had considered leaving Concord with a view to finding his place and making his living elsewhere. Eight years earlier, between college terms at Harvard, he had taught with Orestes Brownson for six weeks in Canton, Massachusetts. But his temporary return to Cambridge brought him thence to Concord. Three years later, just out of college and standing on a more apparent threshold, he had written to his older brother John who was then teaching in Taunton:

> I have a proposal to make. Suppose by the time you are released we should start in company for the West, and there establish a school

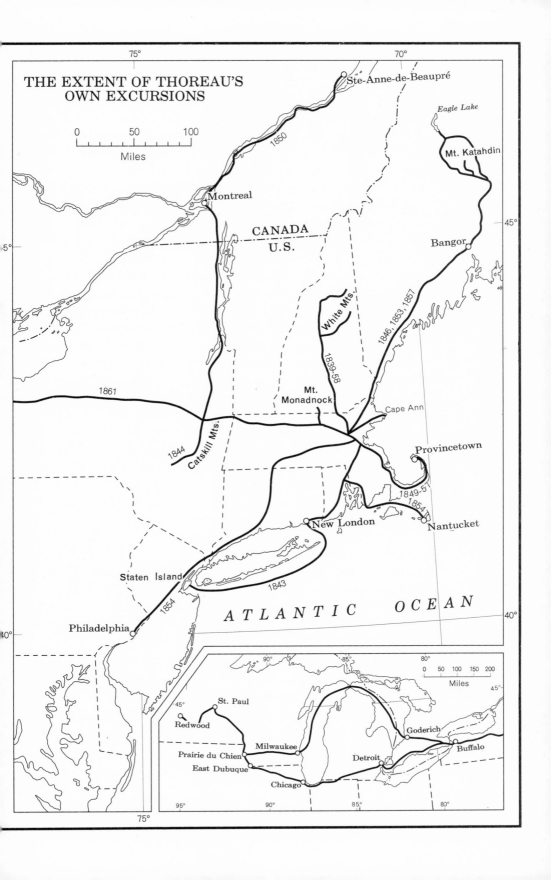

THE EXTENT OF THOREAU'S OWN EXCURSIONS

0   50   100
Miles

Ste-Anne-de-Beaupré

Eagle Lake

1850

Mt. Katahdin

Montreal

CANADA
U.S.

Bangor

White Mts.

1846, 1853, 1857

1839-58

Mt.
Monadnock

Cape Ann

1861

Provincetown

1844

Catskill Mts.

1849-51

1854

New London

Nantucket

Staten Island

1843

1854

Philadelphia

ATLANTIC OCEAN

St. Paul

Redwood

Goderich

Milwaukee

Buffalo

Prairie du Chien

Detroit

East Dubuque

Chicago

jointly, or procure ourselves separate situations. . . . Go I must, at all events. . . . I wish you would write soon about this. It is high season to start. The canals are open, and travel comparatively cheap. I think I can borrow the cash in this town. There's nothing like trying.[16]

The plan was taken seriously by all the Thoreau family, as Miss Prudence Ward, then staying at the Thoreaus' rooming house, indicated in her letters to her relatives at the time.[17] In the end it was abandoned, however, and Thoreau attempted a less adventurous remove from Concord, going to Maine "to look for a school," but without success.

It was now five years since his last abortive attempt at departure, and changes which had since affected Thoreau's life made this present move considerably more crucial for him. Except for such intimacy as he could enjoy with his own family or allow himself with Lidian Emerson, he was more alone than he had ever been. A young man who yearned for intimacy saw himself increasingly deprived of intimates. It had now been a year and a half since his brother John's sudden death by lockjaw, and the close companionship of their last voyage together was only for vivid memory, stored away for safekeeping in Thoreau's Journal. The present tutoring job offered him by William Emerson was no longer end but means and seems to have held no particular relish for Thoreau. Unlike the young teacher at Canton who had shown an interest in pedagogy, or the fresh college graduate who was able to anticipate a career in teaching, this Thoreau confided to Emerson upon arriving at his new home:

> I do not feel myself especially serviceable to the good people with whom I live, except as inflictions are sanctified to the righteous. And so too, must I serve the boy. I can look to the Latin and mathematics sharply, and for the rest behave myself. But I cannot be in his neighborhood as an Educator, of course, but as the hawks fly over his head. I am not attracted toward him but as to youth generally. He shall frequent me, however, as much as he can, and I'll be I.[18]

All evidence indicates that Thoreau was now looking to different talents and for different nourishment. His desires, no matter how cryptically exposed, were pretty much those recognized by his close friends: a craving for new and enriching experience, of an amplitude healthy for a writer; the need for greater personal independence, both intellectually and materially; and not least, a Yankee's curiosity about that "knowledge of the world" with which the peoples and environs of a greater national metropolis (as New York was fast becoming) tempt the uninitiated.

Thoreau's plans to leave Concord were not momentous to him alone. They were commented upon by most of his acquaintances and observed with silent interest by many a Concord resident. Emerson could sail for England, Alcott spend most of his time out of town, Channing move in and out, and Margaret Fuller appear constantly in transit, but Thoreau was already regarded as a fixture of the place. Now rumor, his own preparations, and the expectations of his closest friends indicated that he was, at last, "leaving home." The arrangements for the Staten Island position had been confirmed in February, an advance payment for his services made to Thoreau in March, and the date for his departure, after several postponements on Thoreau's part, finally set for the first of May. Those closest to Thoreau had had ample opportunity to reflect upon the import of his move.

His immediate family, increasingly disturbed by uncertainties regarding his life's plans, hoped that Concord would indeed "conquer New York" (as Thoreau had suggested to Emerson it might) and that Henry would find there proper recognition of his literary talents. They were to be forgiven their desire to see him returning to Concord just as soon as possible; it was characteristic of their faith in him that they hoped he would return an appreciated and remunerated author almost as strongly as they hoped he would return. Outwardly they displayed an attitude of optimistic resignation, counting upon this "sojourn" to appease the yearnings they half sensed in his moods.

Emerson, who had arranged the departure, was less naïve about the prospects of quick literary achievements. He certainly did not look upon the departure as a "sojourn." He hoped that Thoreau could be launched upon a more congenial career of partial self-support by attracting the attention of good editors, and to this end he had done his best to offer him open doors to influential friends in the city. He also felt that his young friend could profit from exposure to a more cosmopolitan life and culture than Concord afforded. He saw Thoreau searching for a writer's experience and opportunities, and the

SALEM COLLEGE LIBRARY
WINSTON-SALEM, N. C.

"great things" which he now expected from him suggested the need for emancipation from the Thoreau rooming house as well as from the Emerson garret. He viewed this departure of his friend as a first, portentous step on a route which could lead far from Concord, an attitude reflected in his first letter to Thoreau after the latter's arrival at Staten Island: "I am sure that you are under sacred protection if I should not hear from you for years. Yet I shall wish to know what befalls you on your way." And it was Emerson who reported to Thoreau the typical view of his departure, voiced by their mutual friend Ellery Channing: "He remembers you with great faith and hope, thinks you ought not to see Concord again these ten years, that you ought to grind up fifty Concords in your mill." [19]

Hawthorne too expressed his views on Thoreau's plans, during a leisurely talk with Thoreau at the Old Manse on an April afternoon. Deserted by his Sophia, who had left for a visit with relatives in Boston, Hawthorne had been saved from the stickier perils of journalizing his moods of ennui and loneliness by a call from Thoreau, one which Hawthorne, the better for mood and subject matter, summarized in his journal as soon as Thoreau left.

> I was interrupted by a visit from Mr. Thoreau, who came to return a book, and to announce his purpose of going to reside at Staten Island as a private tutor in the family of Mr. Emerson's brother. We had some conversation upon this matter, and upon the spiritual advantages of change of place, and upon the *Dial*, and upon Mr. Alcott, and other kindred and concatenated subjects. I am glad, on Mr. Thoreau's own account, that he is going away; as he is physically out of health, and, morally and intellectually, seems not to have found exactly his guiding clue; and in all these respects, he may be benefitted by his removal;— also, it is one step towards a circumstantial position in the world. On my account, I should like to have him remain; he is one of the few persons, I think, with whom to hold intercourse is like hearing the wind among the boughs of a forest-tree; and with all this wild freedom, there is high and classic cultivation in him too.[20]

The compatibility between the two men to which this session attests did not rest principally upon the fact that both were writers. Hawthorne at thirty-eight was a recognized author of two editions of short stories, while Thoreau at twenty-five was unknown outside of Concord, his only publications a few essays in the privileged pages of the *Dial*. Although on the threshold of a move designed to develop his literary career, Thoreau showed no interest in Hawthorne's fiction. He was of course aware of Hawthorne's long experience in periodical publication and more specifically of his friendship with John O' Sullivan, the editor of the *Democratic Review*, whom Thoreau had met at the Hawthornes' in January and on whom he was now counting for assistance in New York. But this April call was obviously no visit to exploit advantageous "contacts" in the literary world, any more than were the compatibilities which provoked and sustained it rooted in matters of practical advantages for either man. The bonds which Thoreau enjoyed with people were not features of distinction for the market place. He was invariably drawn to less conspicuous traits of character, those hidden attitudes of mind and heart lying in the nooks and corners of a person's nature or personal history, often nuances of taste or temperament which even in oneself come into focus only from another's peculiar illumination of them. This seems to have been the case with Thoreau and Hawthorne. Their empathy for one another as individuals had little to draw on other than those secret wellsprings of desire apt to honeycomb reserved and withdrawn natures. One senses the force of this same extracting influence on Hawthorne from Melville's devotion a few years hence, as indeed one can of Emerson's upon this young Thoreau. For the brief companionship of Hawthorne and Thoreau one must look to intimate sympathies, even if the identification of them by either man remained no more than implicit.

We could say it was as seaman's grandson to sea captain's son that the two found common ground with least strain. Thoreau had sealed his friendship with Hawthorne the previous summer by selling him his boat the *Musketaquid*, emblem of his own most significant and extensive "voyage" (up the Concord and Merrimack rivers); and by all evidence Hawthorne appears to have enjoyed his companion-voyager as much as his vessel.[21] This newly domesticated Hawthorne who had just settled down in Concord to try married life (even while his younger neighbor was preparing to break domestic ties and venture "abroad") was still only a step away from the young Hawthorne of Salem who shadowed the town haunts of a sea-captain father lost at sea, spending his afternoons listening to sea yarns in the taverns and his evenings in his garret reading travel books. We can assume that talk of travel filled in much of the discussion between the two friends that April afternoon, even as we can presume that Hawthorne's reference to the conversation "upon the spiritual advantages of change of place" affirmed Thoreau's view as well as his own. We can be certain that Hawthorne, genuinely concerned for his young friend's welfare, put forth his own opinions on the subject. And we know what his attitude was toward travel and change of place. In 1861, when he thought himself (as others now thought Thoreau) settled too firmly in Concord, Hawthorne wrote to his seafaring friend Horatio Bridge:

> The worst of it is that I must give up all thought of drifting about the world any more; and try to make myself at home in one dull spot. It is rather odd, that, with all my tendency to stick in one place, I get great delight in frequent change; so that, in this point of view, I had better not have burdened myself with taking a house on my back. Such change of quarters as makes up the life of you Naval men might have suited me.[22]

It was not a point of view with which Thoreau was at all unsympathetic even as early as 1843, as we shall see. We are alerted by the familiar ring of Hawthorne's second sentence and reminded that its echo occurs in the pages of *Walden*.[23] It is interesting to note that, even as Thoreau proceeded to test the theory of the "spiritual advantages" which Hawthorne pressed upon him, Hawthorne himself proceeded to share vicariously his friend Bridge's last voyage (this one to Africa) and to instruct his older friend in the art of travel writing.[24] Both Hawthorne and Thoreau could claim as their inheritance a feel for the voyage and the venture, and it is not surprising that Thoreau, on the eve of testing his, should turn for talk of change of place to this quiet neighbor.

One month after his visit with Hawthorne, Thoreau left Concord. So vacillating was he about his actual moment of departure that few of his biographers have managed to identify the date correctly.[25] A letter in April from Emerson to his brother William forecast May 1, but biographers have proved more precipitous than Thoreau and less accurate than Emerson, who recorded in his journal for May 7, "Yesterday went our brave youth, Henry Thoreau, into the great city." As

Thoreau himself faithfully reported to his family, he arrived at Staten Island on Sunday morning, May 7, having left Concord the day before for New London, where he took the boat for the Island.[26] On the sixth of May, then, he was off, armed with letters of recommendation to Emerson's friends, his music box,[27] and a new inkstand and steel pen from his Concord neighbor Elizabeth Hoar, who had written in her note to him, "I am unwilling to let you go away without telling you that I, among your friends, shall miss you much, and follow you with remembrance and all wishes and confidence." [28]

The history of Thoreau's Staten Island venture is brief but significant. Six months later he was back in Concord, this time for good. These few months away proved to be his last long absence from home. His decisions to return for the Thanksgiving holiday, and then to accept Emerson's request for a November Lyceum lecture while he was home, were clear cracks in the resolve. His subsequent return to New York was scarcely even a gesture, lasting at most for only a week, apparently no longer than was necessary for clearing up all commitments. From the moment of his final return home in early December, he was rooted solidly in Concord, and never again did he show any serious inclination to change this feature of his destiny. To the reader of his nostalgic letters to his family and the Emersons during the six months away, and of the unpublished Journal which he kept scantily during the period, it seems probable that such a destiny was already set for him from his first pang of homesickness on the morning of May 7 as his ship "curtseyed up to a wharf just the other side of their Castle Garden" and he self-consciously declared himself an outlander among foreigners, "very incurious about them and their city." [29]

Exactly how hopeful Thoreau himself was of this experience we shall probably never know. As to El Dorado, "that is far off yet," he reminded his family.[30] He was painfully conscious of effort and obligation. "I must not know anything about my condition and relations here till what is not permanent is worn off. I have not subsided," he cautioned himself in a letter. "Give me time enough, and I may like it. All my inner man heretofore has been a Concord impression; and here come these Sandy Hook and Coney Island breakers to meet and modify the former." [31] But in spite of all fair play and genuine effort, this exposure to "foreign" influences never really "took." Rather than forging new pieces from the experiences of his new environment, Thoreau turned back in the midst of a Staten Island summer to work upon an account of a winter's walk in Concord. He confessed on May 23 to Emerson: "I have had no later experiences yet. You must not count much upon what I can do or learn in New York. . . . Everything there disappoints me but the crowd; rather, I was disappointed with the rest before I came." [32] He was constantly aware of "the roar of the sea and the hum of the city" and left no doubt as to which he preferred. After an initial bout of illness, he took himself to the beach, where "you only remember New York occasionally," or climbed the hills overlooking the Atlantic from which he could see "more than thirty vessels going to sea" but where his thoughts, refusing to follow, turned instead to Concord and the cherished friend whose letter he had brought to that solitary spot to read. [33] Later, on home soil, he was to renew these experiences quite differently; in his first book, written in the years immediately following his return to Concord, he could give such scenes their full measure of appeal: "From an old ruined fortress on Staten Island I have loved to watch all day some vessel whose name I had read through the telegraph glass, when she first came upon the coast and her hull heaved up and glistered in the sun." [34] But now the view was less vivid than another which lay fair in the mind's eye. "Have you had the annual berrying party?" he inquired of Lidian Emerson. To Emerson he exclaimed: "What are the cities of Asia? . . . Staying at home is the heavenly way." [35] His letters home were filled with inquiries regarding friends.

His tie with Concord transcended that of personal friendships, of course. His yearning for new knowledge could not uproot the nourishing sense of belonging and an intense feeling for the familiar and the already intimately known. He evaded the core of his feelings when he spoke in his letters of missing the people in Concord; it was their context that mattered. It was the character of Concord as a place—the features of its landscape, the smell and sounds of its days and nights, its secret recesses and its local landmarks, its rivers and streets and fields, even that horizon which could only be seen from its pastures or the shores of its ponds, these and many more specific visions of its face, all of them thoroughly familiar from a cultivated intimacy—that made this geographical spot for young Thoreau "still a cynosure to my eyes," one which, he now confessed, he found hard to attach, even in imagination, to the rest of the globe. He registered a growing sense of panic, a loss of touch with the pole-center of his habits, an inability to distinguish hub from spokes.

Yet it was not simply a matter of place either, and in the same breath with which he labeled Concord a "cynosure" Thoreau added, "Places are strangely indifferent to me." [36] In the particular sense in which a good Transcendentalist meant it, the statement was an honest one. We need only be reminded of Emerson's assertion in "Self-Reliance" that "our first journeys discover to us the indifference of places." A place was but a symbol of transcendental reality, for the head and heart to interpret. Concord had become Thoreau's particular means of linking the concrete and the abstract, the real and the ideal, matter and spirit. The concrete realities of this particular place he had tested on his pulse; from them emanated philosophical principles which had already begun to fulfill themselves for him in that "total act" of living described by Emerson. For Thoreau it was enough that Concord should be the core to his life to the extent that it furnished him the sources of belief. In *Walden* he could describe how a personal renascence made indifferent all times and places, but an experience which finally transcended geography was first fed by it, as his very title made clear.[37] The role which Concord's inhabitants played in such a context had little to do with how they felt about Thoreau, indeed if they felt about him at all, although Thoreau flattered himself that they did. In a letter written in July to Emerson he gave himself away honestly. Not only latitudes and longitudes colored his nostalgia; time joined space and helped to fix the features of Concord in an imaginary history:

> In imagination I see you pilgrims taking your way by the red lodge and the cabin of the brave farmer man, so youthful and hale, to the still cheerful woods. And Hawthorne too, I remember as one with whom I sauntered, in old heroic times, along the banks of the Scamander, amid the ruins of chariots and heroes. Tell him not to desert, even after the tenth year. . . .
>
> And Elizabeth Hoar, my brave townswoman, to be sung of poets,— if I may speak of her whom I do not know. Tell Mrs. Brown I do not forget her, going her way under the stars through this chilly world. . . .

And least of all are forgotten those walks in the woods in the ancient days.[38]

No matter how nostalgic he was for the familiar intimacy of Concord, however, nor how unchallenged by his present "foreign" vantage point, Thoreau did not refuse to look about him. He wrote to his father and mother four days after his arrival:

> I have already run over no small part of the island, to the highest hill, and some way along the shore. From the hill directly behind the house I can see New York, Brooklyn, Long Island, the Narrows, through which vessels bound to and from all parts of the world chiefly pass. . . . From the pinnacle of one Madame Grime's house, the other night at sunset, I could see almost round the island. Far in the horizon there was a fleet of sloops bound up the Hudson which seemed to be going over the edge of the earth; and in view of these trading ships commerce seems quite imposing.[39]

He visited telegraph stations, Sailors' Snug Harbor, the Seaman's Retreat, "Old Elm Trees, where the Huguenots landed," Bretton's Mills, and all the villages on the Island. He found himself well situated to observe the western movement from the Old World, sixteen hundred immigrants arriving each day at the quarantine ground while their vessels underwent purification. He saw the steamship *Great Western*, the Croton waterworks, and the picture gallery of the National Academy of Design. He met Horace Greeley, Edward Palmer, and Henry James, Sr. in New York. His visits to museums provoked violent reactions against their preserved death and "dried histories." [40] He watched a canoe race on the Hudson (although all was lost to view "as is everything here in the mob"). He crossed the bay "twenty or thirty times," "read a good deal," and was by his own admission "pretty well known in the libraries of New York." And he canvassed the periodicals, one after the other, for congenial and remunerative outlets for his writings. He was constantly seeing people, so many from day to day in fact that he came to have less respect for flesh and bones, and wondered if it did not exert a bad influence on children to see so many human beings at once, "mere herds of men." [41]

When all is said, however, the rewards proved meager compared with the riches culled from Concord experiences. And contempora-

A VIEW OF THE NARROWS FROM STATEN ISLAND

"From the hill directly behind the house I can see . . . the
Narrows, through which vessels bound to and from all parts
of the world chiefly pass."

neous with the sparse accounts of the eye were fragmentary indices in
his Journal to a truer account which the heart was rendering:

> Monday 24th [September]. Who can see these cities and say that
> there is any life in them? I walked through New York yesterday—and
> met with no real and living person.
>
> Thursday 27th. How much more wretched could the world of men
> be if there was the same formality and reserve between him and his
> intercourse with nature that there is in human society.
>
> Perhaps I may say that I have never had a deeper and more mem-
> orable experience of life—its great serenity, than when listening to
> the thrill of a tree-sparrow among the huckleberry bushes after a
> shower. It is a communication to which a man must attend in solitude
> and silence, and may never be able to tell his brothers.
>
> Friday 29th [28th?]. I am winding up my music box, and as I pause,
> meanwhile the strains burst forth like a pent up fountain. . . .
> [Music] awakens and colors my memories.[42]

The greater world which Emerson had sent him forth to meet, Thoreau could not really take the measure of, standing as he was on for-

eign soil remote from his particular cynosure. Unable in this way to attach Concord to the rest of the globe, he returned to his "poplar tree" at the backdoor in Concord, and to that central vantage point which he never again deserted.

The fact of Thoreau's decision and subsequent practice can not be questioned. The trouble starts when the facts are used as leverage for erecting a superstructure of supposition and syllogism relating to the circumference of Thoreau's horizon—which is precisely the use to which these particular facts are usually put. It is too tempting to assume that Concord supplied Thoreau all his resources as well as his inspiration, furnished him the view as well as the vantage point. It is habit now to celebrate Thoreau for the concentration of his geographical knowledge rather than for its range, just as it is critically fashionable to stress the depth of Thoreau's insight as substitute for a breadth of acquaintance. A critical appraisal which rationalizes Thoreau's inspection of minutiae is very apt to have its premise embedded in the "fact" of his geographical provincialism. The first object of these pages must be to upset that "fact." But an approach which is by now assumed uncontestable has a strong presumptive claim, even if that is all it has; which requires that we proceed to contradict it with care and deliberateness. The conclusions toward which we shall work, then, must have this value at least: that they rest not upon preconceived notions but upon factual evidence by which any conclusions we shall draw can be tested. Let us look first at the evidence, before we seek common ground on a new premise and a fresh view of this Concord recluse. The delight is often as much in the search as in the findings, and I would cheat the reader as well as myself if I did not share some of the stages of that search.

৺ CHAPTER II ৶

The Substitute Route

The biography of a man who has spent his days in a library, may be as interesting as the Penninsula Campaigns. . . . To my mind he travels as far when he takes a book from the shelf as when he went to the barrows of Asia.

Journal, November 9, 1840

To emphasize the inevitability of the view of Thoreau as a confirmed provincial is not to demonstrate the soundness of such a view. Let us permit ourselves a resource of the Transcendentialists for a moment, one of those trying observations that seem intent upon squeezing the truth through incompatibilities and contradictions. One of the best means of steadying our view of Thoreau at this point is by laying firm hold of a paradox, one which any reader of Thoreau can confirm for himself. Open the pages of these "local" travel accounts of Thoreau's which on the surface seem to reflect his insularity, and you are met with a startling global familiarity. For here are references and allusions to every portion of the world. A list of the geographical names alone reads like an index of an atlas, references covering the four quarters of the world, from Arctic to Antarctic, the Caribbean archipelago to Ceylon; they range from Tierra del Fuego to Greenland, from the East Indies to the West. Colombia, Peru, the Congo and Guinea, Syria, Persia, and Japan—the names spread across the map in any direction one chooses. In addition to references to every major continent, there appear comments pertaining to the seven seas and a galaxy of islands stretching from Norfolk in the Pacific to the Canaries in the Atlantic. Nor are the references confined to the obvious geographical familiarities of the schoolboy. Thoreau refers easily to such places as Dahomey, Hodeida, Kamchatka, Lokoja, Murzuk, Tadoussac, and Valdivia, such rivers as the Arabis, Marañón, and Moselle, such lakes as Koko Nor, Ngami, and Van, and to hundreds of other unusual and remote nooks of the world. At first glance his geographical acquaintance seems almost esoteric.

But more important than the mere number of geographical references scattered throughout his writings, impressive as this number is,[1] is the suggestion of intimate familiarity with foreign places which these references usually convey. Thoreau is insulted when told at a menagerie that the hyena comes from South America. He knows that a kudu is an antelope and that the springbok is another name for the gnu. He can describe in detail the Spanish coasts as seen from the Mediterranean or the trip overland from the Brenner Pass to Verona. He knows how horses are corralled in Buenos Aires, how the Egyptians cultivate hatching eggs, how the women of Malamocco sing to their fisherman husbands at sea. He seems as familiar with the breaking up of winter in Labrador as he is with spring in the Louisiana bayous. He knows that in Hindustan one can freeze ice on summer nights. He describes a stretch of Concord pasture in winter as it reflects the snowy details of a pass through the Wind River Range. He knows that pearls come from Coromandel, a sweet gum from Senegal, and an opium drug from the Kát tree on Mount Sabir in Arabia. His familiarity extends with equal ease and preciseness to the customs of the Eskimos, the Yezidis, the Tierra del Fuegans, the Montrosideri of Africa, the Pawnees, the Chinese, the Fiji Islanders. He is acquainted with the furniture of the Arabs, the fortifications of the East Indians, the routine of the sealers of the South Pacific, the local superstitions of the villages of Brittany and Ireland, the dress of the Polynesians, and the diet of the Hottentots. From a man who never really put to sea come facile references to equinoctial gales, coral reefs, reefs knots, spritsails, and "constant trades."[2]

Fascinating as it is to cull such illustrations from Thoreau's pages, the process seems endless, and one soon becomes curious about the sources for this amazing geographical versatility. The evidence suggests a remarkably well-traveled man. In the case of Thoreau, we can only conclude that this globe-trotter is traveling on the feet of others rather than on his own, and that the vast familiarity which he shows is entirely secondhand, derived from travels imaginary over routes unmistakably real. And so our search is on.

Personal names are often linked significantly with some piece of geographical information in Thoreau's pages: Parry, for instance, with polar bears, the French traveler Botta with Jidda and Arabs, John MacTaggard with the Columbia River, M. Huc with the Mongol Tartars, Sleeman with India, Kane with icebergs, Ferris with Utah. Sometimes proper names are embedded in mere fragments of texts: "those Arnolds of the wilderness"; "Josselyn the voyager"; "Forbes says that the guides who crossed the Alps with him lost the skin of their faces." Here emerge the clues to the owners of those feet upon which Thoreau is traveling and of the eyes with which he sees. These are the names of travelers the globe over whose adventurous journeys supplied the public of Thoreau's day with an inexhaustible array of popular literature.

In his Journal Thoreau often acknowledges his sources directly and fully. The entry for December 30, 1850, for example, opens: "In R. Gordon-Cumming's 'Hunter's life in South Africa,' I find an account of the honey-bird, which will lead a person to a wild bee's nest, and having got its share of the spoil will sometimes lead to a second (Vol. I, page 49)"; the entry continues to record chronologically from Thoreau's reading a veritable hodgepodge of information from Gordon-Cumming's book through page 106 of the first volume. True to Channing's claim, Thoreau seems to be reading with pen in hand. On June 8, 1851, we find him summarizing in the Journal two and a half pages of material from "F. A. Michaux's (i.e. the younger Michaux's) 'voyage a l'ouest des Monts Alleghanys, 1802,' printed at Paris, 1808." Three days later begin the extensive notes from "Charles Darwin's 'Voyage of a Naturalist round the world,' commenced in 1831." On April 28 of 1852 he opens his entry with the explanation: "I scarcely know why I am so excited when, in Huc's book, I read of the country of the Mongol Tartar as the 'Land of Grass,' but I am, as much as if I were a cow"; in July of the same year he quotes Wafer on the Indians of Darien and refers to Drake's *Collection of Voyages*. In December, 1853, he refers to his reading of Austen Layard's discoveries and travels, and in June, 1854, he quotes from "Herndon, in his 'Exploration of the Amazon.'" On October

18, 1855, he reflects upon an evening spent reading "Howitt's account
of the Australian gold-diggers." Journal entries between December 19
and 29 of 1856 are rife with references to the arctic region where
Thoreau was apparently determined to experience a winter to outdo
Concord's, as he read Elisha Kane's *Arctic Exploration*. Even in December of 1860 he was still acknowledging such specific geographical
sources as Richard Burton's *Lake Regions of Central Africa*.

It is apparent from these continual references in his Journal that
Thoreau was enjoying a well-indulged habit. As he confessed in 1856,
the "travel book" shared a significant place beside his standard fare of
poetry and philosophy. He painted a pleasant winter evening scene
for December 9: "Now for a merry fire, some old poet's pages, or else
serene philosophy, or even a healthy book of travels, to last far into
the night." Only a year before his death, a letter to a friend reflected
the honors which his solid interest in the classical writers and in texts
on natural science shared with the travel book: "I also read the *New
York Tribune*: but then, I am reading Herodotus and Strabo, and
Blodget's 'Climatology,' and 'Six Years in the Desert of North America' as hard as I can to counterbalance it." [3] It was a day when travelers' accounts were enjoying unprecedented popularity. In the short
period during which Thoreau was assisting Emerson in editing the
Dial, that relatively unpopular periodical printed accounts of the
Creoles in the West Indies, a discovery in the Nubian pyramids of
Egypt, the exploring expedition of Captain Wilkes to the Antarctic
and the Oregon Territory, travels in Spain, and voyages to
Puerto Rico and Jamaica. It is not only Thoreau who can surprise us
by showing an avid interest in a genre so gauged to the public taste.

The fact that Thoreau read and enjoyed travel books is clear to any
careful reader of his published Journal. Less apparent but also clear
when reconstructed is the evidence in his writings outlining for us his
manner of indulging in this particular habit. To piece together the
picture of an author's reading practice from his writing is apt to be a
difficult matter under any circumstances. To do so from the complex
welter of written records (both published and unpublished) which
Henry Thoreau amassed during his lifetime will require us to concentrate like scholarly detectives upon the faint clues and indirections

within these writings. If the footnotes seem to have moved for a while into the body of the text, it will be reminder again that in many instances the routes through Thoreau's record expose as much about his practice as do the conclusions to which they lead.

A first clue to his practice appears in his Journal. His reading in the travel genre seems to have been self-perpetuating. Like Coleridge, quick to pick up cross-references in his reading, he was apparently sent frequently from one traveler's account to another's. It was characteristic of travel books to represent an inevitable inbreeding. They often covered the same territory, and the resources offered by a predecessor's account of the route, a route in most cases still unknown to most readers, tempted some authors to rely more upon others' experiences than their own. Sometimes the practice was reversed, and a writer developed his own observations with an uninhibited flair for fancy and originality no matter how incompatible they might be with previous accounts; it was, after all, simply a case of one traveler's word against another's. To derive reliable guidance from the reading of travel accounts, a reader needed to practice discrimination and skill. As we might have expected, this Thoreau seems to have done. While apparently following up many references to further travel works, he did so only upon the recommendation of writers whose knowledge and performance he thought he could trust.

His note-taking from Darwin's *Voyage of a Naturalist round the World* in his Journal for 1851 illustrates his practice. Darwin he trusted; as we shall see later, he depended upon him for much more than mere geographical information, attesting to the respect in which he held him as a scientist, observer, and philosopher. Thus we find him paying particular attention to Darwin's references to other travelers' accounts. Thoreau interrupts his note-taking from the *Voyage* frequently to remind himself "vide Kotzebue" or "vide Voyages Round the World Since Cook," or to note "I should like to read Azara's voyages," "Would like to see Sir Francis Head's travels in South America—Pampas perhaps," or "Darwin refers to Hearne's Journey, p. 383, for. . . ." It is interesting to note that of the nineteen different travel works referred to by Darwin in the *Voyage*, Thoreau read nine, and all but one after reading Darwin.[4] And just as Darwin had referred to such travelers as Hearne, Head, Back, Park, Lewis and Clark, Buffon, Humboldt, and Tschudi, all of whom Thoreau went on to read, so John Richardson, in his *Arctic Searching Expedition*, an equally reliable travel book which Thoreau owned, referred to such fellow explorers in the north as Wrangel, Cook, McKenney, and Schoolcraft, all of whom Thoreau also read.[5] The flyleaf of Richardson's book, like so many travel editions, added a list of "Fresh Books of Travel and Adventure" with a brief description of the contents of each. Walter Colton's *Three Years in California*, which Thoreau read in 1850, recommended Dana, Fremont, and Wilkes as good sources of pre-gold-rush pictures of California, and Thoreau proceeded to read all three. While this Journal evidence must stand as circumstantial, it is enough to remind us how easily Thoreau's reading of travel books could become a self-stoking process.

The six thousand pages of Thoreau's Journal are a crucial source of evidence for any study of Thoreau's reading. They span the longest stretch of his life covered by him in any single record, from the age of twenty and his graduation from Harvard in 1837 to five months before his death. Not yet, however, has sufficiently scholarly study been made of the processes by which Thoreau constructed this massive twenty-five-year record.[6] His own description of it proves only half accurate: "It is always a chance scrawl, and commemorates some accident,—as great as earthquake or eclipse. Like the sere leaves in yonder vase, these have been gathered far and wide. Upland and lowland, forest and field have been ransacked."[7] The Journal is indeed a vast granary of gathered experiences—experiences as cosmic as earthquakes or eclipses—but it is no product of chance scrawls. The final version which the thirty-nine manuscript notebooks in Thoreau's hand represent is the product of repeated revisions, additions, subtractions, and recopyings, a process which continued up to the last weeks of his life. The Journal was a reservoir of best ideas and carefully defined experiences, from which Thoreau drew constantly, sometimes tearing out the pages containing the matter reused elsewhere, sometimes recopying whole stretches of the pruned record.[8] It was his habit to keep rough notes on several days' experience, whether in the field or in the study, and then rework them into more literary reports, polishing them scrupulously for style and structure. As he explained:

> I would fain make two reports in my Journal; first the incidents and observations of to-day; and by tomorrow I review the same and record what was omitted before, which will often be the most significant part. I do not know at first what it is that charms me. The men and things of to-day are wont to lie fairer and truer in tomorrow's memory.

This description, made in March, 1857, proves a particularly apt one for the Journal from 1851 on, when its pruned and cultivated "reports" tend to represent varying proportions of direct observation on the one hand and thoughtful reflections and criticisms and imaginative musings on the other. The earlier Journal offers more evidence of the recopying and reuse which Thoreau originally made of his Journal reservoirs and shows less finality and fullness by virtue of being linked more immediately and erratically to field or notebook versions.[9]

Particularly significant for the tracer of Thoreau's reading practices is the fact that the Journal is not only a chronological record but a precisely dated one. Its author was for the most part scrupulous in keeping his experiences in their original context so far as the date of original entry went. (Other aspects of their context underwent considerable metamorphosis, as we shall later see.) When sometime after July 10, 1852, Thoreau wrote up his entries for the preceding days, he mixed his notes and included by error under the July 9 entry an observation of a purslane "just in flower, bright yellow, in the garden." The mistake in dating he hastened to correct by explaining clearly in the margin beside the original entry, "Should have been in next day, 10th." His dating of his reading, like that of any other experience, can generally be trusted, for his record of it shared a similar immediacy for Thoreau as it became a part of a faithful record of the realities of actual day-to-day awareness. In every instance where there is opportunity to cross-check dating—and fortunately there are many such—the evidence confirms the reliability of the Journal record.

A few entries will illustrate this facet of the Journal. The entry for June 13, 1852, contains a report of two separate activities: a walk to Conantum taken in the afternoon (specifically at 3 P.M., as Thoreau is scrupulous in recording in the heading to his entry) and some reading done presumably in the evening. The written report of both is a polished version, not necessarily done contemporaneously with either experience, but the final version remains scrupulously true to the original calendar and clock time. Thoreau was often to remind himself that this was the fullest justification for a Journal in the first place: "I do not know but thoughts written down in a journal might be printed in the same form with greater advantage than if the related ones were brought together into separate essays. They are now allied to life, and are seen by the reader not to be far-fetched." The walk to Conantum furnishes a good portion of the details for the first part of the record.

> A warm day. It has been cold, and we have had fires the past week sometimes. Clover begins to show red in the fields, and the wild cherry is not out of blossom. The river has a summer midday look, smooth to a cobweb. . . .
> What a sweetness fills the air now in low grounds or meadows, reminding me of times when I went strawberrying years ago. . . . Saw four cunning little woodchucks nibbling the short grass, about one third grown, that live under Conant's old house. Mistook one for a piece of rusty iron. . . .
> I think I know four kinds of cornel besides the dogwood and bunchberry; one now in bloom. . . .
> Orobanche uniflora, single-flowered bloom-rape (Bigelow). . . . C found it June 12 at Clematis Brook. Also the common fumitory (?), methinks; it is a fine-leaved small plant.

Interspersed with these natural observations is an animadversion upon Gray's naming of the *Clintonia borealis* after a New York governor and some discussion of ways in which nature "imitates all things in flowers . . . at once the most beautiful and the ugliest objects, the most fragrant and the most offensive to the nostrils." The second portion of the entry, without other external evidence, might appear to be a continuation of Thoreau's train of thought, to derive its context from a possible association of ideas just as logically as from the accident of time.

> Captain Jonathan Carver commences his Travels with these words: "In June, 1766, I set out from Boston, and proceeded by way of Albany and Niagara, to Michillimackinac; a Fort situated between the Lakes Huron and Michigan, and distant from Boston 1300 miles. This

being the uttermost of our factories towards the northwest, I considered it as the most convenient place from whence I could begin my intended progress, and enter at once into the regions I had designed to explore." So he gives us no information respecting the intermediate country, nor much, I fear about the country beyond.

But whatever pertinence Thoreau's response to the opening pages of Carver's book has for his own activity recorded in the preceding portion of the entry is clear bonus here, for the records of withdrawals from the library of the Boston Society of Natural History for 1852 show that Thoreau withdrew Carver's *Travels throughout the Interior Parts of North America* from this very day, June 13, until he returned it himself July 26.[10] The reference is Thoreau's first to Carver's book. We can be reasonably confident that the Journal accurately identifies a time at which Thoreau was actually reading the first portion of Carver's account.

An entry for April 27, 1854, records a similar scrap of information, but in this instance one completely irrelevant to the concerns which surround it: "Forbes says that the guides who crossed the Alps with him lost the skin of their faces—apparently from the reflection of the snow." Once again we have evidence to corroborate the immediacy of Thoreau's response to his reading: that he withdrew James David Forbes's *Travels through the Alps of Savoy and Other Parts of the Pennine Chain* from the Boston Society of Natural History library from March 14 to May 9 of 1854. We also have Thoreau's copy of excerpts from Forbes in an unpublished Extract Book,[11] excerpts bounded chronologically on one side by excerpts from a New York *Times* account of an address delivered before the American Geographical and Statistical Society on February 16, 1854, and on the other by excerpts recorded from a travel book, John Hunter's *Memoirs of a Captivity among the Indians of North America*, withdrawn by Thoreau from the Harvard Library on December 7, 1854. We can once again assume, then, that Thoreau was reading Forbes's book between February and December of 1854, more precisely yet, between March 14 and May 9 of that year and thus in all probability on April 27, the Journal date to which he attributes his response to an interesting phenomenon encountered on page 243 of Forbes's account.

A Journal reference to Thoreau's reading of Herndon's *Exploration of the Amazon* on June 8, 1854, constitutes the major portion of an entry preceded by otherwise totally unrelated observations upon the day's special character ("A.M.—Gentle, steady rainstorm") and activities ("P.M.—On river"), plus some particular attention to calendar accuracy ("The Rosa nitida bud which I plucked yesterday has blossomed to-day, so that, notwithstanding the rain, I will put it down to to-day"):

> Herndon, in his "Exploration of the Amazon," says that "there is wanting an industrious and active population, who know what the comforts of life are, and who have artificial wants to draw out the great resources of the country." But what are the "artificial wants" to be encouraged, and the "great resources" of a country? Surely not the love of luxuries like the tobacco and slaves of his native (?) Virginia, or the fertility of soil which produces these. The chief want is ever a life of deep experience.

Herndon's book was published late in 1853. We know that Thoreau owned both Part I and Part II of the *Exploration*. Part II was by Lieutenant Gibbon and was not published until the spring of 1854.[12] We also know that Thoreau plucked this very observation upon Herndon from its place in his Journal for illustrative matter in a lecture titled "Getting a Living" (later to be renamed "Life Without Principle") delivered in New Bedford in the late fall of this year 1854, a lecture which shows considerable debt to other portions of his early 1854 Journal. We know that the lecture was inspired by his concern over the Fugitive Slave Law issue in May of this year. So the calendar period for Thoreau's reading of Herndon's four-hundred-page book narrows down to a span stretching at the utmost from the fall of 1853 to that of 1854, in more likelihood to the spring of 1854. At this stage of the proof, then, we permit Thoreau the benefit of further circumstantial evidence and the accuracy of his own dating, to conclude with reasonable surety that as of June 8, 1854, he is reading or has recently read at least to page 254 of Herndon's book.

From cumulative experience with such detection one can soon identify prevailing patterns of reliability—in this case, the conscious accuracy of the Journal's dating. Its contemporaneous tone is on the whole a sound index to its chronological integrity, no matter how much the actual immediacy of the observation or reflection proves to be simulated through artful rewriting. It remains the backbone for any study of when its author read what, as Thoreau meant that it should. "From all points of the compass, from the earth beneath and the heavens above, have come these inspirations and been entered duly in the order of their arrival." [13]

Only occasionally did Thoreau take liberties with chronology in adding illustrative material. When he did, he plunged future students of his work into scholarly dilemmas. Arthur Christy, observing that Thoreau quoted in the Journal for October 3, 1855, an excerpt from a travel book by Thomas Atkinson, *Oriental and Western Siberia*, which was not published until 1858, confessed to being unable to explain the discrepancy in dates; he added that "Thoreau might have seen newspaper accounts." [14] But there were no newspaper accounts of Atkinson's trip as early as 1855, nor do any later ones I can find carry the material Thoreau quotes. The page reference which Thoreau scrupulously adds to his quotation refers unmistakably to the 1858 edition. A glance at the manuscript version of the Journal entry, however, offers evidence which Bradford Torrey's published version camouflages. The Atkinson excerpt has been copied in a different ink and obviously at a different time into the original entry of 1855, squeezed almost indecipherably between the earlier lines in fine, thin handwriting. The reconstruction of Thoreau's probable procedure is not without significance. Reading in Atkinson's book, probably in the year in which it was published, he came upon the first of Atkinson's descriptions of the crimson "Salsola plant" which grew by the margins of the salt-water lakes of the Kirghiz Steppe: on page 425 of his book Atkinson declares that he could tell a salt lake from a distance by the crimson margins which encircled it. Perhaps Thoreau just happened to be revising the October portion of his own 1855 Journal at this time. But coincidence is less likely an answer here than Thoreau's automatic habits of memory. He knew his Journal well, as his frequent and facile borrowings from it attest. Most probably his reading of his passage in Atkinson recalled a similar sight which he himself had observed as he walked along the shores of Acushnet three years earlier, when the samphire (also a flowering phenomenon of salt-water margins) was, as he had recorded in his Journal at the time, "turning red in many places, yielding to the autumn." [15]

Whereupon he turned back to his Journal record of his experience to insert this parallel of Atkinson's on the other side of the world. We shall later be confirming in detail how acutely conscious he was of such parallels in experience, particularly by 1858.

Accurate as the Journal record of Thoreau's reading remains, however, it does not tell the whole or even the greater portion of the story of Thoreau's way of reading. Although he began his Journal as a depository for all his written records, including all note-taking from his reading, he decided rather soon that the Journal was to be principally a record of his own thoughts and experiences, and he proceeded to establish other depositories for specific information derived from his reading which he wished to retain for possible future use. Thus the Journal is only one of a host of commonplace books, fact books, and extract books of many kinds and sizes, few of which have ever been published. In addition to many fragmentary collections of notes and records on special subjects among extant Thoreau manuscripts, there are ten separate notebook sources in Thoreau's handwriting which contain material pertaining specifically to his travel reading, sources which are scattered among five libraries and which range in size from a single-volume notebook of 31 pages to an eleven-volume depository of 2,949 pages. They remind us of the proportion of writing a good writer does to prime that instrument which can furnish eventually the pure draught from the well of inspiration.[16]

Although dating these commonplace books often rests upon internal evidence, it is possible to establish their chronology fairly accurately. Interestingly enough, it is Thoreau's reading activity itself which assists us. For example, from a study of Thoreau's note-taking from Darwin's *Voyage* and from Peter Kalm's *Travels into North America*, one discovers that, sometime between his note-taking from Darwin in his Journal for June, 1851, and his reading of Kalm's *Travels* in September of the same year, he established a special Extract Book to which he could now relegate the bulk of his reading notes from Kalm. Another source book (the "Indian" Notebook) was apparently started a bit earlier, while he was still reading Darwin, in time to receive appropriate portions of the Darwin reading, whereas the Extract Book was apparently not yet available for its share.[17]

Moreover, the chronology of Thoreau's reading by year and often by month can be established for many of these undated notebook records. Thoreau did not always copy his excerpts from his reading into his notebooks at the very time he first read them. (Presumably he often took "notes," sometimes mere page numbers, reminding him of matter he wanted to store in one or another notebook, an activity to which he gave his usual systematic attention.) But he did, of course, have to return to the book for his final transcribing; the record was made with the book in hand. And the order of entry in the notebooks is fixed chronologically in one sense, for these notebooks give no evidence of the recopying and cancellations which we know characterized the writing of the Journal. The entry appears to be the first and final version of a formal, scholarly record. Since scarcely a single record of Thoreau's reading needs to stand alone, upon its own internal evidence, there remains, in addition to the contemporaneous Journal, a matrix of notebook entries to support one another. Like the tension of a good bridge, the cooperating weight and balance of all evidence supports the parts by best supporting the whole.

The result can be illustrated if we start with a reconstruction of the order of some recordings in the Indian Notebook. Here we find Thoreau copying excerpts from Josselyn's *Account of Two Voyages to New England* (which he withdraws from Harvard Library on January 9, 1854), before recording portions of Kane's account of the first Grinnell expedition; then some excerpts from Mayne Reid's *Young Voyagers*, from John Heckewelder's and John Tanner's respective narratives, and from John Hunter's *Memoirs* (a book he later owns, but does not now, since he must borrow it from the Harvard Library on December 7 of this year). Next he adds excerpts from Schoolcraft's *Narrative*, with which he was already familiar from earlier reading, and from Herndon's *Exploration*, which we have already found him reading in June of this year. Finally he records material from both Sagard's *Le Grand Voyage* and his *Histoire*, and then excerpts from William Wood's *New England Prospect* (which he withdraws from Harvard on December 25).

When we submit this chronology of the notebook entries to the further test of clues in the Journal's chronology for 1854, we find such corroborative evidence as the following: January 23 and February 8: quotations from a current reading of Josselyn; February 26: quotations from Kane; March 9: report of a deliberate confirmation of an observation of Mayne Reid's in *Young Voyagers* (together with proof that he has not as yet read Franklin's own account of his arctic voyages—a book soon to be read, early in 1855); March 29 and April 21: reference to arctic voyages and to Sir John Franklin (the renowned object of Kane's arctic searches); May 16: reflections on Herndon's descriptions of the repulsiveness of crocodiles on the Amazon; June 8: a quotation from Herndon's book; June 21: a quotation from the "second part of the story of Tanner"; January 20, 1855: "In Sagard's History I read . . . "; January 25: quotations from Sagard's *Voyage*. The evidence, as the jurist might say, is certainly not at odds with itself. The three batches of recordings for the dating of which there is no evidence other than that internal to this notebook, excerpts from Captain Sitgreaves' *Expedition down the Zuni and Colorado Rivers* (1853), Theodore Irving's *Conquest of Florida, by Hernando de Soto* (1851), and Randolph B. Marcy's *Exploration of the Red River* (1853), appear in this order between the excerpts from Tanner and those from Hunter, placing them sometime between May and December.

A chronology once established for a portion of one notebook can in turn be used to confirm the dating of other notebook records. The parallel, for instance, between the order and identity of recordings in the Indian Notebook for 1854 through early 1855 and that of the Extract Book mentioned earlier will illustrate this resource:

Indian Notebook	*Extract Book*
Josselyn	Josselyn
Kane	Kane
Reid's *Young Voyagers*	Reid's *Young Voyagers*
Heckewelder	Forbes's *Alps*
Tanner	Sitgreaves
Sitgreaves	Marcy
De Soto	Hunter
Marcy	Sagard
Hunter	Franklin
Schoolcraft	Howitt
Herndon	
Taylor's *Eldorado*	
Sagard	
Wood	
Franklin	
Howitt	

New references in the Extract Book also carry new bodies of evidence for their dating, of course (as we have already seen in the case of the Forbes entry). So the process of verification can go on, weaving that complex but solid web of reading time which an insatiable reader like Thoreau spent his years spinning.

That these notebooks furnished Thoreau an important adjunct to his Journal is apparent from the frequent references to them which pepper the pages of the Journal itself, signposts for Thoreau to all the corners of his extensive and voluminous file. As we should expect, it took some years to accumulate these additional resource piles, and it is only by 1855 and later that we find Thoreau tapping them readily and frequently. "Vide Indian Book," he notes in parentheses in a Journal entry in 1855, a reference to the special notebook of "Indian material." By 1860 this particular depository had mushroomed to eleven separate notebooks, and it was necessary to refer more exactly to material quoted "near the beginning of Indian Book No 9." [18] An inscription on the inside bricks of a chimney ruin in Concord reminds him on February 15, 1857, of previous data on old houses which he has stored away in yet another notebook, and in parentheses he directs himself: "Vide Book of Facts."

We might travel this reference route with Thoreau for a moment. In September, 1856, he saw in Brattleboro, Vermont, the skin and skull of a panther, "the most interesting sight I saw in Brattleboro"; and the information which a local authority gave him on the habits of the animal is followed in his Journal by the following reference: "Vide Lawson, Hunter, and Jefferson in Book of Facts. Hunter when near the Rocky Mountains says, 'So much were they [cougars] to be apprehended . . . that no one ever ventured to go out alone, even on the most trifling occasions.' He makes two kinds." [19] This particular "Books of Facts" is the Extract Book which survives today among Thoreau's unpublished material, its two volumes residing impractically in two great libraries more than one hundred miles apart.[20] If we follow the cross-reference from the Journal as directed, we find in this Extract Book, falling in the year 1856 and wedged between excerpts from Mayne Reid's *Young Voyagers* and William Vincent's edition of *The Voyage of Nearchus*, an excerpt from "p. 172" of John Hunter's *Memoirs of a Captivity among the Indians of North*

America on, sure enough, the "Cougar," followed by an instruction "v. Lawson below," where there follows a mass of information "Of the panther" from John Lawson's *History of Carolina*. Although I cannot find the reference to Jefferson in this particular notebook, I imagine either it was there or Thoreau had a good reason to think it was. Four years later Thoreau withdrew Jefferson's *Notes on the State of Virginia* (to which he here probably refers) from the Harvard Library in order to copy into his Indian Notebook eight pages of excerpts.

Now that the subject of the American panther has moved us from Journal to Extract Book in the workable fashion that Thoreau set up for himself, a closer inspection of this latter notebook exposes further evidence of Thoreau's reading habits. Significantly, there is almost no overlapping of recorded material between the Journal and the Extract Book even though there are many instances where different excerpts from the same book are recorded simultaneously in both depositories. The notebook, then, seems to have been intended from the start as a supplementary resource, a depository for such interesting matter from Thoreau's reading as spilled over from the Journal. And what is true of this particular notebook in this regard is in turn true of the other notebooks in which Thoreau recorded his reading. He seems to have decided, as he read, just where he wished to record the particular material that interested him. His principle of assignment is fairly clear. He worked into the Journal those borrowings which provoked him either to comment upon them immediately or to use them to illustrate some idea or experience of his own.[21] He then copied into the array of commonplace books kept contemporaneously with the Journal those excerpts which interested him but for which he had as yet no immediate use.

At times the notebooks offer revealing glimpses into Thoreau's process of making such assignment. In the Indian Notebook for 1853, for example, after extensive excerpts copied without comment from Charles Pickering's *The Races of Man*, appears the following start of a comment by Thoreau: "P. gives California to the Malay Race,"—a comment meant to introduce a quotation from Pickering but which strangely ends with the comma, followed by an expanse of conspicuously empty page (and it was not Thoreau's habit to waste page space). What the comment actually led to, indeed was doing so even as he wrote it down in his notebook, was a view of Thoreau's own on the implications of the passage he had just read in Pickering and was about to copy for filing, a view which readers may find for themselves in the entry in the Journal for September 1, 1853, where Thoreau felt it properly belonged. We can see him hastily lifting his pen from his notebook page and turning to copy the provocative passage, with his own sly interpretive comment, onto another sheet for inclusion in his Journal, where it now stands.[22]

One suspects that the range and size of this handwritten "library" even caused its owner to lose touch with his vast holdings at times. One of the few observations recorded in full in both the Journal and a notebook is one made in the Extract Book in connection with Thoreau's reading of W. H. Sleeman's *Rambles and Recollections of an Indian Official* in 1852: "Sleeman says no boy in India ever robs a bird's nest. Are they heathenish in that?" It is the kind of response we would expect Thoreau to relegate to his Journal, and, sure enough, he did (on July 9, 1852). But in this instance he may well have lost it there, for although Torrey in the published *Journal* gives it the attention of a separate paragraph, albeit between two entirely irrelevant ones, in Thoreau's original copy it enjoys not even this distinction. It is wedged inconspicuously and completely irrelevantly into the middle of a solid-page paragraph.

While the Extract Book is still before us, it will repay us to look more inclusively at its contents. The Journal evidence suggests an extensive reading of travel books. The Extract Book supplies the confirmation of the extent. Recordings from travel accounts fill the greater portion of its pages, recordings which also illustrate the variety of information that Thoreau was prompted to copy. The category suggested by the formal title of the notebook—"Extracts, Mostly from Natural History"—hardly prepares one for the range of material recorded; Thoreau's own shortened title for it, "Book of Facts" or "Fact Book," is better. A quick glance through some of its pages will illustrate the diversity. The excerpts which follow are all from travel books, are picked at random, and are given in their entirety, although I have not included more than one from any single book. Thoreau usually prefaced his excerpts from a work with formal identification of the edition. He was irregular about giving the excerpts subject headings of his own, but he was scrupulous in distinguishing directly quoted material from his own summary of information read. Here are some sample entries.

Tartary "is a boundless prairie, sometimes broken up by immense lakes, majestic rivers, imposing mountains, but rolling away always into vast and immeasurable plains. You feel alone in its green solitudes, as in the midst of the ocean."

Custom in pregnancy in Java

"The pregnant woman must afterwards wash her body with the milk of a green cocoanut, on the shell of which has been previously carved two handsome figures, one of each sex, by which the parents intend to represent a standard of beauty for their expected offspring, and to engrave on the imagination of the mother, impressions which may extend to the lineaments of her infant. The nut must be opened by the husband."

(Although it is seldom that Thoreau ever comments directly upon the material which he copies into the Extract Book, the quotation above elicits the comment, "A modern as well as ancient custom.")

Warmth of ice

"With an atmosphere whose mean is below zero throughout the year, and a mean summer heat but 4 degrees above the freezing point, these great Polar glaciers retain a high interior temperature not far from 32 degrees, which enables them to resume their great functions of movement and discharge readily, when the cold of winter is at an end, and not improbably to temper to some extent the natural rigor of the climate. Even in the heart of the ice nature has her compensations."

The Peepul Tree of Jubbulpore in India

"Three or four young peepul trees have begun to spread their delicate branches and pale green leaves rustling in the breeze from the dome of this fine temple, which these infant Herculeses hold in their deadly grasp and doom to inevitable destruction. Pigeons deposit the seeds of the peepul tree, on which they chiefly feed, in the crevices of the buildings.

"No Hindoo dares, and no Christian or Mohammedan will condescend to lop off the heads of these young trees, and if they did, it would only put off the evil and inevitable day; for such are the vital powers of their roots, when they have once penetrated deeply into a building, that they will send out their branches again, cut them off as often as you may, and carry on their internal attack with undiminished vigor.

"No wonder that superstition should have consecrated this tree, delicate and beautiful as it is, to the gods. The palace, the castle, the temple, and the tomb—she rises triumphant over them all in her lofty beauty, bearing high in air amidst her light foliage fragments of the wreck she has made."

Sand fleas

"The children [in the interior of southern Brazil] even of rich people go without shoes and stocking, but before they go to bed, it is necessary to examine their little feet, and take out the sandfleas that may have nestled in them—an operation which is commonly performed by the elder negro children with a pin."

Caravan Journey from Mossal in Mesopotamia to Ravandus. Through a mountain pass. With the noise of stones which they set in motion rolling down into the abysses.

"We had been going along thus for about an hour, when the moon all at once became covered with thick clouds, and the darkness was so total that we could scarcely see a step before us. Our leader kept constantly striking fire with a flint, in order that the sparks might enable us to see in some measure where we were going; but this was not sufficient, and the animals began to stumble and slip; and soon there was nothing for it but to halt and stand motionless one behind another —as if we had suddenly been changed to stone—till morning. But with the dawn of light our life returned again, and we cheerfully urged on our steeds, and soon found ourselves in an indescribably beautiful circle of mountains. Right and left, before and behind, they rose one above another, and far in the background towered above all a mighty giant crowned with snow."

Slaves

Lane's Modern Egyptians, vol 1, p. 244. "Three days trial is generally allowed to the purchaser of a slave girl in Cairo; during which time, the girl remains in his, or some friend's harem, and the women make their report to him. Snoring, grinding the teeth, or talking during sleep, are commonly considered sufficient reasons for returning her to the dealer." [23]

There is scarcely a stopping place, once one launches forth into the exotic and variegated regions the Extract Book offers to the curious. The 675 pages of its two volumes are crowded with a conglomeration of information, scenes, reflections, opinions, anecdotes, natural and social phenomena culled from one travel account after another, sources carefully acknowledged, usually to edition and page. Here are descriptions of a buffalo lick in Georgia, the Puri Indians near Rio de Janeiro, a Chinese lady's foot, the "red snow" of the Arctic, an African river lost in sand, the ruins of Babylon, bee hunting in Peru. There is information on the Tahitian's capacity for smelling gold, the lost tribe of Atures on the Orinoco, the burning of widows in India, the letter writing of Turkish cadis, turtles, crocodiles, giraffes, and ostriches. And we have no more than scratched the surface.

We must remember, moreover, that this notebook is only one of the ten notebooks in which Thoreau recorded his specific reading of travel literature. The distinctions among these notebooks are neither narrow nor hard and fast in spite of their rather specialized titles. Each notebook reflects much the same diversity of material. The Indian notebooks, for example, abound with impressions of all corners of the globe, foreign sights and facts packed solidly between the covers of notebooks which grew larger and thicker with the years, a vast eleven-volume potpourri, including not only much Indian history and lore but accounts of primitive peoples in all quarters of the earth, descriptions of the Peruvians, the Eskimos, facts of climate, geology, botany, and zoology, any and all matters environmental and anthropological that relate in any way to the context and character of aboriginal life. The same range of interest is reflected in the single-volume Canadian Notebook titled by Thoreau "Extracts from works relating to Canada, etc." which we shall explore more closely in a later chapter; only the final abbreviation in its title sets the limits to its content.

The range and variety of these reading notes have implications which we would do well to face before filing Thoreau's practice of travel reading too quickly under any single category of "special" interest. We are dealing with a reader of so many and such broad interests that their common denominator becomes peculiarly elusive. This we soon discover when we search for a single interest, or even for several quite distinct and separate interests, into which we can fit in Procrustean fashion all the multitudinous evidence of Thoreau's constant responsiveness. If Thoreau remains today an interesting person, it is because he remained, up to the moment of his death, such an intently interested one. And soon we discover that his interests were never narrow ones, even during those last years of his life which it is fashionable to label ones of growing "specialization" along the lines of botany and the American Indian. For Thoreau the American Indian fused with all "primitive life," and what proved important about the *Vaccinia* in the Concord oak woods was its global lineage, as he made perfectly clear when he spoke of it.[24] His interests were continuously mushrooming, and his final difficulties in controlling and using the mass of data which he was accumulating stemmed not from its narrow limitations but from its boundlessness. Only to the young mind was everything individual, standing by itself, specialized and categorized. Thoreau was Emerson's scholar, whose mind

> finds how to join two things and sees in them one nature; then three, then three thousand; and so, tyrannized over by its own unifying instinct, it goes on trying things together, diminishing anomalies, discovering roots running under ground whereby contrary and remote things cohere and flower out from one stem.[25]

This is not to say for a moment that by the late 1850s Thoreau was growing in ground-creeper fashion; it can hardly be said that he ever did that. But the fact is worth stressing—and nowhere better illustrated than in his travel reading—that, for the nutriment which his expanding interests furnished him, he sent his roots wide as well as deep.

ᴇᏙ CHAPTER III Ꮟᴇ

The Summing Up

I read one or two shallow books of travel in the intervals of my work.
Walden, 1854

In following the route of discovery into Thoreau's travel reading, we have up to now begged the question of the amount of such reading which Thoreau did. Taking the measure of his reading in this genre is somewhat like measuring an iceberg. Each new sounding in each new source (and what an amorphous mass of unpublished source material there is!) exposes greater size and more solid substance. But it is time we at least saw some outline of its dimensions.

Numbers do not tell the whole story, but they can begin it. We shall restrict ourselves, for the emphasis of this book, to those narratives describing travels outside New England. The amount of such reading which the evidence exposes is impressive.[1] In his published writings (including the *Journal*) Thoreau refers directly to his reading in at least eighty-three different travel works. The unpublished Extract Book contains a record of reading in fifty-six different travel books, twenty of which are in addition to those directly acknowledged in the published writings. The Indian notebooks record the reading of ninety different travel accounts, forty-two of which are additions to the record of both the published writings and the Extract Book. The Extract Book and the Indian notebooks between them present a record of reading in one hundred and forty-six different travel books.

It is worth noting that these represent travel books read completely through, carefully, from cover to cover, as the unpublished notebooks prove, substantiating the position that Thoreau's acquaintance with works to which he refers anywhere is based on a reading *of* them rather than simply *in* them. His quotations from Karl Andersson's *Lake Ngami; or, Explorations and Discoveries during Four Years' Wanderings in the Wilds of South-western Africa* are typically illustrative of the thoroughness of his reading. From a book of 451 pages he records in his Extract Book material from pages 101, 104, 136, 180, 212, 213, 217, 240, 248, 250, 251, 254, 256, 257, 267, 384, and 425; while in the Indian notebook he records material from pages 64, 90, 94, 151, 174, 181, 189, 199, 202, 203, and 441. The amount of copying in longhand which he did took hours of his life. We find him recording long passages from fifty-four pages of James Swan's *The Northwest Coast; or, Three Years' Residence in Washington Territory*, commencing on page 27 and ending on page 415;[2] he copied from sixty-two pages of the first volume of David Crantz's *Greenland*, pages evenly distributed between the Introduction and the end of the book.[3] Inserted in one of the volumes of the Indian notebooks are loose slips of paper solid with page numbers containing references to a book from which Thoreau had already copied some twenty pages of excerpts.

The published writings and unpublished notebooks pick up Thoreau's reading record principally after 1842 and most fully after 1850. Two further sources supply additional evidence, some of it for a yet earlier period. The records of Thoreau's withdrawals from the Harvard Library show that he borrowed at least sixteen different travel books during his four years as an undergraduate, the reading in many of which is confirmed in his later writings. From 1849 to 1860, the period during which he resumed his withdrawals from the library,[4] he took out twenty-eight more travel books, in addition to John Nevins' *New Collection of Voyages and Travels* and several volumes of the *New-York Historical Society Collections* and the *Historical Collections of Louisiana* containing early voyages of exploration. Altogether his withdrawals of travel works represented over one fifth of his total recorded borrowings from the Harvard Library. It is not unreasonable to suppose that travel literature also represented a fair proportion of his borrowings from the Boston Public Library, the Concord Library, and the library of the Massachusetts Historical Society, all three richly stocked with such works.[5] Moreover, we know that Thoreau's own library, refined as it was to a preponderance of classical works, standard editions of English literature, textbooks, and scientific "reference" works, also included some twenty travel books, several of them double-volume editions rare to its shelves.[6]

Gathering together our bibliography of Thoreau's reading in this particular genre, then, from all the sources left us, and relying only on such evidence as proves unquestionable rather than circumstantial or conjectural, we are able to identify, in many cases to the very edition, a minimum of one hundred and seventy-two separate travel accounts read by Thoreau. This total does not include at least nine separate collections of travels and voyages in which we know he read and which contain accounts not included in our count of individual travel works. Nor does this total figure include any of those periodical accounts of travels which we have good reason to suppose Thoreau followed extensively. Unlike many magazine readers, however, he did not accept a periodical report as substitute for a full account; he went on to the book.

Time appears to have been ample for reading as well as for copying. The "original" work to Thoreau meant the "whole" work, and in a day when condensed versions of travel books were not only popular but sensibly expedient, Thoreau characteristically refused to compromise. Occasionally he refrained from going on to the second volume of a work, as with Gordon-Cumming's two-volume *Five Years of a Hunter's Life in the Far Interior of South Africa*; but such instances are rare, and in the case of Gordon-Cumming the decision was based upon Thoreau's distaste for a dull chronicle of the slaughter of wildlife. Although Thoreau's final word upon the value of Austen Layard's monumental accounts of travels and excavations in the Near East was not particularly appreciative,[7] he did not give it until he had read to the last page of Layard's three volumes, 1,264 pages in all. In the face of a widely accepted one-volume condensation of Alexander von Humboldt's travels in South America made by a well-known naturalist whose scientific studies Thoreau had read,[8] Thoreau still turned to the original translated edition of Humboldt's *Personal Narrative* in three volumes. Of the two editions of Livingstone's *Travels* in South Africa brought out simultaneously by Harper and Brothers in 1858, one a whittled down 440-page version of the full 728-page volume, Thoreau chose the full one. His practice in this regard is almost without exception. Thus we must add to our numerical evidence of titles the more weighty evidence of bulk, reminding ourselves that Thoreau's reading in this genre included 850 pages of Pike's two-volume *Account of Expeditions to the Sources of the Mississippi*, the 800 pages of William Howitt's *Land, Labor, and Gold; or, Two Years in Victoria* in two volumes, the 900 pages of Kane's two-volume account of the second Grinnell expedition to the Arctic, and such single-volume tomes as J. D. Forbes's *Travels through the Alps* of 560 pages, Charles Wilkes's *Voyage round the World* of 670 pages, and Lewis and Clark's *Expedition* of almost 700 pages, to mention only a few examples. The single-volume accounts read by Thoreau averaged 400 pages. The year 1852, for instance, found him reading at an absolute minimum 8,849 pages of travel literature—a creditable expanse of print for even a devoted scholar to traverse in his exclusive area of specialty. And this total for the year does not include the reading he also did in Purchas' *Pilgrimes* and Drake's *Collection of Voyages*. It does represent his reading of the travelers Pfeiffer, Head, Talbot, Richardson, Lahonton, Arnold, Huc, Carver, Sleeman, Osborn, Humboldt, Culbertson, Long, Verrazano, Schoolcraft, Gregg, and Maximilian.

Not only was Thoreau's travel reading extensive and solid; it appears to have been, as it would almost have had to be, a concentrated reading of works one by one. For this assumption the evidence is circumstantial, but it is consistent enough to round out our picture. The notebooks with their excerpts from books which Thoreau did not even take from the library, excerpts copied on those many days which he spent in the Boston or the Harvard Library and reported in his Journal under the designation "Cambridge," reflect attentive, rapid, thorough reading of one work at a time. The systematic résumés which appear in the Journal up to 1852, before the notebooks took over this feature, are in every instance limited exclusively to a single source at a time. Even after 1852 we can often trace from references and allusions in the Journal the span of Thoreau's reading in a particular work where no acknowledged record of reading time is indicated. It is possible, for instance, to trace in the pages of the Journal for March, 1852, meandering like a slow but distinct thread of current through placid pages filled with scenes of Concord's winter landscape, his reading of John Richardson's *Arctic Searching Expedition*. The considerable evidence which the Journal furnishes us suggests that Thoreau did not take very long or waste many hours in finishing a book once he began to read it. Although it would be folly to attempt to hold a stopwatch on him even had we the sure evidence for doing so, we can assume, for example, that from one chronological résumé of his reading in Darwin's *Voyage* to the next (when he picks up his record again with "June 15. Sunday, Darwin still") Thoreau read in the intervening three days at least two hundred and twenty-eight pages; not a staggering total, to be sure, but ample enough to consume the major if not the exclusive portion of the time left him after three full days of his usual outdoor activity plus in this instance the somewhat less usual indulgence of a long evening walk by moonlight on each of the three nights.[9]

Extensive, substantial, concentrated as his travel reading was, it was also persistent. At no time in his life after the age of sixteen, when he entered Harvard, did Thoreau turn his back on the travel account. Assigned an essay in his rhetoric class at Harvard with instructions to "give your ideas of the anxieties and delights of a discoverer of whatever class: Columbus, Herschel, or Newton," Thoreau picked the traveler.[10] And from this point on there is scarcely a year for which there is not concrete evidence that he journeyed with some travel writer into parts of the world foreign to him, and usually with many over a variety of routes. During the years for which we have the fullest record of his reading and which in turn represent his maturest years, the decade of the 1850s, we find him averaging between twelve and thirteen new travel works a year. Over these ten years travel books represent a steady, reliable, rather evenly distributed proportion of his reading. Only occasionally in the fifties does the evidence indicate fewer than ten new travel books read in a year. Neither are there exceptional concentrations of such reading to suggest that his interest in the genre was only temporary or momentarily aroused.[11] His friends seem to have been perfectly familiar with his steady interest in such literature. Whereas the presentation to him of forty-five volumes of Oriental philosophy and literature in 1855 by his English friend Thomas Cholmondeley seems to have postdated what *was* a particular interest of Thoreau's, Cholmondeley ran no such risk when he recommended to him Du Chaillu's *Explorations and Adventures in Central Africa*, "the book of the season," in a letter of April 23, 1861. "I suppose you will have seen Sir Emerson Tennent's 'Ceylon,'" Cholmondeley added, "perhaps as complete a book as ever was published." [12] The book had 1,255 pages, and Cholmondeley's supposition seems quite reasonable.

Most important of all, Thoreau's reading in travel literature remained up to date. His interest in such writings was predominantly a contemporary one, the works he read mostly nineteenth-century publications. Almost three fourths of them were published after 1800, and of these over half were published in the three decades during which Thoreau was reading them, from 1832 to 1862. This of course does not reflect any neglect of earlier travel accounts, for he used and reused the rich collections to be found in Purchas, Drake, Nevins, Brosses, Bry, Hakluyt, and Ramusio. He read the early Spanish voyagers: Columbus, Ojeda, Nicuesa, Balboa, Ponce de León. He read the sixteenth- and seventeenth-century accounts of Frobisher, Verrazano, Cartier, De Soto, Champlain, Dablon, Hennepin, Laet, Lescarbot, Montanus, Sagard, John Smith, Tonti, Wafer, Hudson, De Vries, Druilletes. He traveled with Bartram, Loskiel, Bossu, Carver, Charlevoix, Cook, Hearne, Josselyn, Kalm, Lahontan, Lawson, Post, Volney, and a host of others in the 1700s. But his interest was a continuing one that kept up with travels and discoveries as they occurred around the globe, and his own day proved rich in such activity. The first half of the nineteenth century saw the penetration of the Arctic and Antarctic, the opening up of Japan from its isolation since 1624, the first extensive coverage of the Far East, glimmerings of light from the heart of the Dark Continent, such expansive travel and exploration in South America that the period has been described as the "Rediscovery of America," [13] and such western travel in North America between 1801 and 1855 that the area of the "unexplored" was pushed from the Mississippi into the Pacific and there was added to United States possession virtually every acre of territory west of the Mississippi today included within our nation's continental boundaries.

As we would expect, travels and explorations of such extent were bound to arouse public interest and to promote a staggering output of records to satisfy and promote that interest. One compiler has listed 562 titles of travel accounts for the period 1800 to 1860 bearing upon the state of Illinois alone; another lists a minimum of 45 guide-books and gazetteers on the Middle Western frontier for the period 1809–40, while his bibliography of travel books on this territory for the same period runs to thirty-three pages.[14] Thoreau would have had all he could do to keep up with even the most interesting and significant accounts appearing each year. The majority of the excerpts in his unpublished notebooks are transcribed from travel works during the year of their publication. He read Colton's account of California and Gordon-Cumming's narrative of Africa just as soon as they were published. He must have taken Ross Cox's two-volume *Adventures on the Columbia River* and Sir George Back's *Narrative of the Arctic Land Expedition* out of the Harvard Library almost the minute they were shelved. In 1860 he read five travel books published in that year; in 1859 he read one marked with the publishing date of 1860, four published in 1859, and one published in 1858. His reading of a review of Paul Emile Botta's *Travels in Arabia* in the *Athenaeum* for January 1, 1842, and of an equally contemporary review of James Clark Ross's *Voyage of Discovery and Research to Southern and Antarctic Regions* in the *North British Review* for November, 1847, suggests that the periodicals helped to keep him up to date.[15] He was constantly checking up on new travel books as they came out. In this area of his reading he was no antiquarian.

It is time to remind ourselves that this collating of evidence, offered on the very heels of our bow to Thoreau's predilection for a quiet country village in eastern Massachusetts, has but exposed contradictions and identified a paradox. Although I think we shall find it one which comforts even while it mocks, our attention rests for the moment upon the contrasts which it italicizes: that of a man who on the one hand reiterates his disdain for travel and on the other peppers his writings with its products; a writer who urges his readers to concentrate upon a knowledge of their own local plot of ground at the same time that he makes sure in his writing that their acquaintance with the world be nothing less than global; the seemingly contented provincial who is all the while devouring the accounts of other men's furthest travels.

So stands the paradox which the facts of the Thoreau record reveal.

The very route which has led to its disclosure, however, encourages the exploration of new latitudes and fresh views, even the suggestion of a new angle of vision on Thoreau from which apparent contradictions may look less like true incompatibles than provoking complements. To discover the resolution of this paradox will require tracing the uses which Thoreau made of his imaginary travels. And back of such use is an attitude on Thoreau's part toward his reading and its subject matter. We must appreciate more specifically those feelings and thoughts of his about travel before we observe where he went or what he found.

PART II

The Traveler

◄§ CHAPTER IV ξ◄◄

The Voyageur Sublimed

A traveler. I love his title. A traveler is to be reverenced as such. His profession is the best symbol of our life. Going from—toward; it is the history of every one of us.

Journal, July 2, 1851

"Live at home like a traveler," Thoreau advised a friend.[1] We could search long in Thoreau's writing for a single statement epitomizing as succinctly the core to the paradox we have just defined. Here is Thoreau offering, in characteristic phrase, a partial definition of the resolution which he made of this paradox, for the advice which he gives exactly describes what he himself did in the nineteen years following December, 1843. As a young man, he had observed that there was "something pathetic" in the sedentary life of men who had traveled. "They must naturally die when they leave the road." [2] Thoreau himself never left the road. Even in his last months, when the "excursions" were over and his walks about Concord curtailed because of ill-health, he continued to read his travel books, traveling from his couch over roads as varied and remote as ever.

He had good cause to debate in his own mind so often and so vehemently the correlation between Concord's hold upon him and the appeal of open roads and beckoning seas for the traveler, for he shared the responses, even the yearnings, of the latter.

The snow-dust falls,
The otter crawls,
The partridge calls
    Far in the wood;
The traveler dreams,
The tree-ice gleams,
The blue-jay screams
    In angry mood.[3]

Thoreau's dreams were usually the traveler's, and they were not limited to winter. His reveries saw in the low western sky "a splendid map, where fancy can trace islands, continents, and cities beyond compare," at times New Hollands and Borneos. He threaded his way through hedge and thicket to stand upon the edge of a lost meadow-swamp, impenetrable except in midsummer, "as far off as Persia from Concord"; a large snapping turtle looked "terrible even as a crocodile." [4] Or on a winter's evening he took a "journey" on his skates along the course of the meandering Concord River, "as full of novelty to one who sits by the cottage fire all the winter's day, as if it were over the polar ice, with Captain Parry or Franklin." Even the apple trees under the snow were "travelers bending to the storm under white mantles." [5] Sometimes he stayed indoors to read "with a thrill of delight, when the snow covers the ground, of the magnolia, and the Florida keys, and their warm sea breezes; of the fence rail, and the cotton tree, and the migrations of the rice-bird; I seem to hear the melting of the snow in the forks of the Missouri as I read. . . . There is a singular health for me in those words Labrador and East Maine." In the spring he stood by the river and followed in imagination the route taken by the timber fragments it had floated, some of which, "no doubt, were carried down to the Merrimack, and by the Merrimack to the ocean, till perchance they got into the Gulf Stream and were cast up on the coast of Norway, covered with barnacles, or who can tell what more distant strand?"—fragments destined to be shouldered by whales, then finally collected as driftwood by some faraway native. [6]

Any biographer of Thoreau is reminded of the pride he took in his nautical knowledge and ancestry. It was not enough that his grandfather, the first John Thoreau, had been a merchant seaman and a privateer, whose books on navigation were now part of his own library; Thoreau liked to consider himself descended from a branch of an Old Norse family and thereby related to the earliest and most daring voyagers of all. [7] No sailor ever appreciated his ship more than Thoreau his boat, and it is questionable whether Melville's Ishmael hanging in the crow's-nest over the waters of the Pacific concentrated more imaginatively upon the exhilarations of voyaging. As one of his biographers reminds us, Thoreau's travels in Concord became more and more fluvial.[8] "I sail with a smacking breeze to-day, and fancy that I am a sailor on the ocean." The bream under his bow gave the impression "of vast size like halibuts or whales." It was pleasant to hear the sound of the waves and feel the surging of the boat—"an inspiriting sound, as if you were bound on adventures"; the creaking sound made by one of his oars, "like a block in a harbor," seemed such a sound "as would bring tears into an old sailor's eyes." "No wonder men love to be sailors," he proclaimed, "to be blown about the world sitting at the helm, to shave the capes and see the islands disappear under their sterns—gubernators to a piece of wood. It disposes to contemplation, and is to me instead of smoking." [9] For Thoreau, as for Ishmael, water and meditation seemed wedded. Like Ishmael too, Thoreau was prone to take to sea for his health, even though the voyage was no farther than across Massachusetts Bay to Provincetown. Occasionally he sailed to Nantucket, where he checked up on the latest whaling grounds, spent an evening with a Captain Gardiner listening to watery tales of leviathans and sea hunters, and inspected in a museum various South Sea implements brought home by whalers. At New Bedford he was intrigued to find, through conversation with him, that a "rather dull and contrified fellow for the neighborhood" had actually been a master of a whaler and "been to most all parts of the world." [10]

From that early day on Staten Island when his eyes followed the ships as they seemed to pass over the edge of the earth, Thoreau was constantly allowing his mind's eye to travel to the farthest corners of the world upon the slightest provocation. From the beach of Cape Cod it was "a poetic recreation" to watch distant sails steering for half-fabulous ports. As he walked the stretch of sand which rimmed the Cape on its most eastern front, between the Highland Light and Truro, he was less interested in the shells at his feet than in those places from which an ocean separated him. He could match a knowledge in natural history with one of European geography, as he showed in his description of his walk.[11] The enthusiastic approval of commerce which he so often expressed seemed rooted more firmly in his instinctive yearning for an identification with all parts of the world, for a kind of spiritual global barter, than in any strong views on the role of trade in the world's economy. Commerce was "adventurous." As he declared rhapsodically in a long passage in *Walden,* he found himself "refreshed and expanded" when the freight train rattled past and he smelled "the stores which go dispensing their odors all the way from Long Wharf to Lake Champlain, reminding me of foreign parts, of coral reefs, and Indian oceans, and tropical climes, and the extent of the globe." Palm leaf, Manila hemp, coconut husks, and torn sails made him feel like a citizen of the world; closed cars smelling of salt fish reminded him of the Grand Banks; the tails on Spanish hides still preserved "the twist and angle of elevation they had when the oxen that wore them were careening over the pampas of the Spanish Main." [12] In *A Week on the Concord and Merrimack Rivers* he drew an evocative picture of his excitement as a boy at seeing the occasional canalboat laden with stores come up the Concord River, "stealing mysteriously through the meadows and past the village," that "huge traveler" one summer day moored at some meadow wharf, the next day gone. "In after years I read in print, with no little satisfaction, that it was thought by some that, with a little expense in removing rocks and deepening the channel, 'there might be a profitable inland navigation.' I then lived somewhere to tell of. Such is commerce, which shakes the cocoanut and bread-fruit tree in the remotest isle, and sooner or later dawns on the duskiest and most simple-minded savage." [13]

These instincts of a Marco Polo which commerce provoked, instincts that his grandfather the sailor-merchant could perhaps best have explained, were akin to those which took Thoreau, as sure as Ishmael, waterwards in the cities he visited. "When I go to Boston, I go naturally straight through the city down to the end of Long Wharf and look off, for I have no cousins in the back alleys." [14] In his Journal for May 9, 1854, a visit to Boston is reported in its entirety as follows:

> Sat on end of Long Wharf. Was surprised to observe that so many of the men on board the shipping were pure country men in dress and habits, and the seaport no more than a country town to which they come a-trading. I found about the wharves, steering the coasters and unloading the ships, men in farmer's dress. As I watched the various craft, successively unfurling their sails and setting to sea, I felt more than for many years inclined to let the wind blow me to other climes.

BOSTON HARBOR, 1832

"As I watched the various craft, successively unfurling their sails and setting to sea,
I felt more than for many years inclined to let the wind blow me to other climes."

The reveries, musings, imaginings continued throughout Thoreau's life, often enriching the experience of the present moment, occasionally tingeing it with unmistakable nostalgia and yearning. On a rainy afternoon in November, 1855, Thoreau took his usual walk (described in his Journal, under the date November 7):

> I find it good to be out this still, dark, mizzling afternoon; my walk or voyage is more suggestive and profitable than in bright weather. The view is contracted by a misty rain, the water is perfectly smooth, and the stillness is favorable to reflection. . . . My thoughts are concentrated; I am all compact. The mist is like a roof and walls over and around, and I walk with a domestic feeling. . . . My attention does not wander. The world and my life are simplified. What now of Europe and Asia?

So it was often with his response as traveler and voyager to the world about him. So strongly and persistently did the remote features of the globe encroach upon his view that at times it is almost as if he had to wipe the vision from before his eyes deliberately, even violently—to concentrate all his attention upon a particle of his world, or to defend vehemently an extreme provincialism of which he was in no way guilty—to the end that his attention might not "wander" and the appeal of Europe and of Asia and of Timbuktu might not blind the traveler in Concord to what lay in his immediate path.

For better or worse, a "traveler" and "voyager" Thoreau considered himself to be, whether in or out of Concord. He was proud of the titles, of both their philosophical and their literal implications, and his persistent use of them to designate the major portion of his activity proved so apt that Emerson could declare of him, "Here is the precise *voyageur* of Canada sublimed, or carried up to the seventh power." [15] Thoreau liked the stalwart, adventuresome connotation of the French term and tried to live up to it. He was for most of the afternoons of his life a traveler in Concord and its vicinity. Spring and fall were seasons for farther travel, when he extended his trips for several days or even weeks at a time, to Wachusett, the Berkshires and the Catskills, the Maine woods, Cape Cod, Plymouth, to Vermont, the White Mountains, Cape Ann, Nantucket, and Mount Monadnock. His letters to his friends ("travelers" all themselves, it should be noted) were apt to be filled with accounts of the latest trips he had been taking.[16] He had every right to sign himself, in a letter to Alcott, "Your fellow-traveler."

He was concerned with society's attitude toward the traveler, a concern which identified him with travelers the world over. As he journeyed through the White Mountains in 1858 he expressed his antipathy to being "barked along through the country, from door to door." It was difficult to journey in an already crowded New England with the same freedom and immunity of a McKenney about the Great Lakes or a Marcy in Louisiana. He was reminded that even in Virginia the traveler Peter Kalm was arrested while in a meadow catching frogs.[17] He read with feeling of Goethe's "gefahrliches Abenteuer" with the suspicious townspeople of Malsesine,[18] and he knew enough of the vicissitudes of Eastern travelers in particular, those of Wolff and Parrott, Burton and St. John, to fit his own reactions into the context of a universal problem.

> Consider how so many, perhaps most, races—Chinese, Japanese, Arabs, Mussulmans generally, Russians—treat the traveler. What fears and prejudices he has to contend with. So many millions believing that he has come to do them harm. Let a traveler set out to go round the world, visiting every race, and he shall meet with such treatment at their hands that he will be obliged to pronounce them incorrigible fools.[19]

Thoreau read of the curious lama service in Tibet which M. Huc witnessed: that of scattering in the wind from the top of high mountains handfuls of paper horses thought to be changed by Buddha into real horses which offered themselves to exhausted travelers in all the four quarters of the world.[20] He himself benefited more directly from the water-troughs by the roadsides in Maine, supported, he was informed, by the state legislature and maintained by a resident in each school district for the use of travelers, "a piece of intelligence as refreshing to me as the water itself." [21]

The excursions which Thoreau took were planned like those excursions undertaken by the most conscientious explorers.[22] He was as scrupulous as a Humboldt or a Brackenridge about clothing and outfit. When he set out for Minnesota in 1860 (on which occasion he compromised his ideal by carrying a carpetbag in place of the usual brown-paper parcel), he carefully recorded a complete inventory of his equipment at the start of the trip.[23] To read it reminds us of his

remark about the traveler and naturalist Linnaeus setting out for Lapland, who surveyed his comb and spare shirt, his leathern breeches
and his gauze cap to keep off gnats, with as much complacency as
Bonaparte would have inspected a park of artillery to be used in the
Russian campaign.[24] Channing gives us a picture of Thoreau which
emphasizes not only his equipment but also his systematic habit of
note-taking, no matter how brief or local the trip:

> In these walks, two things he must have from his tailor: his clothes
> must fit and his pockets, especially, must be made with reference to his
> outdoor pursuits. They must accommodate his notebook and spy-glass;
> and so their width and depth was regulated by the size of the notebook.
> It was a cover for some folded papers, on which he took his out-of-door
> notes; and this was never omitted, rain or shine. It was his invariable
> companion, and he acquired great skill in conveying by a few lines or
> strokes a long story, which in his written Journal might occupy pages.
> Abroad he used the pencil, writing but a few moments at a time, dur-
> ing the walk; but into the notebook must go all measurements with a
> foot-rule which he also carried, or the surveyor's tape that he so often

TIBETAN LAMAS OFFERING HORSES TO TRAVELERS

From Huc, *Tartary, Thibet, and China*

had with him. Also all observations with his spy-glass—(another invariable companion for years), all conditions of plants, spring, summer, and fall, the depth of snows, the strangeness of skies,—all went down in this note-book. To his memory he never trusted for a fact, but to the page and pencil, and the abstract in the pocket.[25]

No traveler ever considered himself a better authority on foot travel than Thoreau; what he did not know from his own experience he learned from the accounts of others, and those persons who knew him well were accustomed to turn to him for advice.

Every trip Thoreau took became subject for a written account. A "journal" was, strictly speaking, a record of a journey. The great majority of his published writings were accounts of journeys fluvial or pedestrian. The notes taken on his trips, and the accounts later rendered in his Journal (often only sketches, middle versions between the original notes and an elaborated account), attest to the seriousness and appropriateness with which he assumed the traveler's role. Most of the reports in the Journal are too long to quote, but one of the briefest is also one of the most interesting and characteristic, packed with the fragments of Thoreau's kaleidoscopic interests and impressions.

[1854] Nov. 20. To Philadelphia. 7 A.M., to Boston; 9 A.M., Boston to New York, by express train, land route. Saw the reddish soil (red sandstone?) all through Connecticut. Beyond Hartford a range of rocky hills crossing the State on each side the railroad, the eastern one very precipitous, and apparently terminating at East Rock at New Haven. Pleasantest part of the whole route between Springfield and Hartford, along the river; perhaps include the hilly region this side of Springfield. Reached Canal Street at 5 P.M., or candle-light.

Started for Philadelphia from foot of Liberty Street at 6 P.M., via Newark, etc., etc., Bordentown, etc., etc., Camden Ferry, to Philadelphia, all in the dark. Saw only the glossy panelling of the cars reflected out into the dark, like the magnificent facade of a row of edifices reaching all the way to Philadelphia, except when we stopped and a lanthorn or two showed us a ragged boy and the dark buildings of some New Jersey town. Arrive at 10 P.M.; time, four hours from New York, thirteen from Boston, fifteen from Concord. Put up at Jones' exchange Hotel, 77 Dock Street; lodgings thirty-seven and a half cents per night, meals separate; not to be named with French's in New York; next door to the fair of the Franklin Institute then open, and over against the Exchange, in the neighborhood of the printing-offices.

Nov. 21. Looked from the cupola of the State House, where the Declaration of Independence was declared. The best view of the city I got. Was interested in the squirrels, gray and black, in Independence and Washington Squares. Heard that they have, or have had, deer in Logan Square. The squirrels are fed, and live in boxes in the trees in winter. Fine view from Fairmount water-works. The line of the hypotenuse of the gable end of Girard College was apparently deflected in the middle six inches or more, reminding me of the anecdote of the church of the Madeleine in Paris.

Was admitted into the building of the Academy of Natural Sciences by a Mr. Durant of the botanical department, Mr. Furness applying to him. The carpenters were still adding four stories (!) of galleries to the top. These four . . . were to be devoted to the birds. It is said to be the largest collection of birds in the world. . . . The Academy has received great donations. There is Morton's collection of crania, with (I suppose a *cast* from) an Indian skull found in an Ohio mound; a polar bear killed by Dr. Kane; a male moose not so high as the female we shot; a European elk (a skeleton) about seven feet high, with horns each about five feet long and *tremendously* heavy; grinders, etc., of the *Mastodon giganteum* from Barton County, Missouri; etc., etc. Zinzinger was named as the geological department.

In Philadelphia and also New York an ornamental tree with bunches of seed-vessels supplying the place of the leaves now. I suppose it the ailanthus, or Tree of Heaven. What are those trees with long, black sickle-shaped pods? I did not see Steinhauser's Burd family at St. Stephen's Church. The American Philosophical Society is described as a company of old women.

In the narrow market-houses in the middle of the streets, was struck by the neat-looking women marketers with full cheeks. Furness described a lotus identical with an Egyptian one as found somewhere down the river below Philadelphia; also spoke of a spotted chrysalis which he had seen in Massachusetts. There was a mosquito about my head at night. Lodged at the United States Hotel, opposite the Girard (formerly United States) Bank.

It is worth noticing that here, in Thoreau's own travel notes, is in miniature a replica of that variety of observations which we found him recording from others' travel accounts in his Extract Book: in place of the plains of Tartary, a glimpse of the Connecticut River valley; instead of barefoot children in Brazil, full-cheeked marketwomen in Philadelphia; rather than a journey by caravan through a mountain pass in Mesopotamia, the description of a night journey by rail through the darkened towns of New Jersey; and in place of the

Peepul Tree, the Tree of Heaven. Round out these summary notes of Thoreau's into full descriptions, the "long stories" of which Channing spoke, and the accounts resulting should certainly bear more than an incidental similarity, in both form and substance, to the many travel accounts he was reading.

CHAPTER V

Part of the Human Journey

I did not wish to take a cabin passage, but rather to go before the mast and on the deck of the world.

Walden, 1854

As a traveler both by inclination and by practice, Thoreau showed an early and continual preoccupation with the requirements for successful travel. Over and over again he expressed himself on the characteristics most appropriate to the traveler, and he soon established a set of criteria by which he tested in turn the value of the many accounts he read. He made the same requirements for himself and for all others, just as he tried to represent in his own writings that quality of experience which he demanded in other travelers' works. In developing his theory of a good traveler, he learned as much from the experience of those travelers whom he read as he did from his own "voyages" and "excursions." Three travelers whom he met relatively early in his reading particularly illustrate this correlation.

In the winter of 1837–38 Thoreau put to use the knowledge of German he had acquired from Orestes Brownson by reading Goethe's *Italienische Reise*.[1] He read it slowly and laboriously (he was not at ease in reading German as he was with French), but with attention and increasing appreciation. Although he was later prone to depreciate his familiarity with Goethe,[2] he also read *Dictung und Wahrheit*, to which the *Italienische Reise* formed the logical sequel, and his personal library contained by 1840 the three-volume edition of *Wilhelm Meister* (translated by Carlyle) presented to him by Emerson. Moreover, his limited acquaintance did not deter him from discussing fully the grounds for his appreciation of what he did read. It was significant that Thoreau should first choose, from the fifty-five-

GOETHE AT THE AGE OF THIRTY-EIGHT IN ROME

volume *Werke* on the shelves of Emerson's library, Goethe's most famous travel book.

Goethe's account, although published twenty-eight years after his trip, reflected feelingly the intimacy and intensity of a young man's travels. Goethe too had relied upon notes taken on his trip and was now re-creating those realities of his experience that "are wont to lie fairer and truer in tomorrow's memory." Although there was much Goethe did not see because he did not look at it, much of that which he did look at he saw and described to Thoreau's great satisfaction, as the latter attested:

> I should say that it is one of his chief excellences as a writer that he was satisfied with giving an exact description of things as they appeared to him, and their effect upon him. Most travelers have not self-respect enough to do this simply, and make objects and events stand around them as the centre, but still imagine more favorable positions and relations than the actual ones, and so we get no valuable report from them at all.[3]

The exacting eye and accurate description were to be paramount in Thoreau's requirements of the traveler. His criticism in 1852 of Jonathan Carver's *Travels throughout the Interior Parts of North America*, that its author gave "no information respecting the intermediate country, nor much I fear, about the country beyond," was as serious a charge as he could level.[4] He criticized the voyagers to the arctic regions for failing to describe honestly enough the peculiar dreariness of the scenery and of the perpetual twilight of the arctic night.[5] The traveler should, above all else, be an honest observer. In Goethe Thoreau found a traveler intent upon learning through his eyes. There was so much to see that often Goethe could find no time to record his descriptions of it. In Rome he confessed both his frustration and his delight, adding,

> Here I am now living with a calmness and tranquility to which I have for a long while been a stranger. My practice to see and take all things as they are, my fidelity in letting the eye be my light, my perfect renunciation of all pretension, have again come to my aid, and make me calmly, but most intensely happy.[6]

Although Goethe might jog along at a snail's pace, Thoreau found him "always mindful that the earth is beneath him and the heavens above him. His Italy is not merely the fatherland of lazzaroni and virtuosi, and the scene of splendid ruins, but a solid turf-clad soil, daily shined on by the sun, and nightly by the moon. Even the few showers are faithfully recorded." [7] His descriptions were dependable ones: "He speaks as an unconcerned spectator, whose object is faithfully to describe what he sees, and that, for the most part, in the order in which he sees it. Even his reflections do not interfere with his descriptions." Fidelity to the scene before one would enable inferior minds to produce invaluable books, Thoreau noted, if this very moderation were not itself the evidence of superiority. [8] "I kept my eyes continually open, and strove to stamp deep on my mind the images of all I saw," declared Goethe; "judge of them I could not, even if it had been in my power." [9] But as Thoreau observed, "How much virtue there is in simply seeing. . . . We are as much as we see." [10]

Thoreau pointed to a further quality which Goethe exemplified as a traveler, observing that, whereas "some, poor in spirit, record plaintively only what has happened to them," Goethe was among those who report "how they have happened to the universe, and the judgment which they have awarded to circumstances." [11] In spite of Goethe's frequent suspensions of judgment and his attempts to keep separate the records of his eye and his heart, no reader could for long regard him as an impersonal or "unconcerned" observer. While "travels" were by their very nature likely to be largely autobiographical, Goethe's Italian experiences were from beginning to end tools used by him for laying bare his inner development. Thus he continually brought to bear upon that which he objectively viewed the calm response and judgment fostered by his fine sensitivity and intelligence. He was the poet traveling, whose sensibilities condition not only his judgments of circumstances but even what he sees. Although he traveled like Thoreau with his spyglass and botany text, in the best tradition of the great scientific movement of the late eighteenth and early nineteenth centuries, he kept the perspective of the poet. [12] Thoreau praised and carried in his mind's eye Goethe's magnificent "objective" description of Venice—he kept conjuring up its scene years after reading *Italienische Reise* [13]—but it was Goethe's personal experience of rapture at the sound of crickets on an autumn evening in the Trent countryside with which Thoreau most closely identified himself.[14] Thoreau's constant statements on the limitations of purely scientific observation are numerous and well known. He found the poet and naturalist looking quite differently at objects, and he regarded the *Annual of Scientific Discovery* as a "poor dry compilation"; "the astronomer is as blind to the significant phenomena, or the significance of phenomena, as the wood-sawyer who wears glasses to defend his eyes against sawdust. The question is not what you look at, but what you see." [15] He expressed still more clearly in 1857 the view which twenty years earlier he found represented in Goethe:

> Sometimes I would rather get a transient glimpse or side view of a thing than stand fronting to it,—as those polypodies. The object I caught a glimpse of as I went by haunts my thoughts a long time, is infinitely suggestive, and I do not care to front it and scrutinize it, for I know that the thing that really concerns me is not there, but in my relation to that. That is a mere reflecting surface. It is not the polypody in my pitcher or herbarium, or which I may possibly persuade to grow in my yard, or which is described in botanies, that interests me, but the one I pass by in my walks a little distance off, when in the right mood. Its influence is sporadic, wafted through the air to me.

Goethe's descriptions were particularly pleasing to Thoreau because, like those which he himself gave, they blended scientific observation with artistic feeling.[16]

Even more important, Thoreau found in Goethe's account the reflection of that aspect of nineteenth-century science which had greatest significance for both poets and Transcendentalists, namely, the organic nature of all phenomena. Goethe's observations upon the people, the fauna, the history, the geology of Italy, fragmentary and varied as they might seem, were constantly being resolved as parts of an organic whole. "And so let me trust, that no matter how things first appear, the order will reveal itself." [17] Goethe's interest in the parts was to discover how and what principles evolved from them. With similar intent, Thoreau was to focus his desire for global familiarity upon the elemental truths of nature and man, expressing only annoyance at information on the petty, incidental or accidental aspects of life. That a cow was run over on the Western Railroad stemmed from no principle of which he needed to learn. "If you are acquainted with the principle, what do you care for a myriad instances and applications?" [18]

Goethe in his traveling was motivated by much the same incentive that Thoreau acknowledged when he confessed himself to be on the trail of his hound, bay horse, and turtledove. Through his Italian journey Goethe attained his understanding of his own ability and mission as a poet. His trip afforded him vantage ground from which he could renew the past and make plans for the future; he continually reminded his reader that the trip's final significance lay in its moral profit, its contribution to his own growth as a person. "I am not making this wonderful trip in order to delude myself but in order to get to know myself through those things which stand around me." [19] For the rest of his life Thoreau was to reaffirm similar convictions regarding the moral test of travel.

> A man fits out a ship at a great expense and sends it to the West Indies with a crew of men and boys, and after six months or a year it comes back with a load of pineapples. Now, if no more gets accomplished than the speculator aims at,—if it simply turns out what is called a successful venture,—I am less interested in this expedition than in some child's first excursion a huckleberrying, in which it is introduced into a new world, experiences a new development, though it brings home only a gill of huckleberries in its basket. . . . The value of any experience is measured, of course, not by the amount of money, but the amount of development we get out of it. If a New England boy's dealing with oranges and pineapples have had more to do with his development than picking huckleberries or pulling turnips, then he rightly and naturally thinks of the former.[20]

He summed up his view succinctly when he declared, "Ultimately the moral is all in all. . . . A man has not seen a thing who has not felt it." [21]

Still another characteristic of Goethe the traveler won Thoreau's admiration. "Above all," said Thoreau, "he possessed a hearty goodwill to all men, and never wrote a cross or even careless word." [22] Thoreau did not demand etiquette or formality or sentimentality from his fellow travelers, but for him as surely as for Emerson all things were moral, and that quality of character which dictated a true sympathy with one's fellow men and a recognition of a common humanity regardless of differences of place, race, or time, that quality he

required of any fellow traveler as he did of any fellow man. He never
absolved a man from practicing, even though he might abjure his
preaching. A bigot was as distasteful to travel with as to live with.
The relation between character and observation was obvious. The
sight was conditioned by the seer, the experience dependent upon the
character of the individual who lived it.

> Men talk about traveling this way or that, as if seeing were all in the
> eyes, and a man could sufficiently report what he stood bodily before,
> when the seeing depends ever on the being. . . . A blind man who
> possesses inward truth and consistency will see more than one who has
> faultless eyes but no serious and laborious astronomer to look through
> them. As if the eyes were the only part of a man that traveled.[23]

Books, Thoreau observed, "should contain pure discoveries, glimpses
of terra firma, though by shipwrecked mariners, and not the art of
navigation by those who have never been out of sight of land. They
must not yield wheat and potatoes, but must themselves be the unconstrained and natural harvest of their authors' lives." [24] Goethe's
book was such a harvest. The travel accounts which Thoreau was to
value most were the intimate and genuine expressions of their authors' lives.

Such a book was Alexander Henry's *Travels and Adventures in
Canada and the Indian Territories between the Years 1760 and
1776*, which Thoreau read at about the same time that he read
Goethe. Thoreau's one adverse criticism of the *Italienische Reise* was
that it reflected too much consciousness of "art," too much time
spent testing an aesthetic "taste" which should need no testing.
"Goethe's whole education and life," he complained, "were those of
the artist. He lacks the unconsciousness of the poet. He says of himself [in his autobiography]: 'I had lived among painters from my
childhood, and had accustomed myself to look at objects, as they did,
with reference to art.' And this was his practice to the last." [25] But if
Goethe's travel account reflected at times too much of the "artist,"
Alexander Henry's book amply compensated by its prosaic natural-
ness. Few books showed less consciousness of art.

Henry was scarcely the poet traveling, although his account in
Thoreau's eyes served the end of poetry, stood in a threshold rela-

tionship to that primitive poetry which obeyed the laws of nature rather than the rules of art. His book read, Thoreau said,

> like the argument to a great poem on the primitive state of the country and its inhabitants, and the reader imagines what in each case, with the invocation of the Muse, might be sung, and leaves off with suspended interests, as if the full account were to follow. . . . It contains scenery and rough sketching of men and incidents enough to inspire poets for many years, and to my fancy is as full of sounding names as any page of history,—Lake Winnipeg, Hudson's Bay, Ottaway, and portages innumerable; Chippeways, Gens de Terres, Les Pilleurs, The Weepers; with reminiscences of Hearne's journey, and the like; an immense and shaggy but sincere country, summer and winter, adorned with chains of lakes and rivers, covered with snows, with hemlocks, and fir trees.[26]

Henry offered that mythological dimension to travel which invested the particularity of a scene with archetypal significance, suggested in part by his direct and unencumbered style which focused selectively upon the clear and basic object or phenomenon itself, identifying elements of nature simply and classically. As Thoreau was to observe, "A fact truely and absolutely stated acquires a mythological or universal significance."

The book's contents were set forth in the Preface in the following formal fashion characteristic of eighteenth-century travel works:

> The heads under which, for the most part, they [the details of this volume] will be found to range themselves are three: first the incidents or adventures in which the author was engaged; secondly, the observations, on the geography and natural history of the countries visited, which he was able to make, and to preserve; and thirdly, the views of society and manners among a part of the Indians of North America, which it has belonged to the course of his narrative to develop.

The divisions did not operate in the narrative itself, however, where all three subject matters were integrated at once into the chronological account of Henry's experiences. His account was plainly written, direct and unpretentious in style, smacking at times of that formal tone peculiar to an unlearned man's sincere attempt to communicate without pretense on the one hand or the distraction due to errors of grammar or syntax on the other. To a remarkable extent Henry succeeded in both, for his style never got in the way of truth or clarity. Thoreau remarked in A *Week on the Concord and Merrimack Rivers:*

> There is a sort of homely truth and naturalness in some books which is very rare to find, and yet looks cheap enough. There may be nothing lofty in the sentiment, or fine in the expression, but it is careless country talk. Homeliness is almost as great a merit in a book as in a house, if the reader would abide there. It is next to beauty, and a very high art.[27]

Thoreau could recall from his reading of another travel account one Hussein Effridi who praised to the French traveler Emile Botta the epistolary style of an Arab pasha because there was not one person in all of Jidda who could understand it.[28] But for Thoreau the test of style was the preciseness and directness with which it communicated an experience or an idea. "A great thought is never found in a mean dress; but though it proceed from the lips of Wolofs, the nine Muses and the three Graces will have conspired to clothe it in fit phrase." [29] The style was but the flower of the man and should possess a sinewy, hearty, even earthy quality to survive the inclemency of time. Robust sincerity might communicate truth where contrived means failed. In the *Week* Thoreau summed up his admiration of Henry's prose. The context of his discussion is interesting, reaffirming as it does the kind of reading which was wont to lie fairest in Thoreau's memory!

> Tuesday   This noontide was a fit occasion to make some pleasant harbor, and there read the journal of some voyageur like ourselves, not too moral nor inquisitive, and which would not disturb the moon. . . . But, alas, our chest, like the cabin of a coaster, contained only its well-thumbed "Navigator" for all literature, and we were obliged to draw on our memory for these things.
>
> We naturally remembered Alexander Henry's Adventures here, as a sort of classic among books of American travel. . . . He has truth and moderation worthy of the father of history, which belong only to an intimate experience, and he does not defer too much to literature. The unlearned traveler may quote his single line from the poets with as good right as the scholar. He too may speak of the stars, for he sees them shoot perhaps when the astronomer does not. The good sense of this author is very conspicuous. He is a traveler who does not exaggerate, but writes for the information of his readers, for science and for history. His story is told with as much good faith and directness as if

it were a report to his brother traders, or the Directors of the Hudson's Bay Company, and is fitly dedicated to Sir Joseph Banks. . . . In what school was this fur-trader educated? He seems to travel the immense snowy country with such purpose only as the reader who accompanies him, and to the latter's imagination, it is, as it were, momentarily created to be the scene of his adventures.[30]

Bits of information and details from scenes in Henry's book found their places later in Thoreau's writings, but it was the over-all tone of Henry's narrative and his manner of expression which most impressed his reader.[31]

Thoreau also admired the way in which Henry traveled: in a simple, primitive, original manner, standing in a true relation to men and nature. In *Walden* Thoreau referred to a proposal he had heard lately "that two young men should travel together over the world, the one without money, earning his means as he went, before the mast and behind the plow, the other carrying a bill of exchange in his pocket." He left no doubt as to which method he deemed proper travel.[32] He applied Sadi's advice to his own practice, maintaining the virtue of as simple, primitive, and unencumbered travel as possible. "The cheapest way to travel, and the way to travel the farthest in the shortest distance, is to go afoot, carrying a dipper, a spoon, and a fish line, some Indian meal, some salt, and some sugar." He looked upon the England of his day "as an old gentleman who is traveling with a great deal of luggage." [33] He upbraided his friend Blake in 1859 for not traveling Cape Cod with sufficient rigor, and criticized his own recent travels in the White Mountains: "I confess that the journey did not bear any fruit that I know of. I did not expect it would. The mode of it was not simple and adventurous enough." [34] In 1860 he mourned that "the traveler is no longer a wayfarer, with his staff and pack and dusty coat. He is not a pilgrim, but he travels in a saloon, and carries dumbbells to exercise with in intervals of his journey." [35] For the same reason he became increasingly annoyed with the travels undertaken by United States Army officers supposedly for exploratory purposes, and with their accounts eventually published at the offhand instruction of Congress and the Secretary of the Interior, often consisting of "a journal of a picnic or sporting expedition by a brevit Lieutenant-Colonel, illustrated by photographs of the traveler's footsteps across the plains and an admirable engraving of his native village as it appeared on leaving it, and followed by an appendix on the paleontology of the route by a distinguished savant who was not there." [36] Henry's narrative, in sharp contrast, reported genuine experiences which could only have been the fruit of elemental and intimate personal relations with the people and the country visited.

Henry's natural manner of travel was connected with one other characteristic which Thoreau found exemplified by the fur trader. The best travel, in Thoreau's eyes, was that most closely related to a man's way of living. It profited one to travel "not as a scientific explorer under government, but a Yankee sealer rather, who makes those unexplored continents his harbors in which to refit for more adventurous cruises." [37] Henry was peculiarly dear to Thoreau because his traveling evolved naturally from his living, primitive and unphilosophical as the occupation of fur trading might be. As Thoreau declared in *Walden*, "The traveler on the prairies is naturally a hunter, on the head waters of the Missouri and Columbia a trapper, and at the Falls of Saint Mary a fisherman. He who is only a traveler learns things at second-hand and by the halves, and is poor authority."

The third book which proves interesting in relation to Thoreau's theories on a successful traveler is one which he read in the spring of 1851 and to which reference has been made in an earlier chapter: Charles Robert Darwin's *Voyage of a Naturalist round the World*.[38] Darwin's book served to confirm and solidify certain of Thoreau's views on the criteria for good travel; at the same time his book gave emphasis to new views peculiarly apt for a confirmed travel addict seeking sure grounds for a very un-Transcendental and even un-Thoreauvian position. Thoreau's reading of Darwin's *Voyage* coincided, perhaps not without significance, with that period which marks a transition in his reading practices, from rather informal and spasmodically recorded ventures into travel literature to more extensive, precise, and scholarly coverage, a shift indicated, as we have already shown, by the inauguration of the special notebooks for cataloguing and recording fully the varieties of information gleaned. At the precise time that he was reading Darwin, Thoreau was also read-

THE YOUNG CHARLES DARWIN SHORTLY AFTER
HIS RETURN FROM HIS VOYAGE ON THE BEAGLE

ing the travels of another naturalist, son of a famous scientist: François André Michaux's *Voyage a l'ouest des monts Alleghanys*.
Although neither book supplied Thoreau his first contact with the
science of the naturalist, Darwin's and Michaux's accounts did represent the most "scientific" approaches which he had yet met among
his travelers.[39]

By the time Thoreau read Darwin's book, there was no question
about the stature of its author as a scientist. Only nine years later
Thoreau was to read and take notes from Darwin's *Origin of Species*.[40] Now he was reading a young scientist's first exposure to travel.
Once again, as with Goethe's account, Thoreau was sharing experiences which had had momentous import for the personal growth of
the traveler. Within a year of his return, Darwin began his notebook
on evolution; he went on to write some twenty books, all stemming
from the original inspiration of this five-year voyage. From the popular title which Thoreau uses and the parenthetical dating by him of
the observations made by Darwin, we know that he read the first
American edition of the *Voyage* published in two volumes in 1846,
which Darwin described in his Preface to the English edition the year
before as follows:

> This volume contains, in the form of a Journal, a history of our voyage,
> and a sketch of those observations in Natural History and Geology,
> which I think will possess some interest for the general reader. I have
> in this edition largely condensed and corrected some parts, and have
> added a little to others, in order to render the volume more fitted for
> popular reading; but I trust that naturalists will remember, that they
> must refer for details to the larger publications, which comprise the
> scientific results of the Expedition.

Thoreau was obviously more interested in Darwin's journal than in
his science.

Aside from the mere volume of data which Thoreau recorded from
Darwin's account and the frequency with which he referred to the
latter's travel experiences in his writings,[41] Darwin exemplified practices and principles of which Thoreau approved. Darwin traveled
simply and appropriately for his purpose. His descriptions of what he
saw were vivid and exact, and unlike those of the traveler whom
Thoreau later scored for "snatching at a fact or two in behalf of sci-

ence as he goes, just as a panther in his leap will take off a man's
sleeve and land twenty feet beyond him traveling down hill," [42]
Darwin's descriptions were full ones thoroughly integrated into the
mainstream of his experience. Thoreau had always been impressed
with how little of concern to the close observer and lover of nature
the ordinary map offered.[43] He was grateful to find Darwin traveling over the face of the land and sea and with his clear and inclusive
eye filling in a good portion of the map of the Southern Hemisphere.

Moreover, like Goethe and Henry, Darwin was the kind of man
Thoreau could admire as a person. Although he observed with the
knowledge of the natural scientist, he did not observe with "scientific" detachment; he neglected neither the subject of his own feelings about that which he saw nor the obligations attendant upon his
moral principles regarding his fellow men. He spoke openly of "the

H.M.S. BEAGLE ENTERING THE NARROWS
AT TIERRA DEL FUEGO

From *Voyages of H.M.S. Adventure and Beagle*

sublimity of the primeval forests undefaced by the hand of man . . .
temples filled with the varied productions of the God of Nature:—no
one can stand in these solitudes unmoved, and not feel that there is
more in man than the mere breath of his body." And on leaving
Brazil he exclaimed:

> Thank God, I shall never again visit a slave-country. . . . Those who
> look tenderly at the slave-owner, and with a cold heart at the slave,
> never seem to put themselves into the position of the latter. . . . And
> these deeds are done and palliated by men, who profess to love their
> neighbors as themselves, who believe in God, and pray that His will be
> done on earth! It makes one's blood boil, yet heart tremble, to think
> that we Englishmen and our descendents, with their boastful cry of
> liberty, have been and are so guilty.[44]

Maintaining such breadth of character as he did, his scientific observations supplementing the findings of his heart and conscience,
Darwin represented to Thoreau the scientist in his most palatable
guise. Although Thoreau did not sell out to the scientists of his day,
and although even when reading them he expressed his distrust of
them as travelers precisely because they were scientists,[45] he yet acknowledged several of the premises which Darwin recommended as a
scientist to the traveler. These premises Darwin summed up at the
end of his *Voyage* in a section called "Retrospect." Travels, declared
Darwin, should be undertaken not dilettantishly but deliberately;
more specifically, they should be made to confirm or advance one's
knowledge of something in which one already had an interest and
thus some knowledge of. Immediately upon finishing Darwin's book
Thoreau stated in his Journal: "I am, perchance, most and most
profitably interested in the things which I already know a little about;
a mere and utter novelty is a mere monstrosity to me." And in 1856
he explained, in regard to his own travels: "I have found my account
in traveling in having prepared beforehand a list of questions which I
would get answered, not trusting to my interest at the moment, and
can then travel with the most profit." [46]

Darwin not only stressed the interdependence of all living things,
and thus that synthesis and organic unity of nature which Thoreau as
poet and philosopher assumed, but he also emphasized the need of
some scientific knowledge for comprehending this wholeness. The

traveler, he noted, should be able to examine all the distinct parts of this whole from a comparative viewpoint, in order to see correlations, not simply distinctions; and this ability, he maintained, depended upon sound knowledge of the natural sciences.

> There is a growing pleasure in comparing the character of a scenery in different countries, which to a certain degree is distinct from merely admiring its beauty. It depends chiefly on an acquaintance with the individual parts of each view; I am strongly induced to believe that, as in music, the person who understands every note will, if he also possesses a proper taste, more thoroughly enjoy the whole, so he who examines each part of a fine view, may also thoroughly comprehend the full and combined effect. Hence, a traveler should be a botanist, for in all views plants form the chief embellishment.[47]

He spoke further of the "group masses of naked rock," of both the "tedious waste" of the ocean and its "heaving surface polished like a mirror," of the boundless plains and the crest of the Cordilleras, of wildlife, fish, fowl, and mammal, of the Southern Cross and other constellations of the Southern Hemisphere: all demanding for their appreciation some exact knowledge of the natural laws and operations of the physical and biological universe.

It is scarcely necessary to point to Thoreau's own training and practice as a natural scientist. Amateur though he may have remained in any single field, and protester throughout his life that science's perspective was untrustworthy, Thoreau's microscope, spyglass, charts, weather tables, presses, and collections, his geological surveys and "Zoological Notes," his perusal of the reports of the Smithsonian Institution, of the Boston Society of Natural History, and of the Massachusetts Agricultural Society, his reading of Audubon, Wilson, Macgillivray, Bechstein, Lyell, and Nuttal, of Loudon, Gray, Harlan, and Lovell, of Fitch, Harris, Kirby, and Spence, of Agassiz and Gould, Abbott, Sowerby, and Chambers, his own field notes and his essays, all attest to the respect and interest which he showed for the natural scientist's acute eye and practiced induction. He cautiously accepted Darwin's reasoning on the formation of coral reefs. He was impressed that Darwin, Agassiz, Gould, and Desor all discussed the ocean as the principal seat of life.[48] It was because the traveler should be a philosopher, interested in laws and principles, that

Thoreau acknowledged with Darwin the desirability of his having some sound scientific knowledge.

One must also remember that in the first half of the nineteenth century it was not really a question of whether or not a traveler should be a naturalist. Most travelers were naturalists in some degree, whether their knowledge was based upon native skill or scientific learning. This was the period when the traveler was opening up the physical world for science. The question was only how good a naturalist one must be, and how such a naturalist, having the necessary capacity for identifying and understanding natural phenomena, could keep from being narrow or detached or amoral regarding his observations and responses. The great naturalists of this period, Humboldts or Darwins, did not represent for a moment the "impersonal" approach of the late nineteenth- and twentieth-century scientist.

It is significant to note that in his "Retrospect" Darwin emphasized the further values from travel of experiencing (1) the sight of the marvels of natural phenomena, (2) a knowledge of primitive man, (3) contact with the wilderness (vast, unknown, timeless, and so perpetually intriguing), and (4) the appeal of the outdoor, uncivilized, adventurous life. And it is of further interest to note that this summary can serve exactly as a summary of values which we find Thoreau specifically acknowledging upon more than one occasion from his own travels immediate and vicarious.

Early in his life, then, and at the time when he was reading two quite different but impressive travelers, Thoreau determined what requisites he himself held for good traveling. His reading of Darwin somewhat later, but still in time to anticipate a major volume of his travel reading, added to and summed up his requirements. The principles thus formed he stuck to firmly thereafter in evaluating both his own and others' travels. Six months after reading Darwin he referred to his own criteria as follows in his Journal: "The question is not where did the traveler go, what places did he see?—it would be difficult to choose between places—but who was the traveler? how did he travel? how genuine an experience did he get?" He did not then fill in the answers to his own questions, but we know now the answers he had in mind.

Who should the traveler be? He should be a scientist in sufficient degree to be able to understand (i.e., distinguish) natural phenomena as he saw them. But he should not be simply a scientist, should not be concerned only with the "scientific" aspects of what he saw and experienced, for then the information which he gave would be only partial, a half-truth; he should have the unconsciousness of the poet, who experiences intuitively that which no objective datum or form can communicate by itself; and he should be a humane and admirable person whose moral character is inevitably reflected in his experiences. Finally, he should be more than a traveler, his travels relegated properly to some other natural activity or occupation which he found most meaningful as a way of life; he should not bear the taint of a "professional" traveler but be a man whose travels relate to his "profession."

How should he travel? He should travel in a simple, primitive, original way, standing in a true relation to men and nature, able to give an exact description of what he saw and its effect upon him. He should travel deliberately rather than dilettantishly, in order to confirm or advance his knowledge of something in which he already had an interest. And he should travel for the purpose of examining the variety of phenomena, natural, human, and social, from a comparative viewpoint, to the end that his understanding of the parts could enable him to comprehend the whole.

How genuine an experience should he get? This answer was the hardest, of course, to define. The experience should be such that he could communicate its intimacy in truth and moderation, without deferring too much to artistry, could report it with good faith and directness as human history. Above all, it should be such an experience as contributed crucially to his growth as a person, significant for what it made him as well as for what it told him, an event of some real moral profit. As Thoreau summed up the case for travel in the pages of his own first travel book, "True and sincere traveling is no pastime, but it is as serious as the grave, or any part of the human journey."

At the same time that Goethe, Henry, and Darwin contributed to Thoreau's formulation of these criteria, they also furnished him literary standards for evaluating the travel books he was to read, standards of such excellence as one would be hard put to match with any other combination of travel books of similar caliber. No matter how often he was forced to compromise these standards in selecting even the best current travel accounts of his day, Thoreau had learned to bring to this phase of his reading, as he did to others, high standards and critical acumen.

◄§ CHAPTER VI §►

More Than the Count of Cats

My desire for knowledge is intermittent, but my desire to bathe my head in atmospheres unknown to my feet is perennial and constant.

"Walking," 1862

In his Journal for November 11, 1851, Thoreau wrote:

> Today you may write a chapter on the advantages of traveling, and tomorrow you may write another chapter on the advantages of not traveling. The horizon has one kind of beauty and attraction to him who has never explored the hills and mountains in it, and another, I fear a less ethereal and glorious one, to him who has. That blue mountain in the horizon is certainly the most heavenly, the most elysian, which we have not climbed, on which we have not camped for the night. But only our horizon is moved thus further off, and if our whole life should prove thus a failure, the future which is to atone for all, where still there must be some success, will be more glorious still.

Three features of his statement are particularly worth noting. In the first place, the passage reflects, through the veneer of somewhat romantic reasoning, the undercoating of self-consciousness which always characterized Thoreau's attitude toward the narrow orbit of his own physical "travels." He had determined to stay at home. Yet in a great bulk of his reading he was contradicting that very determination by traveling at the side of those whose decisions in the matter were opposite to his own. It is scarcely surprising that he showed some self-consciousness. It is interesting that he always expressed his doubts or his rationalizations in relation to his own "voyages" and "excursions," never in relation to those many more vicarious travels which he was taking through his reading. A second feature of the statement worth noting is that, while at first it wavers in regard to the immediate pros and cons of travel, it resolves itself in favor of travel.

I think a careful chronology of all Thoreau's judgments upon travel rendered during his lifetime would find such a resolution characteristic of his questionings. In the third place, both the waverings and the resolutions in the statement are obviously and unashamedly the exclamations of a man who *has* "explored the hills" and camped on the mountain for a night, the confessions of a man who is, willy-nilly, for better or for worse, a hopelessly confirmed traveler himself.

It is time to draw some conclusions about the essential position which travel held in Thoreau's life, and thus cut through some of the confusion which Thoreau creates for us with his voiced vacillations. Placed in the context of his philosophy of life, all travel was but means to an end, in Thoreau's case only one means to the particular end which he pursued: the discovery of the nature of transcendent reality.[1] The end was not, strictly speaking, a philosophical one, for it was to be experienced, not simply understood, its promise the deepest spiritual reward rather than intellectual satisfaction. It was an end approached through more than mere knowledge, involving a much greater commitment of self. The ultimate goal was no less than the secret of life itself, to be "apprehended" in the manner Thoreau described in *Walden*—"by the perpetual instilling and drenching of the reality that surrounds us"—or by what Perry Miller in his *Consciousness in Concord* calls "the royal right of consciousness." [2]

Theoretically it would seem difficult to conceive of anything which could constitute genuine interference with such an end so approached; but empirically Thoreau was frequently finding impediments threatening to swerve him from his goal, obstacles which he could not always handle as directly or as easily as he expected the readers of *Walden* to cope with the nutshells and mosquitoes' wings on the rails that threatened to throw them off their tracks. So in describing his stay at Walden Pond he would lash out at the inconsequential value of travel reading compared with the reading of Homer, establishing a hierarchy of values fitted to the moment, and probably experiencing no little guilt that his energies were not focused entirely upon the immediate acreage which offered him for these months its concentrated realities. When any activity in which he was engaged, whether a study of paleontology or a "sojourn" at Walden, came into conflict with the end to which it was but contributory, Thoreau felt compelled to belittle it, either by dramatically dismissing it or by whittling it down to a relative size. When that travel which he so impulsively enjoyed and which he one moment justified with the most extravagant extolment seemed to be overtempting him or to be usurping too much of his time and attention, when it threatened to corrupt commitments to the nobler end, then Thoreau turned upon it. The rending which ensued accounts for most of the direct contradictions in his evaluations.

But such uneasiness also furnished reinforcement for the paradoxical position which travel came to hold in his thought and art. For while it was exceedingly difficult to throw overboard the appeals of the traveler and the values of travel, to denounce travel outright in favor of staying at home, it was inspirational to defend staying at home as a form of travel. It was peculiarly so when the two activities were literally so linked in Thoreau's own practice. Gradually defense and extolment fused, travel at home incorporated any amount of travel abroad, and only in his more direct and labored rationales of his position did Thoreau wind himself in verbal contradictions on the subject. And these dilemmas were for the Journal and the man; the artist, as we shall see, managed not only to resolve them but thereby to give his literary art its most distinctive stamp.

In a passage in the Journal for November 20, 1857, Thoreau tried to place in proper perspective ends and means in relation to travel. Although on this particular occasion he was inclined to play down the value of his own journeying, his position regarding the relationship between travel and, as he put it, the deepest living is one which makes a good deal of sense if one attends to the substance of his explanation, almost in spite of the hyperboles of his expression.

> In books, that which is most generally interesting is what comes home to the most cherished private experience of the greatest number. It is not the book of him who has traveled the farthest over the surface of the globe, but of him who has lived the deepest and been the most at home. If an equal emotion is excited by a familiar homely phenomenon as by the Pyramids, there is no advantage in seeing the Pyramids. . . . A man is worth most to himself and to others, whether as an observer, or poet, or neighbor, or friend, where he is most himself, most contented and at home. There his life is the most intense and he loses the fewest moments. Familiar and surrounding objects are the best symbols and

illustrations of his life. If a man who has had deep experiences should endeavor to describe them in a book of travels, it would be to use the language of a wandering tribe instead of a universal language. The poet has made the best roots in his native soil of any man, and is the hardest to transplant. The man who is often thinking that it is better to be somewhere else than where he is excommunicates himself. If a man is rich and strong anywhere, it must be on his native soil. Here I have been these forty years learning the language of these fields that I may the better express myself. If I should travel to the prairies, I should much less understand them, and my past life would serve me but ill to describe them. Many a weed here stands for more of life to me than the big trees of California would if I should go there. We only need travel enough to give our intellects an airing.

This is Thoreau attempting to be reasonable about the whole matter. It was bound to land him in some extraordinary overstatements, the most blatant certainly being that which denies to the major portion of his own published writings, including his first book, any "universal language"—unless we can assume that "deep experiences" here implies some subtle shade of difference between the truths of *Walden* and those of the *Week*, which seems unlikely. We see evidence everywhere, moreover, to indicate that, if "familiar and surrounding objects" were the "best" symbols of life for a writer's use, they were in Thoreau's case by no means the only ones. When he speaks of the "intellect" which travel aired, we must understand him to be speaking of mind in the Transcendentalist's sense, his "cleaver," as he calls it in *Walden*, which "discerns and rifts its way into the secret of things." What is particularly important is that we see, through the welter of specific declarations, the core of his case. It is again the old stand for a vantage point, coupled with the maturer realization of the price which deliberate knowledge costs in time and attention, even when acquired through a "drenching" in immediate reality. Never relinquishing his premise as a writer that "your account of foreign parts which you have never seen should by good rights be less interesting," [3] Thoreau was nevertheless "seeing" more and more foreign parts; the geographical circumference of his area of knowledge was actually widening at the prodigious rate, and the demands upon him for close scrutiny and full understanding of it grew proportionately. His full answer to the way in which travel contributed to his life was even for him a complex one, only gradually arrived at, and only adequately assimilated in his art. It remains most properly an answer for us to deduce, not one for him to state to us outright.

Thoreau built his incentives for travel, as he did for travel reading, upon the premise that one could learn from it. Undertaken in the manner of which he approved, traveling had much to teach a man. "We are acquainted with a mere pellicle of the globe in which we live," he reminded his readers in *Walden*. The true traveler recognized no physical, no geographical boundaries to what he should and could know. This same desire for the most informative travel was back of Thoreau's theories regarding his travels in Concord. As he put it in his Journal:

> A man must naturally get away some hundreds or thousands of miles from home before he can be said to begin his travels. Why not begin his travels at home? . . . Now if he should begin with all the knowledge of a native, and add thereto the knowledge of a traveler, both natives and foreigners would be obliged to read his book. . . . It takes a man of genius to travel in his own country, in his native village. . . . Such a traveler will make the distance which Hanno and Marco Polo and Cook and Ledyard went over ridiculous.

He even found so worthy a traveler as William Bartram guilty of postponing productive travel, by heading his first chapter of his *Travels* with the words "The author set sail from Philadelphia, and arrives at Charleston, from whence he begins his travels." [4]

Thoreau did not postpone his travels until he got outside his own gate; on the other hand, he also carried them well beyond it. In addition to his travels in "his native village" he traveled via his reading over extensive tracts of "his own country" with a host of Bartram's predecessors and followers. That he never seriously thought of limiting the value of traveling to local travels alone is apparent from the many instances in which he discussed the value of travel in relation to the provincialism of his fellow New Englanders. Not only did he confess that he found the information of the traveler more far-reaching than the villager's; he stated his hope that "no people can long continue provincial in character who have the propensity for politics and whittling, and rapid traveling, which the Yankees have." [5] He contrasted the pioneer of the West, dwelling "within sound of the surf of those billows of migration which are breaking on the shores around him, or near him," with the stagnant provincial retirement of Green, the selectman of Carlisle. He criticized Concord for representing many New England towns, "contented to be countrified, to be provincial." Why should his village not "put itself in communication with whatever sources of light and intelligence there are in the world?" he asked. "If the South Sea Explorers have at length got their story ready, and Congress neglected to make it accessible to the people, why does not Concord purchase one for its grown-up children?" While Thoreau saw the railroad as both blessing and curse for the farmer—"seeing the world all going by as it were"—he recognized quite objectively that it had unsettled the young Concord farmers to the extent that they could not make up their minds to live the quiet, retired, old-fashioned country-farmer's life; they were now "too well aware of what is going on in the world not to wish to take some part in it." [6] And this was not a bad thing. As he observed in a letter to a friend in 1859, "Men may sit in chambers, seemingly safe and sound, and yet despair, and turn out at last only hollowness and dust within, like a Dead Sea apple." He noted in his Journal that "the inhabitants [of the village] are wayworn by the travel that goes by and over them withoout travelling themselves." [7] In a letter written eleven years earlier to the same friend he expressed the alternative:

> To set about living a true life is to go a journey to a distant country, gradually to find ourselves surrounded by new scenes and men; for as long as the old are around me, I know that I am not in any true sense living a new and better life. The outward is only the outside of that which is within. [8]

When its intellectual gains were chalked up, however, there remained incentives and rewards connected with travel which were no less crucial for Thoreau because they fell outside the realm of the rational. It is characteristic of Thoreau, having proclaimed one intelligible premise for his interest in travel, to qualify it with an additional piece of confession. It is as hard to contradict him as it is Emerson, for both men disarm their readers with more truth than it is convenient to include. His statement which heads this chapter proves inescapably relevant to the extensive travel reading which he was doing, now that we know of the latter. Here he might appear to be driving a wedge between the airing of his intellect and the bathing of his senses, but it is the head which is to bathe, just as surely as it is the intellect which discerns and rifts. Factual knowledge, of which his stupendous private reference library held such bulk, was but the raw material which one mined. All the things that gave it significance constituted the variables of motivation for Thoreau's travel reading, just as surely as they were the incentives for the mining at Walden. That they were desires more closely allied with emotions and intuitions than with "knowledge" in no way belittled them. Much of the truest value of his endless global travel Thoreau described for himself just after his first and most rewarding "voyage" on the Merrimack, as he wrote ecstatically in his Journal on March 21, 1840, of the expanding horizons which his travel reading was now opening up to him:

> The world is a fit theatre today in which any part may be acted. There is this moment proposed to me every kind of life that men can lead anywhere, or that imagination can paint. By another spring I may be a mail-carrier in Peru, or a South African planter, or a Siberian exile, or a Greenland whaler, or a settler on the Columbia River, or a Canton merchant, or a soldier in Florida, or a mackerel-fisher off Cape Sable, or a Robinson Crusoe in the Pacific, or a silent navigator of any sea. . . .
>
> I am freer than any planet.[9] No complaint reaches round the world. I can move away from public opinion, from government, from religion, from education, from society. Shall I be reckoned a ratable poll in the county of Middlesex, or be rated at one spear under the palm trees of Guinea? Shall I raise corn and potatoes in Massachusetts, or figs and olives in Asia Minor? Sit out the day in my office in State Street, or ride it out on the Steppes of Tartary? For my Brobdingnag I may sail to Patagonia; for my day's adventures may surpass the Arabian Night's Entertainments. I may be a logger on the headwaters of the Penobscot, to be recorded hereafter as an amphibious river-god, by as sounding a name as Triton or Proteus; carry furs from Nootka to China, and so be more renowned than Jason and his golden fleece; or go on a South Sea exploring expedition to be hereafter recounted along with the periplus of Hanno. I may repeat the adventures of Marco Polo or Mandeville.
>
> These are but a few of my chances, and how many more things may I do with which there are none to be compared!
>
> Thank Fortune, we are not rooted to the soil, and here is not all the world. The buckeye does not grow in New England, the mockingbird is rarely heard here. Why not keep pace with the day, and not allow

of a sunset or fall behind the summer and the migration of the birds? Shall we not compete with the buffalo, who keeps pace with the seasons, cropping the pastures of the Colorado till a greener and sweeter grass awaits him by the Yellowstone? The wild goose is more a cosmopolite than we; he breaks his fast in Canada, takes a luncheon in the Susquehanna, and plumes himself for the night in a Louisiana bayou. The pidgeon carries an acorn in his crop from the King of Holland's to Mason and Dixon's line. Yet we think if rail fences are pulled down and stone walls set up on our farms, bounds are henceforth set to our lives and our fates decided. If you are chosen town clerk, forsooth, you can't go to Tierra del Fuego this summer.

The reader who would see at a glance the development of Thoreau's attitude toward travel over the years, most particularly how a paradox of contradictory desires resolved itself into a paradoxical idea, need only place this passage beside its more familiar version which appeared fourteen years later opening the last chapter of *Walden*. Thoreau repeated this description of the exhilaration offered the traveler. But the original passage, written before the decisive Staten Island venture and so obviously referring to the vistas and appeals which literal travel to new and far places then offered Thoreau, is now employed to bring all such wonders to rest in the township of Concord and to transform the traveler's ventures into metaphysical quests best done at home.

To the sick the doctors wisely recommend a change of air and scenery. Thank Heaven, here is not all the world. The buckeye does not grow in New England, and the mockingbird is rarely heard here. The wild goose is more of a cosmopolite than we; he breaks his fast in Canada, takes a luncheon in the Ohio, and plumes himself for the night in a southern bayou. Even the bison, to some extent, keeps pace with the seasons, cropping the pastures of the Colorado only till a greener and sweeter grass awaits him by the Yellowstone. Yet we think that if rail fences are pulled down and stone walls piled up on our farms, bounds are henceforth set to our lives and our fates decided. If you are chosen town clerk, forsooth, you cannot go to Tierra del Fuego this summer: but you may go to the land of infernal fire nevertheless. The universe is wider than our views of it.

Yet we should oftener look over the tafferel of our craft, like curious passengers, and not make the voyage like stupid sailors picking oakum. The other side of the globe is but the home of our correspondent. Our voyaging is only great-circle sailing, and the doctors prescribe for diseases of the skin merely.

Only the last paragraph of the four original is tapped, and the direction of the release which it offers is swerved dramatically by the decisive "Yet" which introduces the next paragraph; indeed, it has already been rerouted by the conversion of the reference to Tierra del Fuego from its literal attachment to an explorer's (Darwin's) voyage of discovery to the most remote tip of the Western world, to a symbol of the spiritual search for self-discovery with its complete denial of physical space, the latter made explicit with reference to infernal regions and a universe "wider" than man's "view" of it. Notwithstanding the passage's metamorphosis, however, the appeal of travel is not disguised on its transfer to metaphysical routes. Fourteen years have not really dimmed the passage or reduced its vigor. By 1854 Thoreau had even better reason to know that there was more to gain from circling the globe than the count of cats in Zanzibar.[10]

PART III

The Route

❧ CHAPTER VII ❧

The Route Taken

Before I walked in the ruts of travel; now I adventured.
Journal, January 2, 1851

His friend William Ellery Channing reported that before Thoreau set out on a journey he collected all the information he could on the routes he was to travel.[1] Yet we must control our temptation to relegate Thoreau's travel reading to such prestudy of route and region. Let us consider for a moment the relation of his travel reading to his "excursions" by looking at one of the few instances in which his physical and vicarious trips took him over the same route outside his New England. The ten-day trip to Quebec in September, 1850, reveals a practice basically different from that described by Channing. By far the greater amount of vicarious travel in southeastern Canada which Thoreau's reading shows him to have done, extensive as such travel was, proved to be the result of his "excursion" there rather than a preparation for it. To be sure, Thoreau had read travel accounts of Canada before accompanying Channing on this autumn trip, but he had read none of them very recently. As a freshman at Harvard he had read Colonel Francis Hall's *Travels in Canada*; it was Hall who referred to Alexander Henry's travels between Quebec and the Rocky Mountains, and it was Hall's route which Thoreau was to parallel roughly: by rail to Montreal, then by boat down the St. Lawrence to Trois Rivières, Quebec, Montmorency, and Ste-Anne-de-Beaupré. By 1848, through his perusal of Charlevoix's and Lescarbot's histories of New France, Thoreau had accompanied a number of early French explorers up and down the St. Lawrence River.[2] But it was in fact immediately upon his return from this trip of 1850 that his intensive travel in Canada really began.

He returned to Concord on October 3. In October and November he read Champlain's narrative of his voyages from 1608 to 1616 about the Gulf of St. Lawrence and up the great river, Cartier's account of his voyages of 1534 and 1535 over the same routes, and Roberval's description of the settlement at Montreal in 1540. He returned to the histories of Lescarbot and Charlevoix.[3] In November he commenced his Canadian Notebook, a fact book which was to accumulate seventy pages of notes in two years. By February it contained, in addition to material from the accounts already mentioned, a record of his reading of Warburton's *Conquest of Canada*, the "Routier" of Jean Alphonse, Bacqueville de la Potherie's voyages to America in 1722, and Richard Biddle's *Memoir of Sebastian Cabot: With a Review of the History of Maritime Discovery*, from which Thoreau took three pages of notes on Cabot's explorations in the Gulf of St. Lawrence.[4] In February he also read Benjamin Silliman's *Short Tour between Hartford and Quebec*. Silliman's itinerary paralleled almost exactly his own, even to the byways. The parallels in this case only illustrated coincidences, however, such as Thoreau's accidental visit to a tomb which Silliman went out of his way to see; Thoreau apparently had no notion whose tomb he was viewing until he read Silliman.[5] In June he was reading John MacTaggard's *Three Years in Canada*, covering the years 1826 to 1829, and in August Peter Kalm's account of his travels of 1749 up the Hudson and through Lake Champlain to Montreal and Quebec. He was still plowing through Charlevoix's three volumes in November, 1851, and he noted for later reading Long's travels in Canada in 1791.[6] He read Montresor's journal of his tour from the Chandiere River to the Kennebec in 1760 and Benedict Arnold's account of his expedition to Quebec in 1775.[7] February, 1852, found him, through the *Voyages du baron de la Hontan*, launched upon an exploration of the whole of Upper Canada.

Thoreau was now the scholar traveling, intent upon studying every scrap of narrative even tangential to the route he had himself taken. On March 16, 1852, buried in that "wilderness of books" which was the Harvard Library, "looking over books on Canada written within the last three hundred years," he noted in his Journal how each account built upon its predecessor's, and reminded himself that it was

necessary to know exactly what book to read on a subject, possibly
only three or four out of the thousand written. He trusted his own
judgment, after sampling a few pages, to tell him what few were
essential. In a particularly vivid passage he spoke of the excitement
which the day's literary explorations held for him:

> I saw that while we were clearing the forest in our westward progress,
> we were accumulating a forest of books in our rear, as wild and unex-
> plored as any of nature's primitive wildernesses. The volumes of the
> fifteenth, sixteenth, and seventeenth centuries, which lie so near on the
> shelf, are rarely opened, are effectually forgotten and not implied by
> our literature and newspapers. When I looked into Purchas's Pilgrims,
> it affected me like looking into an impassable swamp, ten feet deep
> with sphagnum, where the monarchs of the forest, covered with mosses,
> and stretched out along the ground, were making haste to become
> peat. These old books suggested a certain fertility, an Ohio soil, as if
> they were making a humus for new literature to spring in. I heard the
> bellowing of bullfrogs and the hum of mosquitoes reverberating through
> the thick embossed covers when I had closed the book.

He returned that day to Concord with Edward Talbot's *Five Years'
Residence in the Canadas* under his arm. In October of the same
year he began his extensive coverage of the *Jesuit Relations*, which
furnished him with accounts of Canada that spanned the seventeenth century; he withdrew from Harvard Library between 1852 and
1859 thirty-nine volumes of the *Relations*, which were published
annually between 1632 and 1673.[8]

His immediate reading revived memories of his own trip, as his
commentary in the Journal shows. His firsthand experience served to
transform into "realities" for him what were formerly "books only."
But in the same breath he defended his habit of reversing the procedure, of viewing the actual scene, even at firsthand, through the eye-
glass of his reading.[9] This was not only the richer practice for him; all
our evidence suggests that it was almost in the nature of an instinctive response with him, a way of using the re-created sights of the
inner eye as lens for viewing all immediate realities. Does not the
noble doubt constantly suggest itself to the reader of the Journal that
the Thoreau who at times so riveted his eye to the material minutiae
of the scene before him was the poet at war with his imagination
rather than, as he would have us believe, satiating it? the visionary

valiantly and at times compulsively maintaining his hold on the real world, compelled by a sober recognition and perhaps even the Yankee's instinctive distrust of his imaginative strengths?

In the case of his Canadian travel, it is apparent that Quebec had had far less appeal when he actually visited it than it had for him now that he was inspecting it at second hand.

> Of course we assign to the place the idea which the history or poem suggested. Quebec, of course, is never seen for what it simply is to practical eyes, but as the local habitation of those thoughts and visions which we have derived from reading of Wolfe and Montcalm, Montgomery and Arnold. It is hard to make me attend to the geology of Cape Diamond or the botany of the Plains of Abraham.[10]

So, in reading of Cartier's reactions to the magnificent sweep of the St. Lawrence, he found himself bringing his own experience into harmony with that experience of three hundred years before. Now he was particularly conscious of experiences of his own which paralleled those of Silliman.[11]

Such concentrated reading as this upon a single region stands out conspicuously as a rarity in the total picture of Thoreau's travel reading. In this case its deliberateness suggests a specific provocation, as indeed there was: the preparation, not for travel, as Channing would have it, but of a travel account. Thoreau began planning the narrative of his trip to Quebec immediately upon his return from Montreal. The first product was the proverbial lecture. On the opening page of the Canadian Notebook is a first draft of a crabbedly disparaging introduction: "I lecture on Canada because I find that I must give my account of it sooner or later—but I have not got much to say. What I got by going to Canada was a cold. And not till I get a fever shall I know how to appreciate it." But by early 1852 the report had shaped itself into a full narrative, the first three installments of which appeared anonymously in *Putnam's Magazine* beginning in January, 1853, titled "Excursion to Canada."

In his Journal many years later Thoreau remarked: "I think it will be found that he who speaks with most authority on a given subject is not ignorant of what has been said by his predecessors. He will take his place in a regular order, and substantially add his own knowledge to the knowledge of previous generations." [12] Like others before him, Thoreau set out to build his account upon the foundation of others' discoveries as well as his own. To do so took homework, most of which showed in the end. Every traveler from whose work Thoreau recorded material in his Canadian Notebook made a direct contribution to the "Excursion." Each one was referred to in connection with some specific observation, and with the single exception of Sir Francis Head, who, although frequently quoted, was always obliquely acknowledged as "an English traveler," each traveler was acknowledged by name. In the five chapters of Thoreau's piece there are some forty-five different references to experiences of other travelers of the route.

The result was distinctly a hybrid. The attempt on Thoreau's part to combine the eighty-four-page account of his trip which he tore out of his Journal for October, 1850,[13] with the seventy-page mass of travel data which he accumulated after his return resulted in an artificial synthesis. Occasionally in his narrative he kept faith with the chronology of his two distinct experiences. Commenting upon the cheapness of labor in Quebec, he confessed: "I have since learned that the English traveler Warburton remarked, soon after landing at Quebec, that everything was cheap there but men." For the most part, however, he fused his later vicarious travels with his original tour. He observed from the deck of his ship about thirty miles above Quebec the uninterrupted succession of whitewashed cottages on each side of the river exactly as Kalm and Lahontan had described them. The sight of dogs harnessed to their miniature milk carts reminded him of Kalm's description of the sledges drawn by dogs through the same streets a hundred years before, and he was prompted to add the date Charlevoix gave for the introduction of horses to New France.[14]

The significance for us of this perfectly defensible literary sleight of hand, this dovetailing of separate experiences, lies in the extent to which the later experiences which Thoreau's reading furnished him clouded or even substituted for the firsthand experience which had been his own. He opened his "Excursion" with the explanation that he wished only "to be set down in Canada, and take one honest walk there as I might in Concord woods of an afternoon." But the walk proved a self-conscious one, showing far less alertness to the immediate than those taken by the afternoon saunterer in Concord. The intense cold of the Canadian winter played as prominent a role in the narrative as the comfortable autumn which he had actually experienced there; it was the winter season which had dominated most of the travel accounts he had since read.[15] By the time he came to his own description of the Falls of Montmorency, he had very little to say. Like a scene viewed too often on postcards, this sight Thoreau had viewed too many times through others' eyes, and a surfeit of description did not help him to present his own. "It is a very simple and noble fall, and leaves nothing to be desired; but the most that I could say of it would only have the force of one other testimony to assure the reader that it is there." And he thereupon turned to Jean Alphonse, Champlain, Warburton, and Kalm for his description of it.[16]

"Excursion into Canada" was not a particular success. It lacked, except in occasional spots, the immediacy of Thoreau's keen observation and involvement that gave vitality to his later accounts of Maine and Cape Cod. Ironically enough, it seems to be the very thoroughness of Thoreau's coverage of others' descriptions of his route that weakened the immediacy of his own observations. The stitching together of physical and vicarious travel in this instance showed its seams. "Well, I thought to myself, here I am in a foreign country," declared the author; "let me have my eyes about me, and take it all in." But there is reason for feeling that by the time he began re-creating his original trip he had too many eyes about him, and that they interfered with the direct perception by his own. Thoreau made no claims for this particular travel account. He could not even make up his mind about the value of the trip itself, as the contrast between the opening and closing sentences of his final account suggests. In a letter to Blake he summed up his view of the piece:

> I do not wonder that you do not like my Canada story. It concerns me but little, and probably is not worth the time it took to tell it. Yet I had absolutely no design whatever in my mind, but simply to report what I saw. I have inserted all of myself that was implicated, or made the excursion.[17]

Fortunately, Thoreau was to write other travel accounts in which more of himself was implicated. But for none of them did his travel reading serve so deliberately or directly as preparation. That such reading obviously failed him as "padding" for his own travel narratives is of utmost significance. His travel reading was not destined to be his homework. It was not to furnish geographical data for filling in chinks in his own observations along routes he himself traveled. Historical background he continued to value, for whatever area his own "excursions" covered—Maine, Cape Cod, or Concord—and early travel accounts often constituted the best source for such history. But his predilection for contemporary travel books showed that he was as conscious of place as he was of time, and to the extent that place was his concern, he grew increasingly satisfied to view new routes *either* through his own eyes *or* through the eyes of other travelers. More important still, as the routes viewed through his own eyes became more restricted and repetitive, those he viewed through others' eyes ranged farther and wider. He continued to use such reading to support his own travel works, but his success did not lie in the procedure used in the "Excursion." It depended on a radically different method, one which brought together divergent routes instead of piling similar ones on top of one another, a technique which was to leave the correlation to the imagination rather than to the cartographer.

In spite of the desire expressed at the end of the "Excursion," Thoreau never made another trip of his own to Canada. The familiarity with routes which he shows years later in a letter to Thomas Wentworth Higginson, when the latter requested advice about a trip to Quebec, is really derived from his reading: "The most direct and regular way, as you know, is substantially Montresor's and Arnold's and the younger John Smith's." [18] With the immediate provocation of a lecture and an article on his own trip out of the way, Thoreau settled down for the rest of his life to secondhand travels through British North America: the *Jesuit Relations*, Sagard's *Grand Voyage*, Dablon's *Relation of the Voyages, Discoveries, and Death of Father James Marquette and the Subsequent Voyages of Father Claudius Alloney*, Susanna Moodie's two books on *Life in the Clearings* and *Roughing It in the Bush*, Mrs. Traill's letters on *The Backwoods of Canada*, John West's *Journal*, Henry Youle Hind's *North-*

west Territory, not to mention the numerous expeditions overland across northern Canada to the Icy Sea, about which we shall speak later.

The early French travelers in Canada to whom he so often returned held a twofold appeal for Thoreau. The first he described in his Journal: "The most poetic and truest account of objects is generally by those who first observe them, or the discoverers of them, whether a sharper perception and curiosity in them led to the discovery or the greatest novelty inspired their report." [19] The appeal of the "first sight" was as exciting for Thoreau as for the great majority of his contemporaries, although, unlike those whose interests were at the superficial mercy of the newest and the latest, Thoreau found value in the initial view regardless of its date. The second attraction of these French "discoverers" he acknowledged in the "Excursion to Canada."

> I am not sure but I have most sympathy with that spirit of adventure which distinguished the French and Spaniards of those days, and made them especially the explorers of the American continent—which so early carried the former to the Great Lakes and the Mississippi on the north, and the latter to the same river on the south. It was long before our frontiers reached their settlements in the West. So far as inland discovery was concerned, the adventurous spirit of the English was that of sailors who land for a day, and their enterprise the enterprise of traders.[20]

Not only did Thoreau share the French and Spanish love of adventure through travel and discovery; he expressed only scorn for those of his fellow men who did not. He commented bitterly in his Journal in 1857: "With all this opportunity how near all men come to doing nothing! . . . The seaboard swarms with adventurous and rowdy fellows, but how unaccountably they train and are held in check! They are as likely to be policemen as anything." [21]

The "adventure" and the "first sight": these were the intangible rewards of his travel reading on Canada, less deliberately harvested than the data which he jammed into the "Excursion," but in the end the more valuable products. At the age of twenty-seven Thoreau wrote:

> I am that age when an unexplored country road furnishes objects of interest enough—when any deeper ravine—a more novel bridge or an

unknown stream—detains one a long time—and one can proceed with the adventurous feeling of childhood, not knowing what we shall see next.[22]

He could have written the same at forty. The adventure of discovery represented much of that satisfaction which he derived from all his travel reading, reading which was to take him over a vast network of routes across the continents and oceans of the globe.

CHAPTER VIII

The Western Impulse

I must walk toward Oregon, and not toward Europe. And that way the nation is moving, and I may say that mankind progress from east to west.

"Walking," 1862

As an undergraduate at Harvard reviewing William Howitt's *Book of the Seasons*, Thoreau quoted with rare enthusiasm a novelist's description of his country: "America . . . with her beautiful and stupendous scenes of nature; her immense lakes; her broad and sweeping rivers; her climes melting into all the varieties of the globe; her solitudes and forests, yet hushed in primeval silence." [1] Fifteen years later he endorsed with equal pride Sir Francis Head's conclusion that "in the northern hemisphere of the New World, Nature has not only outlined her work on a larger scale, but has painted the whole picture with brighter and more costly colors than she used in delineating and beautifying the Old World." [2] One is reminded of Cotton Mather speaking in his "Winter Meditations" of the Divine favors showered upon the New Goshen, or of Thomas Paine describing America in the *Rights of Man* as the only spot in the world where Nature could so gigantically implement the principles of universal reformation: "where the scene which that country represents to the eye of the spectator has something in it which generates and enlarges great ideas. . . . and he partakes of the greatness he contemplates." [3]

With Paine and Mather, Thoreau shared the recurrent enthusiasm for the paradisaical dream as it seemed realizable in the New World. In his day this dream, keeping its tie with each new El Dorado, focused most specifically upon the American West, just as it had earlier upon the eastern shores of the continent. By the 1830s it found its expression not so exclusively in religious fervor or political idealism as in a literary and economic nationalism which celebrated the potential for self-expression and economic independence (the two went increasingly together) in the resources of a vast expanding continent. Most writers who reached their literary maturity by mid-century were receptive in one way or another to its appeals, although their responses took different forms. James Russell Lowell expressed his at one point in an attack upon what he thought was Thoreau's immunity to the vision: "While he [Thoreau] studied with respectful attention the minks and woodchucks, his neighbors, he looked with utter contempt on the august drama of destiny of which his country was the scene, and on which the curtain had already risen." [4] So effective was this sweeping pronouncement in 1865, aptly coincident with a new postwar wave of nationalism, that it drove Thoreau's defenders back to the line of Concord's stone walls which protected by provincializing, and to a premature capitulation to the view of Thoreau as an eccentric, even among his literary contemporaries, with regard to a feeling for his country. We are still today inheritors of the notion that Thoreau alone remained indifferent to the currents of nationalism that affected, among others, Longfellow, Hawthorne, Whitman, Melville, Whittier, Holmes, and Emerson. Henry Seidel Canby summarized the view in his biography of Thoreau when he concluded that Thoreau had not Whitman's "sense of a continent growing, for his imagination was stubbornly New England and unconcerned with geographical space." [5] It has come to seem inevitable that Thoreau shall bear the burden of contrast with Whitman, as it has for New England to bear exclusive responsibility for any of her sons' provinciality. In this matter, as in others, it is necessary to reconstruct Thoreau's actual latitudes.

We must remind ourselves that Harvard undergraduates of the 1830s were particularly receptive to the literary nationalism of the day. Professor Channing might defer when it came to such talk; Longfellow, Lowell, and Holmes tended to sneer at its extremer manifestations. But it was not that easy to dampen the ardor of Young America or the American Scholar. The *Democratic Review*, which had offered Thoreau congenial outlet for "Paradise (to be) Regained" in 1843, as it already had for pieces by Hawthorne and

Whitman, was a periodical openly crusading in behalf of a national literature, urging American writers to "comprehend the matchless sublimity of our position among the nations of the world." A special vision of America's significance and destiny was not only an inevitably strong formative influence on Thoreau but a perpetual concern, influencing in particular his outlook upon the American West.

Thoreau's preoccupation with this portion of his country appears continually in his writings. "How many are now standing on the European coast whom another spring will find located on the Red River of Wisconsin!" he exclaimed early in the Journal in March, 1840. "Today we live an antediluvian life on our quiet homesteads, and tomorrow are transported to the turmoil and bustle of a crusading era." [6] A few months later in the Journal the nationalistic overtones were even more explicit: "Man looks back eastward upon his steps till they are lost in obscurity, and westward still takes his way till the completion of his destiny." [7] At Staten Island, where he watched the western movement get under way, he wrote: "We must look to the West for the growth of a new literature—manners, architecture, etc. Already there is more language there which is the growth of the soil than here." [8] Man's literary and national destinies were again fused in an essay on Carlyle in 1847: "Literature speaks how much still to the past, how little to the future, how much to the East, how little to the West." [9] In January, 1851, he reiterated in his Journal the "need of America" in the history of poetry. [10] In 1855 he attributed what he labeled the "retrograde" character of the Australian migration to the fact that it was a "southeastern" movement rather than a southwestern one. [11]

As such affirmations suggest, Thoreau's feelings about America were actually closer to those of Whitman than to those of his fellow literati in Concord. In a remarkably neglected essay parochially titled "Walking" [12] Thoreau took pains to summarize the significance which he felt the West had for his day and the hold it had upon him. His essay takes its place provocatively beside Whitman's Preface to his first *Leaves of Grass* in 1855. Like the latter, it offered the vision of a national literary destiny based upon the illimitable resources and inspiration of the American continent, and anticipated for art and thought a New World mythology to succeed that of the Old. Like

Whitman's credo, which was continually reformed and reasserted over subsequent years, this statement of Thoreau's kept abreast of his expanding views and represented both a continuum and a synthesis of his thoughts on the subject. A lecture in 1851, the summary underwent revisions and amplifications during the remaining ten years of its author's life. To it were added passages from his current Journal and reading. One of his last literary activities was a final reading of the proofs for its forthcoming publication in the *Atlantic Monthly* which he did not live to see. Here it was published in June, 1862— not the most auspicious moment for its debut, with an impending civil war clouding visions of America's Westward Dream.

In "Walking" [13] Thoreau identified his preference for a western direction to his walk with the prevailing tendency of his countrymen and with an instinct in the human race for "enterprise and adventure." He approved the European geographer Guyot's conclusion:

> As the plant is made for the animal, as the vegetable world is made for the animal world, America is made for the man of the Old World . . . who sets out upon his way. Leaving the highlands of Asia, he descends from station to station toward Europe. Each of his steps is marked by a new civilization superior to the preceding, by a greater power of development.[14]

He cited the eastern Tartars as people stagnated by their inability to conceive of anything west beyond Tibet except "a shoreless sea"; it was unmitigated East where they lived. The garden of the Hesperides was but the Great West to the ancients. And as it had been the foundation for the great fables of the past, even now he found the West preparing new ones:

> The valleys of the Ganges, the Nile, and the Rhine having yielded their crop, it remains to be seen what the valleys of the Amazon, the Plata, the Orinoco, the St. Lawrence, and the Mississippi will produce. Perchance, when, in the course of ages, American liberty has become a fiction of the past—as it is to some extent a fiction of the present—the poets of the world will be inspired by American mythology.

So the Atlantic was the Lethean stream "in our passage over which we have our opportunity to forget the Old World," and the Pacific yet another, "three times as wide," and perhaps mankind's last chance before the Styx. From this "great western impulse" Thoreau found all the commerce and enterprise of modern times springing. The vast and fertile regions of the American West became naturally the common meeting ground for all inhabitants of the globe—a phenomenon which augured well in Thoreau's eyes. He pointed with pleasure to the experience of the younger Michaux in his travels west of the Alleghenies in 1802; Michaux found that the common inquiry in the newly settled West was, "From what part of the world have you come?" If the heavens appeared higher and brighter in America (and Thoreau expressed no doubt but that they did), then he trusted these "facts to be symbolical of the height to which the philosophy and poetry and religion of her inhabitants may one day soar."

> I trust that we shall be more imaginative, that our thoughts will be clearer, fresher, and more etherial, as our sky,—our understanding more comprehensive and broader, like our plains,—our intellect generally on a grander scale, like our thunder and lightening, our rivers and mountains and forests,—and our hearts shall even correspond in breadth and depth and grandeur to our inland seas. . . . Else to what end does the world go on, and why was America discovered? . . . As a true patriot, I should be ashamed to think that Adam in Paradise was more favorably situated on the whole than the backwoodsman in this country.

It is easy to imagine the dismay, if not disdain, with which Lowell or Holmes would have looked upon this panegyric, with its implicit suggestions of Tom Paine's naturalism; men could be as humane in garrets as they could be inhuman on the prairie, they would have retorted. There was little in Thoreau's vision of America's "manifest destiny" (or in Whitman's for that matter) which guaranteed compatibility with Lowell's view. John O'Sullivan's catch phrase was already distasteful to Thoreau by the fifties, smacking generally of the evils of exploitation and more particularly of political identification with the Mexican War. Thoreau's perspective upon the western movement, while a committed one, was also a critical one. He could refer feelingly to "those scamps" in California who wantonly cut down the redwoods simply because of the challenge of their size, at the same time that he could eulogize the life of the lumbermen in the Northwest.[15] Did he not, after all, express his most decisive indictment of the hunter while voluntarily on a moose hunt in Maine?[16] He found the gluttonous scramble for gold as disgusting when it took place in the new territory of California as when it gutted the countryside of the newly settled continent of Australia (and he read, by travelers Colton and Howitt respectively, graphic firsthand accounts of both).[17]

It was repugnance toward such insensitive materialism that provoked him to explode in a letter to his friend Blake in 1853 and appear to provide a literal basis for Lowell's verdict. "The whole enterprise of this nation," he exclaimed, "which is not an upward, but a westward one, toward Oregon, California, Japan, etc., is totally devoid of interest to me, whether performed on foot, or by a Pacific railroad." [18] Thoreau's susceptibility to hyperbole landed him in more than one dramatic contradiction in his lifetime, but perhaps never more demonstrably than here. This explosion was one of those exaggerated responses which he confessed to, "those reckless and sweeping expressions I am wont to regret that I have used." The remainder of his tirade to Blake shows the particular direction of his criticism. Blake had, by confessing to some doubts of his own, provoked Thoreau into defending the comparative value of his own "cheap hours" against the "World's way." Thoreau's answer suggests that the bumbling Blake may have added insult to injury by identifying the western "prospector" with the "rewards" to be gained from the world's route westward. Thoreau always peculiarly indulged himself with Blake, writing him long letters particularly oracular and impersonal in their address; in this case he warmed to his own feelings and continued:

> It [the enterprise of the nation] is not illustrated by a thought; it is not warmed by a sentiment; there is nothing in it which one should lay down his life for, nor even his gloves,—hardly one which one should take up a newspaper for. It is perfectly heathenish,—flibustiering *toward* heaven by the great western route. No; they may go their way to their manifest destiny, which I trust is not mine. May my seventy-six dollars, whenever I get them, help to carry me in the other direction! I see them on their winding way, but no music is wafted from their host,—only the rattling of change in their pockets. . . . What aims more lofty have they than the prairie dogs?

The tone is plainly that of outraged disappointment, not indifference. Thoreau's preference in this letter for "the other direction" must be placed beside his consistent predilections expressed in "Walking," where, concurrent with the outburst to Blake, he was asserting, "Our sympathies in Massachusetts are not confined to New England; though we may be estranged from the South, we sympathize with the West. There is the home of our younger sons, as among the Scandinavians they took to the sea for their inheritance." Even more forthright was another letter by Thoreau, this one to his friend Cholmondeley just three years later in which he wrote:

> The *great west* and *north west* stretching on infinitely far and grand and wild, qualifying all our thoughts. That is the only America I know. I prize this western reserve chiefly for its intellectual value. That is the road to new life and freedom—if ever we are dissatisfied with this, and not to exile in Siberia.[19]

It should go without saying that Thoreau spoke in "Walking" of a western inheritance for Concord's younger sons not storable in banks or gunny sacks. For him the fulfillment of the paradisaical dream lay in the farthest creative reaches of man's consciousness. The material resources which the West offered by way of economic independence meant as much to him as to Lowell, but on strikingly different terms. Thoreau's were summarized in the chapter on "Economy" in *Walden,* where the necessities of life were placed in relation to the ends for which man was heated, sheltered, clothed, and fed. His celebration of the western movement, like that of a sojourn at Walden Pond, while attesting quite properly to man's daily attention to the material resources of life, was fundamentally a paean to man's imaginative quest, not to his larder.

Backing up his explicit words on the subject of the West are the surer reminders of Thoreau's interest: his own travels and his travel reading. The trip to Maine instead of to the West at the age of twenty was Thoreau's first, not last, compromise with a strong desire. Only at the age of forty-three, dying with tuberculosis and faced with a required remove from New England for his health, did he spend, not his seventy-six, but one hundred and seventy-six dollars to take him at last in the direction of his first choice. Advised by his doctor to travel south to the West Indies, Thoreau "selected" instead Minnesota, the Mississippi, and a touch of the American prairie. We are reminded that Irving, Melville, Cooper, Bryant, Whitman, and Emerson all demonstrated their "national" sympathies by traveling

West, usually to the prairies, trips which they took some pains to advertise as illustrating their appreciation of the West's significance for the American writer. Thoreau's trip was not strategic for such exploitation. We can not know for sure what he would have made of it had he recovered his health. But we do know that the clues to such an answer lie in those writings of his which span the ten or twelve years preceding his Minnesota trip and in the essay "Walking" which kept pace with them. For Thoreau's trip West in 1862 was but the last of a long series of travels westward across the continent which he had been taking through his reading, such a number that this last actual one may have suffered some loss of immediacy by virtue of being an anticlimax.

Lowell did not identify the particular "drama of destiny" toward which he found Thoreau contemptuous. The curtain on the drama of the Civil War had of course been raised for a good portion of Thoreau's lifetime, exposing a stage of national conflicts and forces few of which Thoreau proved indifferent to. But still further backstage loomed the major force of the times with respect to the national consciousness: the unexampled expansion of the continent itself. For this chapter in his nation's "august drama of destiny" Thoreau showed, not contempt, but persistent and indefatigable interest. The evidence of his reading shows him following as closely as he could this "enterprise of the nation"—whether performed on foot, horseback, river raft, or sailing ship!

Thoreau's twenty-five-page analysis in "Cape Cod" of the earliest discoverers and explorers of North America [20] attests not only to historical scholarship but to avid travel reading: of Monts, Champlain, Poutrincourt, Ogilby, Sir Ferdinando Gorges, Pring, John Smith, Cabot, Verrazano (Thoreau read accounts of both his voyages), Gomez, Gosnold, Roberval, the third volume of Ramusio's *Navigationi et Viaggi* (relating to America), Hakluyt's *Divers Voyages Touching the Discovery of America*, and Rafn's tracts on the discovery of America by the northmen. He also read extracts from the journal of Henry Hudson's voyage to the coast of America in 1609, and noted carefully in Volume 8 of his Indian Notebook the voyages in Purchas' *Pilgrimes* which related to his own continent, among them Drake's touch upon the west coast and De Soto's visit to Florida in 1532. He was familiar with Montanus' description of the New World and the *Remarkable Voyages Thither* of 1671 (the English translation of the Dutch.) He read Best's *True Discourse of the Late Voyages of Discoveries for the Finding of a Passage to Cathaya by the North-West under the Conduct of Martin Frobisher* of 1578; translations of two seventeenth-century accounts: David Pietersen de Vries's voyages made to America and Adriaen van der Donck's *Description of the New Netherlands*; and Jean Bossu's record of three voyages to Louisiana in the 1800s.

In spite of his devotion to early reports of the discovery and exploration of that "New England" which he knew at firsthand—to "Old Josselyn's" *Account of Two Voyages to New England*, Young's *Chronicle*, Winthrop's *Journal*—Thoreau's reading of travel accounts written before his day carried him considerably further. With explorers of the seventeenth and eighteenth centuries he converged upon his continent from the north, east, and south. He missed only the Spanish travelers who pushed up from Mexico to explore parts of the Southwest, but he did not neglect the voyages and discoveries of De Soto and Ponce de León along the Mississippi and in Florida.[21] With the French, with Cartier, Champlain, the Jesuits, La Salle, Jolliet and Marquette, Hennepin, Lahontan, and Charlevoix he pushed inland and Southwest from the St. Lawrence, and with Henri de Tonti west from Louisiana to the South. He traveled with the English, from Hudson Bay to the Rockies with Hearne and Mackenzie in the north, from the east coast northward in search of the passage to the western sea with Gosnold and Pring, and into Virginia and the middle South with John Smith and William Bartram; he read portions of William Strachey's *Second Book of the First Decade of the Historie of Travaile into Virginia Brittania* covering the years 1602–7. Turning to those travels which pointed more exclusively westward toward the end of the eighteenth century, he read C. F. Post's *Second Journal* of his journey from Philadelphia to the Ohio, Peter Kalm's travels into western Pennsylvania, Jonathan Carver's account of his adventures beyond the Mississippi, and the younger Michaux's report on his journeys into Ohio, Kentucky, and Tennessee.

The volume of western travel and exploration rolled like a gigantic snowball into the nineteenth century, and Thoreau proved intent upon keeping up with the major accounts. Like his most impressionable fellow Americans he relied upon the contemporary travel works for immediate knowledge of a country still largely unknown. As he exclaimed in 1858, "Like the English in New Holland, we live only on the shores of a continent even yet and barely know where the rivers come from which float our navies." [22] The records show that he read at least forty separate books of travel relating to the West in America in his own day. His reading of them is mainly distributed over the decade from 1850 to 1860.[23] Ten of them became part of his personal library. To trace the routes he covered would be to honeycomb the continent west of the Mississippi: There is scarcely a single major traveler who now looms large in the history of American western expansion, between the years 1803 and 1852 whose first account of his trip Thoreau did not read.

He owned Lewis and Clark's journal of the expedition of 1803–6. He also owned Major Pike's account of the journey which took him, at the same time that Lewis and Clark were crossing the Rockies, up the Mississippi to the Northwest, and later, from 1806 to 1807, to the headwaters of the Arkansas and Red rivers. Pike's clipped and factual entries, similar to Thoreau's own daily field-notes, undoubtedly appealed to him for their honesty. But it is not likely that Thoreau found particularly congenial the person who could conceive of no motive sufficient to keep men contented in the wilderness other than a desire for Indian women. From 1811 to 1813 the "Astorians" covered the area between St. Louis and the mouth of the Columbia River in establishing the fur-trade empire of John Jacob Astor; and although there is no evidence that Thoreau read Washington Irving's *Astoria,* which was published in 1836 and which summarized this important venture, he did own after 1854 Gabriel Franchère's *Narrative of a Voyage to the North West Coast of America,* a translation of the 1820 work which Irving used for his source. Moreover, Thoreau was reading as early as 1833, and again in 1837, *Adventures on the Columbia River* by Ross Cox, another "Astorian." Cox's romantic description of the Sandwich Islanders stuck in Thoreau's memory, as readers of *Walden* can recall, as did his accounts of the Nez Percé Indians of the northwest coast.[24] Cox's five-page sketch of the Canadian *voyageurs*, together with Henry Brackenridge's description of them in his *Journal of a Voyage up the River Missouri* (also read by Thoreau in 1837), probably constituted Thoreau's fullest introduction to these much admired guides.

In 1852 Thoreau read William Keating's compilation of Major Stephen Long's famous third expedition of 1823 to explore the St. Peter River (now the Minnesota) and the country to the north. In the same year he read Henry Schoolcraft's account of his trip in 1832 through Minnesota, distinguished for its discovery of Itasca Lake, a source of the Mississippi. (Thoreau, like Longfellow after him, went on to read Schoolcraft's works upon the Indians.) He also showed interest in the earlier account of Jean Baptiste Perault (*Relation des traverses et des aventures d'un marchand voyageur dans l'Amerique Septentrionale*, 1783), the manuscript of which Schoolcraft had used in his narrative. Still in this same year Thoreau took a side trip with Thaddeus Culbertson to the upper Missouri, an expedition undertaken only two years before, the journal of which had just been published in the annual report of the Smithsonian Institution.

Upon its publication in 1854, Thoreau read Benjamin Ferris' account of the migratory trek of the Mormons during the year 1846–47. The same year saw him reading Randolph Marcy's *Exploration of the Red River of Louisiana, in the Year 1852*, a book which became part of his personal library sometime after he took his extensive notes from the copy in the Harvard Library. Like the other explorations he had been sharing, this one too was an important "first" journey of discovery. As Marcy testified, it was doubtful whether the region he penetrated, a country which had repelled all earlier attempts to explore it, had ever before been known to civilized man. Although his edition was burdened with appendices, Marcy's descriptions were full and graphic, and Thoreau gathered plentifully from them; it was in this work that he read of the phenomenon known as "Red River raft" to which he liked later to allude.[25] In 1854 he also acquired for his library Captain Sitgreaves' *Report of an Expedition down the Zuni and Colorado Rivers*, published by the Thirty-second Congress.

Thoreau's indubitable familiarity with Frémont's expeditions apparently came from the record in Charles Upham's *Life, Explorations, and Public Service of John Charles Frémont*, published in

1856, which Thoreau owned, rather than from Frémont's original narrative published by Congress in 1844–45. In 1856 Thoreau turned back to two earlier explorations of importance along the upper Mississippi in 1838 and 1839, both by Joseph Nicollet. Although Nicollet published no narrative of his travels, Congress rendered a "Report" in 1855 which Thoreau read. By this time he had had his fill of Congressional travel publications, giving vent to the annoyance which we cited in an earlier chapter, directed apparently at William Emory's *Report of the United States and Mexican Boundary Survey*, published in two volumes by Congress in 1857. Emory as traveler was no stranger to Thoreau; he owned his *Notes of a Military Reconnaissance*, the account of an undertaking in 1846–47 between Missouri and California. In 1860 Thoreau turned to a French translation of the *Report on the Exploration of the Country between Lake Superior and the Red River Settlement* made by Henry Youle Hind and others and just published, this time by the Canadian Legislative Assembly.

A great deal of Thoreau's reading about the West was, however, of quite unofficial documents, accounts by trappers and traders who, like Alexander Henry, could get close to both the land and its inhabitants: such a classic as Josiah Gregg's *Commerce of the Prairies* by a man who made eight expeditions across the "Great Western Prairies" in the forties; or the narrative of Kit Carson, "the Nestor of the Rocky Mountains," as reported by DeWitt Peters in 1858. As the "first" or "official" accounts grew rarer and thinner by the 1860s, Thoreau had to rely increasingly upon the hunters to take him west: *The Life and Adventure of James P. Beckwourth, Mountaineer, Scout, and Pioneer* (1856), *The Adventures of James Capen Adams, Mountaineer and Grizzly Bear Hunter of California* (1860). A good portion of his reading was on a thoroughly "popular" level: such accounts as Colton's *Land of Gold, or Three Years in California* (1850); Maximilian's *Travels in the Interior of North America* (1843); William Cullen Bryant's *Letters of a Traveller* (1850), written from Illinois in 1841; Bayard Taylor's *Eldorado* of 1850; Richard Henry Dana's voyage to California in 1834 in *Two Years before the Mast*; two accounts in a popular boys' series by a favorite author of Thoreau's: Mayne Reid's *Desert Home* (1852) and *Boy Hunters*

(1853); and Frederick Law Olmsted's *Journey through Texas* (1857). Whenever he could borrow a pair of feet and eyes, Thoreau pursued his westward travel. One week it was with Father Smet in Oregon (*Oregon Missions and Travels over the Rocky Mountains, in 1845–1846*); the next with Colonel Doniphan on a military campaign in New Mexico. And we recall the notebook excerpts copied from fifty-four separate pages in James Swan's account of his three years' residence in Washington Territory.

With the notebook record alone supplying ponderous evidence of continued attention on Thoreau's part to all the realities of the western portion of the continent—its history and lore, facts of its climate, terrain, and life, its natives and its settlers, its social customs and institutions, its commerce, politics, religions, habits of dress, eating, and entertainment, literally all things environmental and natural—it seems safe to suggest his interest in more than Concord woodchucks. Those critics who find it difficult to savor Thoreau's wry humor will have herculean difficulty with his straight-faced reply to an admirer named Calvin Green in 1857: "Dear Sir, You are right in supposing that I have not been Westward. I am very little of a traveller." [26]

Thoreau added in the later part of his essay "Walking" a point of view as both cause and effect of his interest in the West. Placed with the values he underlined in *Walden*, it proclaims once more that fusion of spiritual self-fulfillment with the national destiny which the vision of America's West offered so many of Thoreau's literary peers.

> Eastward I go by force; but westward I go free. . . . It is hard for me to believe that I shall find fair landscapes or sufficient wilderness and freedom behind the eastern horizon. . . . The West of which I speak is but another name for the Wild; and what I have been preparing to say is, that in Wilderness is the preservation of the world.[27]

The "wilderness" was inexhaustible, virginal, regenerative, containing within it the always unexplored and undiscovered; it was still, in the mid-nineteenth century, symbol for the American writer of a timeless frontier, the line of the horizon. And to match the splendor of the vision was the physical grandeur of the country to sustain it: of this the hundreds of travel accounts of the day bore firsthand testimony. The American West gave peculiar luster to the macrocosm of which Thoreau felt himself a part, even as its appeal tapped the springs of his spiritual needs. Thoreau's original lecture had been titled "Walking, or the Wild." In one of his commonplace books he listed thirty words and their derivations from Richard Chenevix Trench's recent book *On the Study of Words,* among which appears the following entry: "wild—participle of to *will,* self-willed." [28] The real challenge of the West in Thoreau's eyes was that of the potential fulfillment of the will, of the self-will, the sturdiest test of man's freedom. As Mr. Canby once declared, Thoreau's West was of the spirit.[29] But it had considerable "body" to it too, more than has since been acknowledged. Thoreau was not a man to leave his visions ungrounded; his castles had their foundations. It would be truer, in view of the concrete familiarity with his continent of which he could have boasted (but never did), to say that Thoreau's West was of both the spirit and the body, neither one denied, both as real as the Brahma and the woodchuck he found in his own backyard.

❦ CHAPTER IX ❦

The Voyage Out

To tell the truth, I saw an advertisement for ablebodied seaman when I was a boy, sauntering in my native port, and as soon as I came of age I embarked.

"Life Without Principle," 1862

Surprising as it may strike one to be traveling up the Rio Grande or across the Rockies with Thoreau, it is yet more startling to re-create even a partial picture of Thoreau's hours of travel abroad. He appears so indigenous to his own land, regional or continental, that he stands in image less easily and fittingly on soil foreign to America. Open the pages of such a book as Thomas Atkinson's *Travels in the Regions of the Upper and Lower Amoor* or J. Ludwig Krapf's *Travels . . . in Eastern Africa,* and after your so solid sense of the place where you stand begins to slip away in favor of a mountain pass in Outer Mongolia or the blistering sands of the Libyan Desert, place Thoreau there with you if you can. So set is our image of the Concord saunterer that only the insistent reminder that Thoreau actually held the book and read the pages forces us to hold him, in our mind's eye at least, to these strange and foreign routes.

The first step in simulating the realities of Thoreau's participation is, of course, to travel some of these pages with him. Travel books are, in a rather insidious manner, one of the most dominating of literary genres. They assert their imaginative sway over the reader, after the first few pages, simply by insisting that one always *travel*. One cannot get at a sight or a fact without actually going the journey: of this the author makes sure. And journeying involves an extraordinary amount of activity—starting out, stopping for the night, following a path or charting a course, coping with knapsacks, camels, windlasses, food, mosquitoes, the natives, the weather—a perpetual busyness which tugs one along with the persuasion of active involvement in getting to, looking at, and returning from whatever it was the reader may originally have convinced himself he wanted to see. I dare say no one who dislikes traveling ever read a travel book with pleasure. But Thoreau's peripatetic leanings were tailor-fitted to the genre, and we can be confident that he never resisted a route in favor of a sight, any more than he avoided a process for a conclusion. A good surveyor, he was in the habit of measuring where he was by how he got there. His inclinations were all geared to the imaginative operation of the travel book. In spite of conflicts we may experience with our habitual visions of him in familiar settings, we shall have to imagine Thoreau not only sailing into Shanghai harbor or crossing the Andes on a llama, but taking perpetual pleasure in the trip itself.

As late as March 25, 1860, Thoreau recorded in his Journal:

> The ice of the night fills the river in the morning, and I hear it go grating forward at sunrise. As soon as I can get it painted and dried, I launch my boat and make my first voyage for the year up and down the stream, on that element from which I have been debarred for three months and a half. I taste a spring cranberry, save a floating rail, feel the element fluctuate beneath me, and am tossed bodily as I am in thought and sentiment. Then longen folk to gon on *voyages*.

Thoreau's physical "voyaging," like all his own travel, was but the offshoot of vicarious voyages which he enjoyed the year round. He was constantly setting out from land, touched by imaginary sea breezes from his reading which turned him seaward as surely as did those mementos of beach and seashell's roar which he retained from his Cape Cod excursions.

Like his contemporary Herman Melville, he saw a good deal of the "watery parts of the world," but almost all at second hand. The sight of seals in the Boston harbor, mammals which he had always associated "with Esquimaux and other outlandish people," reminded him that, although the wilderness of the land at his back might soon be tamed, the ocean was a wilderness reaching round the globe. He found himself looking at the whole earth as seashore.[1] He observed in *Walden* that it was "well to have some water in your neighborhood, to give buoyancy to and float the earth. One value of the smallest well is, that when you look into it, you see that earth is not continent but insular." As the Eskimos, "one of the littoral people," inquired with surprise of the explorer Richardson, "Are not all lands islands?" [2]

On July 14, 1852, Thoreau wrote in his Journal: "Is it not more attractive to be a sailor than a farmer? . . . not better to plow the ocean than the land? . . . You may go round the world before the mast, but not behind the plow." The preaching emanated from the practice, for at that very moment Thoreau was plowing the oceans of the world through the pages of Drake's *New and Universal Collection of Authentic and Entertaining Voyages* (1768). Sea travel it had been which first lured man into the unexplored, and Thoreau delighted in learning of all ventures from land. We find him reading, at one time or another, in at least nine separate collections of voyages undertaken during the sixteenth, seventeenth, and eighteenth centuries, voyages covering all the major oceans of the globe.[3] Although he traced the routes of sea exploration back to 340 B.C., sailing from the mouth of the Indus River up the Persian Gulf with Nearchus, his voyaging for the most part followed in the wake of Columbus and in the great Age of Discovery. With Columbus he sailed through the "weedy sea" of the South Atlantic, off the coast of South America through waters covered with tortoises, the air above filled with clouds of gaudy butterflies. His memory of Columbus' feelings upon first sensing a land breeze after the long voyage repeatedly colored his own responses to the sweet spring wafts from the Concord meadows.[4] He discovered with Martin Pinzon, forty miles off the mouth of the Amazon, water from the sea so fresh that casks could be filled with it for drinking. He floated for three months and twenty days on the glass of the Pacific sharing Magellan's torturous becalmment. He enjoyed the fragments of tradition and myth which he met with in so many of the early accounts, the earliest stories of Atlantis, for example, or in Josselyn when he read: "June the first day, in the afternoon, very thick foggy weather, we sailed by an enchanted island." [5] He could appreciate the heroism of the old navigator Sir Humphrey Gilbert, "of whom it is related, that being overtaken by a storm on his return from America in the year 1583, sitting abaft with a book in his hand, just before he was swallowed up in the deep, he cried out to his comrades in the Hind, as they came within hearing, 'We are as near to Heaven by sea as by land.' " [6] He understood the admiration whch the voyager Lahontan expressed for the *coureurs de bois* when he declared that they "lived like sailors ashore." [7]

Closer to his own day were the three voyages made around the world from 1768 to 1780 by Captain James Cook, the greatest explorer of his age. Gone now were the enchanted islands, to be replaced by the scores of substantial ones which Cook discovered in the Pacific while disproving the existence of the fabulous "southern continent." With Alexander von Humboldt, sailing at night under the Southern Cross, Thoreau watched the bands of porpoises plowing the surface of the waters and leaving behind them tracks of brilliant phosphorescent light. He made the circumnavigation of the globe on the H.M.S. *Beagle* from 1831 to 1836. He seems to have endured the thundering platitudes of Captain Benjamin Morrell for four voyages, from 1822 to 1831, to the South Sea, the North and South Pacific oceans, the China Sea, the South Atlantic Ocean, and the Indian and Antarctic oceans, including the discovery of the "Massacre Islands" (a group of the Solomons), "where thirteen of the author's crew were eaten by cannibals." [8] Could the pompous humility of Morrell's introduction (comprising a "Brief Sketch of the Author's Early Life," for thirty pages) have failed to affect the young student reader, particularly the remarkable declaration by the author that "ever anxious to avoid even the appearance of egotism, he has thus introduced himself to the reader in the third person; but in telling his own story, he finds it more convenient to adopt the first"? This reader, able to discern the speciousness of Morrell's façade for a book all about its author, made a point of introducing his own most personal account twelve years later with the observation, "In most books, the I, or first person, is omitted; in this it will be retained; that, in respect to egotism, is the main difference. We commonly do not remember that it is, after all, always the first person that is speaking." More scientific than Morrell was Charles Wilkes's exploring expedition to the South Pacific in 1838–42. The Harvard sophomore went no further than the first volume of Enoch Cobb Wines's *Two Years and a Half in the Navy*; but although the first volume barely got its sailor to Gibraltar, Thoreau apparently read it for its methodical introduction to every feature of a sailing vessel. He picked up still more knowledge of the sailor's life from Dana's *Two Years before the Mast*. His own library offered him Commodore Perry's voyages in the China seas, and he sailed in 1852 with Ida Pfeiffer on her "adventurous" voyage around the world (as he was to describe it in *Walden*).

As he covered the oceans, he did not fail to supplement his knowledge of many of the "islands" at which his ships paused. He read David Crantz's description of Greenland and Howitt's account of two years in Victoria, Sidney, and Van Diemen's Land. He owned his friend Cholmondeley's account of New Zealand. He made three visits to Madagascar with the Reverend William Ellis, studied the East Indian archipelago intently through Walter Gibson's narrative of his misfortunes there, and probably took a "Peep at Polynesian Life" through Melville's *Typee*.[9] He showed particular interest in the island of Teneriffe;[10] he climbed the mountain originally with Humboldt and again in 1856 with C. P. Smyth, and he read Sir John Barrow's *Voyage to Cochinchina* in which the author found Teneriffe's summit (together with the elephants of Cochin China and a storm at sea) one of only three objects in nature that surpassed any idea of them which imagination could form.

"It is remarkable that men do not sail the sea with more expectation," he declared as he stood on the shore of Cape Cod in July, 1855, and looked out over the Atlantic. "Even the expeditions for the discovery of El Dorado and the Fountain of Youth led to real, if not compensatory discoveries."[11] Thoreau knew well of these "real" discoveries. He had first sighted the shores of South America in his reading, as early as 1834, of the voyages of Columbus and his companions in Washington Irving's three-volume account. It was natural that he should skip from Columbus to Humboldt, from the discoveries of the southern continent in the late fifteenth and sixteenth centuries to those of the late eighteenth and nineteenth. For almost two centuries the other great "American" continent had lain behind Spain's iron curtain—a dark interim of blood and exploitation which Thoreau had read of in Ranking's *Conquest of Peru*. Now the rediscovery of the continent was taking place in his own day.

His first travels in South America were taken in Colombia, when as an undergraduate at Harvard he read Charles Cochrane's *Journal of a*

Residence and Travels in Colombia. Cochrane's book contained a preponderance of alligators and historical data and probably only served
to fill in the historical background which Ranking supplemented for
Thoreau the following year. Humboldt's *Aspects of Nature* tantalized
him with its colorful glimpses of the great rivers, rain forests, and
plains of the continent; but they were glimpses only. With Charles
Darwin he commenced his real exploration.

Darwin recorded in his *Voyage* the ecstasy of his first day on South
American soil:

> Bahia, or San Salvador. Brazil, Feb. 29th.—The day has passed delight-
> fully. Delight itself, however, is a weak term to express the feelings of
> a naturalist who, for the first time, has wandered by himself in a
> Brazilian forest. The elegance of the grasses, the novelty of the parasiti-
> cal plants, the beauty of the flowers, the glossy green of the foliage,
> but above all the general luxuriance of the vegetation, filled me with
> admiration. A most paradoxical mixture of sound and silence pervades
> the shady parts of the woods. The noise from the insects is so loud, that
> it may be heard even from the vessel anchored several hundred yards
> from the shore; yet within the recesses of the forest a universal silence
> appears to reign. To a person fond of natural history, such a day as this
> brings with it a deeper pleasure than he can ever hope to experience
> again. . . . I was overtaken by a tropical storm. I tried to find shelter
> under a tree, which was so thick that it would never have been pene-
> trated by common English rain; but here, in a couple of minutes, a
> little torrent flowed down the trunk.[12]

Thoreau, recording his impressions of Darwin's route, noted particu-
lary this tree that attested to the force of a tropical rain, just as he
continued to copy a rich assortment of scenes and details from Darwin's account:[13] the lazy manner of hunting partridges at the mouth
of the Río de la Plata, by circling them on horseback in a closing
spiral; the skill of General Rosa in breaking wild horses; the Gaucho
sharpening his knife on the back of the armadillo before he killed it;
the floating islands of Lake Taguatagua in central Chile. Darwin's
trek up the Santa Cruz River introduced Thoreau to a phenomenon
which particularly appealed to him. "Rowing up a stream which takes
its rise in a mountain, you meet at last with pebbles which have been
washed down from it, when many miles distant. I love to think of
this kind of introduction to it," wrote Thoreau.[14] Three years later

the roar of the sea on the eastern coast of Cape Cod reminded him of Darwin's experience on the shore of Chiloé; and he contrasted his own attempt to discern the masts of vessels on the distant horizon of the Atlantic with Darwin's clear view of the Pacific from the base of the Andes.[15]

Having been carried by Darwin around the coast and over the pampas and cordilleras of the south, Thoreau next turned to Alexander Humboldt for exploration of the northwest portion of the continent. Darwin himself had deferred to Humboldt when it came to describing in proper vividness the feelings experienced on first entering the tropics. Even Irving had used Humboldt's description of the "grassy sea" in describing Columbus' voyage through it.[16] Thoreau did not record with similar fullness his particular impressions of Humboldt's account, but we know he visited with Humboldt the cavern of Ataripe near Maipures on the upper Orinoco, the strange sepulcher of an entire extinct nation: he noted in his Extract Book that at the time of Humboldt's visit "an old parrot was shown at Maipures, of which the inhabitants said, and the fact is worthy of observation, that 'they did not understand what it said, because it spoke the language of the Atures.' " [17] Whereas Darwin had barely rambled inland, Humboldt took Thoreau deep into the interior of an unexplored tropical wilderness, across the llanos of Venezuela, up the Orinoco to its connection with the Río Negro and the Amazon, over the Andes to Ecuador, and within 3,000 feet of the summit of 21,000-foot Mount Chimborazo, thought in Humboldt's day to be the highest mountain in the world. Having preceded his reading of Humboldt's *Narrative* with his *Aspects of Nature*, Thoreau indicated his continued interest in the geographer by reading his biography when it appeared in 1855.[18]

"Of some of the great rivers, like the Nile and Orinoco (?), men still only conjecture the sources," observed Thoreau in 1852.[19] The question mark indicated a scholarly caution; the latest word he had read on the Orinoco had been Humboldt's in 1847. Humboldt had raised the question as to which of South America's three great rivers was the most impressive.[20] Thoreau had by now traveled up two of them: three hundred miles up the Río de la Plata with Darwin and all the way up the Orinoco with Humboldt; the third and longest

awaited him, together with the entire central portion of the continent which it drained, a mammoth tropical rain forest of over two
and one-half million miles. He had confessed his desire to read the
Travels of Von Martius and Von Spix, who had botanized on the
Amazon for three years, but we do not know that he went through
with his intention.[21] But his interest was now ripe for traveling this
vast hinterland deserted by both padres and peasants, hanging at this
particular moment in history between exploitation and apathy, momentarily given over to the aboriginal tribes which honeycombed it
and to the rampant luxuriance of tropical wildlife and vegetation. It
is no surprise to find added to his library the two volumes of *Exploration of the Valley of the Amazon*,[22] by Lieutenants Herndon and
Gibbon respectively. They proved to be less congenial fellow travelers
for Thoreau than either Darwin or Humboldt. He indicated his basic
disapproval of their motive even while reading their accounts, provoked as he was by William Herndon's frequent expressions of contempt for the natives and assumptions as to slavery's expansion in
this "new" area. (Gibbon's attitude, in the second volume, was far
more sympathetic.) In a lecture given in 1854 he referred bitterly to a
Lieutenant Herndon "whom our government sent to explore the
Amazon, and, it is said, to extend the area of slavery," and who proceeded to criticize the standard of living of the Amazon natives. But
in spite of his disgust with some of the Lieutenant's premises,
Thoreau seems to have followed the routes attentively, particularly
Herndon's, which took him inland from Lima on the Peruvian coast,
over the Andes, down the river Huall to the Amazon, and thence to
the Atlantic. Herndon's account gave vivid details of the region: a
cobweb ten yards in diameter mantling the whole of a large lemon
tree, glistening in the morning sun like delicate drapery laid over the
rich-looking fruit beneath; the perfect stillness of the interior jungles,
where the scratch of the author's pen had only the faint scratching of
a tiny lizard on his table as competitor. Once again clues attest to
Thoreau's imaginative involvement in his travel reading. During his
reading of Herndon, his own Journal is filled with particularly "tropical" experiences of river travel on the Concord and Sudbury: lush
descriptions of the river banks in their "summer aspect," of great
fringed orchids growing in the luxuriant swamps, of towering ferns,

of turtles, and of fireflies in the muggy evenings.[23] Herndon also told stories of the Campas, who held undisputed control of the upper waters of the Ucayali, who appeared to be, from the extent of their territory, "the most numerous body of savages in America." Thoreau showed particular interest in all the Indians Herndon was able to observe: the Panos, Omaguas, Yameos, Sencis, Cobibos, Sipibos, Setibos, Piros, Remos, Amahuacas, and Yaguas; he noted their making and shooting of arrows, their canoes, their customs in securing wives.[24] Herndon had no hesitation in predicting, at the conclusion of his travels, that within fifty years Rio de Janeiro would be a village compared to Pará, Santarém would be the St. Louis of Brazil, and Manáos its Cincinnati. He compared the Amazon, as Thoreau himself had the Mississippi, with the Rhine.[25]

One account of the region of the Amazon basin combined fiction with fact and so differed from all the others which Thoreau read. It is not difficult to see what Thoreau found so appealing in Mayne Reid's "Books of Adventures for Boys," a series of narratives of travel in different regions of the Americas. Although the travel was fabricated, the route was not; Reid presented the facts of natural history accurately and clearly, and introduced his young readers to a region in a manner which we might imagine Thoreau imitating for the young people of Concord. Thoreau read each book in the series as soon as it came out. *The Forest Exiles; or, The Perils of a Peruvian Family amid the Wilds of the Amazon*, published in 1855, was fourth, and Thoreau read it early in 1856. Reid's family traveled over the cordilleras of the Andes east of Cuzco and down into the basin of the Amazon, then sailed down the Purus River on a balsa raft to the Amazon and thence fifteen hundred miles to its mouth. Every mile of the trip presented phenomena peculiar to the country, and Thoreau responded to everything. He noted carefully the descriptions of the tapir, the sloth, and the jaguar. He learned the features of the great Montaña of South America and of the classification of South American rivers: the Río Blanco whose waters were almost as white as milk, and the Amazon itself, both "white rivers"; the "blue" rivers of the Amazon valley whose courses lay through rocky countries and whose waters were clear and transparent; and the remarkable "black" streams, which ran through the most thickly wooded regions and, when deep, looked like rivers of ink, while their sandy bottoms, when they could be seen, gave the appearance of gold. He responded to a peculiar feature of these last rivers, noting with emphasis in his Extract Book, "Mosquitoes are not found on their banks!!!" [26]

In 1856 with Edmond Reuel Smith he took a *Tour among the Indian Tribes of Southern Chile* and the same year read Thomas Ewbank's *Life in Brazil,* both accounts just published. In 1857 he returned to Colombia with the naturalist Isaac Holton, reading his *New Granada: Twenty Months in the Andes,* a narrative which covered the thirty-year gap in geographical information about that portion of the continent since Cochrane's account. In his own library Thoreau possessed a translation of the zoologist Tschudi's *Travels in Peru,* the account of a trip undertaken in the 1840s. Altogether his reading provided him with travels in South America sufficient to take him literally the length and breadth of that vast continent.

But Thoreau's zest for traveling the South American continent was only representative of the interest which he was simultaneously showing for continents to the East. Although Columbus sailed westward to the Americas, he had charted his route for India, and Thoreau was not one to be cheated short of any destination. As he exclaimed in his Journal the same year he was reading of Columbus' and Humboldt's voyages, "The whole world is an America, a New World." [27] The great clipper ships, the *Samuel Russell,* the *Oriental,* the *Flying Dragon,* the *Northern Light,* the *Jacob Bell,* raced for China in futile attempts to beat the stunning record of 74 days, 14 hours set by skipper Robert Waterman and the fabled *Sea Witch* in 1849. It was the riches of trade with the Orient that inspired the Lows of Salem to revolutionize the merchant sailing ship and, following England's Opium War with China and the opening of that country to full commerce in 1845, to establish the United States, with her clipper ships and her whaling fleet, as emperor of the seas. From Salem and Boston harbors the ships Thoreau watched rigged at the Long Wharf now sped not only around the Horn to California but around the other Cape to India and Canton. The era of the clipper ship was to surfeit itself in a short two decades, but it centered in the precise period during which Thoreau did his travel reading. Prodigious wealth was its spur, speed the test, daring seamanship the challenge, the opening of an eastern continent the prize. We have only to turn to the familiar pages of W*alden* to find the eastern enterprise as Thoreau knew it at firsthand accurately recorded in an ecstatic metaphor faithful to both its immediate reality and its spirit.

> If your trade is with the Celestial Empire, then some small counting house on the coast, in some Salem harbor, will be fixture enough. You will export such articles as the country affords, purely native products, much ice and pine timber and a little granite, always in native bottoms. These will be good ventures. To oversee all the details yourself in person; to be at once pilot and captain, and owner and underwriter; to buy and sell and keep the accounts; to read every letter received, and write or read every letter sent; to superintend the discharge of imports night and day; to be upon many parts of the coast almost at the same time—often the richest will be discharged upon a Jersey shore;—to be your own telegraph, unweariedly sweeping the horizon, speaking all passing vessels bound coastwise; to keep up a steady dispatch of commodities, for the supply of such a distant and exorbitant market; to keep yourself informed of the state of the markets, prospects of war and peace everywhere, and anticipate the tendencies of trade and civilization—taking advantage of the results of all exploring expeditions, using new passages and all improvements in navigation;—charts to be studied, the position of reefs and new lights and buoys to be ascertained, and ever, and ever, the logarithmic tables to be corrected, for by error of some calculator the vessel often splits upon a rock that should have reached a friendly pier,—there is the untold fate of La Perouse;—universal science to be kept pace with, studying the lives of all great discoverers and navigators, great adventurers and merchants, from Hanno and the Phoenicians down to our day. . . . It is a labor to task the faculties of a man.[28]

But Thoreau's trips to the Middle and Far East deserve a chapter to themselves. They afford us an opportunity to move closer yet to the tone of the page and the detail of the route. Directed by the guide rails and signposts scattered through Thoreau's recordings in his notebooks, and with the pages of the travel books open before us, we can more fully share the journey.

~§ CHAPTER X §~

Eastward over the World

Was not Asia mapped in my brain before it was in any geography?
                                          Journal, March 23, 1842

Sure as Thoreau was of his intuitive sympathies with that Oriental thought which "Sanscrit contains or Sir W. Jones has unlocked," his persistent exploration of the physical and cultural environs in which such thought flourished kept him traveling to and through the Middle and Far East long after he had confessed bewilderment over what to do with the library of Oriental philosophy and history furnished him by Cholmondeley. The Asian continent was geographically mapped for Thoreau through his travel reading, most of it subsequent to his confident outburst of insight and predilection in 1842. Indeed, the very provocation for this early declaration of intellectual affinity was not (as Thoreau implied in his Journal) his "New England noontide" but his reading of a periodical review of Paul Emile Botta's discoveries on an expedition into Yemen in 1837, a small spot on the map of Arabia currently illuminated by the scientific reports of a geographer, naturalist, and archaeologist.

As a Harvard student Thoreau had read Sir John Barrow's *Voyage to Cochinchina* and Hugh Murray's *History of India*, and under Emerson's influence he had later resumed his study of Oriental thought. But it is to the traveler in the East that he turns for his closest and most sustained backward look "eastward over the world." The backward look offered as much new discovery as the forward one. The older world no less than the new one beckoned to explorer and traveler, offering itself for hazardous rediscovery by Occidentals in the nineteenth century. While the merchants mapped the sea routes east, it was left to the Christian missionaries to penetrate the

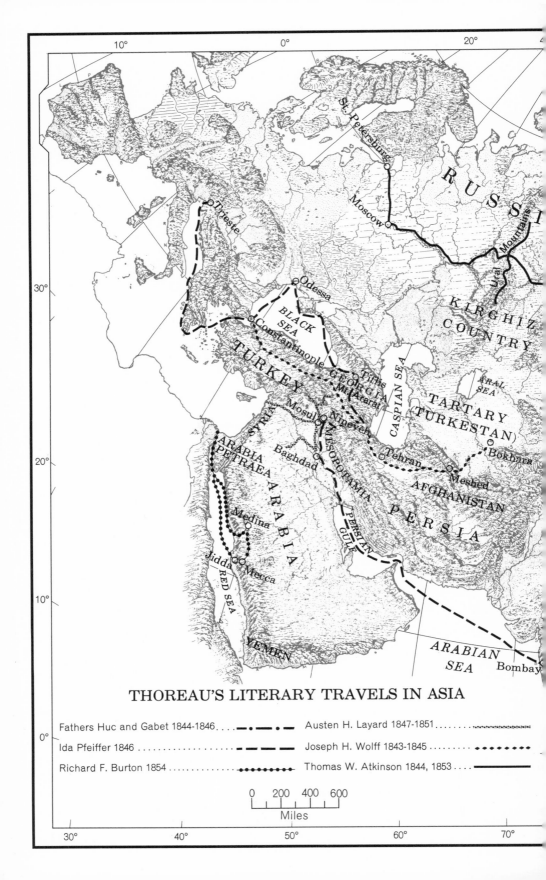

THOREAU'S LITERARY TRAVELS IN ASIA

Fathers Huc and Gabet 1844-1846 .... —··—··— Austen H. Layard 1847-1851 ....

Ida Pfeiffer 1846 .... —————— Joseph H. Wolff 1843-1845 ....

Richard F. Burton 1854 .... •••••••••• Thomas W. Atkinson 1844, 1853 .... ————

0 200 400 600
Miles

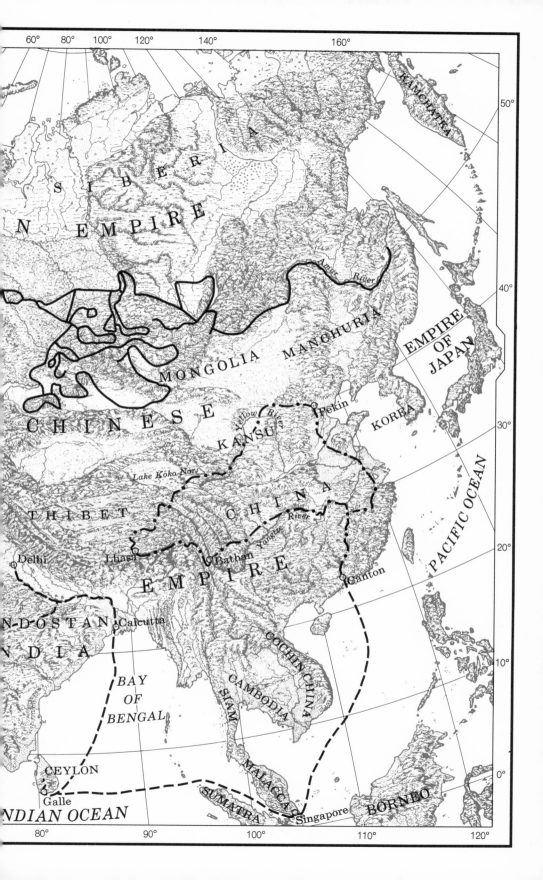

land of the "infidels." In these latter cases, fortunately a devotional zeal often combined with scholarly and scientific skills, assets which gave the new "crusade" greater promise than earlier ones.

On the whole, these missionaries were a humble, resourceful, and knowledgeable breed of travelers. No better representative could be cited than Joseph Wolff, son of the rabbi of Württemberg who became a convert to Christianity and by Thoreau's day an Anglican priest in England and a keen Oriental scholar. By 1847 Thoreau had read Wolff's last and most popular work, *Narrative of a Mission to Bokhara*, the account of a search for two missing Englishmen; the book went through seven editions between 1845 and 1852. Wolff was a traveling companion with whom Thoreau could find ready congeniality. He adventured and observed as directly and honestly as he wrote. He set forth his reasons for taking his trip with characteristic forthrightness in a letter to the English authorities:

> 1st. To perform a Christian act, by attempting the liberation of fellow-creatures, of two gallant officers of my adopted country.
> 2nd. To liberate *a friend, an intimate friend of mine*, in the person of Conolly.
> 3rd. To be useful to England.
> 4th. To perform a promise given to the prime minister of Bokhara, that I would remove the prejudice from the Europeans, caused by the calumny of the Persians, that the people of Bokhara were *murderers of guests*.
> 5th. To show to Asiatics how highly an Englishman and a Christian values the lives of his fellow-creature, by exposing myself to the fatigues and dangers of a journey from the Thames to the Oxus; and thus to inspire respect for the name of an Englishman in the minds of the Usbegs and their Prince.[1]

Leaving a young son in the care of the missing Conolly's brother-in-law, Wolff set off on a route that took him to Constantinople, then across Turkey to the Persian border and to Teheran, from there to Ashkhabad and into southern Central Asia to the great cultural and commercial center of the Moslem world. Once in the city of Bokhara, he conducted a compaign of intellectual maneuver and dialogue to save his life from the machinations of the deceitful nawab of the Ameer of Bokhara, whose treachery had already caused the execution of the two officers he sought. Wolff's skills in this duel were considerable, not the least of which were linguistic. In a Thoreauvian vein he declared it "distressing to see how often a person sets out for the East on a journey of pleasure, without knowing one single word of the language, and then comes back, after a few months (when he could only have observed that the Eastern clergy wear beards) and writes a nonsensical pamphlet, pompously styling it, *The State of the Eastern Churches*." [2] Eventually Wolff extricated himself from his danger and returned to England to write his own book.

We can reconstruct Thoreau's reading of Wolff's narrative without great difficulty. He was attracted to Wolff's brief official inventory of his items of itinerary, pared to the essentials of his mission:

1. I shall take with me a clergyman's gown and cassock, my hood, and a shovel hat.

2. One dozen or two of Hebrew Bibles and Testaments of the Common Prayer Book in Hebrew, for the Jews of Bokhara, Shahr Sabz, Khiva, Samarcand, Balkh, and Khokand.

3. Two or three dozens of silver watches, for the grand mullah and mullahs of Bokhara, the Khans of Khiva, Shahr Sabz and Khokand. The Ameer of Bokhara shall not get one single thing, in case he was the cause of their death.

4. Two or three dozens of maps in the Arabic characters. . . .

5. Three dozens of *Robinson Crusoe*, translated into Arabic. . . .
I distributed a great many copies of this book, when at Sanaa and Loheya, in Arabia, and I assure you that it excited a great sensation.[3]

Recalling this "sensation" in the *Week*, Thoreau quoted Wolff's further statement that "Robinson Crusoe's adventures and wisdom were read by Mohammedans in the market-places of Sanaa, Hodyeda, and Loheya, and admired and believed!" even adding Wolff's footnote that "on reading the book which I gave them the Arabs exclaimed, 'Oh, that Robinson Crusoe must have been a great Prophet!' " [4] Wolff's experiences often emphasized one world and one family of believers, and Thoreau's immediate response to his reading was provoked by such details: "The Missionary Wolff says, 'All the Brahmins I met with had an unlucky habit of affirming that what I said was in the Shastor, and used no further argument,' Christians do the same." [5] Wolff showed qualities of character which we should expect to win Thoreau's admiration: a firm integrity with relation to any fellow men he met; a liberality and adaptability (asked if he would prostrate himself before the Ameer of Bokhara three times and wish him peace and long life, Wolff declared that he would do so thirty times if necessary; on another occasion he responded to an invitation of the sheikh ul Islam, the first mullah of the Mohammedan religion at Constantinople, with characteristic tact: "Though I am not used to take snuff, I consider it such a high honour to take snuff with so distinguished a personage, that I would take a very hearty pinch" [6]); a vigor and hardihood as a traveler, as he demonstrated en route to Constantinople in February: "My previous habits made me support the voyage better than my fellow-travelers. I walked about on deck without a hat, and every morning had sea water poured over me." [7] Here also was a traveler who took pleasure in conversation with the pasha of Erzurum and his commissioner Envery Effendi about Arabic and Persian literature and history, who from his captivity in the city could satisfy the Ameer of Bokhara's arbitrary demand for a life of Mohammed with an extemporaneous forty-page document that created a sensation in Bokhara for its completeness and authenticity. [8]

As his own scrupulous translator, Wolff offered the reader interested in language and its uses authentic insight into its cultivated employment in Mohammedan culture. Wolff, ordered to sit upon a stone inside the palace gate at Bokhara and wait until properly introduced to the Ameer, submitted a sheaf of letters to fulfill this courtesy, letters which he identified for his readers as follows:

1. Two letters from the Sultan.
2. A letter from His Majesty Muhammed Shah of Persia.
3. A letter from Haje Mirza Aghassee, Prime Minister to the King of Persia, addressed to the so-called Vizer of the King of Bokhara, but who in fact is nothing else but the chief of the custom-house, and who is not allowed to receive or open any letter without the Ameer's permission.
4. A letter from his Excellency Count Medem, Russian Ambassador at Teheraun, to the Ameer himself.
5. A letter from the Sheikah al-Islam of Constantinople, to the Cazi Kelaun (grand judge) of Bokhara, for I knew that none of the dignitaries of Bokhara, not even a merchant, are allowed to receive letters without first of all being perused by the Ameer.
6. Letters from the Assaff-ood-Dowla written to myself, in which he stated to me that all the presents he had sent to the King of Bokhara

were sent on my account, and he further wrote to me, that if Dil Assa Khan should betray me at Bokhara, he would burn his father.

7. A copy of the letter sent by the Assaff-ood Dowla to Dil Assa Khan himself, warning him not to betray me.[9]

This load of epistles was to assuage a sensitive sovereign who had once regarded as a deadly affront a response to his message to the queen of England which came by way of the governor-general of India instead of the queen herself. Wolff gives his readers literal translations of each of these letters, but an introductory portion of only one will illustrate the style:

> From the Shah of Persia to the Ameer of Bokhara:
> The Enlightener of the dawn of Sovereignty and Dominion, the Personage worthy to occupy the throne of power and government, the Exalted Star in the heaven of splendour and greatness, the Illustrious Sun in the firmament of magnificence and felicity, the Best of the rulers of illustrious rank, the Most Excellent of the sovereigns illustrious for their generous deeds, the Chosen of the pillars of the governments of Islam, the Assister in the path of the religion of Mustapha Ameer Nusr Ollah: May your greatness and splendour not perish! May the glory of splendour, sovereignty, and dominion, be with you! . . .
> Now as the High in Rank, the Possessor of genius and understanding, the Endowed with sagacity and judgement, the prop of the learned among the followers of Messiah, the Chief among the wise people of Christendom, the English Padre Wolff has the intention of proceeding in that direction, urged by the sincere friendship which exists between us, and in order to promote the unanimity of Islam, we are induced to issue this auspicious friendship-denoting letter, the love-increasing zephyrs of affection being reflected towards your benevolent mind, and the opportunity being favorable for announcing the ties of friendship which of old and now bind us.[10]

One tries to imagine the response to this by the Concord reader who observed: "As for style of writing, if one has anything to say, it drops from him simply and directly, as a stone falls to the ground." [11] Promising more understanding, however, would be Thoreau's further realization: "What men say is so sifted and obliged to approve itself as answering to a common want, that nothing absolutely frivolous obtains currency. . . . Only the ethics of mankind . . . give point and vigor to our speech."

Not all travelers whom Thoreau accompanied in the Middle East were missionaries by profession, however. Austen Layard, to whose *Nineveh and Its Remains* (1849) Thoreau turned his attention in 1850, was a young man exactly Thoreau's age who had traveled in most of the larger European countries before he was twenty, had stood on the banks of the Tigris at the age of twenty-three, and had at the age of twenty-eight begun excavating archaeological remains around Mosul, between excursions into southeastern Asia. His book, which Thoreau read immediately upon its publication, was divided into two volumes, the second containing descriptions of the excavations at Nineveh, the site of which Paul Emile Botta had discovered a few years earlier; the first volume offered narrations of almost continuous journeys throughout the Ottoman Empire, Syria, and Mesopotamia, with full accounts of the country and its inhabitants, the subtitle of the book calling particular attention to "An Account of a Visit to the Chaldaean Christians of Kurdistan, and the Yezidis, or Devil-Worshippers." We find Thoreau recording his responses to Layard's experiences in his Journal between June 9 and 15, notes stored in the Journal prior to the establishment of the Extract Book. He was impressed with the frequent discussions on doctrinal points which Layard had with Chaldean Christians in the Kurdish Hills, and in one instance with a Turkish cadi, an event which Thoreau recalled later when he read in old town records of the doctrinal issues affecting the selection of ministers for the town of Eastham on Cape Cod.[12] He noted the religious ceremonies of the Yezidis, fire worshipers or worshipers of the Devil, which Layard observed at the village of Baadri north of Mosul on the Tigris.[13] But long before Layard reached the Yezidis and page 240 of his first volume, he had offered his sympathetic fellow traveler any number of vivid experiences in these remote regions. As he announced:

> I had traversed Asia Minor and Syria, visiting the ancient seats of civilization, and the spots which religion has made holy. . . . I now felt an irresistible desire to penetrate to the regions beyond the Euphrates, to which history and tradition point as the birthplace of the wisdom of the West. Most travellers, after a journey through the usually frequented parts of the East, have the same longing to cross the great river, and to explore those lands which are separated on the map from the confines of Syria by a vast blank stretching from Aleppo to the banks of the Tigris. A deep mystery hangs over Assyria, Babylonia,

Chaldea. With these names are linked great nations and great cities dimly shadowed forth in history; mighty ruins, in the midst of deserts, defying by their very desolation and lack of definite form, the description of the traveller; the remnants of mighty races still roving over the land; the fulfilling and fulfilment of prophecies; the plains to which Jew and Gentile alike look as the cradle of their race. After a journey to Syria the thoughts naturally turn eastward.[14]

Layard was a competent writer and showed skill in grounding the impressions of his senses in concrete details. He did not belittle his feelings, only his capacity to justify them to the reader:

The exhilaration caused by the air of the desert in spring, and the feeling of freedom arising from the contemplation of its boundless expanse, must have been experienced before they can be understood. The stranger, as well as the Arab, feels the intoxication of the senses which they produce. From their effect upon the wandering son of Ishmael, they might well have been included by the Prophet amongst those things forbidden to the true believer.[15]

Yet Layard was not quite at such a loss as he proclaimed, as the following depiction may illustrate:

The middle of March in Mesopotamia is the brightest epoch of spring. A new change has come over the face of the plain of Nimrood. Its pasture lands, known as the "Jaif," are renowned for their rich and luxuriant herbage. In times of quiet, the studs of the Pasha and of the Turkish authorities, with the horses of the cavalry and of the inhabitants of Mosul, are sent here to graze. Day by day they arrived in long lines. The Shermutti and Jesesh left their huts, and encamped on the greensward which surrounded the villages. The plain, as far as the eye could reach, was studded with the white pavilions of the Hytas and the black tents of the Arabs. Picketed around them were innumerable horses in gay trappings, struggling to release themselves from the bonds, which restrained them from ranging over the green pastures.

Flowers of every hue enamelled the meadows; not thinly scattered over the grass as in northern climes, but in such thick and gathering clusters that the whole plain seemed a patchwork of many colors. The dogs, as they returned from hunting, issued from the long grass dyed red, yellow, or blue, according to the flowers through which they had forded their way.[16]

While Thoreau read these descriptions, spring was abroad in his own land, the evidences of which he too was etching in words. The moderate spring rain "makes the grass look many shades greener. . . . I too revive as does the grass." "In all my rambles I have seen no land-scape which can make me forget Fair Haven. I sit still on its Cliff in a new spring day, and look over the awakening woods and river, and hear the new birds sing. . . . It is as sweet a mystery to me as ever, what this world is." Bucolic scenes far removed from one another must have enhanced each other while Thoreau read Layard.

> There is the time when they begin to drive cows to pasture—about the 20th of May. . . . I sometimes see a neighbor or two united with their boys and hired men to drive their cattle to some far-off country pasture, fifty or sixty miles distant in New Hampshire, early in the morning, with their sticks and dogs. . . . The herdsman in some distant pasture is expecting them.[17]

Even as he wrote down these observations of his own, Thoreau was reading in Layard:

> When I returned in the evening after the labor of the day, I often sat at the door of my tent, giving myself up to the full enjoyment of that calm and repose which are imparted to the senses by such scenes as these. . . . The bleating of sheep and lowing of cattle, at first faint, became louder as the flocks returned from their pastures, and wandered among the tents. Girls hurried over the greensward to seek their father's cattle, or crouched to milk those which had returned alone. . . . Some were coming from the river bearing the replenished pitcher on their heads or shoulders; others, no less graceful in their form, and erect in their carriage, were carrying the heavy load of long grass which they had cut in the meadows. Sometimes a party of horsemen might have been seen in the distance slowly crossing the plain, the tufts of ostrich feath-ers which topped their long spears showing darkly against the evening sky. They would ride up to my tent and give me the usual salutation, "Peace be with you, O Bey," or "Allah Aienak, God Help you." Then driving the end of their lances into the ground, they would spring from their mares, and fasten their halters to the still quivering weapons. Seating themselves on the grass, they related deeds of war and plun-der, or speculated on the site of the tents of Sofuk, until the moon rose, when they vaulted into their saddles and took the way of the desert.[18]

How easy it is also, while reading of such pastoral scenes on the plains of Mesopotamia, to recall Thoreau's evening idyls in *Walden*, when from the door of his cabin at evening "the distant lowing of some cow in the horizon . . . sounded sweet and melodious," the delicious evening made the whole body one sense that "imbibes delight through every pore," and the observer gave himself up to the sounds and sights of his setting.[19]

Thoreau showed interest in Layard's findings at Nineveh as well as in his travels, going on to read Layard's second book when it was published in 1853, *Discoveries among the Ruins of Nineveh and Babylon, with Travels in Armenia, Kurdistan, and the Desert.* He copied copiously from pages 109, 220, 221, 354–56, 408, 506, 612, 663–64, and 674 of the huge volume, material ranging from Layard's description of the Arab's regard for his horses, to matter from the Appendix, written by Sir David Brewster upon the chemical properties of the ancient glass found in the ruins.[20] But Thoreau was less archaeologist than traveler, and his comments upon Layard's preoccupation with excavations and ancient inscriptions suggest decreasing sympathy after the first four hundred pages of reading. Layard's eager and perilous climb up a precipice to inspect some inscriptions he had been told were graven there high above Lake Van, only to find some "modern" scratching and be disappointed "as many a traveller has been under similar circumstances," elicited from Thoreau the Journal comment: "They were not old enough; that was all. Wait a thousand years and you will not be disappointed."[21] Thoreau copied into his Extract Book two interesting descriptions by Layard of the ruins of Babylon:

Site of Babylon

On all sides fragments of glass, marble, pottery, and inscribed brick are mingled with that peculiar nitrous and blanched soil, which, bred from the remains of ancient habitations, checks or destroys vegetation, and renders the site of Babylon a naked and hideous waste.

The Mujelibe or Kasr, a mound ruin of Babylon

Upon nearly every brick is clearly and deeply stamped the name and title of Nebuchadnezzar, and the inscribed face is always placed downwards. . . .

This ruin has for ages been the mine from which the builders of cities rising after the fall of Babylon have obtained their materials. To this day there are men who have no other trade than that of gathering bricks from this vast heap and taking them for sale to the neighboring towns and villages, and even to Baghdad. There is scarcely a house in

Hillah which is not almost entirely built with them; and as the traveller passes through the narrow streets, he sees in the walls of every hovel a record of the glory and power of Nebuchadnezzar.[22]

But his reaction to such description was voiced in his Journal on December 9: "Above all, deliver me from a city built on the site of a more ancient city, the materials of the one being the ruins of the other. There the dwellings of the living are the cemeteries of the dead, and the soil is blanched and accursed." [23] The sight remained with him, vivid and repulsive. Four years later he could as readily recall it, exclaiming in his Journal, "I would rather be the barrenest pasture lying fallow than cursed with the compliments of Kings, than be the sulphurous and accursed desert where Babylon once stood." [24] When Thoreau wrote his friend Blake on December 22 that the Turkish cadi's letter with which Layard concluded his volume was "a capital comment on the whole book which precedes it," he was siding with that "Oriental wisdom" which he found speaking through the cadi, an attitude which Layard criticized as an unappreciative "spirit in which Eastern philosophy and Mussulman resignation contemplate the evidence of ancient greatness and civilization, suddenly rising up in the midst of modern ignorance and decay." [25] The cadi's letter was written to a friend of Layard's in reply to some inquiries as to the commerce, population, and remains of antiquity of an ancient city, in which the cadi dwelt. Thoreau copied the letter entire into his Extract Book, but the opening portion will identify his sympathies.

My illustrious Friend and Joy of my liver!
The thing you ask of me is both difficult and useless. Although I have passed all my days in this place, I have neither counted the houses nor have I inquired into the number of the inhabitants; and as to what one person loads on his mules and the other stows away on the bottom of his ship, that is no business of mine. But above all, as to the previous history, God only knows the amount of dirt and confusion that the infidels may have eaten before the coming of the sword of Islam. It were unprofitable for us to inquire into it.
Oh my soul! Oh, my lamb seek not after the things which concern thee not. Thou camest unto us, and we welcomed thee: go in peace.
Of a truth, thou hast spoken many words; and there is no harm

done, for the speaker is one and the listener is another. After the fashion of thy people thou hast wandered from one place to another until thou art happy and content in none. We (praise be to God) were born here, and never desire to quit it. Is it possible then that the idea of a general intercourse between mankind should make any impression on our understandings? God forbid!

It would be vain, observed Layard, to speak to such a man "of the true objects of researches, the knowledge they impart, the lessons they teach, or the thoughts they beget." Thoreau was no antiquarian, and his final appraisal of the sight of Nineveh's remains brought him closer in spirit to the cadi than to the archaeologist. As early as 1840 he had written in his Journal:

> The true art is not merely a sublime consolation and holiday labor which the gods have given to sickly mortals . . . but such a masterpiece as you may imagine a dweller on the table-lands of Central Asia might produce, with threescore and ten years for canvas, and the faculties of a man for tools,—a human life . . . not the bald imitation or rival of Nature, but the restored original of which she is the reflection. . . . Not how is the idea expressed in stone or on canvas, is the question, but how far it has obtained form and expression in the life.[26]

We must caution ourselves once again, however, from concluding that these few critical statements summarize Thoreau's view of Layard's accounts. While he suggested that Layard's major concerns were basically inappropriate, he read 1,366 pages describing them. Clearly the annoyance was only one side of his response, not even the determining one. His own discovery of an early date upon the chimney ruins of the Lee house in Concord which had just burned to the ground (in February, 1857), and his attempt to bring away the evidence in a piece of brick and mortar only to have it crumble in his hands, instinctively allied him with the earlier excavator:

> I was reminded of the crumbling of some of the slabs of Nineveh in the hands of Layard as soon as brought to light, and felt a similar grief because I could not transport it entire to a more convenient place than that scorching pile, or even lay the crumbling mass down, without losing forever the outlines and the significance of those yet undeciphered words. But I laid it down, of necessity, and that was the end of it. There was our sole Nineveh slab, perhaps the oldest *engraving* in Concord.

LAYARD'S IMPRESSION OF A CLAY TABLET FROM THE RUINS OF KOUYUNJIK

THOREAU'S DRAWING IN HIS JOURNAL OF THE DATING ON A PIECE OF CHIMNEY FROM THE RUINS OF THE LEE HOUSE IN CONCORD, 1857

He had profited from his initiation in the deserts of Syria, for he had learned to take those proper preliminary steps before attempting to remove archaeological evidence; from the precious slab in the ruins of the Lee house he first made his drawing exactly reproducing the inscriptions, a record which he reproduced in the pages of his Journal as faithfully as Layard had his in the pages of his book.[27]

Thoreau's reading of Sir Thomas Stamford Raffles' *History of Java* in 1851 was more for evoking the present realities of the place than for learning of its past, as can be seen from the numerous excerpts which he copied into his notebook.[28] William Sleeman's *Rambles and Recollections of an Indian Official*, which he read a year later, offered him comparable coverage of modern India, and from a work which offered generous proportions of history with its firsthand reports Thoreau filled his Extract Book with ten pages of gleanings from the two-volume, 937-page account: descriptions of hornets that could rout "six companies of infantry"; of the burning of widows or "suttees"; of wheat blights, the supernatural causes to which they were attributed and a long account of herculean cures; of Nerbudda, a sacred mountain whose sight alone could bless and purify, in contrast with the Ganges the water of which one had to bathe in or drink.[29] But more characteristic of the actual journeying which he did in the East was *A Journey to Mount Ararat*, the account of a trip which he took in 1851 with Frederick Parrot (the first man to reach the peak of that mountain, in 1829) and to which we shall be referring again in a subsequent chapter. It was not the mountain alone which impressed Thoreau. Parrot traversed the steppes of Georgia and Armenia, filling his account with myriad details of the land and its natives. Here Thoreau met the Kalmucks, whose territory gave for years the only name to a vast region of southern Russia. Their attachment to the roving life offered as extreme an illustration of the avoidance of ties and impedimenta to travel as Thoreau was to find in his reading.

So great is their attachment to a roving life that I was assured by one of their priests that it would be looked upon as a sort of violation of religious principle if they were to attempt to provide a supply of hay in summer to secure their horses and oxen from the danger of perishing of hunger in the winter, because it would seem an approximation to habits to which their national practices are too obstinately opposed.[30]

Of particular interest to Thoreau, in addition to the ways of life of the Kalmucks, were the town houses of Tiflis in Georgia; he noted the way in which they were constructed, their roofs overgrown with weeds. He copied down a vivid picture from Parrot of the inhabitants' novel custom of refreshing the green of their thatched roofs by burning the dry weeds in the summer, "so that the fire, which soon seizes on this inflammable vegetable matter will often present the startling and beautiful spectacle of a wide body of flame sweeping over the city in the night." [31]

Thoreau was back in Tiflis a few months later with Ida Pfeiffer, as he came to the concluding portion of her *Lady's Voyage round the World* which had just been published (1852). As was almost inevitable with travel books, routes overlapped from one account to the next. It is interesting to speculate about Thoreau's apparent immunity to the usual tediousness of too many return trips. He seems content, if not indeed actually eager, to retravel a route and reexperience it as many times as he can find travelers to take him over it. Perhaps he was anxious to render the foreign routes as familiar as were his

A KALMUCK RESTING

Sketched by Atkinson in his *Oriental and Western Siberia*

own retraced ones at home. With Mme Pfeiffer he not only visited Georgia in Asiatic Russia again but once more traveled over the plains within a few miles of Ararat to inspect again that "magnificent mountain," although not to climb it. Once again he traveled to Mosul and Nineveh, over routes crisscrossed by Layard; once more he inched by caravan across the same perilous mountain pass from Mosul to Rawanduz which Layard's caravan trip introduced him to only months before, taking time this trip to record a vivid moment of peril and beauty.[32] For those areas which Thoreau had already traveled with others, Mme Pfeiffer's narrative must have proved relatively superficial. He probably expected no more than he got; he appears to have read her book originally only on the recommendation of Emerson, who was considerably less demanding of his travel reading. Thoreau's reference in *Walden* to Mme Pfeiffer's adaptation in Asiatic Russia to the demands of "a civilized country . . . where people are judged by their clothes" [33] avoids reference to her own attitude toward a custom to which she was only too willing to acquiesce. But travel she did, and the greater part of her 300-page book from her arrival at Canton on page 50 described her routes honeycombing the Far and Middle East.

Perhaps it was enough for Thoreau that, as traveler, Mme Pfeiffer kept moving. Her chapter titles traced the route and the pace of her journey: "China," "Singapore," "Ceylon," "Benares," "Allahabad, Agra, and Delphi," "Journey from Delhi to Bombay," "From Bombay to Bagdad," "Mesopotamia," "Mossul and Ninevah," "Persia," "Tabreez," "Asiatic Russia—Armenia, Georgia, and Mingrella," "European Russia," "Constantinople and Athens." Her editors prefaced her book with a self-portrait that revealed much about inclinations:

> From my earliest childhood I had always the greatest longing to see the world. When I met a travelling carriage I used to stand still and gaze after it with tears in my eyes, envying the very postilions, till it vanished from my sight. As a girl of ten or twelve, I read with the greatest eagerness all the books of travel I could get hold of, and then I transferred my envy to the grand traveller who had gone round the world. The tears would come into my eyes when I climbed a mountain and saw others still piled up before me, and thought that I should never see what lay beyond. I afterwards, however, travelled a good deal. . . . I cared little for privation; my bodily frame was healthy and

hardy; I had no fear of death; and as my birth-day dated from the last century, I could travel *alone*.[34]

Thoreau recorded excerpts in his Extract Book from her rapid and kaleidoscopic accounts and commented upon others in his Journal: the judgment of persons by their clothes in the "civilized" country of Asiatic Russia he openly termed "another barbarous trait" in his Journal entry; but he expressed evident satisfaction in reporting from his reading that "barbarous as we esteem the Chinese, they have already built their steamboat." [35] His excerpts included such domestic details as the familiar names the Arab children near Nineveh used for their parents, and a Chinese lady's manner of binding her feet to force fashionable height in place of practical length and breadth.[36] Mme Pfeiffer added to the scenes of the Far East which Raffles and Sleeman had furnished. With her, Thoreau visited both Hindu and Buddhist temples, further etching in his memory the details and impressions he later recalled readily in his Journal (although he proved remarkably careless in distinguishing his recalled edifices by religious sect).[37] His Journal entries for January 15 and 16 are sprinkled with responses to his reading of Chinese funerals in Singapore and of Parsi worship in Bombay.[38] A "ramble" with Mme Pfeiffer at night about the streets of Delhi offered a rich assortment of sights: princes riding up and down the streets on elephants decked with carpets and cashmere shawls, hangings trimmed with gold lace and festooned with gold cords and tassels; laden camels and fine Arab horses and *bailis* drawn by white buffaloes in scarlet trappings with painted horns and feet; beggars, snake charmers, and conjurors who changed the color of their pupils, spit fire, and drew from incisions in their skin ell after ell of silk thread and narrow ribbon.[39]

It may have been the rapid rate of Mme Pfeiffer's travel (she was compulsively arriving and departing)that prompted what appears to be Thoreau's lasting impression of her account. He wrote in his Journal, at the very time that he was reading her V*oyage*, the following comment upon travel:

> The traveller's is so apt to be a progress more or less rapid toward his home (I have read many a voyage around the world more than half of which, certainly, was taken up with the return voyage; he no sooner is out of sight of his native hills than he begins to tell us how he got home again) that I wonder he did not stay at home in the first place.[40]

The reference here is unprecise, but no circumnavigation by a man that Thoreau had read up to this time answers even faintly to the indictment; and five years later almost to the day, Thoreau is provoked by another traveler in the Middle East, this time Richard Burton, to make an additional comment upon traveling, inveighing against that kind which grows so out of restlessness and dissatisfaction as to constitute a "disease" (a "prevalent" one, "which attacks Americans especially, both men and women"), the "opposite to nostalgia," yet, he adds, "does not differ much from nostalgia. I read the story of one voyageress round the world, who, it seemed to me, having started, had no other object but to get home again, only she took the longest way round." [41] This time the reference was made considerably clearer.

Mme Pfeiffer took her whirlwind trip "East to West" in 1846; in 1852 Thoreau also joined two extraordinary travelers, the Lazarist Fathers Huc and Gabet, for a far more extensive *Journey through Tartary, Thibet, and China, during the Years 1844, 1845, and 1846.* Huc's account had just been published in Appleton's Popular Library, in two small volumes, and during April and May Thoreau concentrated upon Huc's five-hundred-page narrative. This Roman Catholic missionary, with his assistant M. Gabet, undertook a daring journey across Tibet, having already worked among the scattered Christians in Tartary and acquired knowledge of the Chinese and Mongol languages. The pair set out in 1844, affecting a ruse which attested to their skill in acting almost as much as to their courage and originality; they cut off the pigtails they had assumed for the sake of their Chinese converts and put on the dress of lamas, a role which they played so well that they crossed forbidden borders with immunity. Upon entering the Chinese province of Kansu, Huc could declare, "The triumph we had thus obtained in a country admission even to which was prohibited to us under pain of death, gave us prodigious courage." [42] The missionaries set forth into the plains of Tartary, the "Land of Grass" for which Thoreau expressed such excited interest from almost the outset of his reading.[43] In spite of a slow start (because of inexperience in handling camels), "our march soon became regular." The first night was spent at one of the lonely inns frequently found in the deserts of Tartary, not far from the frontiers of China. Here travelers converged in picturesque and genial comfort, where the protocol of landlords matched the politeness of robbers (duly noted by Thoreau in extensive notebook excerpts, and perhaps recalling his own early essay on "The Landlord" [44]). From a green knoll near the Lincoln and Concord lines Thoreau showed contagious excitement, observing in the distance the hedged waterway of the winding Concord River "like a lake in Tartary; there our camels will find water." He had come from reading that M. Gabet "gave a loud shout and made a gesture with his hand"; advancing to meet him, the caravan, tortured by thirst, discovered that Providence offered them a small pond, the waters of which were half hidden by thick reeds and marsh plants; "hungry, thirsty, fatigued as we were, we could wish for nothing better. The camels had scarcely lain down before we ran each with his little wooden bowl to the pond, and filled it from between the reeds." [45]

The boundless prairie over which the Fathers journeyed made them feel as alone in its green solitudes as in the midst of an ocean. But the feeling was one of exhilaration, as they passed through the "delightful meadows" of the border country lying in a 400-mile square to the north of the Great Wall of China. Here life was, as Thoreau observed, "as on our prairies. Dried dung served as fuel." Huc explained: "Those who have never led the nomadic life will have some difficulty in comprehending how . . . when you have the

THE TRAVELERS SETTING OUT
ON THEIR JOURNEY

From Huc, *Tartary, Thibet, and China*

good fortune to find suddenly among the grass an argol remarkable for its size and dryness, you experience one of those sudden pleasurable emotions that for the moment make you happy." [46] Entering western Tumet after more than a month in the desert, the missionaries found their taste "insensibly modified, and our temperament accommodated by its silence and solitude, and on re-entering cultivated lands, the agitation, perplexity, and turmoil of civilization oppressed and suffocated us; the air seemed to fail us, and we felt every moment as if about to die of asphyxia." It is hardly surprising to find Thoreau calling such experience to the attention of his own readers of "Walking." [47]

The Mongol's character and customs were peculiarly congenial to travelers. On the one hand, they were themselves nomadic.

> When the Tartars travel during the night, it often happens that they do not give themselves the trouble to dismount in order to sleep; and you may see a caravan stop when it has reached a fat pasture, and the camels disperse themselves this way and that, and begin to graze, while the Tartars, astride between their humps, are sleeping as if they were in their beds.[48]

On the other hand, the Mongols showed strong feelings toward family, brotherhood, hospitality. Etiquette forbade the entrance into a dwelling with a stick, since it would imply "in their own figurative style" (because sticks were necessary for protection against the dogs guarding Tartar tents) that the inhabitants were dogs. "All men are brothers," declared the old Mongol who generously entertained the French Fathers with food and minstrelsy supplied by a wandering troubadour of the desert (reminding them of "the rhapsodists of Greece"); "but those who dwell beneath tents are united as the flesh and the bone." As Thoreau jotted down, "A Tartar debt is never paid." [49] It was as common for Huc to "meet with a family in China remarkable for hospitality," as Thoreau noted, as it was for the Mongol to present himself frankly, simply, and free to another person. Thoreau wrote in his Journal for May 3:

> The salutations and commonplaces of all nations, which sound to us formal often, are always adapted to their circumstances, and grow out of their necessities. The Tartar inquires, "Has the rain been abundant? Are your flocks in prosperity? Have your mares been fruitful?" and the

answer is, "All is at peace in our pastures." Serene and Biblical, and no man's invention.[50]

As the Fathers entered Manchuria, the Chinese whom they encountered in this remote part of the Chinese Empire had yet heard word of the China War and the English, "the Rebels of the South," who "never dare to quit the sea; as soon as ever they come on shore they tremble and die like fish." Here too the travelers discovered the peculiar advantages of their assumed role.

> The vagabond Lamas visit all the countries accessible to them—China, Mantchoria, Khalkas, Southern Mongolia, Ounang-Hai, Kou-Kou-Noor, north and south of the Celestial Mountains, Thibet, India, and sometimes even Turkistan. There is not a river they have not crossed; a mountain they have not ascended; a Grand Lama before whom they have not prostrated themselves; a people among whom they have not lived, and of whom they do not know the manners and the language. Losing their way in the desert is not possible, since all ways are alike to them. Travelling without any object, the places they arrive at are always those where they desire to go. The legend of the Wandering Jew is exactly realized in the persons of these Lamas. One would say they are under the influence of some mysterious power, which drives them incessantly onward; and it seems as if God had caused to flow in their veins something of that motive force which urges worlds forward in their course, without ever permitting them to rest.

Thoreau copied it all down faithfully in his Extract Book, this with other descriptions of the lamas' way of life.[51] Traversing Kansu province, the Fathers met a living Buddha on his way from his native Tibet to the great lama convent in the country of the Khalkas not far from the Russian frontier. The Buddha spoke of the route to Tibet and of "the terrible journey we should have to make to get to it—seeming to doubt whether we were strong enough for such an undertaking. The words and the manner of this Grand Lama were full of affability, but we could not accustom ourselves to the strange look of his eyes." [52] The warning about the route proved pertinent, although not the doubts about these travelers' strength. Having already crossed the Yellow River in flood period, with camels helpless in the marshy area and unable to swim, having already crossed the Great Wall three times, the first time "without dismounting," the Fathers paused at the frontier town of Keou-Eul or Dangkar ("Nobody walks the

streets without a great sabre at his side") and listened to accounts of
the road ahead to Lhasa.

> A journey of four months had to be made across countries entirely
> uninhabited and where travellers were often frozen to death or buried
> under the snow. During the summer, it was said many were drowned;
> for it was necessary to cross great rivers without bridge or boat; and
> besides this, these deserts were ravaged by hordes of robbers who
> plundered those who fell into their hands even of their clothes, and
> left them naked and starving in the wilderness.[53]

Waiting at Keou-Eul for the annual Chinese embassy to Tibet,
which had just left Peking and which they must accompany, the
missionaries studied Tibetan with the scholars of the lamaseries, then
with the coming of summer proceeded to Koko Nor or "Blue Sea," a
great salt sea, by which they pastured their camels until the embassy
arrived with a great Mongol caravan (2,000 men and 40,000 horses,
yaks, and camels).

On the fifteenth of November they left the fertile plains for the
country of the Tsaidam Mongols. "Here the landscape underwent a
great change, and became wild and gloomy, and the dry and stony
soil bore nothing but brambles impregnated with saltpetre." Then
came the ascent of the "dreaded" Bourhan-Bota (Burchan Buddha)
Pass enveloped in poisonous vapors:

> In a short time the horses appeared to be incapable of bearing their
> riders;—every one slackened his pace, all faces turned pale, the heart
> beat faintly, the limbs refused their office;—many lay down, then got
> up again, made a few steps, then lay down again, and in this deplorable
> manner toiled up the side of the famous Bourhan-Bota.

The passage of the Bourhan-Bota proved only their apprenticeship;
another mountain range—the Shuga—put strength to yet greater
test:

> The wind began to blow with constantly increasing violence, while the
> snow was so deep on the sides of the mountain that it was up to the
> bellies of the cattle, and many . . . were left to perish. The gale was
> so icy and cutting that it almost took away our breath and wrapped up
> as we were in furs, we feared being frozen to death. In order to avoid
> the whirlwinds of snow that the wind lashed in our faces, we . . .
> mounted our horses backwards, leaving them to go as they would.[54]

When they had crossed the mountain and could open their eyes, they saw many a frozen face, including that of M. Gabet. "Fainting with hunger, numbed with cold, as we were, we had not, like the Alpine traveller, a hospitable convent wherein to find shelter and warmth, but we had to pitch our tent in the snow, and go on a long search for a few fragments of argols, which just made fire enough to melt some large lumps of ice that we cut with a hatchet from a frozen pond." From here on the fury of snow and wind and cold augmented each day. "The deserts of Thibet are, beyond all contradiction, the most frightful that can be imagined. . . . and we had still two months' journey before us, and that in the depth of winter!" Early in December the diminished caravan climbed the mountain chain of Bayan Kara, extending southeast to northwest between the Yellow River and the Kinsha Kiang (river of golden sand), a feat accomplished by clinging to the tails of their animals preceding them. Crossing the upper reaches of the Yangtze on the ice (where a herd of wild oxen were frozen in the river, their heads and fine antlers above the ice, their bodies solidified in swimming gestures, their eyes pecked out by eagles and ravens), the caravan dragged itself for twelve days over the great plateau 16,000 feet above sea level which is the source of the Yangtze, the Salween, and the Mekong rivers, the final barrier to Lhasa. Here men joined cattle to be left by the way:

> More than forty men perished thus in the desert. When they could no longer eat or speak, or support themselves on their horses, they were left on the road, though still alive, a small bag of oatmeal and a little wooden bowl being placed beside them as a last mark of interest in their fate. When every one else had passed by, the crows and vultures were seen to wheel round them in the air, and probably they began to tear the unfortunate men before they were fairly dead.[55]

M. Gabet, whose hands, feet, and face were frozen, was tied his whole length on a camel to save him from a similar fate. At last began the final descent and on January 13, 1846, "issuing from a defile at the foot of the mountain, we saw lying before us the renowned Lha-Ssa, the metropolis of the Buddhist world, encircled by a multitude of grand old trees, which form with their foliage a girdle of verdure around it; its white houses, with their terraces and turrets; its numerous temples, with their gilded roofs; and high above all, the majestic palace of the Tale Lama." [56] Observed Thoreau in his notebook, "For the Tartars there is nothing beyond Tibet. 'The world ends there,' say they, 'beyond there is nothing but a shoreless sea.' "[57]

It is the straightforward, humble character of these two strange travelers that remains with one after accompanying them across the breadth of southern Asia. They were sensible, practical men, adaptable and open-minded in matters of custom and need, intrepid and not a little stubborn regarding principles. Their performance in the presence for the first time of a living Buddha was characteristic.

> As soon as the inn was quiet, this singular personage apparently felt inclined to indulge his curiosity; and he travelled all over the house, going into every room, and speaking to every body, though without sitting down or stopping anywhere. As we expected, he came also to our room. We were waiting for him, and we had seated ourselves gravely on the kang, and purposely did not rise to receive him, but merely made him a slight salutation. He appeared much surprised, but not disconcerted; and he stopped a long time in the middle of the room, and looked at us one after the other. We remained profoundly silent, making use meanwhile of the same freedom, and examined him also from head to foot.[58]

KANG OF A CHINESE-TARTAR INN
From Huc, *Tartary, Thibet, and China*

Huc blamed Christians themselves for their oppression in China: "When one of them is dragged before the tribunal, the others all hide themselves, instead of coming to his assistance and repressing by their boldness the insolence of the Mandarins. In China, as every where else, we are only free when we will be so, and this will results only from the spirit of association." [59] But with the dedication to principle went a basic sweetness of nature which consistently aligned these missionaries with the oppressed, the sensitive, and the victimized. It was impossible for Huc to refrain from taking the hand of the frozen man found sitting alone on the Tibetan desert stiff and immobile except for the slightest turn of a glazed eye, a man already among the companion dead left behind by native travelers. It was characteristic of Huc to make a lasting friend of the Buddha he so uncompromisingly inspected, as it was to chronicle so honestly and sympathetically each of the distinctive religious ceremonies which he witnessed, whether it was the festival of the Loaves of the Moon among the Mongols, the Feast of the Flowers at Tang-Keou-Eul, or a "touching custom" at Lhasa:

> In the evening, as soon as the light declines, the Thibetan men, women, and children cease from all business, and assemble in the principle parts of the city, and in the public squares. As soon as the groups are formed, every one sits down on the ground, and begins slowly to chant his prayers in an undertone, and the religious concert produces an immense and solemn harmony throughout the city.

Thoreau shared Huc's impression of the Tibetans' chants, storing in his Extract Book this evening scene, together with much further information about specific prayers and their meanings, particularly the six-syllable, unvaried chant for the dead, "Om mani padme houm!" whose literal sense Huc gave as "O the jewel in the lotus! Amen." The jewel was the emblem of perfection, the lotus that of Buddha. "The Lamas assert that the doctrine contained in these marvellous words is immense, and that the whole life of man is insufficient to measure its depth and extent." [60]

Richard Burton's *Personal Narrative of a Pilgrimage to Al-Madinah and Meccah*, published in 1855, had already created a popular sensation as a travel book by the time the first American edition appeared a year later and Thoreau read it. It established the fame of an author who was to give far more solid evidence of his exploratory skills in Africa in 1856, recounted in an equally popular book published in 1860 (which Thoreau also read).[61] This first journey which Burton took proved less remarkable than his colorful account of it, for Burton showed a flair for projecting his "personality" into his pages, vaunting a cynical humor and a reckless insobriety of opinion in frank and pungent language. He left little doubt that he was an adventurer, although he went through the motions of justifying his indulgence by playing the role of scientist and explorer. His later fame as the translator of the *Arabian Nights* proved his most fitting epitaph. But Thoreau did not live to know this last sixteen-volume work; he was to test Burton as traveling companion rather than as storyteller, which exactly misjudged him. Nevertheless, Burton himself waved the false banner under which he marched. He roamed uncharted regions where pure adventure could be dignified by "geographical service." By the time Thoreau picked up his book, his name was associated with Arabia on far more pretentious grounds than later history accords him.[62]

In his first chapter Burton explained that in 1852 "I offered my services to the Royal Geographical Society of London, for the purpose of removing that opprobrium to modern adventure, the huge white blot which in our maps still notes the Eastern and the Central regions of Arabia," an offer which Burton explained was gladly accepted but which was balked by the petulant refusal of the chairman of the East India Company to grant him three years' leave. "However, being liberally supplied with the means of travel by the . . . Society; thoroughly tired of 'progress' and of 'civilization'; curious to see with my eyes what others are content to 'hear with ears,' namely, Moslem inner life in a really Mohammedan country; and longing, if truth be told, to set foot on that mysterious spot which no vacation tourist has yet described, measured, and sketched," he marshaled his resources for a shorter sojourn and set out to cross the Arabian Peninsula. Even this design was "balked" by warring tribes, with the result that he went no further than Medina and Mecca. Instead he accompanied the Moslem hadj to the holy cities, in the guise of an Indian Pathan or "Darwaysh." Burton was neither the first nor the last to succeed in such a ruse, but he was one of the most clever, proving thoroughly proficient in a complicated ritual and familiar with the minutiae of Eastern manners and etiquette. His attitude toward his religious dissembling was thoroughly characteristic:

> The home reader naturally inquires, Why not travel under your English name?
>
> For this reason. In the generality of barbarous countries you must either proceed like Bruce, preserving the "dignity of mankind," and carrying matters with a high hand, or you must worm your way by timidity and subservience; in fact, by becoming an animal too contemptible for man to hit or injure. But to pass through the Moslem's Holy Land, you must either be a born believer, or have become one; in the former case you may demean yourself as you please, in the latter the path is ready prepared for you. My spirit could not bend to own myself a *Burma*, a renegade—to be pointed at and shunned and catechised, an object of suspicion to the many and of contempt to all. Moreover, it would have obstructed the aim of my wanderings. . . . Firmly as was my heart set upon travelling in Arabia, by Heaven! I would have given up the dear project rather than purchase a doubtful and partial success at such a price. Consequently I had no choice but to appear as a born believer.[63]

The necessaries for travel which Burton itemized add the finishing touches to a traveler's outfit which contrasted somewhat with that of the naturalist-explorer of Thoreau's preference: a large wardrobe of clothes including a very grand suit for critical occasions ("it is a great mistake to carry too few clothes"), a goat-skinned water bag and a Persian rug, a cotton-stuffed chintz-covered pillow, a blanket, and a sheet, a substantial "housewife" (a roll of canvas garnished with needles and thread, cobbler's wax, and buttons), a pea-green medicine box with red and yellow flowers, a dagger stuck in the belt, a brass inkstand and penholder, a "mighty" rosary ("which on occasion might have been converted into a weapon of offense"), and, to shade the whole ensemble, a huge bright-yellow cotton umbrella.[64] There is pure ironic delight in imagining Thoreau's visualization of this creation, as there is in placing this image of the English traveler in Arabia beside that "Knight of the Umbrella" whom Daniel Ricketson sketched in New Bedford in 1854.

It is a passage by Burton that starts out with superficial affinities

SKETCH OF THOREAU BY
DANIEL RICKETSON

The sketch accompanied Ricketson's description of Thoreau's
arrival at New Bedford in 1854:
"I perceived a man walking
towards me bearing an umbrella
in one hand and a leather
travelling-bag in the other. . . .
As he came near to me I gave
him the usual salutation . . .
supposing him to be either a
peddler or some way-traveller."

with a Thoreau view that finally provoked from Thoreau a criticism
unmistakably aimed at Burton himself. Describing the desert, Burton
announced:

> To the solitary wayfarer there is an interest in the Wilderness unknown
> to Cape seas and Alpine meadows, and even to the rolling Prairie,—
> the effect of continued excitement on the mind, stimulating its powers
> to their pitch. Above, through a sky terrible in its stainless beauty, and
> the splendours of a pitiless blinding glare, the Samún caresses you like
> a lion with flaming breath. Around lie drifted sand-heaps, upon
> which each puff of wind leaves its trace in solid waves, flayed rocks,
> the very skeletons of mountains, and hard unbroken plains, over which
> he who rides is spurred by the idea that the bursting of a water-skin,
> or the pricking of a camel's hoof, would be certain death or torture,—
> a haggard land infested with wild beasts, and wilder men,—a region
> whose very fountains murmur the warning words "Drink and away!"
> What can be more exciting? What more sublime? Man's heart bounds
> in his breast at the thought of measuring his puny force with Nature's
> might, and of emerging triumphant from the trial. This explains the
> Arab's proverb, "Voyaging is victory."

Thoreau immediately responded in his Journal:

> Burton, the traveller, quotes an Arab saying, "Voyaging is a victory,"
> which he refers to the feeling of independence on overcoming the

difficulties and dangers of the desert. But I think that commonly voyaging is a defeat, a rout, to which the traveller is compelled by want of valor. The traveller's peculiar *valor* is commonly a bill of exchange. He is at home anywhere but where he was born and bred. Petitioning some Sir Joseph Banks or other representative of a Geographical Society to avail himself of his restlessness, and if not receiving a favorable answer, necessarily going off somewhere next morning. . . . Snatching at a fact or two in behalf of science as he goes, just as a panther in his leap will take off a man's sleeve and land twenty feet beyond him when travelling down-hill, being fitted out by some Sir Joseph Banks.[65]

Thoreau settled for the abridged version of Burton's *Narrative*, scrupulously making note of the fact.[66] Burton's scathing disdain for the East Indians with their "open rudeness" to the white man (e.g., the pleasure they took in demonstrating their doctrines of equality and liberty to one's face), "of all Orientals, the most antipathetical companions to an Englishman," could not but have won Thoreau's disdain in turn, most particularly when Burton went on to an oversimplified picture of the African and North American Indian in favorable contrast. But as in the case of other traveling companions with whom Thoreau shared little basic accord, the route retained its reality and appeal in partial compensation for the most idiosyncratic of travelers. In the case of Burton, Thoreau culled pages of excerpts from the most valuable portion of his experience: the "inside" views of Mohammedan pilgrimages and religious ceremonies. Nor were some features of Arabian travel without their permeating influence upon the reader who, while reading of Burton's waits for caravan accompaniment before hazarding desert expanses, looked upon his own unbroken snow fields as untrodden regions "which wait, as it were, for some caravan to assemble before any will traverse them." [67] Burton's voyage over the "summer sea" to Alexandria with the band performing

> There we lay
> All the day,
> In the Bay of Biscay, O!

was reflected in the refrain which Thoreau chose to shout to the waves of the summer Atlantic from the outer shore of Cape Cod, possibly only a few months later.[68]

In the next two years Thoreau was to go, for his last trips east, on a

remarkable series of journeys and explorations in central and southeast Asia, in Siberia, Mongolia, the Kirghiz Steppe, Chinese Tartary,
and the length of the Amur River. His eyes and feet in this instance
belonged to a traveler with every asset for compatibility. Thomas
Witlam Atkinson was an English architect who became interested in
central Asia through the works of Humboldt, went to St. Petersburg
in 1844, and from there set off upon an extraordinary trip across the
Russian steppes over the plains of Siberia into central Mongolia and
Chinese Tibet. Over a period of seven years he wandered quite literally throughout central Asia, for the most startling feature of Atkinson's feat was not simply that so much of the territory he traveled
was at this time unknown to Europeans but that for great stretches of
his journey he traveled on foot. At night he knocked politely upon
remote doorways and took what fare hospitality offered the wayfarer;
by day he explored, either by himself or in company with some interested native who directed him to a local spot of beauty or curiosity,
always with his sketchbook in hand, in which he employed his skills
in painting and drawing to record for the pages of his accounts etch-
ings and paintings of scenes heretofore unseen by Western man.
When he returned to England in 1853, Atkinson estimated that he
had traveled some 30,000 miles, much of it in areas into which he was
the first European to venture. Thoreau read of his travels as soon as
the accounts of them were published, in 1858 in *Oriental and Western Siberia: A Narrative of Seven Years' Explorations and Adventures,* and in 1860 in *Travels in the Regions of the Upper and Lower
Amoor, and the Russian Acquisitions on the Confines of India and
China.*

We noted in an early chapter Thoreau's response to Atkinson's
view of the salsola margins to the salt lakes of the steppes. From the
composition of yurts, the skin dwellings of the steppes, to feats of
hunting and the artistic tastes of the Manzas and the Goldi natives
on the Amur, Atkinson furnished his share of knowledge for Thoreau's record.[69] And as usual, the details of the route which appear in
the pages of Thoreau's notebooks indicate the deliberateness with
which Thoreau traveled the entire route with Atkinson. They were
not details found in the latter's account by way of an index or a special subject matter; they could only have been "come upon" in the

course of the trip, met as Atkinson himself met them, a phenomenon suddenly disclosed around the bend of a river or information spontaneously supplied in the isolated context of a moment's experience. It is fair, as always, to keep vividly before us the image of the author as participant in the experiences he describes, for we can be sure that this is exactly where Thoreau joined him as he could.

Such scenes as the following were bound to have their familiar identities. Atkinson reported that, after his boat was pulled ashore on the bank of the Chusovaya River at the base of the Ural Mountains,

> Our traps were taken out and carried a short distance into the forest to some large pine-trees, where they were piled up to keep off the cold blast. A large fire was soon kindled. . . . Presently the singing of the tea-kettle was soon heard above the crackling of the logs.
>
> After supper I took my rifle and rambled into the forest to some distance from our encampment, but found no game. I, however, beheld what was more agreeable to me, flowers pushing through the thick brown grass—the first indications I had met with of spring, and I hailed them with delight.
>
> The crew, having also enjoyed themselves, were singing merrily. I listened for a while to their songs, then wrote up my journal by the light of our blazing fire.[70]

Atkinson's account often retained the immediacy of his journal record; like Thoreau he was at times deliberately careless about obliterating his more contemporaneous original source. "The change [to spring] is so delightful, I have already decided to spend tomorrow (Sunday) at this place. This is a glorious morning—a bright sun, and a sky without a cloud, while a gentle breeze is bringing scents from the larch and birch trees, now almost in full leaf." Atkinson even offered Thoreau that touch of dry humor and sly perspective which the reader finds so infectious in Thoreau's pages, the detachment which enables Thoreau to observe as much about his own appearance in a scene as that of his company and surroundings. Atkinson described a furious "conversation" with some natives on the Ural River, a discussion that continued into the night in language totally incomprehensible to the Englishman:

> The tea-drinking continued a long time, which gave my two companions the opportunity of putting a series of questions, few of which I could understand. They talked very fast, however, and I listened attentively, saying ("Dah!" "Neate!") Yes or No, in Russian, as the

case appeared to require. At length I got tired of this, and began an oration in English, speaking as fast as I could, by which I got the advantage, for they ceased immediately. But the moment I had left off addressing the chair, one or the other began to catechise me again. As a last resort, I was driven to try some snatches of poetry, which fairly silenced them.[71]

Atkinson had certain affinities with that traveler-mentor of Thoreau's, Alexander Henry, in spite of his far different cultural background. From Atkinson's context in the region of the Ural Mountains in Siberia, Thoreau was reminded that "the fir and lumber trade is an old story to Asia and Europe." [72] Atkinson's account reported travel undertaken simply but deliberately for personal satisfaction. He moved uncluttered and unconfused over routes of his own choosing, always the observer but naturally and comfortably participant as well. His pages, particularly of his first book (his second deferred to popularity with long insets of romantic adventures reported secondhand), were full of the land and the lonely and isolated people who lived in it, of the hard living imposed by the wilderness, and of the rugged grandeur of its beauty. Although Thoreau would scarcely have condemned him for yielding to the picturesque, Atkinson was more original in his narrative than in his sketches. In his words he permitted the details of his experiences to establish authenticity: his shoulders ache from carrying his load on the portages; he melts the ice from his clothes over the pine fire; he accepts the board bench offered him for his bed ("I was used to hard fare and hard beds, and content with whatever turned up"); he examines the rocks, the lichen, the pools, the pine needles, the bear's teeth, the Kalmucks' stew. He is an Englishman who goes four years without a haircut without self-consciousness or apology either to the reader or to the Cossacks (who shaved their heads regularly).

Atkinson had done no new traveling by 1860, and his second book offered accounts stored in his journal for over ten years. He lacked Thoreau's peculiar resources for activating remote experience, and his *Travels* was too padded with secondhand accounts and appendices. But Thoreau would naturally have read a new travel book by him. One only wishes that this return to him, Thoreau's last trip to Asia, might have proved as satisfying as had been his earlier rejoinings with Layard and with M. Huc.

CHAPTER XI

Young Africa

Is not the midnight like Central Africa to most? Are we not tempted to explore it, to penetrate to the shores of its Lake Schad, to discover the sources of its Nile, perchance in the Mountains of the Moon? Who knows what fertility, what beauty in the animal and vegetable kingdom are there to be found, what primeval simplicity and reflection of truth among its dusky inhabitants?

Journal, February 1, 1852

In January, 1855, after delivering a lecture in Worcester, Thoreau met a young Negro who introduced himself as a native of Africa and a lecturer on the subject "Young Africa." Thoreau was impressed; as he confessed afterwards, "I never heard of anything but old Africa before." [1] Thereupon he recommenced a consistent reading of travel accounts of Africa for the first time since his disillusionment over Gordon-Cumming's account of 1850. Interestingly enough, he first took another chance with a hunter, this time reading *The Adventures of Gerard, the Lion Killer . . . among the Wild Animals of Northern Africa,* just translated (1856) from the French. We must not be too quick to attribute an irregularity in Thoreau's reading pattern to some immediate provocation, however, for a careful appraisal of his travel reading on Africa reveals a timing dictated by the travelers themselves and the history of the continent's exploration. Thoreau traveled where and how he could when he could, and his reading practice in this instance shows no basic deviation from this primary characteristic.

During his college years Thoreau had commenced his travel in Africa with a group of adventurers and explorers of the twenties (Denham, Oudney, Clapperton, and Waddington) whose accounts also appeared in that decade. Thereafter, sometime probably in the forties, he retraced Mungo Park's famous explorations undertaken at the turn of the century but described in a number of editions following his death in 1805, including a popular edition in the Harper's Family Library in 1840.[2] In 1840 Thoreau caught up on Constantin Volney's *Travels through Syria and Egypt* taken in the late 1700s. From 1850 on, we find him traveling the African continent as contemporaneously with the explorers as they permitted, reading of their trips just as soon as they published their accounts. Except for two works (one a popular narrative by a sailor named Riley wrecked on the west coast of Africa in August of 1815,[3] the other Bayle St. John's *Adventures in the Libyan Desert and the Oasis of Jupiter Ammon*, published in 1849), every book which Thoreau read represented the first account of a contemporary venture: Andersson's in 1856, Livingstone's in 1858, Barth's in 1859, Burton's and Krapf's in 1860. The gap between a Clapperton in the twenties and a Livingstone in the forties and fifties was a reality of African history rather than a symptom of averted interest on Thoreau's part. For the serious follower of exploration in this portion of the world, there was little else but the play of a Gordon-Cumming to fill the interim.

It is relevant for Thoreau's experience to remind ourselves of two further facts. By the beginning of the nineteenth century the continent of Africa, except for Egypt, had been more neglected by serious travelers than any comparable land area of the world. Its interior was less known to "civilized" man than Australia or New Zealand. In the second place, the extraordinary exposure of this "darkest" continent took place during a few decades in Thoreau's life and can be viewed from our practical angle as the story of three rivers, the Niger, the White Nile, and the Zambezi.[4] Allied to the tracings of these flowing bodies of water were the tangential accounts of Africa's vast inland lakes. All exploration in Africa turns into a search for its waters. Around the three great arteries are grouped the major explorations of the continent up to the time of Thoreau's death. As had been the case with both the American continents, rivers were once again, as Thoreau observed, the "guides which conducted the footsteps of the first travelers," the "lure . . . to distant enterprise and adventure."

Neither the source, the mouth, nor the direction of the flow of the

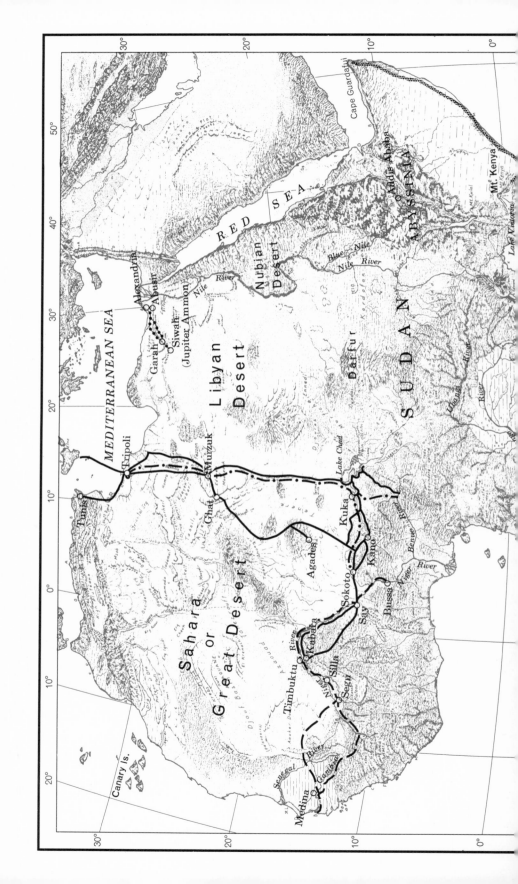

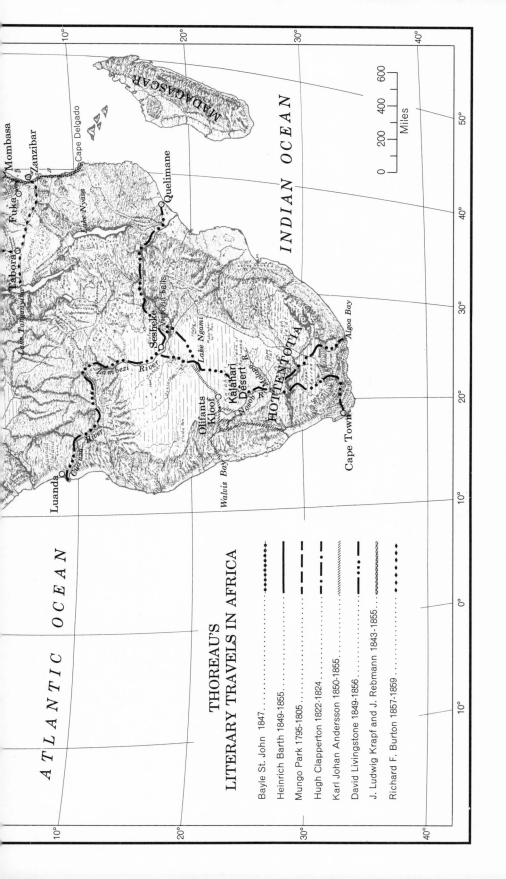

ATLANTIC OCEAN

INDIAN OCEAN

MADAGASCAR

Mombasa
Zanzibar
Fuke
Tabora
Cape Delgado

Lake Nyasa
Lake Tanganyika
Central

Quelimane

Victoria Falls
Sesheke
Zambezi River

Lake Ngami
Kalahari Desert
Olifants Kloof
Walvis Bay

HOTTENTOTIA

Algoa Bay

Cape Town

Ouanza River
Luanda

THOREAU'S
LITERARY TRAVELS IN AFRICA

Bayle St. John 1847 . . . .

Heinrich Barth 1849-1855 . . . .

Mungo Park 1795-1805 . . . .

Hugh Clapperton 1822-1824 . . . .

Karl Johan Andersson 1850-1855 . . . .

David Livingstone 1849-1856 . . . .

J. Ludwig Krapf and J. Rebmann 1843-1855 . . . .

Richard F. Burton 1857-1859 . . . .

Miles
0   200   400   600

Niger was known when the English surgeon Mungo Park offered his services in 1795 to the African Association to promote British interest in Africa. Thereupon the river or its environs was to draw early travelers from the north and west into the central interior of the continent. Park set out specifically to explore the river. He studied the Mandingo language and the customs of the various races who came to trade with the English at the Gambia River. From this point he commenced a long journey inland through the domain of the Mandingos and the Fulah of Bondou, to the Senegal, "a beautiful but shallow river, moving slowly over a bed of sand and gravel." Crossing the river, he proceeded through kingdom after kingdom whose native kings subjected him to a series of humiliations and harassments either because he was a Christian (the Moors had penetrated the area from the borders of the Sahara), or because of his white skin, a phenomenon literally unbelievable to most of the tribes he met; the natives of Bondou, convinced of its artificiality, attributed it to his having been repeatedly dipped in milk as an infant. Travel took place at night to avoid the daytime attacks. Having pushed for six months through the savanna and bush woodlands, Park finally approached Segu where he was to have his first sight of Joliba, or the Great Water, as the natives called the upper Niger:

> We rode through some marshy ground, where, as I was anxiously looking round for the river, one of them called out, "Geo affilo" (see the water); and looking forward, I saw with infinite pleasure the long object of my mission, the long-sought and majestic Niger, glittering to the morning sun, as broad as the Thames at Westminister, and flowing slowly *to the eastward*. I hastened to the brink, and having drank of the water, lifted up my fervant thanks in prayer to the Great Ruler of all things for having thus crowned my endeavors with success.[5]

Not permitted to cross the river to Segu, Park dropped down the north bank and crossed it safely at a lower point, then "worn by sickness, exhausted with hunger and fatigue, half naked and without an article of value," he turned west back toward Gambia, ascending the Niger to its headwaters near the valley of the Senegal. Here he observed the gold washing and identified the source of the gold of the Ethiopians mentioned by Herodotus. But here also he suffered his greatest hardships, at one point being robbed even of his clothing to find himself "in the midst of a vast wilderness, in the depth of the rainy season, naked and alone, surrounded by savage animals, and men still more savage." As the traveler stretched himself on the forest floor to die, "at this moment, painful as my reflections were, the extraordinary beauty of a small moss in fructification irresistibly caught my eye. I mention this to show from what trifling circumstances the mind will sometimes derive consolation; for though the whole plant was not larger than the top of one of my fingers, I could not contemplate the delicate conformation of its roots, leaves, capsula without admiration." [6] Rescued and reaching Manding, he described the burning of the grass plains in scenes matching those of the burning prairies of North America which were later to so impress Thoreau, very possibly because they offered him familiar reminders of such a scene as the following:

> In the middle of the night I could see the plains and mountains, as far as my eye could reach, variegated with lines of fire; and the light reflected on the sky made the heavens appear in a blaze. In the daytime pillars of smoke were seen in every direction; while the birds of prey were observed hovering round the conflagration, and pouncing down upon the snakes, lizards, and other reptiles which attempted to escape from the flames.

Park even has a note referring to comparable scenes on American prairies, for which he cited the very source which Thoreau was later to share with him.[7]

With the dry season, Park journeyed the last five hundred miles to Gambia, where he had long been given up for dead. Still intent upon following the Niger to its mouth (his own view was that it might become the Congo), Park returned to Gambia from England in 1805 and insisted upon starting his decisive voyage down the river, in spite of terrible losses through death and sickness to the rest of his party. On the day of his departure Park wrote his last letter: "With the assistance of one of the soldiers I have changed a large canoe into a tolerably good schooner, on board of which I this day hoisted the British flag, and shall sail to the east with the fixed resolution to discover the termination of the Niger or perish in the attempt." [8] Perish he did, in the Bussa Rapids several hundred miles down the river. It was another traveler whom Thoreau read, Hugh Clapperton, who visited the rapids in 1826 and recorded final confirmation of Park's death.

The "White Man's Grave" was the ominous name given the west coast of Africa, one which Thoreau found fully exploited by James Riley in his *Authentic Narrative*, but which both Park and Clapperton confirmed. Hugh Clapperton, too, perished in the interior bordering the Niger, at Sokoto, leaving his companion Lander to make the return to the coast alone, and eventually to solve the mystery of the Niger's mouth by penetrating its forest-clad delta in 1830. Thoreau apparently did not read Lander's accounts and consequently did not take Clapperton's last trip in 1826. His travel with Clapperton took place earlier in 1823 on the long route from the north across the Sahara from Tripoli on the Mediterranean. Moreover, he appears to have shared the adventures of this trip only through the journal of Major Dixon Denham, who with Dr. Oudney accompanied Clapperton. Denham was a narrator whom a later traveler of the same route was to discredit for accuracy. But Thoreau read Denham twenty-three years before he read Heinrich Barth's more reliable account, and in the intervening years the vividness of the "Great Desert" was to be firmly etched for him.[9]

Thoreau was constantly reminded "that in some parts of the globe, sand prevails like an ocean." This was the "trackless" Sahara, "where caravans and cities are covered," the great waste that figured as prominantly in his metaphors as either jungle or steppes.[10] Denham permitted him to travel it a day at a time, its variety recorded in a traveler's journal of a caravan journey south from Murzuk.

> The presence of nothing but deep sandy valleys and high sand hills . . . masses of loose sand, fully four hundred feet high, ready to be tossed about by every breeze. . . . We had now passed six days of desert without the slighest appearance of vegetation. . . .
>
> While I was dozing on my horse about noon, overcome by the heat of the sun . . . I was suddenly awakened by a crashing under his feet, which startled me excessively. I found that my steed had, without any sensation of shame or alarm, stepped upon the perfect skeletons of two human beings, cracking their brittle bones under his feet, and, by one trip of his foot, separating a skull from the trunk, which rolled on like a ball before him. . . . During the last two days we had passed on an average from sixty to eighty or ninety skeletons each day.

Here we had a gale of wind from the northeast for three days. Our tents were nearly buried in the sand, and we were obliged to roll ourselves up in blankets nearly the whole time. . . . We lost more than twenty of our camels this day, by their straying out of the path.

Our road lay over loose hills of fine sand, in which the camels sank nearly knee-deep, desert wilds, where hills disappear in a single night by the drifting of the sand, and where all traces of the passage, even of a large kafila, sometimes vanish in a few hours.[11]

"As indistinct as a camel track between Mourzuk and Darfur," Thoreau liked to observe.[12] But the face of the desert was not without its beauty and its humanized landscapes.

At 2:40 started with a beautiful moonlight, over a sandy plain. . . . About a mile from Bilma is a spring of beautiful clear water, which rises to the surface of the earth, and waters a space of two or three hundred yards in circumference which is covered with fresh grass.

Clapperton was sitting on the top of a high sand hill, and so pleased with the view, that he called out several times for me to dismount from my camel and enjoy the treat. A deep sandy valley, without vegetation, and containing only two large groves of date trees; within each a fine lake was enclosed. The contrast between the lofty sand hills, and the two insulated spots, was the great cause of the sensation of beauty.[13]

"These salmon-colored clouds" mused Thoreau under a Concord summer sky, "like a celestial Sahara sloping gently upward, an inclined place upward, to be traveled by caravans bound heavenward, with blue oases in it." [14]

Thoreau accompanied at least four other travelers in addition to Denham and Clapperton onto the sands of northern Africa. But like Humboldt's famous description of his first night in a tropical jungle, it may have been the description of another first night, this one spent on the edge of the Libyan Desert by the last traveler whom Thoreau accompanied into these regions, Bayle St. John, that epitomized the desert's continuing appeal for Concord's walker of sand dunes.

I shall often think of the night I spent near the well of Tanum. . . . We were yet new in the Desert, and the first tumult of our impressions had hardly subsided. Our senses were wide awake to catch every characteristic of the scene, and seemed, if I may use the expression, rather baulked at first by the fewness of the objects that presented themselves to our notice. Our familiar companions the moon and stars, with some brilliant meteors that gleamed near the horizon, and numbers of those heavenly rockets which, say the Arabs, are hurled by angels guarding the gates of heaven upon demons who approach too near; a ridge of rocks to the south; to the north a broad and shallow valley, dim with a light mist, that remained cold and dull even beneath the shining beams that were shed from that Oriental sky, and scarcely allowed the shrubs and bushes to appear athwart it; beyond all this the sombre sea—these, with the exception of the ungainly form of a camel, as, despite its fettered legs, it went slowly from the bivouac to browse; our little group of donkeys, the scattered luggage, the sleeping Bedawins and domestics, were all the objects that met the eye; whilst there was nought to appease "the famine of the ears" save only the shrill shriek or measured chirp of two Desert birds, and the monotonous chinck of thousands of grass-hoppers. But if disappointment was the first feeling, a sense of the sublime—a perception of the simplicity of nature's operations—a feeling of intense solitude—of separation from the busy nuclii round which men congregate—and ultimately of cheerful self-reliance succeeded. I felt my imagination kindle, and that steady, enduring enthusiasm begin to take possession of my mind, which is the necessary companion of all who encounter fatigue, and even danger, actuated by the mere thirst of knowing "how wonderfully and strangely" God's world is con-structed—what kind of people inhabit its remoter parts—and what the wilderness and the waterless desert have to say about the commerce and civilization of past ages.[15]

Clapperton's expedition finally reached the steppe grasslands that girdle the African continent from the Senegal to the Nile, and soon, "on ascending the rising ground . . . the great lake Tshad, glowing with the golden rays of the sun in its strength, appeared to be within a mile of the spot on which we stood." [16] The remainder of Denham's account described the excursions taken from Kukawa about the great lake's shores, an area heretofore untraveled by a white man. On the borders of the lake flocks of geese and wild ducks, of a most beautiful plumage, were quietly feeding. "Pelicans, cranes, four and five feet in height, grey, variegated, and white, were scarcely so many yards from my side, and a bird, between a snipe and a woodcock, resembling both, and larger than either; immense spoonbills of a snowy white-ness, widgeon, teal, yellow-legged plover, and a hundred species of unknown water-fowl were sporting before me." The water was found to be sweet and pleasant, abounding in fish which native women caught by wading into the lake and driving them in schools onto the shore. "Two elephants were seen swimming in the lake this day. . . . Two buffaloes stood boldly grazing, nearly up to their bodies in

ELEPHANTS ON THE SHORES OF LAKE CHAD,
DESCRIBED BY DENHAM, CLAPPERTON, AND BARTH

From Barth, *Travels and Discoveries*

water; on our approaching them they quickly took to the lake: one of them was a monstrous animal, fourteen feet in length from the tail to the head. . . . We disturbed hippopotami, buffaloes, enormous fish, and innumerable hosts of insects . . . the buzz from the insects was like the singing of birds; the men and horses groaned with anguish." When the explorer's route left the lake shore to penetrate the forests, "birds of the most beautiful plumage were perched on every tree. Guinea fowls were in flocks of eighty to one hundred; and several monkeys chattered at us imprudently." He went eastward, to get a sight of a great herd of elephants ("upwards of one hundred and fifty") : "I found them about six miles from the town, in the grounds usually overflowed by the waters of the lake, where the coarse grass is twice the height of a man; they seemed to cover the face of the country." He reported enormous snakes, "measuring eighteen feet from the mouth to the tail"; bees so numerous as to obstruct the passage of travelers; and giraffes pursued over the plains in chases forecasting that unbroken line of temptation for all African visitors.[17]

When Thoreau returned to Kukawa with Heinrich Barth twenty-three years later, he was taking a yet more inclusive trip, for Barth's route, as described in his *Travels and Discoveries in North and Central Africa* (1860), took him not only from Tripoli to Kukawa and Lake Chad but southward into the Sudan, also unknown country. He reached the Benue, a tributary of the Niger, then proceeded to Yola in Adamawa, and into Baguirmi. Here he experienced the trying custom of commercial exchange which proved of interest to Thoreau, who copied it into a notebook: "In all these inland countries of central Africa the kurdi (cyprae a moneta) are not, as is customary in some regions near the coast, fastened together in strings of 100 each, but are separate and must be counted one by one. . . . We at length succeeded, with the help of some five or six other people, of counting 500,000 shells." [18] Barth finally reached Timbuktu. When Thoreau referred to life on the upper reaches of the Merrimack as reminding him of descriptions of Timbuktu, he had substantive visions for comparison, for Barth's was his last, not his first, trip to the African town. In the *Week* Thoreau had been affected by earlier and less accurate accounts which stressed the scattered and quite isolated location of the town's houses,[19] a picture which by Barth's trip had changed its

BARTH'S ARRIVAL AT TIMBUKTU

From his *Travels and Discoveries*

character, as Timbuktu now recovered its position as a commercial center after its fading pose as a cultural and religious anachronism. Here in the remote interior of a continent was a well-populated community.

> The city is situated a few feet above the average level of the river, and at a short distance of about six miles from the principal branch. . . . The streets are entirely shut in, and the dwellings form continuous and uninterrupted rows. . . . There are about 980 clay houses, and a couple of hundred conical huts of matting, the latter, with a few exceptions, constituting the outskirts of the town on the north and northeast sides. . . . The town is laid out partly in rectangular, partly in winding streets, or, as they are called here, "tijeraten," which are not paved, but for the greater part consist of hard sand and gravel, and some of them have a sort of gutter in the middle. Besides the large and small market there are few open areas, except a small square in front of the mosque of Yahia, called Timbutu-bottema. . . . The private life of the people runs on very tranquilly. I scarcely imagine that there is in Europe a person more attached to his wife and children than my host was.[20]

Barth made the return trip from Timbuktu north across the Sahara once again, reaching Tripoli in 1844. "Although the impression made upon my mind by the rich vegetation of the gardens which surround the town, after the long journey through the desert waste, was very great, yet infinitely greater was the effect produced upon me by the wide expanse of the sea, which in the bright sunshine of this intermediate zone, spread out with a tint of the darkest blue." Leaving African soil for the last time, Barth summarized without false modesty his five-year journey:

> I resolved upon undertaking, with a very limited supply of means, a journey to the far west, in order to reach Timbuktu, and to explore that part of the Niger which, through the untimely fate of Mungo Park, had remained unknown to the scientific world. In this enterprise I succeeded to my utmost expectation, and not only made known the whole of that vast region, which even to the Arab merchants in general had remained more unknown than any other part of Africa, but I succeeded also in establishing friendly relations with all the most powerful chiefs along the river up to that mysterious city itself.[21]

That "other" parts of Africa were better known by 1860 was in great measure the achievement of two African explorers whom Tho-

reau accompanied into the interior from the south: the Swedish explorer Karl Johan Andersson and Africa's greatest explorer, David Livingstone. Shortly after Thoreau read in *Harper's* for December, 1855,
a review of the Reverend John Leighton Wilson's new book, *Western Africa: Its History, Condition, and Prospects, with Numerous
Engravings*,[22] he traveled with Karl Johan Andersson to Lake Ngami,
reading his *Lake Ngami; or, Explorations and Discoveries during
Four Years' Wanderings in the Wilds of South-western Africa*, published in 1856.

Andersson, while a somewhat fatuous writer, was a stubborn and
indefatigable explorer who prided himself upon traveling on foot
whenever feasible. He first explored the land of the Damara and the
Ovampo, tribes and territory unmapped in 1850, which he entered
from Walvis Bay on the west coast above Cape Town. This required
crossing both the Namib Desert bordering the coast and the northwest portion of the Kalahari Desert inland. "The first appearance of
the coast, as seen from Walfisch Bay, is little calculated to inspire
confidence in the traveller about to penetrate into the interior. A desert of sand, bounded only by the horizon . . . assuming, in one direction, the shape of dreary flats—in another, of shifting hillocks;
whilst in some parts, it rises almost to the height of mountains." [23]
Andersson described his route inland, over desert and semidesert,
through grasslands, into primeval forests where the stems of the baobab trees were from forty to sixty feet in circumference. Thoreau
copied pages of detail from Andersson's account, much of it dealing
with the observations upon natural history in which the author confessed himself to have been interested since childhood and "a subject
on which he therefore feels conversant," and with the superstitions
of the tribes visited, described by one who also declared that "too
much attention . . . cannot be paid to the mythological traditions
of savages." [24] Andersson's second trip in 1855 took him, again from
Walvis Bay, across the Kalahari toward Lake Ngami, once again with
wagons and oxen and a large expeditionary force of tribesmen, on a
route which wound east to the Nosob River, then northeast, through
Olifants Kloof, to the great lake. It was a route which Andersson
hoped would, as "the shortest and best . . . be adopted as the one by
which commerce and civilization may eventually find their way to the

Lake regions." Here in climax came Andersson's "first sight" of another of Africa's great inland lakes:

> I myself kept well a-head in hope of obtaining the first glimpse of Ngami. The country hereabout was finely undulated; and in every distant vale with a defined border I thought I saw a lake. . . . On reaching the top of one of these ridges, the natives, who were in advance of our party, suddenly came to a halt, and pointing straight before them, exclaimed—"Ngami! Ngami!" In an instant I was with the men. There, indeed, at no very great distance, lay spread before me an immense sheet of water, bounded only by the horizon—the object of my ambition for years, and for which I had abandoned home and friends, and risked my life.
>
> The first sensation occasioned by this sight was very curious. Long as I had been prepared for the event, it now almost overwhelmed me. It was a mixture of pleasure and pain. My temples throbbed, and my heart beat so violently, that I was obliged to dismount, and lean against a tree for support, until the excitement had subsided. The reader will no doubt think that thus giving away to my feelings was very childish; but "those who know that the first glimpse of some great object which we have read or dreamt of from earliest recollection is ever a moment of intensest enjoyment, will forgive the transport." [25]

Thoreau does not appear to have been drawn to such protestation of cause and effect. Having his own respect for the potential impact of the first sight, he did not need the feeling defended. He looked rather to the proportion of visible, or invisible, truth which the affected party was able to discern—in the case of Andersson, obviously very little. Andersson's response is in interesting contrast to that of the man whose first sight of the same lake six years earlier was literally the first sight by a white man. Thoreau read in Livingstone's *Travels and Researches in South Africa,* when it appeared two years after Andersson's book in 1858 the following report of that traveler's discovery of Lake Ngami, as different from Andersson's response as lens from mirror:

> Twelve days after our departure from the wagons at Ngabi-sane we came to the northeast end of Lake Ngami; and on the first of August, 1849, we went down together to the broad part, and, for the first time, this fine-looking sheet of water was beheld by Europeans. The direction of the lake seemed to be N.N.E. and S.S.W. by compass. The southern portion is said to bend round to the west, and to receive the Teoughe

from the north at its northwest extremity. We could detect no horizon where we stood looking S.S.W., nor could we form any idea of the extent of the lake, except from the reports of the inhabitants of the district; and, as they professed to go round it in three days, allowing twenty-five miles a day would make it seventy-five, or less than seventy geographical miles in circumference. Other guesses have been made since as to its circumference, ranging between seventy and one hundred miles. It is shallow, for I subsequently saw a native punting his canoe over seven or eight miles of the northeast end; it can never, therefore, be of much value as a commercial highway.

And so Livingstone continues, in matter-of-fact manner, to report further matters of its shore line, its seasonal rise and fall, its temperature, and the taste of its water, all deduced from the evidence offered by attentive observation of the object "sighted." [26]

In Livingstone, Thoreau found a traveler whose achievements were to place him ahead of all other explorers of Africa, who could afford to understate his case, whose manner and purpose of travel were of all African travelers the most commendable in Thoreau's eyes: a committed friend of the natives, he undertook all his explorations to facilitate the abolition of black slavery. Here, moreover, was a man who wrote of his youth, "In reading, every thing that I could lay my hands on was devoured except novels. Scientific works and books of travels were my especial delight." Cutting himself off from all European society in order to share language and customs with the Africans with whom he was to live for the remainder of his life, Livingstone practiced his missionary labors among the Bechuana from 1841 until 1849, when he took Thoreau upon his first trip north from the Cape, across the Kalahari Desert to Lake Ngami. Having returned to his base south in Kolobeng, Livingstone set out for Ngami once again in April, 1850, this time with his wife, three children, a native chief, and friendly aid from the great conquering chief of the Makololo 200 miles further north. The route lay across a "dreary scene," the only vegetation being a low scrub in deep sand, with neither bird nor insect to enliven the landscape, and with water dwindling in face of thirsty children: "The less there was of water, the more thirsty the little rogues became. The idea of their perishing before our eyes was terrible." [27] But the hardships were survived, and 130 miles to the northeast of Sesheke, at the invitation of the friendly Makololo, Livingstone and a friend Oswell discovered the Zambezi in the very center of the continent. As Livingstone put it, in classic understatement:

> This was a most important point, for that river was not previously known to exist there at all. . . . We saw it at the end of the dry season, at the time when the river is about at its lowest; and yet there was a breadth of from three hundred to six hundred yards of deep, flowing water. Mr. Oswell said he had never seen such a fine river even in India. At the period of its annual inundation it rises fully twenty feet in perpendicular height, and floods fifteen or twenty miles of land adjacent to its banks.[28]

Faced with the harassment and intolerance of the Boers in the south, Livingstone returned to the Cape (for the first time in eleven years) to place his family on a ship bound for London and return north alone "with a view to exploring the country in search of a healthy district that might prove a centre of civilization and open up the interior by a path to either the east or west coast." With deceptive mildness he launched upon this his longest journey in a life the whole remainder of which was to be devoted to almost continuous travel in Africa: "Wagon-travelling in Africa has been so often described that I need say no more than that it is a prolonged system of picnicing, excellent for the health, and agreeable to those who are not over-fastidious about trifles, and who delight in being in the open air."

Leaving Linyanti and traveling north and west up the Zambezi, accompanied by a party of the Makololo, crossing the watershed into the basin of the Congo in February, 1854, Livingstone finally reached Luanda and the Atlantic on May 31. Here the Makololo had their first view of the sea, which they looked upon with awe: "On describing their feelings afterward, they remarked that 'we marched along with our father, believing what the ancients had told us was true, that the world has no end; but all at once the world said to us, "I am finished: there is no more of me!"' They had always imagined that the world was one extended plain without limit." [29] While Livingstone recovered his health preparatory to turning about and retracing his route (but this time straight east all the way across the continent to the Indian Ocean), his native fellow travelers were given the job by the Portuguese of loading coal, the "stones that burn" (a phrase that Thoreau carefully noted for future use).[30]

Reaching Linyanti again after a two-year absence, Livingstone paused only long enough to deny the rumors of his death, then proceeded down the Zambezi. Here he was balked by increasing rapids and finally challenged by advance word from the natives of "smoke that sounds" in a great fall anciently called Shongew, observed by them in awe only from a distance. In one of the most vivid scenes in all the travel literature read by Thoreau, Livingstone described his first sight of the spectacular falls to which he gave "the only English name I have affixed to any part of the country," Victoria Falls.

> After twenty minutes' sail from Kalai, we came in sight, for the first time, of the columns of vapor appropriately called "smoke," rising at a distance of five or six miles, exactly as when large tracts of grass are burned in Africa. Five columns now arose, and, bending in the direction of the wind, they seemed placed against a low ridge covered with trees; the tops of the columns at this distance appeared to mingle with the clouds. They were white below, and higher up became dark, so as to simulate smoke very closely.

The approach lay between banks and islands lush with tropical foliage, many of the trees at this season "spangled over with blossoms." "Trees have each their own physiognomy"—the towering great burly baobab, "each of whose enormous arms would form the trunk of a large tree"; groups of graceful palms, "their feathery-shaped leaves depicted on the sky"; the silver mohomono, like the cedar of Lebanon, in contrast with the dark color of the motsouri "whose cypress-form is dotted over at present with its pleasant scarlet fruit"; some trees resembled the spreading oaks, others the elms and chestnuts, thickening the ridges on either side of the river which rose to a height of three to four hundred feet, walls laced with trunks and branches through which appeared the red soil. "The whole scene was extremely beautiful. . . . It had never been seen before by European eyes; but scenes so lovely must have been gazed upon by angels in their flight." With skillful canoeing, Livingstone finally reached the island which is today marked as a memorial to him, "situated in the middle of the river and on the edge of the lip over which the water rolls."

> But though we were within a few yards of the spot a view from which would solve the whole problem, I believed that no one could perceive where the vast body of water went: it seemed to lose itself in

the earth, the opposite lip of the fissure into which it disappeared being only eighty feet distant. At least I did not comprehend it until, creeping with awe to the verge, I peered down into a large rent which had been made from bank to bank of the broad Zambesi.

In looking down into the fissure on the right side of the island, one sees nothing but a dense white cloud, which, at the time we visited the spot, had two bright rainbows in it. (The sun was on the meridian, and the declination about equal to the latitude of the place.) From this cloud rushed up a great jet of vapor exactly like steam, and it mounted two hundred or three hundred feet high; there, condensing, it changed its hue to that of dark smoke, and came back in a constant shower, which soon wetted us to the skin. This shower falls chiefly on the opposite side of the fissure, and a few yards back from the lip there stands a straight hedge of evergreen trees, whose leaves are always wet. From their roots a number of little rills run back into the gulf; but, as they flow down the steep wall there, the column of vapor, in its ascent, licks them up clean off the rock, and away they mount again. They are constantly running down, but never reach the bottom. . . . On the left of the island we see the water at the bottom, a white rolling mass moving away to the prolongation of the fissure. . . . The walls of this gigantic crack are perpendicular, and composed of one homogeneous mass of rock. . . . The rock is dark brown in color. . . . Here we have a good view of the mass of water which causes one of the columns of vapor to ascend, as it leaps quite clear of the rock, and forms a thick, unbroken fleece all the way to the bottom. Its whiteness gave the idea of snow, a sight I had not seen for many a day. As it broke into (if I may use the term) pieces of water all rushing on in the same direction, each gave off several rays of foam, exactly as bits of steel, when burned in oxygen gas, give off rays of sparks. The snow-white sheet seemed like myriads of small comets rushing on in one direction, each of which left behind its nucleus-rays of foam.[31]

Although Livingstone declared to Chief Sekeketu that after this sight there could be nothing else worth showing in his country, he was not deterred from proceeding eastward. He left the Zambezi and traveled northeast across the Botoka plateau, where game abounded, then remet the river at its confluence with the Kafue, and finally reached Quelimane on the coast. He had established Africa's east-west passage, opening up a vast region of hitherto unknown interior to trade and antislavery action. Although an armchair scholar barely beat him by first announcing the theory in print, Livingstone was the first traveler to substantiate on his own feet and from direct observation the geographical fact that "the peculiar form of the continent was . . . an elevated plateau, somewhat depressed in the centre, and with fissures in the sides by which the rivers escaped to the sea." As he summarized this early phase of his travels, "Most geographers are aware that before the discovery of Lake Ngami, and the well-watered country in which the Makololo dwell, the idea prevailed that a large part of the interior of Africa consisted of sandy deserts into which rivers ran and were lost. During my journey in 1852–6 from sea to sea, across the south inter-tropical part of the continent, it was found to be a well-watered country occupied by a considerable population; and one of the most wonderful waterfalls in the world was brought to light." Although Livingstone was to continue his travels and add to his discoveries from 1856 until his death in 1873, this was the last trip with him which Thoreau lived to take.

Sympathies and compatibilities between Thoreau and travel writers are in many cases only inferences at best, assumptions which rest perhaps logically and probably upon the amount of time spent with an individual traveler. Grant Thoreau his critical acumen concerning this literary genre upon which he was by now something of an expert, however, and the distinctions of one traveler from another would inevitably have affected him. Livingstone was among the dozen or so travelers who could hold their own as travel companions with their select counterparts whom Thoreau enjoyed at home. By day it might be Ellery Channing; in the evening it was Champlain, Humboldt, Parrot, Kane, Livingstone. Those compatibilities which linked Thoreau to the company of any traveler were compounded of common elements fired in the same forge for the same purposes. In the case of Livingstone, these elements can be mined at random from his pages, from the vividness of his senses to the tone of his feelings.

> Heavy rain now commenced; I was employed the whole day in cutting down trees, and every strike of the axe brought down a thick shower on my back, which in the hard work was very refreshing, as the water found its way into my shoes.

> As it became dark they [the Bushmen] showed their politeness—a quality which is by no means confined entirely to the civilized—by walking in front, breaking the branches which hung across the path, and pointing out the fallen trees.

We were close to the reeds, and could listen to the strange sounds which are often heard there. By day I had seen eater-snakes putting up their heads and swimming about. There were great numbers of otters (Lutra inunguis, F. Cuvier,) which have made little spoors all over the plains, in search of the fishes, among the tall grass of these flooded prairies; curious birds, too, jerked and wriggled among these weedy masses, and we heard human-like voices and unearthly sounds, with splash, guggle, jupp, as if rare fun were going on in their uncouth haunts.

This being the only hill we had seen since leaving Bamangwato, we felt inclined to take off our hats to it.[32]

Ptolemy placed the source of the Nile in twin lakes fed by the Mountains of the Moon. Denham found the Arabs of the Sahara claiming its source to be Lake Chad.[33] While James Bruce had discovered the source of the Blue Nile in 1768, that of the White Nile remained the lure for enticing the last two travelers whom Thoreau accompanied into the interior of Africa. Thoreau's recognition that the source of the Nile was only "conjecture" was appropriate in 1852 when he made the comment in his Journal;[34] it was still so when he reused the Journal passage containing the reference in a lecture in 1854, and even when he left the allusion in "Night and Moonlight" during his revision of that piece in the last weeks of his life. Only by the time this essay actually appeared in print after his death, in 1863, was the statement at last inaccurate. It is ironic that as late as 1860 Thoreau, traveling into Central Africa from the east coast with two explorers in search of this very source, actually shared the discovery of the great lake that later verification was to establish as one of the Nile's true sources. But such proof came two months after Thoreau's death, only in time to outdate his scrupulous exactitude.

It was not the northern portion of the Nile, the land of the Pharaohs, the pyramids, the Nubian Desert, or the Blue Nile that Thoreau now traveled. Volney, St. John, Edward Lane's *Account* of "Modern Egypt" of the 1830s had all given him his fill of that portion of Africa; he preferred Pliny and Aristotle on that ancient land, the past of which he summarized in *Walden* by suggesting that it had been nobler had its inhabitants drowned themselves in their river instead of building their pyramids. In 1852 expeditions up the Nile were not quite accurately summed up by remarking that they "extend but to the Cataracts, past the ruins of Thebes, or perchance to the mouth of the White Nile." One expedition had in the early 1800s penetrated through the sudd area as far as 4° 42′ N; but written accounts of contemporary approaches to the mystery were limited to two major accounts of travels inland from Mombasa and Zanzibar, both published in 1860, the year Thoreau read them.

The Reverend Dr. J. Ludwig Krapf and his missionary brother the Reverend J. Rebmann, from their missionary station at Mombasa, were enticed by accounts from Arab caravan leaders of great lakes and mountains to the northwest. While Livingstone was proceeding from the south toward the east coast, Krapf and Rebmann were moving from the northeast to almost the same point. But preceding Livingstone in eastern Africa, Krapf commenced all "modern" exploration of that area from his arrival at Mombasa in 1844. He visited Fuka in 1848 and again in 1852; he traveled into Ukambani twice, in 1849 and 1851, and explored the whole of the coast from Cape Guardafui to Cape Delgado in the course of his missionary activity. Although neither traveler was an exact scientist nor even a particularly accurate geographer, the failures in reporting locations and mileages reliably, while throwing scientific discredit upon their discoveries, did not compromise the reality of their experiences. They were not given to lying, and what they saw they reported as best they could. They traveled a vast area of eastern Africa, in the course of which Rebmann sighted the snowclad peak of Kilimanjaro and Krapf that of Mount Kenya, those "salt-covered" peaks of Arab tales, mountains which up to Thoreau's death were still reputable candidates for the *Montes Lunae* and the Nile's source.[35]

Speaking of the Ndsharo, as the Teita people called the mountain (Kilima meaning simply "mountain"), Krapf reported that Rebmann had slept at its base and even by moonlight could distinctly make out snow. "He conversed with the natives in reference to the white matter visible upon the dome-like summit of the mountain, and he was told that the silver-like stuff, when brought down in bottles proved to be nothing but water, that many who ascended the mountain perished from extreme cold, or returned with frozen extremities, which persons unacquainted with the real cause ascribed to the malignant influence of dshins or evil spirits." In spite of scorn

and derision which greeted this early report in 1852, Krapf repeated it
with vigor in his account of his own discoveries and those of Rebmann (from the latter's "Journal") in 1860, in his *Travels and Researches in Eastern Africa*.[36] From the multitude of rivers flowing
down from these mountains in all seasons, from all corroborative evidence, he insisted upon the presence of perennial snow in eastern
Africa. In a long Appendix to the 540-page description of his and
Rebmann's travels was added a report devoted to "The Probable
Sources of the White River, or Nile," containing the latest evidence
of Speke's discovery of Lake Victoria and his yet unproven theory
that the lake was the major source. Its conclusions made tentative
but sensible accommodation of Speke's view that "the swelling of the
Nile is caused, not indeed by snow-water, but by the tropical rains
swelling the Victoria Nyanza," rains which came from mountains rising in the west of the lake to the height of 6,000 feet, the latest
Montes Lunae, as well as from the peak of Mount Kenya on the eastern shore of Lake Nyanza. But the mystery was still unresolved, although on the verge of solution; the report concluded that "probably
a single journey of a scientific traveler . . . would suffice to solve
definitely this famous geographical problem; and that such a journey
will soon be accomplished." [37]

In an Introduction to Krapf's book, rendering it more scientifically
"acceptable," a Fellow of the Royal Geographical Society offered "A
Concise Account of Geographical Discovery in Eastern Africa," from
which Thoreau derived new information on the travels of Livingstone since the latter's book in 1858. This included the discovery of
the mouth of the Zambezi, a trip up the Shire from the Zambezi, and
the discovery of Lake Shirwa early in 1859; and the yet more significant discovery of Lake Nyasa and the exploration of "Nyasaland" in
the autumn of that year. Also in this Introduction was a capsule
résumé of expeditions up the upper Nile, especially those made by
the Roman Catholic missionaries of Gondokoro, evidence which rendered even less accurate Thoreau's reference to the mouth of the
White Nile as the uppermost limit of travel. Finally, there was a reminder that it was to test the accuracy of Krapf's and Rebmann's
findings that the Royal Geographical Society had resolved to send out

the expedition under Major Richard Burton, accompanied by his former traveling companion Speke.

Krapf's book contained a footnote reporting that Burton's account of this expedition was in the press. Thoreau was reading it by December of 1860, his second travel experience with this controversial adventurer.[38] The first 450 pages of Burton's book constituted the narrative of the expedition, or as the subtitle promised, "A Picture of Exploration." The remaining 100 pages of *The Lake Regions of Central Africa* contained an exposition of the village life, character, religion, government, and slavery of the East Africans, from which Thoreau took copious notes in his Indian Notebook. But as we could safely have assumed, he took the trip first, reading Burton's entire narrative. In one most spectacular regard, it was an account which cheated Thoreau of a "first sight" the implications of which he was given no chance, through Burton's eyes, of even guessing; for Burton's petulant treatment of Speke's discovery of the second largest lake in the world, made while Burton remained at Tabora for reasons of health, relegated this most famous and as it turned out most significant portion of the venture to a virtual footnote, and a barely acknowledged one at that. Speke's excited premonition that he had at last discovered the Nile's source was scathingly ridiculed by Burton, as was even the character of his traveling companion (whom Burton refrained from acknowledging by name). It is small wonder that Thoreau gave little credence to "stories" of a serious solution of the Nile's mystery. It was not until 1863 that Speke's own story appeared in book form.

Burton's resentment did not prompt him to skimp on details of his own trip. He left Zanzibar on June 26, 1857, traveling west into the interior over the Ugogo tableland, which begins about a hundred miles from the coast and rises some 3,000 feet above sea level, until he reached the great inner plateau of Unyamwezi, with an elevation of some 3,400 feet, the "Land of the Moon"; then after a long halt at Tabora, a trek west on the leading declining plain ended in his discovery of Lake Tanganyika on February 13, 1858.

Nothing, in sooth, could be more picturesque than this first view of the Tanganyika Lake, as it lay in the lap of the mountains, basking in the gorgeous tropical sunshine. Below and beyond a short foreground of rugged and precipitous hill-fold, down which the footpath zigzags painfully, a narrow strip of emerald green, never sere and marvelously fertile, shelves toward a ribbon of glistening yellow sand, here bordered by sedgy rushes, there cleanly and clearly cut by the breaking wavelets. Farther in front stretch the waters, an expanse of the lightest and softest blue, in breadth varying from thirty to thirty-five miles, and sprinkled by the crisp east wind with tiny crescents of snowy foam. . . . Villages, cultivated lands, the frequent canoes of the fishermen on the waters, and on a nearer approach the murmurs of the waves breaking upon the shore, give a something of variety, of movement, of life to the landscape, which, like all the fairest prospects in these regions, wants but a little of the neatness and finish of art . . . to rival, if not to excel, the most admired scenery of the classic regions.[39]

The want was not one Thoreau was apt to feel, and his travel with Burton this second time was probably less compatible for him than it had been before. But unlike the companions of his firsthand excursions, these travelers with whom he journeyed could not always be of his own choosing if he was to travel the route at all. For it was the route and the discoveries and the identity with place which now kept Thoreau as riveted to the African terrain as to that of a dozen other "foreign" terrains of the world. By the 1860s the last hidden continent in the world save one was midway to full exposure. Next to the Antarctic, Africa was the land of "newest" world discoveries at the time of Thoreau's death. In keeping with the times as well as with the interests of his correspondent, Cholmondeley recommended to a sick Thoreau in 1861 that he read the latest account of Africa, Du Chaillu's tome, *Explorations and Adventures in Equatorial Africa,* just published.[40] But by this time Thoreau's natural pattern was so radically disrupted as to require him to sacrifice a vicarious trip in favor of a real one, and one which health more than interest required him to take.

❦ CHAPTER XII ❧

Winters to Rival Concord's

From the hill beyond I get an arctic view northwest. The mountains are of a cold slate-color. It is as if they bounded the continent toward Behring's Straits.

Journal, December 24, 1853

One further area covered by Thoreau's travel reading needs special mention. Like the other routes we have traced, this was not one he ever expected to travel in person, as he indicated at the end of the "Excursion to Canada" when he reported his expenses for that journey (twelve dollars and seventy-five cents) and added, "I do not suppose that I have seen all British America; that could not be done by a cheap excursion, unless it were a cheap excursion to the Icy Sea, as seen by Hearne or Mackenzie." The great ice barriers at the two poles of the globe, a frozen continent at one and a frozen sea at the other, presented as lively challenges to the discoverers of Thoreau's day as any portions of the unknown world. We find Thoreau following the travels in these regions as closely as published narratives permitted.

The exploration of the Antarctic which Cook had inaugurated was continued first by a Russian expedition in 1819 and then simultaneously from 1838 to 1842 by the United States Exploring Expedition under Charles Wilkes and the voyages of Sir James Clark Ross. From 1843 on, however, there followed a period which Mill in his classic *Siege of the South Pole* called one of "averted interest," as all eyes turned northward to follow an era of arctic travel and exploration which did not really end until 1924 with the advent of polar aviation, and which in Thoreau's day reached feverish pitch with the search for a missing explorer in the 1850s.[1]

In 1818 a map of the Arctic showed the features of the ragged

northern coast of Siberia already traced by Russia's Great Northern
Expedition of the eighteenth century, but of the northern coastline
of America there was nothing but two widely separated points where
Hearne and Mackenzie had explored the Coppermine and Mackenzie rivers to their mouths. Any attempt at the Northeast Passage
looked insuperable, but the route along the northern American coast
toward the Northwest Passage appeared deceptively easy. The challenge invited the English to attack the Arctic with a concentration
second only to that which Americans were focusing upon the western
portion of their own continent. Parry made two voyages in 1819–20,
Sir John Franklin two overland journeys from 1819 to 1822, Sir
George Back an overland expedition from 1833 to 1835, to mention
only the major ones; then, following the disappearance of the sea expedition under Franklin in 1847, Americans joined the British in a
dramatic search that inspired forty separate expeditions within the
next ten years, foremost among them Sir John Richardson's along the
northern coast during 1847–55, Lieutenant Sherard Osborn's voyage
of 1852 to 1854 in the first steam vessel used in the polar seas, and
Captain Francis McClintock's voyage in Lady Franklin's *Fox* from
1857 to 1859, from which he brought back final intelligence of
Franklin's fate.

With the single exception of the early Russian explorations, Thoreau read the account of every one of the expeditions cited above.
Of the second Grinnell expedition he read two accounts: E. K.
Kane's two-volume *Arctic Exploration* (1856) and Isaac Hayes's *Arctic Boat Journey* (1860). The accounts were invariably the "official"
ones, of course. Having read the reports by Hearne, Back, Parry, Richardson, Osborn, and Kane (the first Grinnell expedition), he turned
back in 1855 to Franklin's original *Narrative of a Journey to the Polar
Seas*.[2] By 1857 he was so well informed on the progress of arctic
travel that he took time to retrace his steps, reading first the narrative
by the Russian Ferdinand von Wrangel of his explorations in the
early 1820s (the last attempt made by the Russians to determine the
geographical relationship of Asia and America) and then in 1859 the
two volumes of Mackenzie's narrative. Aside from these three instances of backtracking, he followed the routes north into the Arctic
as they were charted. Alert to latest reports on the Franklin search,

ARCTIC

EXPLORATIONS

IN THE YEARS 1853,'54,'55

BY

ELISHA KENT KANE, M.D., U.S.N.

VOL. I.

PHILADELPHIA

CHILDS AND PETERSON,

124 ARCH STREET.

1856.

THE TITLE PAGE OF KANE'S BOOK

he slipped into his Indian Notebook a clipping from the Boston *Journal* for January 11, 1860, summarizing McClintock's report of his findings in a paper read before the Royal Geographical Society.[3] And in addition to the travels we have mentioned, he read such earlier accounts as that of Martin Frobisher's three voyages in search of a Northwest Passage in 1576, 1577, and 1578, Hudson's account of his similar attempt for the Dutch in 1609, and the journal of Captain Cook's last voyage to the Pacific Ocean with its descriptions of Cook's exploration of the Bering Sea. Once acclimatized to northern temperatures and arctic terrain, he pursued his travels in the frozen region with guides other than those official explorers whose routes made history. He read and reread Mayne Reid's *Young Voyagers; or, The Boy Hunters in the North.* Sir Francis Head's *Emigrant* gave him a picture of the Hudson Bay Territory, while Louis Agassiz and Alfred Maury instructed him in the "Arctic Zones." [4] The standard authority upon Greenland, David Crantz's *History* of the eighteenth century, to which Parry and subsequent travelers so frequently referred, Thoreau took out of the Harvard Library in November of 1860 to copy pages of excerpts into his Extract Book.

The thrill of the "first sight" operated as powerfully for Thoreau at the poles as it did anywhere else. After reading a review of Ross's *Voyage of Discovery and Research in the Southern and Antarctic Regions*, he criticized the reviewer for reducing what should have been the discoverer's moment of wonder as he gazed upon his impressive discovery (nothing less than the Antarctic continent itself) to a mere consciousness of facts and grog; he found the reviewer demonstrating how too many men were commonly impressed by an object of sublimity.[5] Thoreau's arctic reading tested his own appreciative responses continually with the sights it offered him: Parry's description of the splendor of the arctic sky in spring ("the edges of the clouds near the sun presenting a fiery or burning appearance, while the opposite side of the heavens was distinguished by a deep purple about the horizon, gradually softening upward into a warm yet delicate rose-color of inconceivable beauty"); Osborn's description of the arctic moonlight during the winter twilight; [6] the Humboldt Glacier which Kane explored and named; the first sight of the Polar Sea as experienced by Mackenzie and Back; the dreary expanse of the tun-

KANE'S SHIP FROZEN INTO AN ARCTIC HARBOR

From his *Arctic Explorations*

dra or barren grounds traversed by Franklin; Kane's sight of the "red snow" on Ross's "Crimson Cliffs," a view which Thoreau copied into his Extract Book:

> The patches of red snow, from which they derive their name, could be seen clearly at the distance of ten miles from the coast. It had a fine deep rose hue, not at all like the brown stain which I noticed when I was here before. All the gorges and ravines in which the snow had lodged were deeply tinted with it. I had no difficulty in justifying the somewhat poetical nomenclature which Sir John Franklin applied to this locality; for if the snowy surface were more diffused, as it is no doubt earlier in the season, crimson would be the prevailing colour.[7]

But rather than "spectacles," it was apt to be the day-to-day observations that claimed the attention of the arctic traveler. Movement was more circumscribed, pace far less hurried; the entire rate of awareness took on a more leisurely deliberateness with these arctic observers. Frozen into the ice pack for months at a time, or pushing their slow way across frozen tundras or over lethargic glaciers, they covered less ground and lived closer to the minutiae of their setting. Their winter walks from their ships or their camps moved in modest radii from a cynosure to which they hastened back after a few hours' exploration—a symmetry of travel which exactly matched Thoreau's own winter activities in Concord. The richness for sense and thought that a snow-padded Walden offered the author of "The Pond in Winter" and "Winter Visitors" had ample parallels in the pages of these arctic narratives. The eye that observed so closely the ice on Walden had read pages of such detailed descriptions as this by Parry:

> A great deal of the ice over which we passed to-day presented a very curious appearance and structure, being composed, on its upper surface, of numberless irregular, needle-like crystals, placed vertically, and nearly close together; their length varying, in different pieces of ice, from five to ten inches, and their breadth in the middle about half an inch, but pointed at both ends. The upper surface of ice having this structure sometimes looks like greenish velvet; a vertical section of it, which frequently occurs at the margin of floes, resembles, while it remains compact, the most beautiful satin-spar, and asbestos when falling to pieces.[8]

Parry offered also a two-page description of the thawing process almost as minutely detailed as Thoreau's own observation in "Spring":

> In the second week of April any very light covering of sand . . . upon the snow sheltered by the ship from the wind might be observed to make its way downward into holes. . . . We could now perceive the snow beginning to leave the stones from day to day. . . . In the ravines, it could be heard trickling under stones. . . . After this the thawing proceeded at an inconceivably rapid rate, the whole surface of the floes being covered with large pools of water rapidly increasing in size and depth.[9]

The animated scene evoked by Osborn's description of the frantic ice cutters swarming over Melville Bay with their "triangle" rigs and their ten-foot saws, their loud laughs crackling over the sharp chipping of saws on ice, is a fair copy of the view of the ice cutters from Thoreau's cabin at Walden.[10] With an arctic spring, even loons, in this case hundreds of them, sported in these northern bays, to Osborn's and Thoreau's delight.

The accumulation of arctic details in the notebooks attests to an ever increasing absorption of detail and activity on Thoreau's part derived from the explorers of these regions. He copied Osborn's corroborative evidence for that "Boreal repose" (as Thoreau had called it in "A Winter Walk"):

> Nothing strikes the traveller more strongly than the perceptible repose of Nature, although the sun is still illuminating the heavens, during those hours termed night. . . . The inhabitants . . . as well as the animals, retire to rest with as much regularity as is done in more southern climes; and the subdued tints of the heavens, as well as the heavy banking of clouds in the neighborhood of the sun, gives to the arctic summer night a quietude as marked as it is pleasant.[11]

Osborn pictured the unredeemed loneliness of the polar regions ("Give me, I say, death in the deserts or the 'afflicted lands of Assyria,' with the good sun and a bright heaven . . . rather than the solitary horrors of such scenes as these"), but Thoreau also recorded Richardson's response to too much sun in this zone: "The irritability of the human frame is either greater in these northern latitudes, or the sun, notwithstanding its obliquity, acts more powerfully upon it than near the equator; for I have never felt its direct rays so oppressive within the tropics as I have experienced them to be on some occasions in the high latitudes." [12] The boreal data multiply year by year: elk, polar bear, musk ox, walruses, white wolf, snow fleas, and reindeer; ice, its temperatures, dimensions, sounds, colors, texture, taste; arctic plants, trees, birds, and fish; Eskimos and sled tracks and the aurora borealis. The interests of the recorder are as inclusive as those of the travelers. The observations, at the same time, appear less exotic and blend more readily with the affluence of seasonal observations that fill the winter record of the Journal.

They were well made for each other, these arctic narratives which were so often in the form of journal entries, kept during the long night which restricted the "excursions" of the arctic explorer, and the pages which Thoreau's own Journal offered the winter traveler in Concord. It took little stretch of imagination to move from the pages of the immediate to those of the remoter traveler, to such entries as the following by Elisha Kane, made in January, 1851, at Baffin Bay, over two thousand miles north of the place in which Thoreau was reading them in February of 1854:

> January 1, Wednesday. The first day of 1851 set in cold, the thermometer at −28, and closing at −31. We celebrated it by an extra dinner, a plumcake unfrosted for the occasion, and a couple of our

THE "BOREAL REPOSE": WINTER NOON IN THE ARCTIC

From Kane, *Arctic Explorations*

residuary bottles of wine. But there was no joy in our merriment: we were weary of the night, as those who watch for the morning.

It was not till the 3rd that the red southern zone continued long enough to give us assurance of advancing day. Then, for at least three hours, the twilight enabled us to walk without stumbling. I had a feeling of racy enjoyment as I found myself once more away from the ship, ranging among the floes, and watching the rivalry of day with night in the zenith. There was the sunward horizon, with its evenly-distributed bands of primitive colors, blending softly into the clear blue overhead; and then, by an almost magic transition, night occupied the western sky. Stars of the first magnitude, and a wandering planet here and there, shone dimly near the debatable line; but a little further on were all the stars in their glory. The northern firmament had the familiar beauty of a pure winter night at home. The Pleiades glittered "like a swarm of fire-flies tangled in a silver-braid," and the great stars that hang about the heads of Orion and Taurus were as intensely bright as if day was not looking out upon them from the other quarter of the sky. I had never seen night and day dividing the hemisphere so beautifully between them.

January 23. . . . We were called up by the deck-watch to see for ourselves a "ball of fire floating up and down above the ice field." It was there sure enough, a disk of reddish flame, varying a little in its outline, and flickering in the horizon like a revolving light at a distance. I was at first as much puzzled as the men; but glancing at Orion, I soon saw that it was nothing else than our dog-star friend, bright Sirius, come back to us. Refraction had raised him above the hills, so as to bring him to view a little sooner than we expected. His color was rather more lurid than when he left us.

February 23, Sunday. . . . A fresh wind makes the cold very unbearable. In walking today my beard and mustache became one solid mass of ice. I inadvertently put out my tongue, and it instantly froze fast to my lip. This being nothing new, costing only a small pull and a bleeding abrasion afterward, I put up my mittened hands to "blow hot" and thaw the unruly member from its imprisonment. Instead of succeeding, my mitten was itself a mass of ice in a moment; it fastened on the upper side of my tongue, and flattened it out like a batter-cake between the two disks of a hot griddle. It required all my care, with the bare hands, to release it, and that not without laceration.

March 27. . . . Let me make a picture for you without a jot of fancy about it. The sun was low, very low; and his long, slanting beams, of curious indescribable purple, fell upon us . . . as we sat on a craig of ice which overhung the sea. The chasm was perhaps a mile wide, and the opposite ice-shores were so painted by the glories of the sunshine, that they appeared like streaks of flame, licking continuous water. The place to which we had worked ourselves had been subjected to forces which no one can realize, so chaotic, and enormous, and incomprehensible were they. A line of old flow, eight feet thick and four miles long, had been powdered into a pedragal of crushed sugar, rising up in great efflorescing knobs fifteen and twenty feet high; and from amid these, like crystal rocks from the foam of a cataract, came transparent tables of blue ice, floating as it were, on unsubstantial whiteness. Some of these blocks measured eight feet in thickness by twenty-two long, and of indeterminate depth, one side being obliquely burked in the mass. On one of these tables, that stretched out like a glass spear-point, directly over the water, we were straddled. . . . Underneath us the narwhales were passing almost within pole-reach. As they rolled over, much after the fashion of our porpoises, I could see the markings of their backs, and the great suction of their jaws throwing the water into eddies. Seals, breast-high, were treading water with their horizontal tails, and the white whale was blowing purple sprays into the palpable sunshine.

April 16. . . . . This afternoon a solitary snow-bunting was seen flitting around our vessel. . . . He paused at the treasures which surround our ship, refreshed himself from our dirt pile, and then flew away again on his weary journey.

April 17. A memorable day. We put out our cabin lamps, and are henceforward content with day light, like the rest of the world.[13]

It is small wonder that Thoreau's travel in the Arctic possessed that characteristic power which we have attributed by implication to all his travel reading: the power to usurp his immediate awareness, to lay hold of all his faculties in a manner and intensity similar to that which held him to the footpath up Monadnock or the beach at Nauset. So closely did Thoreau identify himself with the travelers on these routes that he found it difficult to leave their company. He did much of his travel reading about the Arctic in the winter months (as, interestingly enough, he did much of his vicarious tropical traveling in the summer), when the world outside the kitchen window lent itself with particular congeniality to his imaginings. When he finally put down his book to pursue his daily outdoor activities, so close to the surface lay the experiences of his reading that like the icebergs on his northern routes they were constantly looming through the Concord landscape, polar "refractions" against a New England background.

During the month of March, 1852, Thoreau was reading Richardson's *Arctic Searching Expedition*. Richardson naturally brought to mind the arctic travels which Thoreau had previously made with Parry, Ross, and Cook; Parry's narrative sat upon his bookshelf. Immediately following his reading of Richardson, he turned to Osborn's *Arctic Journal*. A glance at Thoreau's own Journal for the period between March 4 and April 4 reveals the routes he was traveling. In the entry for March 4 he invoked an arctic scene of towering icebergs, driving snow, and twilight sun for symbol of the short winter days. A walk on the 7th over crusted snow lighted by the full moon brought him upon the countless tracks of boys' sleds, shining like silver in an upland beanfield, and he felt he had reached the region of perpetual twilight where even the sport seems more deliberate and significant performed at night. That Thoreau had his arctic travelers in mind is revealed when we find him later in his Journal describing how impressed he had been with the fact that arctic voyagers forced them-

selves to engage in sports and amusements during the long winter
night, an activity the ironical deliberateness of which Parry had described at length, emphasizing that so irrelevant to sporting moods
were the exercises that more than once the men performed them
without shouts or words to one another, in silent pantomimes of violent gestures in the arctic stillness.[14] Even as Thoreau stood in his
moonlit field musing over the traces of a winter's sport, he found the
stillness exaggerated, more impressive than any sound, "a monumental stillness, whose void must be supplied by thought." On March 23,
after seventeen pages of snowy observations, he figuratively pinched
himself back to Concord:

> As I cannot go upon a Northwest Passage, then I will find a passage
> round the world where I am. Connect the Behring Straits and Lancas-
> ter Sounds of thought; winter on Melville Island, and make a chart of
> Banks Land; explore the northward-trending Wellington Inlet, where
> there is said to be a perpetual open sea, cutting my ways through floes
> of ice.

Two pages later he quoted Richardson on the Eskimos; on March 30,
the frost nearly out of the ground, he confessed that "the Greek word
eap runs in my head in connection with the season and Richardson's
book"; the next day he recorded in full the discoveries and deduc-
tions made by Richardson at "Cape Riley" in Lancaster Sound upon
finding relics of Franklin's expedition there, and later in the same day
he mused upon the large destinies of the small song sparrows: "Do
they go to lead heroic lives in Rupert's Land?" Standing on the
frozen rim of Flint's Pond on April 1, he exclaimed, "How unexpect-
edly dumb and poor and cold does Nature look, when, where we had
expected to find a glassy lake reflecting the skies and trees in the
spring, we find only dull, white ice!" He found the pond worth coming to, all the same, because he could easily fancy it indefinitely
large: "It represents to me that Icy Sea of which I have been reading
in Sir John Richardson's book." On April 3 the thaw turned his
thoughts (they hardly needed turning) to that northernmost sea
called "Polina." The next day it was the Peterboro Hills which took
him northward in imagination:

> Though the ground is bare from the seashore to their base, I presume
> it is covered with snow from their base to the Icy Sea. I feel the north-

west air cooled by the snow on my cheek. Those hills are probably the dividing line at present between the bare ground and the snow-clad ground stretching three thousand miles to the Saskatchewan and Mackenzie and the Icy Sea.

The arctic traveling in Concord continued into the 1860s. Journal entries for the winter of 1853–54 reflect his travels with the first Grinnell expedition, with Reid, and with Franklin.[15] The reading in 1856–57 of Kane's account of the second Grinnell expedition prompted him not only to fill five pages of his Journal with Kane's arctic observations but to look over his own shoulder constantly upon an "arctic scene," to compare the Eskimo's isolation to his own, to recognize in a shelf of ice adhering to the banks of the river "what arctic voyagers call the ice-belt or ice-foot," to be transported by the perennial snow buntings to Grinnell Land. January 20 found him on his hands and knees inspecting Eddy Emerson's snowhouse and later recording in his Journal with unfeigned excitement his realization of a "good deal of Esquimau life." [16] His frequent adaptation of the term "brash" to his local surroundings showed him affecting arctic terminology.[17] Wilkes in the Antarctic conditioned him to seeing in the local ducks so many penguins, just as Parry at the opposite end of the world had prompted him to see in the fox on the ice of Concord River the polar bear on the ice floe at Lancaster Sound.[18]

Thoreau had to endure none of the "dried meats and Pemmican" on which those who made their way through the waste oceans of the barren grounds survived.[19] These excursions of his to the Icy Sea were, by his own confession, cheap and comfortable ones. They were also persistent and numerous, and, as he declared of those "good solid winters" which Concord offered—"intense cold, deep and lasting snows, and clear, tense winter sky"—every trip into these winters of the Arctic and Antarctic was "a good experience to have gone through with." Although his excursions left him searching out the catkins of the willow or the alder along the frozen banks of the Musketaquid, he was reminded, even as he looked upon these familiar shrubs, that "when I read of them in the accounts of northern adventurers, by Baffin's Bay or Mackenzie's River, I see how even there I could dwell." [20]

PART IV

The Reward

CHAPTER XIII

The Physical Macrocosm

I too love Concord best, but I am glad when I discover, in oceans and wildernesses far away, the material of a million Concords.

Letter to Blake, August 9, 1850

The more one tracks Thoreau through his travel reading the less likely one is to come to a single or simple definition of his intentions, on the basis of either the route he takes or the interests that keep him on it. But this does not justify a stance of awe before a mystery, though complexity there is. Many of his motives were originally, and remained at core, emotional ones. As Joseph Wood Krutch wisely said of him, the boatman was antecedent to the philosopher.[1] Thoreau's thoughts had to adjust to his feelings about his travel reading. While such adjustments may have begun as rationalizations, they soon became philosophical convictions which provided genuine sanctions for the strong promptings of his heart: for his impulse for freedom, for emancipation, for the most spacious release from confinements physical or mental—the farms to which one could be tethered or the intellectual closets in which one could so easily be shut; for the excitement of experiencing life with anyone anywhere, with the least or the most remote of the world's inhabitants, so long as they had found the marrow; and, not least, for that yearning which Perry Miller in his *Consciousness in Concord* confessed to finding so impossible, and the Transcendentalists found so easy: what we can identify as a form of cosmic empathy, but empathy with a cosmos that is in evidence at all times, safely circumscribed by those symbolic galaxies, by mountains and wells and the meal in the firkin. Since none of these promptings were thoughtless responses, to disentangle thought from feeling in regard to any one, in hope of isolating original motives, would be tortuous; time enabled the feelings to become more integrated with the thinking, and the fusion resulting offered its own emanations. Rather than "motives" let us speak of "rewards," and of the most apparent ones first. What were the results of that "airing" of his intellect which Thoreau attributed to his travel reading? What particular resources did Thoreau's travel reading offer him that could feed his thought even while they satisfied his feelings?

One of the earmarks of the Transcendentalists was the conviction that tasting a single portion of the world was tantamount to tasting the whole. "A leaf, a drop, a crystal, a moment of time, is related to the whole, and partakes of the perfection of the whole": so Emerson announced the theory of the macrocosm and the microcosm, wherein the American character and experience became identical in form and substance with the character and experience of man everywhere, and an individual tested the realities of life for all men on his own pulse.[2] Thoreau's attempt to reconstruct the whole pattern of human life through his own in Concord had comforting foundation in such a doctrine. As he himself was all men in little, so Concord stood for all New England past and present, and New England for all the world. The mixing of the waters of Walden Pond and the Ganges at the end of *Walden* symbolized that universality of time and place of which Emerson preached and which Thoreau experienced. The peculiar integrity of Thoreau's experience with this doctrine has not been fully appreciated, perhaps because the most reliable basis for it has remained so unacknowledged and unexplored. In this matter Thoreau's travel reading proved crucial.

Faced with a philosophic invitation to generalize at will from a knowledge of the smallest part, Thoreau showed a restraint in ways which differed in degree, one might almost say in kind, from those practiced by other Transcendentalists of his day. In the first place, both his keen enjoyment of his sensory responses and his interest in the principles which the inductions of natural science were exposing kept him close to the specific and the concrete. While the Idealists tended to deny the existential "thing-in-itself," that order of nature which it was said men must discover and obey in order to survive, Thoreau gave the objective factor of the independence of nature much of his attention, even while he also acknowledged the subjective element of the mind's creativity.[3] As Mr. Canby has observed of him, "If he aspired to any science which was more than classification and collecting it was geography, a science scarcely adolescent in Thoreau's day, although with Humboldt and the younger Darwin it had been brought out of infancy." [4] In his desire to know of the relation of man and nature, although ultimately he may have wished to consider it without reference to specific locality, he spent the greater portion of his research on study of different and distinctive natural environments.

In the second place, with such a penchant for concretions and distinctions, it was not surprising that Thoreau should confess the need to limit his concentration. As he frequently acknowledged, he could not hope to know all places as he knew Concord. "With the utmost industry we cannot expect to know well an area more than six square miles, and yet we pretend to be travelers, to be acquainted with Siberia and Africa!" [5] It was the "pretense" that he intended to avoid. Eager to taste the world and digest it, he was yet the sensible Yankee who knew that the most refreshing draught came from the deepest well. But while acknowledging the inadequacy of a wide but shallow knowledge, the pitfall, after all, of William Howitt's *Book of the Seasons* that had once so impressed him, Thoreau recognized with equal sureness the danger of that provincialism which kept one's view of life under one's own house eaves. This was the flaw in Gilbert White's *Selborne*, the book to which his own *Walden* was to be so inappropriately compared. One had to know as much about the rest of the world as possible in order to validate any comparisons one drew. It was characteristic of Thoreau not to take an assumption of the Transcendentalists for granted. He would test it for himself. Had he possessed the financial means and a clearer emancipation from family ties, he would most certainly have traveled, to the West he had first dreamed of, perhaps to Oregon, to the West Indies and the "Tropics," to Canada again, and even to Hudson Bay, possibly to Europe and the Far East. Unable to learn at firsthand, he nevertheless took nothing for granted about the world which lay beyond Concord, not even on the basis of his own Concord experience. Curious, in fact downright anxious, to know the truth about all the globe even while limited in practicality to a few square miles of it, he made a perfectly sensible compromise: to study Concord as thoroughly as firsthand experience enabled him to, and the rest of the world as thoroughly as secondhand knowledge and time permitted.

Thus every investigation which a study of the Concord scene inspired at home Thoreau extended through his reading to as many different areas of the globe as possible, and with a thoroughness different only in degree from that which he applied to Concord. His notebooks recording reading of foreign places show the same increase in thoroughness and inclusiveness in later years that characterizes the later records of Concord in the Journal. His declaration that "only that traveling is good which reveals to me the value of home and enables me to enjoy it better" [6] reflected an essential truth about his travel reading. In pursuing it so vigorously he could say honestly that he was not indulging secret or peculiar interests. His writing attested consistently to his concern with nature and man; to interests in the natural world, and in man's basic relations to this natural world as well as to his fellow man in the *communitas* and to the "Higher Laws" which governed him. It is the extent to which his travel reading fed these basic and familiar interests that now takes on new emphasis.

"Nature will bear the closest inspection," Thoreau declared in his essay "The Natural History of Massachusetts." [7] When he suggested in 1859 that if Henry Ward Beecher knew so much more about God than another he should publish it in *Silliman's Journal,*[8] his choice of that scientific periodical was not entirely facetious. On the other hand, he did not mean to rely only upon the latest authorities among the natural scientists. As he observed while reading a 1608 translation of Konrad von Gesner's *History of Animals:*

> The old naturalists were so sensitive and sympathetic to nature that they could be surprised by the ordinary events of life. It was an incessant miracle to them, and therefore gorgons and flying dragons were not incredible to them. The greatest and saddest defect is not credulity, but our habitual forgetfulness that our science is ignorance.[9]

The poet's sensitivity to nature was in the long run more important. Utilizing all his own sensitized responses, Thoreau proceeded to accumulate a vast range of material from his travel reading on the wonders of the natural world.

His attitude toward nature can not for one moment be attributed to a local view. There were few distinctive terrains on the globe with which he was not acquainted. He was facinated with the steppes of eastern Asia and Tartary, as he traveled them with Huc and Atkinson, and in their equivalent in South America, the pampas over which Darwin passed. Gregg's *Commerce of the Prairies* and Hind's report on the Northwest supplied him with vivid impressions of the North American prairies. As interesting to Thoreau as the profusion of vegetation in the primeval forests of the tropics was its complete absence in great areas of the earth: the bleak wastes of the Galápagos and the barren St. Paul Rocks (where Darwin found the only life to be insects and spiders), above all, the arid deserts, those "seas of sand" as Humboldt had called them. With Clapperton, Pfeiffer, Barth, and St. John, Thoreau crossed the northern deserts of the African continent, as we have seen; he traveled into Egypt with Volney and over the deserts of Syria and Arabia with Parrot and Burton. He was under no romantic illusions regarding any of these regions. He found much of the bleak Middle East "an accursed land, unfit for the habitation of man." In contrast was the great plain of India, which he described in the *Week*; he would not dispute the story that the primeval race was "received" there.[10]

Amateur botanist that he was, Thoreau gathered from his travel reading a variety of data commensurate with the range of the earth's surface he was covering. He recorded Hind's description of the vivid carpeting of the prairies of the American Northwest and Howitt's description of the grasses waist-high on the plains of Australia.[11] He was impressed with the great pine trees along the Columbia River described by MacTaggard "which would require sixteen feet in the blade to a cross-cut saw to do anything with them,"[12] and with Osborn's description of the dwarf birch tree at Disko Island in the Arctic, "full 13 inches high . . . the monarch of an arctic forest!"[13] He found no end to the variety of vegetable life which crowded the globe.

He learned of all seasons and climates. He collected weather tables and charts on remote regions as assiduously as he did those on Concord. One notebook, for example, in addition to mass data on the climate of Greenland and Rupert's Land, contains tables recording the days of Indian summer in the Canadian Northwest from 1840 to 1859 inclusively.[14] He recorded the intense cold of the Arctic, when Kane's instruments indicated minus 70° Fahrenheit in February, chloroform froze and ethylene chloride congealed, and Andersson's report of heat rising to 110° Fahrenheit in the shade only twenty miles inland on the southwest coast of Africa, an atmosphere so fiery that every article of horn or wood shrank and contracted, and the ink dried on the pen the instant it left the stand.[15] His notebooks captured graphic pictures of the winter sea off Greenland smoking like turf with the so-called frost smoke, mist in the cold air congealed to hoarfrost, the subtle icy spicules, discerned "like fine needles or glittering atoms, especially when the sunbeams stream through an opaque shade," overspreading the water with a concretion like a spider's web.[16] He noted the bitter snow- and sandstorms of Persia, the *kulaghs,* which Wolff found could kill in an instant both horse and rider with blasts of chillness. He copied down descriptions of such celestial marvels as the aurora borealis in the Arctic and the "Twilight Bow" on the prairies.[17] With the southern voyagers he gazed upon new heavens, sharing the experience of the traveler in the Torrid Zone who felt himself finally separated from home by finding himself under an unknown firmament.

He spent almost as much of his traveling time on water as on land. He noted that Humboldt declared it still undetermined whether life was most abundant on the earth or in the depths of the ocean.[18] He not only looked into the wells of Concord; he stood on the brink of Otjikoto Well in the dry wastes of southwestern Africa, a chasm four hundred feet in diameter filled with water two hundred and fifteen feet deep at its edges.[19] But his experiences with the wells, waterfalls, lakes, and oceans of the earth were secondary to those which he enjoyed on the rivers of the world.

On September 5, 1838, he recorded in his Journal:

> For the first time it occurred to me this afternoon what a piece of wonder a river is,—a huge volume of matter ceaselessly rolling through the fields and meadows of this substantial earth, making haste from the high place, by stable dwellings of men and Egyptian Pyramids, to its restless reservoir. One would think that, by a very natural impulse, the dwellers upon the headwaters of the Mississippi and Amazon would follow in the trail of their waters to see the end of the matter.

The following summer he was sailing up the Concord and Merrimack rivers, and later he saw the St. Lawrence and the Mississippi from midstream. But the greater portion of his river travel he made through his reading. There was scarcely a major river in the world which he did not float on at some time or other. And all the time he was accumulating fluvial minutiae matching in their exactness and their vividness the fine gems of observation which his own eye discovered on the river bottoms or through the pond-ice in Concord. He copied, for instance, Livingstone's account of the Vaal River in eastern Africa where one could hear literally thousands of stones grinding against each other: "This attrition, being carried on for hundreds of miles in different rivers, must have an effect greater than if all the pestle and mortars and mills of the world were grinding and wearing away the rocks." [20] He recorded Hind's experience on the shores of Lake Manitoba in Canada, where the sounds produced by the waves beating upon the beach resembled the ringing of distant church bells: "So close, indeed, is this resemblance, that several times during the night I woke with the impression that I was listening to chimes." [21]

But it was to bring this multitude of impressions of other regions into some synthesis with his own that Thoreau struggled. While regions had their distinctions, of more significance were their basic parallels. The similarities, he discovered, were literal ones, not simply the analogies we shall speak of in a later chapter. When he declared that for the most part it was as solitary where he lived at Walden Pond as on the prairies, "as much Asia and Africa as New England," he referred not to a state of mind but to the scene. He constantly saw about him views comparable to those he had seen in the Arctic and the tropics. When he read of Kane's account of the crackling sound in the ice up Baffin Bay, "the noise accompanying the aurora," as Wrangel described it, he noted in his Journal, "Is not this the same crackling I heard at Fair Haven on the 19th, and are not most of the arctic phenomena to be witnessed in our latitude on a smaller scale?" [22] He copied Parrot's description of the June drought in Syria to illustrate the parallel which he found in New England summers.[23] Arctic "refractions" and desert "mirages": he liked to test them both by standing on his head to view Concord landscape. Although he could not see the Southern Cross, he stood under the same stars as the Chaldean shepherds.[24]

What most interested him about the plant life was its wide dispersal over the globe, its universality rather than its secularity. He noted a single plant that grew in Oregon, New Zealand, Peru, and Patagonia, and another that could be found in both Oregon and Egypt. Peruvian bark was matched by the shrub oak of Massachusetts.[25] Much of the "strange" plant life which he found travelers admiring as "exotic" on first sight, he knew might prove increasingly "common"; the first explorers of North America had once made much of the huckleberry. It must have pleased him to read in Isaac Holton's *New Granada* that the arracacha was "the root of numerous plants throughout the world, but all allied botanically to the parsnip and the carrot." [26] In the Maine woods he heard at night the sound of trees falling in the forest, an experience identical with that which he recorded in his Extract Book of Kalm's in the wilds of Canada in 1749.[27]

Even when it came to the waters of the globe, Thoreau found his own region, dissected by rivers and bounded by an ocean, adequately representative. "What are the rivers around Damascus to this river sleeping around Concord?" he asked. "Are not the Musketaquid and the Assabet, rivers of Concord, fairer than the rivers of the plain?" The allusion was a literal, not a biblical, one, for Thoreau had viewed the rivers about "El Shan" in Volney's *Travels*.[28]

His travel reading also introduced him to a comparable variety of living creatures. There were the sentinel birds of Africa seen by Andersson and Gordon-Cumming, warning bells for the hippopotamus and rhinoceros, and the snowbirds Kane found the last of all arctic birds to migrate. Thoreau noted the contrast between the plumage of the tropical birds of Africa and the vivid hues of those of Brazil; he recorded reports on the alligators of Alabama to compare them with those of Africa. He filled his notebooks with snatches of strange and contrasting phenomena: the air above the desert of southwestern Africa alive with myriads of lemon-colored butterflies, the sound of their wings resembling the distant murmuring of waves on the seashore; and later in the same notebook, the sky above the northwestern American prairies filled with swarms of grasshoppers dimming the sun with the mass of their transparent wings.[29] How could his fellow men tolerate a moment of dullness, he wondered, when there was such an incessant influx of novelty into the world. His reading told him much about the relation between the wildlife and its physical environment: the capacity of the giraffe, kudu, gemsbok, and eland to go without water on the Syrian Desert; the way in which the elephants in eastern Africa broke paths through otherwise impenetrable jungle; the adaptability of the llamas on the Isthmus of Darien; the insulated den of the grizzly bear in the Yosemite Valley.[30] It pleased him to hear that the skin of most antelopes just killed in Africa emitted the most delicious perfume of trees and grass.[31] Wildlife represented integration with nature at the most elemental level.

Notwithstanding the many peculiarities characteristic of the varied creatures of the earth, again Thoreau found his own environment containing a rich proportion of the earth's teeming life representing that universality which emphasized the wholeness of nature. The cock's salutation sounded literally round the world; the bullfrogs forged a chain of sound from the Atlantic to the Pacific. The ants which he studied with such a Homeric eye in *Walden* had their ant-hills also in southwestern Africa, in Australia, and on the plateaus of New Granada. Even the noxious mosquito seemed a universal emblem of nature's scourge, swatted at alike by Lewis and Clark on the Columbia, Herndon on the Amazon, Livingstone in South Africa, Atkinson in Siberia, Howitt in Australia, and innumerable tortured travelers the world over.[32] Thoreau read of the ocelot of Peru and Mexico, the karakul of Asia, the cheetah of Africa, the ounce of India, and the cougar of Paraguay and North America, all related to the lynx he saw in Brattleboro.[33] He visited every traveling menagerie that came through Concord, though he usually knew more about the captives than did their keepers—"They told me that a hyena came from South America!"[34] He was able to verify the truth of Gerard's tales of lion hunting in Algiers by testing the latter's observations upon the partridge against his own findings in Concord. "It is interesting," he added, "to find that the same phenomena, however simple, occur in different parts of the globe."[35] Under Concord stones he could turn up a spotted salamander, "a trace of Egypt and the

Nile, yet our contemporary." The cat he watched in the meadow
grass demonstrated all the characteristics of the lion. How could his
perspective be less than global when he knew that the goosander he
found in the Concord swamp, shot down by Concord sportsmen,
bred alike in the Russian Empire, the Orkneys, and Lapland, could
be seen in Mississippi, Japan, Iceland, Germany, Holland, France,
Switzerland, Italy, and near the Caucasus, and was often sold in London markets.[36]

Standing upon the fortifications of Cape Diamond in September
of 1850, he observed:

> It is but a few years since Bouchette declared that the country ten
> leagues north of the British capital of North America was as little
> known as the middle of Africa. Thus the citadel under my feet, and all
> historical associations, were swept away again by an influence from the
> wilds and from Nature, as if the beholder had read her history;—an
> influence which, like the Great River itself, flowed from the Arctic
> fastnesses and Western forests with irresistible tide over all.[37]

Thoreau read soberly of the "irresistible tide" of nature, whether of
sand or forest. Many a region of the world demonstrated its triumph
over the antlike efforts of human beings. He did not mind thinking
of nature as universal and eternal, but he read so often of her as over-
powering opponent that he confessed to siding with those who found
many regions of the globe uncongenial to human life. He observed in
his Journal: "One might at first expect that the earth would bear its
best men within the tropics, where vegetation is most luxuriant and
there is most heat. But the temperate zone is found to be most favorable to the growth and ripening of man." [38] It was, after all, man's
understanding of and adaptation to nature that finally and principally concerned him. But he believed that nature in any of her guises
held lessons for man, lessons relevant on the one hand to his eventual
adjustment to his natural setting and on the other to his comprehen-
sion of the universal and eternal principles which nature illustrated.
Not the least of these principles was nature's immutability. It did no
harm for the Hindus of Shiraz to be reminded by their wise man that
"the Dihlah, or Tigris, will continue to flow through Baghdad after
the race of caliphs is extinct." [39]

CHAPTER XIV

Natives to the World

Why are distant valleys, why lakes, why mountains in the horizon ever fair to us? Because we realize for a moment that they may be the home of man, and that man's life may be in harmony with them.

Journal, October 3, 1859

It was his paramount interest in man's relation to nature that kept Thoreau all his life studying men in one kind of natural setting after another. His interest had two special though not necessarily separate aspects: the extent to which man could coexist in harmony with nature, and the extent to which he could simplify his means of living so that he might find and express the truth which nature symbolized. Harmony with nature meant for Thoreau more than cognizance of her; it meant, in the face of an increasingly mechanized age, a direct and elementary contact, rooted as firmly as possible in one's day-to-day living. Thus his own beanfield at Walden: "I came to love my rows, my beans, though so many more than I wanted. They attached me to the earth, and so I got strength like Antaeus." [1] Thus also his respect for the potential strength of the farmer: "I think that the farmer displaces the Indian even because he redeems the meadow, and so makes himself stronger and in some respects more natural." [2]

From this same concern stemmed Thoreau's persistent interest in the "native," whether Concord farmer, Maine Indian, Cape Cod fisherman, or Fiji Islander: that human being whose relation to a region was immediate and sure, who was, like the potatoes which nature grew and the apples which she ripened, a local product. Through his reading he became acquainted with a global cross section of such natives: the Assyrian shepherds, the Bedouins, Bushmen, Ethiopians, Gauchos, Swiss Tyrolian peasants, the Fiskernoes of Greenland, fish-

CHINESE AND TARTARS

A KURD

A MADAGASCAN

EAST AFRICANS

NATIVES OF THE WORLD

ermen of Nova Scotia and of Italy, sealers of the South Seas, bucca-
neers, natives of the Hebrides, Pawnees, New Zealanders, Malayans,
Norsemen. The tragedy of the Irishmen of Concord was that they
had been uprooted and remained so. The Zincali, though wanderers,
still lived in and from nature, their roving a part of nature like her
seasons; but the life of the Irishman, such as it was, rested upon the
railroad ties that lay on top of the earth, and depended upon an occupation whose only remuneration for spirit or body was in coin, arti-
ficially removed from nature's first dividends. The agrarianism which
Jefferson grounded in a political philosophy Thoreau rooted in a religious one, and because it was not simply a matter of political economy, Thoreau's "agrarianism" (if we may call it that) was broader
than Jefferson's, extending alike to farmer, trapper, and *voyageur*.

Thoreau's concomitant interest in the life of the "savage" was only
one aspect of his investigation of the "native." It was inevitable that
an inquiry into man's relation to nature should bring one to man in
nature. Thoreau's day saw the geographer's and naturalist's investigation of the Natural Man whom poets and philosophers had had almost to themselves for half a century. Poet and philosopher though
he was, there is no evidence that Thoreau contradicted the trend or
at any time in his investigation reverted to the presumptions of an
earlier age concerning the Noble Savage. His interest in primitive living derived from his concern for simplified living. Man Thinking
could learn of means from the savage, even when the latter had less
to tell him of the end of life. "It is worthwhile to have lived a primitive wilderness life at some time to know what are, after all, the necessities of life and what method society has taken to supply them,"
Thoreau declared while at Walden in the spring of 1846.[3] Much has
been said about Thoreau's interest in the American Indian, and Albert Keiser's introduction to the Indian Notebooks as long ago as
1928 implied a wide acquaintance on Thoreau's part with primitive
peoples.[4] The travel book was his richest source for such acquaintance, introducing him as thoroughly to the Indians of South America
as of North, to the Puri of Brazil, the Guahibos of Colombia, the
Araucanians of Chile, the Patagonians, and the hundreds of tribes of
the Amazon basin; more important, it took him beyond the Indian to
a familiarity with primitive life of every possible variety: that of the

Fingus, Batoki, Hottentots, and Goldi of Africa, the Kalmucks of Syria, the Mongol Tartars, Polynesians, New Hollanders, and Eskimos, to mention only a few.

It was primarily from his travel reading that Thoreau learned of those "gross necessaries of life" discussed so vigorously in the first chapter of *Walden*. He found certain elemental means of survival required by all human beings throughout the world, taking precedence over all else. The missionary Joseph Wolff had to distribute *Robinson Crusoe* among the Arabs before he did the Bible. These necessaries of life were generally simpler than one might suppose. "It took but a canoe, a paddle, and a sail of matting to people the isles of the Pacific," Thoreau reminded his readers in "Paradise (to be) Regained." [5] Such requirements bore their only necessary relationship to the natural environment, never to social convention. The Hottentots ate the marrow of the kudu raw, the Indian trappers that of the buffalo. Thoreau boiled and ate a handful of rock tripe to share the experience of Franklin at the mouth of the Coppermine River and to test Mayne Reid's account of a similar experience. [6] Whereas some of the savages of the Amazon needed meat only once or twice a year, the Hudson Bay *voyageur* was allotted eight pounds per day. [7]

Shelter, like food, reflected as many different forms of man's ingenuity as there were peculiar regions on the globe, from the houses of earth and clay made by the Georgian natives of Tiflis, to the igloos of the North. "The Scandinavian is not encumbered with modern fashions—but stands free and alert a naked warrior," Thoreau proclaimed after reading Ossian in 1843; [8] but his travel reading presented him with more clothed than naked savages, and ten years later Ossian was less acceptable. Clothing was of every variety, but the more primitive it was, the more closely it was related to the needs of the body in relation to setting. Thoreau read of "fashion" dictating its inevitable distortions of apparel. Huc found the failure to smear one's face with the juice of the tui leaf taken as a sign of bad character in Tibet; women in the East concealed the fact that they had faces, in the West that they had legs. [9] Regarding external warmth, Thoreau found as many varieties of fuel as there were regions requiring fire. The New Englander, New Hollander, Parisian, and Celt still required cut wood; the Greenlander used driftwood; the Tartars and the Indians of the American prairies used dried dung; the Eskimos used blubber.

Beyond an acquaintance with specific instances, Thoreau's reading presented him with a wealth of observations upon the general interrelation between man and nature. He was interested in Wafer's description of the albino Indians of Darien and their biological adaptation to light,[10] as he was in Huc's description of the Mongol's adaptation to his horse. "A Mongol seems out of his element when he sets foot on the ground; his step is heavy; the bowed shape of his legs—his bust always stooping forward—his eyes moving incessantly about,—all announce a man who passes the greater part of his life on a horse or on a camel." [11] He noted that Humboldt found man, "by his mere presence, almost," changing the nature of the trees or primitive forest as no other creature did.[12] He was reminded by Darwin that the easy prevalence of the necessaries of life made the savage, with his reasoning powers only partly developed, the child of the tropics. Moreover, it was by making habit omnipotent and its effects hereditary that nature had fitted the Fuegian to the most miserable country in the world.

It is hardly necessary to point out that Thoreau's two years and two months by Walden Pond represented his own test of the simplification of human survival in the environment of eastern Massachusetts. More important, it proved but the first of many such tests. By the time *Walden* was published, he had drawn conclusions which were derived from such a fusion of vicarious and immediate experiences that it would have been difficult even for him to draw the line. The book was a summation of his lessons about the natives of the world applied to the natives of Concord. Familiar as his conclusions are to readers of *Walden*, three in particular need emphasis here as having been peculiarly supported by his travel reading.

The first was that the basic necessities of man's physical life had not changed much over the long course of the centuries; even the means of acquiring them had changed less than one might suppose. Layard discovered, sculptured on a slab at Nineveh, machines for raising water which corresponded almost exactly to New England's well sweeps. Much of the native's life in the remote corners of the world could be experienced in New England, as Thoreau noted in his travels through the New Hampshire countryside:

> For though the country seemed so new, and no house was observed by us, shut in between the banks that sunny day, we did not have to travel far to find where men inhabited, like wild bees, and had sunk wells in the loose sand and loam of the Merrimack. . . . All that is told of mankind, of the inhabitants of the Upper Nile, and the Sunderbunds, and Timbuctoo, and the Orinoco, was experienced here. Every race and class of men was represented.[13]

A second conclusion followed naturally the first, namely, that many a contemporary Yankee could learn from the savage to simplify his own means of living. He should derive strength from the earth, but not be tied to it; he should be a sojourner in nature, in harmony with it, not a prisoner of it. Why should not his furniture be as simple as the Arab's? Thoreau found a considerable interval, in what was called the "civilized" life about him, between house and inhabitant, a shocking disproportion between the life of man and his conveniences and luxuries. He could contrast such discrepancy with the yurt of willow-trellis and skins, the "castle" of the great and wealthy Kirghiz on the Tartary steppes which Atkinson visited.[14] His reading confirmed a view which he had held as early as 1843 concerning the proper role of material needs:

> Surely all the gross necessities and economies might be cared for in a few years. All might be built and baked and stored up, during this, the term-time of the world, against the vacant eternity, and the globe go provisioned, for its voyage through space, as through some Pacific Ocean, while we would "tie up the rudder and sleep before the wind," as those who sail from Lima to Manila.[15]

The third conclusion in **Walden** was the other prong of Thoreau's second. Together they constituted his formidable weapon against Yankee materialism. Not only was such materialism usurping energies which should be reserved for the fulfillment of mind and spirit; it was not even succeeding on the material level. Thoreau found many a "savage" enjoying better living conditions than certain "civilized" men. He found strength and beauty in the rigorous life of the Iroquois and the Sioux, of the Africans in the villages of Usagari in East

Africa, of the Pueblos in New Mexico, of the Tahitians and the Lapplanders, and of the Caribs of Venezuela.[16] But in proportion as some of mankind had been placed in outward circumstances above the savage, Thoreau found others of his countrymen degraded far below him. In a ringing passage in *Walden*, he contrasted the physical condition of the Irish with that of the North American Indian or the South Sea Islander, indicating the real object of his fire by adding, "It is certainly fair to look at that class by whose labor the works which distinguish this generation are accomplished." [17]

Thoreau's study of the Indian is sometimes spoken of as a final disappointment to him in his search for an ideal life in harmony with nature. Sounder is Mr. Keiser's observation that, whereas Thoreau found many qualities to admire in the Indian, he never overrated him. His fundamental view of the Indian does not change in this regard from the beginning of his investigation to its end, any more than does his view of primitive life of any kind. His reading seemed only to confirm him in three important and consistently held conclusions about man's relation to nature, conclusions which become inevitable as one tracks him through the reading which contributed to them.

In the first place, there is no evidence that Thoreau ever held a brief for primitivism, beyond a recognition of its help in exposing the elementary necessaries for survival. We can now say with confidence that he saw too many of its real features to hold illusions about it. "What a despicable mode of progressing, to be drawn by a pack of dogs!" he exclaimed of the Eskimos.[18] Darwin's picture of a people most "natural" in their living was that of the natives of Tierra del Fuego, "the most abject and miserable creatures I anywhere beheld," he declared.[19] Such graphic scenes as Hind's picture of the ravenously hungry Swamp Indians groveling in the marshes of Lake Winnipeg after the roots of bulrushes would have done little to elevate such aborigines in Thoreau's eyes.[20] He followed up a particular interest when he read in Gibson's account of Sumatra of the wild aborigines called the Orang Kubu living in a state of nature as simple as that of wild beasts—covered with hair, without knowledge of clothing or fire, sleeping in trees and scavenging the primitive jungles for sustenance; four years earlier he had clipped out an article from the

THE FUEGIANS, DESCRIBED BY DARWIN AS
"THE MOST ABJECT AND MISERABLE CREATURES
I ANYWHERE BEHELD"

From *Voyages of H.M.S. Adventure and Beagle*

New York *Tribune* describing this tribe as "of all the races of men of whom we have any knowledge, the lowest in the scale of humanity . . . a picture of degradation." [21]

In "natural" man Thoreau found the "animal man" chiefly developed. Therien, the woodchopper in *Walden,* constituted a challenge because of the suggestion that the intellectual and spiritual slumbered in him, but in his present state he represented no goal. Man had tendency enough to identify himself with earth or the material, "just as he who has the least tinge of African blood in his veins regards himself as a negro and is identified with that race. Spirit is strange to him; he is afraid of ghosts." Thoreau himself was conscious of the feeling, as he confessed in *Walden:* "We are conscious of an animal in us, which awakens in proportion as our higher nature slumbers." But he did not belittle the distance which he had come. "Who shall say that there is not as great an interval between the civilized man and the savage as between the savage and the brute?" [22]

In the second place, Thoreau recognized that as far as man's relation to nature was concerned, simplifying the means of living guaranteed nothing. In 1842 he recorded a visit with an old schoolmate who was leaving to work on the Welland Canal: "He cannot see any such motives and modes of living as I; professes not to look beyond the securing of certain 'creature comforts.' And so we go silently our different ways, with all serenity." [23] With respect to luxuries, Thoreau found the wisest always living a more simple and meager life than the poor, but the reduction of superfluities was to the end that a man's life might then begin in earnest. In 1853 he took issue with the missionaries at the Hawaiian Islands who regarded as a main obstacle to improvement the natives' limited view in respect to "the style of living: 'a little fish and a little poi, and they were content.'" Declared Thoreau:

> The savage lives simply through ignorance and idleness or laziness, but the philosopher lives simply through wisdom. In the case of the savage, the accompaniment of simplicity is idleness with its attendant vices, but in the case of the philosopher, it is the highest employment and development. The fact for the savage, and for the mass of mankind, is that it is better to plant, weave, and build than do nothing or worse; but the fact for the philosopher, or a nation loving wisdom, is that it is most important to cultivate the highest faculties and spend as

little time as possible in planting, weaving, building, etc. . . . The simple style is bad for the savage because he does worse than to obtain the luxuries of life; it is good for the philosopher because he does better than to work for them. . . .

The philosopher's style in living is only outwardly simple, but inwardly complex. The savage's style is both outwardly and inwardly simple.

The real obstacle for the missionaries, therefore, was the natives' limited views with respect to the *object* of living, not to the *style* of living. "It is not the tub that makes Diogenes, the Jove-born, but Diogenes the tub," Thoreau reminded them.[24]

Finally, and consequently, with all his study of the means men employed to survive in nature, Thoreau did not find mere survival of great importance. Although with Layard he discovered the site of Babylon to be a desert where lions and jackals prowled, he found that the Assyrian king who had recorded his military exploits in stone at Nineveh had indeed succeeded by these very means in surviving time; "all was not vanity, quite." [25] The African, docile, patiently learning his trade and dancing at his labor, would survive, Thoreau thought, while the Indian, a hunter refusing to barter his birthright, dancing only at the war dance, would no doubt die.[26] But there was much to learn even from those societies which did not survive. Disillusioned with the legacies of human history preserved in the pyramids, Thoreau turned to the relics of the civilization of the Incas, the Aztecs, and the Toltecs for evidence of man's nobility of spirit, just as he also followed with interest the theory of a superior Indian civilization in the Great Basin of North America.[27] He read of the unknown primitive people whose traces had been lately found at the bottom of the Swiss lakes, relics supposed to be older than the foundation of Rome.[28] And he went about his own plans for preserving a record of the Indian of North America whose way of life in the 1850s was already doomed. What were the skills of the explorer Richardson in search of Franklin but those which the American Indian had perfected? Was not the wildness of the savage but a faint symbol of the awful ferity with which good men and lovers met? [29] In 1859 Thoreau spoke in his Journal in defense of his interest in the Indians:

Even the indigenous animals are inexhaustibly interesting to us. How much more, then, the indigenous man of America! If wild men, so much more like ourselves than they are unlike, have inhabited these shores before us, we wish to know particularly what manner of men they were, how they lived here, their relation to nature, their arts and their customs, their fancies and superstitions. . . . They had their fancies and beliefs connected with the sea and forest, which concern us quite as much as the fables of Oriental nations do. . . .

It is the spirit of humanity, that which animates both so-called savages and civilized nations, working through a man, and not the man expressing himself, that interests us most. The thought of the so-called savage tribe is generally far more just than that of a single civilized man.[30]

What Thoreau here proclaimed in behalf of the knowledge to be gained from study of the American Indian pertained to his study of all natives of the globe. It was not simply their adaptation to nature for survival that concerned him but, more important, the prospect for fulfillment which had been theirs, through which they expressed that "spirit of humanity" which had such perpetual relevance for mankind. "Consider the infinite promise of a man," he marveled, "so that the sight of his roof at a distance suggests an idyll or pastoral, or of his grave an Elegy in a Country Churchyard." [31]

The "infinite promise" of man shone through his ideals, and these in turn were real only as they had their roots in man's religious beliefs and expressed themselves in his social and cultural life. Thoreau's views of society were essentially religious ones, his idea of social improvement grounded in the Puritan concept of self-improvement dictated by one's duty to God rather than to man. But for all his preoccupation with minks and woodchucks (which loomed so large for Lowell), a large proportion of Thoreau's writings had to do with man's social life.

It is perhaps his air of detachment in studying the social and religious life of man, the seemingly scientific and impersonal attitude which he expressed toward the villagers in *Walden*, that tempts us to see in Thoreau the early anthropologist which he never really was. But it is true that his reading acquainted him with a tremendous range of mores. He read the missionary Krapf's account of his many months among the twelve tribes of the Wanika on the coast of East Africa, a confederacy of warriors, and Captain Cook's description, on his first voyage, of the social customs of the Society Islanders. He read

Livingstone's description of the democratic monarchy of the Banyai and Richardson's exposition of the Eskimos' respect for territorial rights. Knowledge of this latter did nothing to increase Thoreau's respect for his own countrymen's attitude toward the Indian or the Mexican. In Sleeman's *Rambles,* the motto of which was Pope's "the proper study of mankind is man," he read of life in modern India, from the systems of religion and caste to relations between parents and children and the state of the police. He read of the modern culture of the Greeks, the full account of their customs, economy, government, and arts by Edmond About; of the Chinese, especially in Huc's and Mme Pfeiffer's accounts; of the modern Egyptians, in Edward Lane's standard account. He scrutinized the social patterns of behavior in such diverse settlements of the globe as Mexico City, New Delhi, Constantinople, Rio de Janeiro, and York Factory. Even his frequent animadversions on the Californians were based on a close acquaintance; Walter Colton's quasi-philosophic description of the new society mushrooming on the west coast pictured each new citizen there supplying himself with a new horse, a mistress, and a pack of cards, in that order. As Colton observed later in his book, speaking of the immense wealth dug from the ground only to be squandered at the gambling table, "There is more practical wisdom in an anthill than is often found in a city." [32] Thoreau found the same corruption of society among the Australians, laboring under the impositions of the English Crown and the stampede of a gold rush. William Howitt's description in *Land, Labor and Gold* forced Thoreau to regard that southeastward migration as a retrograde movement, one which, "judging from the moral and physical character of the first generation of Australians, has not yet proved a successful experiment." [33] As we observed earlier, he did not show uncritical acceptance of the century's watchword of "westward progress," in spite of his high hopes for it. He examined with Puritan care the motive for human action before he labeled the result "progress," and he tested with Yankee caution each nineteenth-century movement for its bearing on man's welfare.

The superficial problems facing man in his relations with his fellow men Thoreau found remarkably similar around the world. Everywhere things were done according to fashion, whether to compress the feet like the Chinese, distort the heads of one's children like the Flatheads, or barter one's soul for the latest finery like the Boston lady. Thoreau saw little difference between the hiring of mourning women in the East to howl and strike their breasts and the hiring of stonemasons in Concord to hammer and blast by the month in order to express one's personal grief on a tombstone.[34] Everywhere material wealth rather than knowledge was likely to be taken for power: "Among the Bedouins the richest man is the sheik, among savages he who has most iron and wampum is chief, and in England and America he is the merchant prince." A man could grow rich even in Turkey if he simply became in all respects a good "subject" of the Turkish government.[35]

The experience of other peoples, when it did not reflect the obvious artificialities and perversions of social behavior which Thoreau could find demonstrated at any time in Concord, frequently offered models for improvement which were relevant and reassuring. He was pleased to see that the inhabitants of California, whatever shortcomings their superficial motives generated, had succeeded without the need of fortifications and thereby put Quebec to shame.[36] He liked the salutations of the Tartars and of the natives of Kelema in East Africa, because both were genuinely adapted to the circumstances and so more than formalities.[37] Was it not in barbarous Tartary, after all, that one met with the venerable lama who invited one to enter his tent with the declaration that all men are brothers? Such hints of man's nobler behavior as a social being, even in primitive-appearing societies, were worth heeding, for as Thoreau observed, "Who are the inhabitants of London and New York but savages who have built cities and forsaken for a season hunting and war? Who are the Blackfeet and the Tartars but citizens roaming the plains and dwelling in wigwams and tents?" [38]

But the contribution of Thoreau's travel reading was of greater significance for his social philosophy. The reverberations of his declaration of passive civil disobedience were felt and renewed round the world because, like that other declaration of principles with which Jefferson had earlier addressed a cause of mankind's, Thoreau's expressed a wisdom about human behavior and aspiration which originated, not in a parochial corner of one man's local society, but in the mainstream of many human societies throughout the world, in the town squares of man's social structures, not at all in nooks or corners. Its author spoke from experience with man's social predicament in all parts of the world, not simply from that of the Massachusetts taxpayer's. He wrote of universal human rights relating to many places and times, not a single one. The more cosmopolitan the experience behind the eyes, the more the words were apt to suffer in proportion to the provinciality with which they were taken. It was Thoreau's knowledge of many societies that gained him his wider audience.

Social action for Thoreau was at base a matter of premise and not prudence. He was more concerned with the root than the branches of social behavior; and the root was religious, as we have noted. While acquainting him with all types of society, tribes to civilizations, Thoreau's travel reading supplied him also with a tremendous bulk of descriptive material on the religious beliefs of his world. Here was his largest source of information on this subject, a more significant one than the relatively few translations of Oriental sacred and secular literature and texts of Eastern history to which he also turned. Lane discussed at length the beliefs of the various sects of "Sunnees" or followers of the traditions of Mohammedanism. In Burton's *Personal Narrative of a Pilgrimage to Al-Madinah and Mecca* Thoreau read one of the fullest accounts of Moslem religious practices to be found anywhere; the preface to the first American edition which Thoreau read stated:

> Burton's narrative is especially valuable for his full and accurate particulars of the religious observances of the pilgrimage, and the various formulas of salutation and prayer. In this respect there is no other work of the kind equal to it. His descriptions of the holy edifices are scrupulously technical and careful; and he gives us, for the first time, sketches of the sacred cities which impress us with their fidelity to nature.

Sleeman's two volumes contained much commentary on the beliefs and practices of the Hindus and of the Parsis of Bombay, last adherents to the Persian theology of Zoroaster. Huc's *Journey through the Chinese Empire* described at length the religions of that country; of the "Jou-kao" or followers of Confucius, the Taoists or "Doctors of Reason," disciples of Lao-tze, and the Buddhists; Huc's descriptions of the Buddhist temples and the monasteries were particularly detailed. Layard's *Nineveh and Its Remains* gave an extensive account of the Chaldean Christians in Turkestan, and both Layard and Wolff described at length the Yezidis or Devil worshipers of the East. In the narratives of Bartram, Cook, Humboldt, Perry, Edmond Reuel Smith, the Jesuits, Kane, Barth, and Livingstone, to mention only a sampling, Thoreau found displayed as great a variety of religious beliefs and practices as there were peoples scattered across the continents of Africa, South and North America, and throughout the islands of the Atlantic and Pacific. The value for his own thought of the knowledge so gained takes on particular significance when we tally the revelations it offered him.

Everywhere he found societies established upon religious premises of one kind or another, but equally striking was the range they illustrated of the degrees to which the social and religious lives of their members fused. He was impressed by expressions of faith that seemed spontaneous and genuine, such as the Hindu's easy belief in miracles, or the popular belief that ascribed to the most celebrated singer in India power of stopping the river Jumna in its course or of splitting a rock with a single note.[39] He liked the "turning prayers" of the Tartars.[40] It pleased him that in Scythia and India the natives made butter and cheese for the soul's larder; one should assume that the Proprietor of the world had an interest in the common activities of daily life. He preferred such elemental integration of a man's religion with his living to the remarkable disputations on doctrinal points heard among the Chaldean Christians.[41] Without such integration one soon approached the stage of the modern Egyptians, who permitted a saint to commit any enormity without its affecting his fame for sanctity. It was perhaps this same dichotomy, Thoreau observed, which accounted for the behavior of "Orthodox deacons"! [42]

He also found, wherever he studied the primitive stages of a religion, that nature supplied the original identification of Spirit. The natives whom Columbus met on his first voyage "pointed towards the heavens, making signs that they believed that there was all power and holiness." Many of the American Indians of Thoreau's day placed their heaven in the Southwest on account of the warmth of the southwest wind. The Swahilis of eastern Africa believed that the earth finished in a great morass in the west of Africa, the end of the world which they called "Usiko wa nit," meaning "burial of the earth." The Yezidis showed their reverence for the sun by making fire the object of their worship, while the Eskimos saw in the aurora borealis spirits at play. In an early Literary Notebook Thoreau recorded a scrap of information about the Bedouin Arabs from Volney's *Travels* that represented a point of view with which he sympathized:

> They even make no difficulty in saying that the religion of Mohammed was not made for them; for add they, "How shall we make ablutions who have no water? How can we bestow alms who are not rich? Why should we fast in the Ramadon, since the whole year with us is one continuous fast? And what necessity is there for us to make the pilgrimage to Mecca, if God be present here?" [43]

The lessons of the spirit were to be learned from those symbols of nature one could read daily and directly and so understand.

But he found all believers prey to similar religious corruptions. He found the English and Americans practicing their "taboos" as readily as the Sandwich Islanders. He placed the cause of the corruption which could sanction the Fugitive Slave Act upon the worship of idols "which at length changes the worshipper into the stone image of himself. Every man worships his ideal of power and goodness, or God, and the New-Englander is just as much an idolater as the Hindu." The American gold rush matched in his mind the infatuation of the Hindus who cast themselves under the car of Juggernaut.[44] By comparison, the suicide of widows or the ritual for the cure of blight in India was harmless indeed. It seemed to him that the God commonly worshiped in civilized countries was no more divine in name than those revered by many savages; too often such a God was but the overwhelming authority and respectability of mankind combined, a God to suit the circumstances, like the "Toahitu" of the Society Islanders—"in shape like a dog; he saved such as were in danger of falling from rocks and trees." Thoreau was reminded that among the latter people a man could make himself a God out of a piece of wood in a few minutes which would frighten him out of his wits.[45]

He found in his reading particular support for his view that the more institutionalized religion became, the further removed it was from the Truth expressed in nature and man's conscience. He saw the church as a sort of hospital for men's souls, making man a hypochondriac, bringing home the sealer of the Pacific to some Sailors' Snug Harbor. He viewed many of New England's religious observances as "pagoda worship"; and as he rested his oars on the Merrimack, listening to the Sabbath bell, he observed:

> It is as the sound of many catechisms and religious books twanging a canting peal round the earth, seeming to issue from some Egyptian temple and echo along the shore of the Nile, right opposite to Pharaoh's palace and Moses in the bulrushes, startling a multitude of storks and alligators basking in the sun.[46]

Worst of all evils fostered by institutionalized religion was the hypocrisy of lip service, in which one's religion, supposedly a matter of inner and personal import, became only a matter of externals and impersonality. He found cosmopolitan examples of such perversion everywhere, from the Brahmins who affirmed the mere presence of an idea in the *Shastar* to be enough for its unthinking acceptance, to the Arabians of El Medinah who covered their voluble personal abuse with interjected prayers of blessing to Mohammed.[47] He found foreign travelers in the East always allowing themselves to be imposed on by a name: coming to a sect of Christians—Armenians or Nestorians—they immediately predicted of them a greater civility, humanity, and civilization than that of their Mohammedan neighbors, with little truth as it turned out. In the West, too, the judgment often went no further than the tag. Thoreau perceived no triumphant superiority in the so-called Christian over the so-called Mohammedan; as he declared feelingly in his Journal:

> That nation is not Christian where the principles of humanity do not prevail, but the prejudices of race. . . . A man of another race, an African, for instance, comes to America to travel through it, and he meets with treatment exactly similar to or worse than, that which Americans meet among the Turks, and Arabs, and Tartars. . . . The traveler, in both cases, finds the religion to be a mere superstition and frenzy, or rabidness.[48]

Thus Thoreau's reading reinforced for him the justice of admiring a genuine reverence for the spiritual wherever it was found. He did not object to holy water or any other symbol so long as it was consecrated by the imagination of the worshiper. So he expressed his respect for the devout in the Cathedral of Notre Dame in Montreal, just as he did for the Indians preserving their intercourse with their native gods in the forest. He recommended the "busk," a ceremony of purification performed by the Mucclasse Indians, to his New England townspeople.[49] It was not the form but the content of worship that counted, not the institution of a Church but the spirit of a faith. He was harder upon the Egyptians than he was upon the cannibals. "The Hindu is not to be tried in all things by the Christian standard, nor the Christian by the Hindu," he declared. It would be hard to find a more liberal religious point of view than that expressed in his Journal in 1850:

> I have no sympathy with the bigotry and ignorance which make transient and partial and puerile distinctions between one man's faith or form of faith and another's,—as Christian and heathen. . . . To the philosopher all sects, all nations are alike. I like Brahma, Hari, Buddha, the Great Spirit, as well as God.[50]

Most importantly, the pictures which his reading supplied him constantly emphasized the cardinal premise and precept of Thoreau's life as well as of Transcendental thought: the preeminence of the individual as the spiritual center of the universe, in whom were to be found all the clues to history, nature, the cosmos itself. Whenever man looked outside himself for the answers to reality, he invented substitutes. Only when he accepted the externals as symbols of that which lay within his own spirit did he come close to finding the hound, bay horse, and turtledove. "Nations! What are nations? Tartars, and Huns, and Chinamen! . . . It is individuals that populate the world." The Chinese philosopher was wise enough to regard the individual as the basis of the empire.[51] Around the globe Thoreau saw men shrugging off the demands and implications of self-knowledge. Even in the deserts of Bokhara one met the theoretical reformers, a party of dervishes who announced the coming of a perfect equality.[52] But reform of the world meant self-reform, just as knowledge of spiritual reality meant self-knowledge. Many of the travelers whose experiences Thoreau read had set out to cure some remote portion of the world from eating green apples (a "drastic philanthropy which seeks out the Eskimo and the Patagonian, and embraces the populous Indian and Chinese villages"[53]) without ever discovering that it was themselves who had the stomach ache. Each man, being a microcosm himself, could just as well and with more integrity bring others back to health by attending to his own cure. Every picture of the peoples of the world which his travel reading afforded him reiterated for Thoreau, stubborn independent that he was, that in individualism and self-knowledge alone were contained all the hopes for human perfection.

Thus Thoreau's secondhand study of the world fused with his first-hand study of Concord. As he contracted the extremities of the outer world through his ever widening acquaintance with it, he magnified his own world through an increasing number of comparisons, until there was feeling neither of shrinkage nor expansion, but only of wholeness. So his travel reading fed that philosophy which, as he settled upon the shores of Walden Pond in July of 1845, expressed itself in his Journal in a burst of feeling: "Here is the world, its centre and metropolis, and all the palms of Asia and the laurels of Greece and the firs of the Arctic Zone incline thither."

Here was a microcosm of the natural world, one hillside illustrating the principle of all the operations of nature. "Next to us the grandest laws are being enacted and administered. Next to us is not the workman whom we have hired, but ever the workman whose work we are. He is at work, not in my backyard, but inconceivably nearer than that." Here were all peoples, from "savage" to "civilized," and all the struggles, prejudices, and superstitions which tested the human race. In the shops and offices and fields of Concord Thoreau found men doing conscious penance in ways more incredible than those practiced by the Brahmins. "The true India is neither east nor west; who has not lived under the Mussulman and Tartar dynasty? You will not have to pierce far into the summer day to come to them." [54]

But here also were all the potentialities for fullest human happiness and fulfillment, hopes for man commensurate with his richest challenges. Here was the yet unexplored. Here over the valley of the Concord and Assabet the sun rose as proudly as over that of the Seine or Tiber. The thin column of smoke which curled up through the trees from the invisible Concord habitation was a universal hieroglyphic of man's life, an ensign that some human life had planted itself—"and such is the beginning of Rome, the establishment of the arts, and the foundation of empires, whether on the prairies of America or the steppes of Asia." [55] One of literature's most vehement expressions of hope for mankind, opening the pages of *Walden*, was directed specifically to the people of Concord: "I would fain say something, not so much concerning the Chinese and Sandwich Islanders as you who read these pages, who are said to live in New England." That the message proved to be an inclusive rather than an exclusive one can be attributed to Thoreau's travel reading—to the fact that its author had already been to China and to the Sandwich Islands.

The Poetic Translation

As we thus rested in the shade, or rowed leisurely along, we had re-course from time to time to the gazeteer, which was our Navigator, and from its bald natural facts extracted the pleasure of poetry.

A Week on the Concord and
Merrimack Rivers, 1849

I have a commonplace-book for facts and another for poetry, but I find it difficult always to preserve the vague distinction which I had in my mind, for the most interesting and beautiful facts are so much the more poetry and that is their success. They are *translated* from earth to heaven. I see that if my facts were sufficiently vital and significant,— perhaps transmuted more into the substance of the human mind,—I should need but one book of poetry to contain them all.[1]

By the time Thoreau wrote this observation in his Journal for February 18, 1852, he was amassing "facts" from his travel reading in at least five separate commonplace books.[2] The two largest, the Extract Book and the Indian Notebooks, had only recently been started, but already he recognized a truth about the character of their contents which later readers of Thoreau have been slower to discern. To see in the data of the Indian Notebooks only a lost cause because Thoreau never wrote a scholarly exposition on the American Indian is to miss the richer harvest which these resources offered him and to which the poet in him was never blind. Whether or not such records would have been adequate resources for a history of the Indians, or of Concord, or of the St. Lawrence River, for example, is beyond finding out, for proof of such lay with Thoreau and he never produced it.

It is not necessary to make Thoreau a scholar in order to excuse him as an artist. He was both, but his success lay in his art rather than in his scholarship. Although he was a thorough reader, he could not confine his eye long to any circumscribed areas. While a meticulous recorder, he could not limit the extent of the data he accumulated. He proved at times to be a painstaking searcher after historical and scientific facts, but he always demonstrated the poet's prerogative of throwing any of them to the wind if they did not meet the demands set by his own imagination. With all due deference to those scholarly habits of mind which Thoreau did possess, it would be ridiculous to presume that they forecast literary works different in kind from those which he produced up to his death, any one of which will strike a reader as being as different from pieces of scholarship as the vine is from the arbor. It is only the titles "Natural History of Massachusetts" and "The Succession of Forest Trees," the first and last essays of Thoreau's to see print during his lifetime, that sometimes suggest technical monographs when compared with such pieces as "A Winter Walk" or "Autumnal Tints." But all four essays are personal paeans to nature, not scientific expositions.

So we return to Thoreau's own affirmation in order to keep ourselves oriented in respect to the facts accumulated from his reading. Borrowing his own suggestion, we should be justified in looking upon all these depositories as one vast book of "poetry." From what we have already seen of the "facts" they contain, it must be apparent that here were nuggets, not simply of scientific data, but of all the colors and shapes of nature, a compendium of human feelings, superstitions, and behavior, scenes, sounds, clues to the visible and invisible, in short, all manner of raw materials, fragmentary but variegated, which formed the stuff from which Thoreau's kind of poetry was made.

Few literary artists stuck closer to the raw material of their art than Thoreau. As F. O. Matthiessen once said of him, concerned as he was with abstract Truth, he was always called back to "the miracle of surfaces." [3] He reminded himself constantly that the route to the spiritual lay through the concrete; he would see, hear, smell, touch, taste that everlasting something to which he was allied. This fusion of the material and the immaterial is his peculiar strength, the metaphysical strain in his prose which can so condition the reader's perspective that he scarcely knows whether he is fishing for perch in Walden

Pond or in the sky for stars, yet can never quite deny the reality of the fishing pole in his hands. Thoreau's scrupulous care to keep his reader close to the natural fact and to the concrete evidence of the senses was not the scholar's endeavor to be accurate or scientifically "real" but the artist's attempt to make substantial and effective the intuitive insights of his imagination. Intuition even for the most thoroughgoing Transcendentalist was never an exclusive means of knowing. The process worked both ways: the seer was vitally dependent upon all the external channels of knowledge, even while he believed in the absolute potentials of intuition. Such a view of the concrete is quite sufficient to keep a fellow traveler like Thoreau on the side of the poet rather than on that of the scholar or scientist. He but grounded his metaphysics in the concrete phenomena of the world about him. This grounding dictated the exactitude of all his titles, whether for articles, books, or chapters: not Alcott's suggestion of "Sylvania" for his second book but the thing exactly, "Walden." The name, like the place, might be transformed through one's experience with it, but it was not to be translated. So also the title "A Week on the Concord and Merrimack Rivers": place, time, event precisely indicated; the extra week's pedestrian trip which took place on the upper reaches of the Merrimack prior to the return voyage was properly excluded.

But this world in which Thoreau grounded his metaphysical thinking was, we need to keep in mind, a vast one indeed, the concrete phenomena of which lay packed solidly in notebooks and Journal. The special views and facts which he stored from his travel reading proved peculiarly rich and relevant for his art; they decisively affected his prose style, for he drew from them allusion and metaphor of such kind and used in such way as to constitute one of the most telling distinctions of his writing. He both summarized and symbolized the process when he paid tribute to his gazetteer in the *Week*.

This metamorphosis is recorded in its more obvious stages in the pages of the Journal. To cite but one example out of many: in December, 1850, when the Journal was still serving as commonplace book, Thoreau recorded from his reading of Gordon-Cumming's book on South Africa several pages of undiscriminated data, including the following item of information, summarized, as was most of

the material from the book, in Thoreau's own words: "The Hottentots devoured the marrow of a koodoo raw as a matter of course." [4]
One month and a half later Thoreau plucked this particular item for
insertion in a paragraph on natural health:

> There is a difference between eating for strength and from mere glut-
> tony. The Hottentots eagerly devour the marrow of the koodoo and
> other antelopes raw, as a matter of course, and herein perchance have
> stolen a march on the cooks of Paris. The eater of meat must come to
> this. This is better than stall-fed cattle and slaughter-house pork.
> Possibly they derive a certain wild-animal vigor therefrom which the
> most artfully cooked meats do not furnish. [5]

It is characteristic of Thoreau to quote his own phrasing as closely as
adaptation permits; this was, after all, one of the values of the Journal
resource. His expansion of the information he originally recorded (to
"other antelopes") remained faithful, we can be sure, to the facts of
Gordon-Cumming's experience; these facts were simply adjusted now
for wider application or easier explanation, or both. Several weeks
later, culminating observations upon the nature of freedom and nature's bases for mythology, with its suggestions of a natural connection between the west and heaven ("The way to heaven is from east
to west round the earth. The sun leads and shows it"), Thoreau concluded with the wish that his neighbors were wilder, "a wilderness
whose glance no civilization could endure."

> He who lives according to the highest law is in one sense lawless. That
> is an unfortunate discovery, certainly, that of a law which binds us
> where we did not know that we were bound. Live free, child of the
> mist. He for whom the law is made, who does not obey the law but
> whom the law obeys, reclines on pillows of down and is wafted at will
> whither he pleases, for man is superior to all laws, both of heaven and
> earth, when he takes his liberty. Wild as if we lived on the marrow of
> antelopes devoured raw. [6]

This time the more familiar antelopes completely displaced the foreign kudus, appropriately for the American devourers whom Thoreau
now addressed. And when he finally tapped these weeks of Journal
practice for a formal composition written in this same year (the early
lecture on "Walking"), he wasted nothing, incorporating both ver-

sions of his exploitation of Gordon-Cumming's fact into passages following up the linkage of the West with the Wild:

> I believe in the forest, and in the meadow, and in the night in which the corn grows. We require an infusion of hemlock spruce or arborvitae in our tea. There is a difference between eating and drinking for strength and from mere gluttony. The Hottentots eagerly devour the marrow of the koodoo and other antelopes raw, as a matter of course. Some of our northern Indians eat raw the marrow of the arctic reindeer, as well as various parts, including the summits of the antlers, as long as they are soft. And herein, perchance, they have stolen a march on the cooks of Paris. They get what usually goes to feed the fire. This is probably better than stall-fed beef and slaughter-house pork to make a man of. Give me a wildness whose glance no civilization can endure,— as if we lived on the marrow of koodoos devoured raw.[7]

In other instances, the metamorphosis which the effluvia from Thoreau's travel reading underwent in the course of his reuse and re-reading suggests subtler amalgamations and multiple sources. When he wrote his college essay on Columbus, Thoreau read Washington Irving's account of the voyage with which every schoolboy was at least superficially familiar.[8] Later in "Paradise (to be) Regained" (1843), Thoreau employed one of Irving's most vivid scenes for an analogy. "Do we not," he wrote, "see in the firmament the lights carried along the shore by night, as Columbus did? Let us not despair nor mutiny." [9] Irving's account, as Thoreau well knew, was greatly indebted to Alexander Humboldt's *Narrative* for its geographical details of the Southern Hemisphere. In 1850 Thoreau copied from Humboldt's *Aspects of Nature* the latter's account of Columbus' response to the land breezes of the New World, the verbatim description of which he then immediately worked into his account of his second Cape Cod trip.[10] In May of 1852 he was reading Humboldt's *Narrative*, copying material from it into his Extract Book. And here too he found the inevitable links with Columbus' experiences; early in his narrative, Humboldt described a night spent on deck as his ship rode off the coast of Africa:

> The night was beautifully serene and cool. . . . The phosphorescence of the ocean seemed to augment the mass of light diffused through the air. After midnight, great black clouds rising behind the volcano [of

Lancerota] shrouded at intervals the moon and the beautiful constellation of the Scorpion. We beheld lights carried to and fro on shore, which were probably those of fishermen preparing for their labours. We had been occasionally employed, during our passage, in reading the old voyages of the Spaniards, and these moving lights recalled to our fancy those which Pedro Gutierrez, page of Queen Isabella, saw in the isle of Guanahani, on the memorable night of the discovery of the New World.

These very pages of Humboldt Irving had already visited before Thoreau, for he plucked, from a paragraph preceding the one above, Humboldt's description of the falling stars in the Southern Hemisphere, a phenomenon Humboldt witnessed in his *Narrative* just before observing the moving shore lights which linked his responses with those of Columbus. And appropriately enough, the linking of the two experiences for Humboldt was sufficient to prompt Irving to transport these exact details of the falling stars from their African setting in Humboldt's narrative to a Caribbean one in his own, where they set his scene for the re-creation of Columbus' memorable sighting of the lights of the New World.[11]

But now Thoreau traveled the reading route in reverse. At the same time that he was being reminded of Columbus' experience by sharing Humboldt's off Africa he was prompted to describe in his Journal one of his own—that of seeing, from his position on "the Lee place rock . . . moon not up . . . Behind Dodd's," the fishermen spear-fishing along the Concord River by night:

> The spearers are out, their flame a bright yellow, reflected in the calm water. Without noise it is slowly carried along the shores. It reminds me of the light which Columbus saw on approaching the shores of the New World. There goes a shooting star towards the horizon, like a rocket, appearing to describe a curve.[12]

During this same spring Thoreau was reading in Purchas' *Pilgrimes* (which included Columbus' first voyage) and in July in E. C. Drake's *Collection of Voyages* (which also included Columbus' voyages). And finally, he even appears to have returned to Irving's account, for in October, in describing an evening walk beneath the stars on the twenty-eighth, he wrote:

> How incredible to be described are these bright points which appear in the blue sky as the darkness increases, said to be other worlds, like the

berries on the hills when summer is ripe! Even the ocean of birds, even the regions of the ether, are studded with isles. Far in this ethereal sea lie the Hesperian isles, unseen by day, but when the darkness comes their fires are seen from this shore, as Columbus saw the fires of San Salvador (?).[13]

This time the lights' original indefinite identification by Irving ("They saw it once or twice afterwards in sudden and passing gleams; as if it were a torch in the bark of a fisherman, rising and sinking with the waves; or in the hand of some person on shore, borne up and down as he went from house to house"), which lent itself so easily to both Humboldt's and Thoreau's evening fishing scenes, was replaced with the more factual suppositions furnished later in his account by Irving (that the lights seen probably came from village fires on land).[14] Even Thoreau's question mark appears to reflect Irving's later conclusion that the light which Columbus saw "may have been on Watling's Island, which lies a few leagues to the east of San Salvador." [15] Herrera's original account, to which Irving turns for these details, was the account appearing in both Purchas' and Drake's collections. From lights carried along the shore, to a single spear-fisherman's light carried along shores, to fires seen from other shores —these varying and modified visions moved through Thoreau's descriptions to fuse with one another as they did in that mind's eye which had by now enjoyed not only its own re-creation of another's firsthand experience but some two or three others' re-creation of it as well.

Thoreau was as thoroughly absorbent of the concrete imaginative experiences in his travel reading as he was of the richness of his own direct encounters. As he wasted none of the versions of his own immediate and firsthand realizations when it came to capturing them in his writings, so we find that he wasted precious little of those multiple versions and variations of vicarious experiences which his travel writers offered him. Fascinating as is the evidence which beckons, time prevents us from searching it all out. Thoreau's work is so filled with illustrations and allusions derived from his travel reading that it has been impossible to discuss his writings this far without citing them in profusion. But while it may not be necessary to add to the examples with which the preceding chapters have been so peppered, it is important to notice some of the specific forms which these geographical comparisons took in Thoreau's writing, to suggest the variety, not simply the extent, of his literary use of them.

Even without discussing here all of his uses of simile and metaphor, it is safe to say that Thoreau's travel reading furnished him material for every kind of comparison or contrast he chose to make. But it was peculiarly pertinent to some kinds and lent primary support to certain conspicuous and crucial features of his style. Of first importance, it enabled him to make local objects suggest their global counterparts. The neighboring town of Bedford as seen from the crest of a hill became the city of Belgrade; the far river-reach of the Musketaquid was compared to a lake in Tartary; the valley of Concord spread out in the morning sun beneath the line of fine-edged pines on the horizon was seen as "a valley amid the Himalaya Mountains, a vale of Cashmere." The herons in the swamps were compared with birds of Syrian lands, and even the cow-droppings in the meadows were associated with the prairies and pampas and steppes, "the great pastures of the world." [16] His reading furnished material for comparisons of man's actions with the natural habits of his "brute neighbors" on all the earth, whether of the migrating buffalo of the West or the guinea fowl on the Cape Verde Islands.[17] It enabled him to make many of his most startling comparisons between two seemingly unlike and incompatible human phenomena, gauged always to embarrass his contemporaries with the shock of hitting hardpan where they least expected it; as when he confronted the Sabbath-school teachers taking their summer recess at the beach with the sweltering pilgrims making their way over the Sahara to Mecca.[18] It supplied him matter for metamorphosing the cow wading the Assabet into the buffalo crossing the Mississippi, for constantly placing the domestic in juxtoposition with the wild, the civilized with the primitive.

The effect of this constant mixing of the local with the global, the nearest with the most remote, the familiar with the strange, is subtler than one might suppose. Since the comparisons root themselves always in specific data and seem to spring spontaneously and consequentially from the author's insights, the mixing appears natural and inconspicuous, yet it works a subtle, permeable alchemy in Thoreau's style. The reader finds himself having experiences that take place in different regions simultaneously without his feet once leaving the ground. This stylistic trait was an early acquisition of Thoreau's. Even such a relatively youthful essay as "A Winter Walk" offered the reader this kind of experience.[19] The features of the winter world through which the author ambled were vividly rooted in the concrete details of the natural scene, but this concrete scene had elements in it from Greenland, Scandinavia, Lapland, Labrador, Spitzbergen, Nootka Sound, the Northwest coast, Finland, and Parry's Antarctic winter harbor as well as from Concord. The scene lost none of its immediacy from such infusion, for none of its natural details were distorted, and the result of a walk with such a seemingly solid, hip-booted, sou'westered hiker as Thoreau left one convinced, in the first flush of the return to the warm kitchen, that one had actually walked the snowy route over Fair Haven Hill. All very well and splendid, but also all illusion. The walk was taken in a region of cold and snow and winter beauty right enough, but as was forecast from the start by that Tartarean light into which Thoreau first stuck his nose after unlatching the door to face the shadowy realm in which he was to take his walk, it turned out to be a region easier to experience through all one's senses and sensitivities than to locate on Fair Haven Hill or indeed ever to return to on one's own. Unlike the routes which to this day devotees so confidently retrace through Concord township, this one remains remote and camouflaged from actual topography, a "Nova Zembla" of Thoreau's own creation.

It is a fine irony that persons who often take most satisfaction in identifying the geography of Thoreau's routes fail because their geographical knowledge is insufficient. They cannot share the trip because they have not traveled enough. There is no real global view behind the eyes. Thoreau would have a feeling of kinship with such present-day Concord saunterers, for he would see them now as he did in his day, as part of one route, rooted features of the Concord scene. Fervent initiates and faithful keepers of the cairn at Walden Pond, all would be cherished for their part in their place. But they can not all travel with him, any more than they ever could. Without sacrifice of one route for another, Thoreau creates a composite that so insistently extends the range of the reader's experience that local rambles become adventures in global geography. "A Walk to Wachusett" becomes also one to Italy and the south of France, to Arabia Petraea, and through the Alleghenies.

Two particular effects of Thoreau's geographical comparisons contributed in peculiar ways to this expansion of local experiences. One was that of comparing the small with the large or a part with the whole. "I am accustomed to regard the smallest brook with as much interest for the time being, as if it were the Orinoco or Mississippi," he explained in his Journal. "What is the difference, I would like to know, but mere size? And when a tributary rill empties in, it is like the confluence of famous rivers I have read of." [20] So the smallest stream was "mediterranean sea," and the Peterboro Hills answered the purpose of the Andes.[21] Thus John Hosmer's "Desert" was but a lesser Sahara to remind one that "in some parts of the globe, sand prevails like an ocean," and even the smallest island pleased Thoreau's imagination "as small continent and integral portion of the globe." [22] Over and over again Thoreau saw in the Concord meadow that "grassy sea" so vividly described by Humboldt, though which navigators in the Southern Hemisphere sailed.[23] Walden Pond became a small ocean.[24]

The other effect was that achieved by a subtle use of place for time. Sometimes the comparison was obvious, as when the walker's associations upon viewing a deserted woodman's hut were likened to the traveler's by the ruins of Palmyra or Hecatompylos.[25] At other times the process was finer. As we noted, in 1850 Thoreau read in Humboldt's *Aspects of Nature* a description of Columbus' approach to the New World, an account which he later copied into a portion of "Cape Cod": " 'The grateful coolness of the evening air, the ethereal purity of the starry firmament, the balmy fragrance of flowers wafted to him by the land breeze, all led him to believe (as we are told by Herrera, in the Decades) that he was approaching the garden of Eden, the sacred abode of our first parents. The Orinoco seemed to him one of the four rivers which according to the traditions of the ancient world, flowed from Paradise, to water and divide the surface of the earth, newly adorned with plants.' " [26] Nine years later, in Thoreau's Journal for May 4, 1859, we find this metaphor: "I, sailing in the spring ocean, getting in from my winter voyage, begin to smell the land. Such a scent perceived by a mariner would be very exciting. I not only smell the land breeze, but I perceive in it the fragrance of spring flowers. I draw near to the land; I begin to lie down and stretch myself on it." The experience once associated with a place was now associated with a season, yet with all its connotations of recurrent discovery. Even such application to locale as carried over from the original image now stressed the idea of renewal through the new and such affirmations of eternal life as both Columbus' "Paradise" and spring suggested. The metamorphosis was one which Thoreau liked, for he went on to use it in only slightly varied forms over and over again.

> The sweetness which appears to be wafted from the meadow . . . is indescribably captivating, Sabean odors, such as voyagers tell of when approaching a coast. Can it be the grape so early?
> (Journal, May 27, 1852)

> The first sight of the bare tawny and russet earth, seen from afar, perhaps, over the meadow flood in the spring, affects me as the first glimpse of land, his native land, does the voyager who has not seen it a long time.
> (Journal, March 16, 1859)

> They [the cocks on a springlike day] are affected like voyagers on approaching the land. We discover a new world every time that we see the earth again after it has been covered for a season with snow.
> (Journal, January 8, 1860)

To this same end—that their features suggest time rather than place—Thoreau maneuvered his images of the primitive. Real as such features as native huts and stone monuments were to the river-travelers whom he had accompanied through his reading, Volney on the Nile or Humboldt on the Orinoco, Thoreau found the route up the Merrimack offering no such touches of the human span, and he was forced, with images of other travelers before him, to create that sense of timelessness which only the fusion of firsthand and vicarious experience could achieve for this new countryside of his that had scarcely moved yet into human history. He painstakingly re-created the white man's first river penetration of the wilderness—the white man "pale as the dawn, with a load of thought, with a slumbering intelligence as a fire raked up, knowing well what he knows, not

guessing, but calculating." [27] When his actual route wanted that
harmony with its setting which might enhance its antiquity, Thoreau
placed behind the immediate scene the negative of other voyages on
other rivers, to reproduce the outlines of that "conciliatory influence
of time on land and water" which he missed.[28] He suggested that the
settlements on this river's banks were as remote as those on the upper
Nile or Timbuktu on the upper Niger. While lying on his oars by the
side of the stream, "slicing the melons which are a fruit of the East,"
his thoughts reverted to Arabia, Persia, and Hindustan, and the
maple and alders became the Kát trees along Botta's route in Yemen.[29] In a sandy tract of "desert" between Tyngsboro and Hudson
he discerned along the shore the exposed "ruins," not of ancient Egyptian temples, but of an Indian wigwam, "a perfect circle of burnt
stones . . . and the bones of small animals which had been preserved in the sand." [30] It is not surprising to find him offering us
next his reminder of the desert scene between Murzuk and Darfur.
He heard the peep of frogs, which was older than the slime of Egypt:
"The newest is but the oldest made visible to our senses." He found
that the revolutions of nature told as fine tales, and made as interesting revolutions, on this river's banks as on the Euphrates or the
Nile.[31] It was its parallel with scenes painted by other travelers elsewhere that finally transformed Thoreau's trip up the river into a venture into the past as well as into the interior and the remote.

> Thus we held on, sailing or dipping our way along with the paddle up
> this broad river . . . eager to double some distant cape, to make some
> great bend as in the life of man, and see what new perspective would
> open; looking far into a new country, broad and serene, the cottages of
> settlers seen afar for the first time, yet with the moss of a century on
> their roofs, and the third or fourth generation in their shadows. Strange
> was it to consider how the sun and the summer, the birds of spring and
> the seared leaves of autumn, were related to these cabins along the
> shore.[32]

But time here, while re-created through other voyages into more
primitive and ancient regions of the world, served only to illuminate
the way in which the living facts of these scenes commended themselves and furnished their own immediate relevance, unlike the pyramids which kept the secrets confided to them. For Thoreau there was

no real distance of time between ourselves and the past, only a distance of relationship (when we are unable to read its "history" correctly). "What if we cannot read Rome or Greece, Etruria or Carthage, or Egypt or Babylon, on these; are our cliffs bare? . . . Here, too, the poet's eye may still detect the brazen nails which fastened Time's inscriptions, and if he has the gift, decipher by this clue." [33] The living fact, of sun and summer as well as of a life or a belief, was that hieroglyphic rendering the living *mythus*.

> If we will admit time into our thoughts at all, the mythologies, those vestiges of ancient poems, wrecks of poems, so to speak, the world's inheritance, still reflecting some of their original splendor like the fragments of clouds tinted by the rays of the departed sun; reaching into the latest summer day, and allying this hour to the morning of creation [34] as the poet says:—
>
> > Fragments of the lofty strain
> > Float down the tide of years,
> > As buoyant on the stormy main
> > A parted wreck appears—
>
> these are the materials and hints for a history of the rise and progress of the human race; how, from the condition of ants, it arrived at the condition of men, and arts were gradually invented.[35]

Every kind of geographical illustration or allusion which Thoreau used, because of the very range of his comparisons, from near to far, small to large, part to whole, immediate to timeless, served the larger purpose of emphasizing that notion of the macrocosm which he was so intent upon conveying—a macrocosm rendered intelligible through language by the poet, "he who can write some pure mythology today without the aid of posterity" because he can find in the fables not only that most ancient history and biography but also those yet older and universal truths, the hidden significances, the ethics running parallel to the poetry and the history. Thoreau turned to the present and the immediate for the illustrations which might outline the slow aggregation of such a mythology. Such metamorphosis of the finite offered him the sure approach to "that universal language which men have sought in vain."

> This final reiteration of the oldest expressions of truth by the latest posterity, content with slightly and religiously retouching the old ma-

terial, is the most impressive proof of a common humanity. . . .

In the mythus a superhuman intelligence uses the unconscious thoughts and dreams of men as the hieroglyphics to address men unborn. In the history of the human mind, these glowing and ruddy fables precede the noonday thoughts of men, as Aurora the sun's rays. The matutine intellect of the poet, keeping in advance of the glare of philosophy, always dwells in this aurora atmosphere. . . .

What though the traveler tell us of the Ruins of Egypt? . . . Carnac! Carnac! Here is Carnac for me.[36]

❧ CHAPTER XVI ❧

Models and Analogies

The murmurs of many a famous river on the other side of the globe
reach even to us here, as to more distant dwellers on its banks.

A Week on the Concord and
Merrimack Rivers, 1849

Thoreau's fine control of the formal elements and structure of
language rivals the best that American authors have offered us. His
skill as a stylist enjoys a just critical acclaim. On the other hand, his
control of those aspects of composition operating on a larger scale,
demonstrating the organization of paragraphs and the more sustained
coherence of systematically developed themes, those called for by the
longer literary pieces which he shaped into extended essays or narrative accounts requiring their ἀρχή, μέσος, and τελευτή, his man-
agement of these aspects of the writer's craft has not enjoyed the
same critical approval. This dichotomy in judgment is understand-
able, for when all is said concerning the integrity of those few works
to which Thoreau did give larger shape and scope, the most appreciative reader of Thoreau is very apt to find their greatest value to be in
their expositional, autobiographical spontaneity, rather than in the
artistry of their narrative frame. They are most successful when they
take for their structures the most natural and undeliberated patterns
of Thoreau's day-to-day way of life—which is to say why the true
reader of Thoreau may ultimately find the twenty-four years of the
Journal the most satisfying structure for Thoreau's art; with this
judgment, at any rate, Thoreau himself would have thoroughly con-
curred. Next in success to the Journal structure, however, come those
particular forms of activity which represented the most natural and
frequent particularized patterns of Thoreau's life: such activities as

that of some daily or seasonal task, most often of some trip taken, some journey or travel undergone, some route traced to a discovery.

To the extent that he employed these latter forms of familiar activities for his compositional structures, in those relatively few works to which he gave finished shape and artistic wholeness, Thoreau did so with great deliberateness and considerable agony of effort. It is no longer possible to ignore or to oversimplify the conscious artistry on the part of this very self-conscious artist. The gap in Emerson's famous eulogy of him has since been filled by as reputable a body of Thoreau scholars and critics as Emerson himself could have hoped for him. From F. O. Matthiessen's criticism in his *American Renaissance* in 1941 to Sherman Paul's *The Shores of America: Thoreau's Inward Exploration* in 1958, appreciative emphasis has been given to the conscious unity which Thoreau attempted to give to every formal piece he ever wrote. Such studies of Thoreau's methods of composition as that of J. Lyndon Shanley in *The Making of Walden* in 1957 have added documentary proof of his careful compositional practices. There is no room in serious Thoreau criticism today for a return to the nineteenth century's image of the solitary and spontaneous wood warbler. Thoreau was fed from as vast, as varied, and as complex an intellectual watershed of actual and vicarious experience as any of his literary contemporaries (and we can remind ourselves that these included Emerson, Whitman, Melville, Hawthorne, and Dickinson), and he in turn converted these resources just as self-consciously and deliberately to his compositional use. We should expect no less from a man whose expressed vocation in life was to write.

We find the influence of Thoreau's travel reading upon the structure and content of his writings disclosing itself in a variety of ways, ranging from the subtle nuances derived from the constant osmosis of specific vicarious travel experiences, to the more deliberate and maneuvered exploitation of these experiences, in whole or in part, for the more formal framework of his finished compositions. We have already cited so many illustrations of the former process that it is scarcely necessary to do more than emphasize the implication of this fusion for those more developed accounts of experiences or more sustained episodes of travel which Thoreau recorded for us. The Journal, as we have shown, is filled with such records, only a very few of which were ever converted by Thoreau into finished literary pieces. They bear the ring of authenticity, not of derivation, and the hooks and eyes that reveal their links with other experiences far removed geographically from their immediate settings are not obtrusive or even readily identifiable until one has traced Thoreau's prior reading experiences to their sources. Nor can one even claim this latter knowledge as an essential prerequisite for the reading of these Journal accounts, for the fact of Thoreau's dual vision lies behind the vividness of his immediate impressions as a negative behind the print, its borrowed portion already converted into the elements stamped upon the new plate. We can no more define the walk to Wachusett Mountain by other walks over remoter terrains than we can the stride of the leg by the food that has energized it or the photograph of the actual by the emulsion which has brought it forth. We are dealing with influences in their least obvious form, which is not, let us add, to say in their least important.

The clues to this kind of influence "by saturation," as we might call it, are sometimes barely perceptible. For such a climb as that which Thoreau took up Mount Monadnock in southwest New Hampshire in June of 1858, for example, a clue may be discovered at the very beginning of his Journal narrative. Describing his first sight of the mountain as he and Channing approached its base (shouldering their knapsacks, the mountain's summit "about four miles off"), Thoreau wrote:

> Almost without interruption we had the mountain in sight before us,— its sublime gray mass—that antique, brownish-gray, Ararat color. Probably these crests of the earth are for the most part of one color in all lands, that gray color of antiquity, which nature loves; color of unpainted wood, weather-stain, time stain; not glaring nor gaudy; the color of all roofs, the color of things that endure, and the color that wears well; color of Egyptian ruins, of mummies and all antiquity; baked in the sun, done brown. Methought I saw the same color with which Ararat and Caucasus and all earth's brows are stained, which was mixed in antiquity and receives a new coat every century; not scarlet, like the crest of the bragging cock, but that hard, enduring gray; a terrene sky-color; solidified with a tinge of earth.[1]

The clue is Mount Ararat, of course: that awesome mountain of antiquity which rose above the plains of Asia Minor over 17,000 feet to dominate its surrounding countryside with a height almost 14,000 feet higher than that of Monadnock's ascendancy over its similar surrounding flatlands; a mountain whose peak had been sacred from the time of Genesis, according to local belief never to be trod by mortal foot. Thoreau had become extraordinarily well acquainted with the physical realities of this geographical wonder of the world by the time he climbed its slighter counterpart. To be precise, he had measured Ararat's dimensions and surveyed its exact location; he had compared sketches of it made from 1686 down to 1849; he had viewed it directly through the eyes of at least three travelers of his own day who offered him full descriptions, and with one of these he ascended its slopes three times, to share at last with Frederick Parrot man's first view from its summit.

His climb with Parrot was characteristic of his vicarious mountain climbs. The Preface to the account of Parrot's *Journey to Mount Ararat*, which Thoreau first read in 1851, reminded its reader, in support of the feasibility of Parrot's accomplishment, of the ascent of the Jungfrau by M. Agassiz and James David Forbes in 1841, an achievement which Thoreau went on to share in 1854 through Forbes's own narrative. The Preface made further reference to Colonel Stoddard's unfulfilled plans to reach Ararat's summit, that colonel "who perished in Bokhara," familiar to Thoreau through Joseph Wolff's narrative. Even more immediate associations were pricked by the reminder in the Preface that as both traveler and philosopher "Parrot merited Humboldt's eulogy of him"; Thoreau had just been reading Humboldt once again. In the narrative proper, Thoreau joined Parrot and his companion on their first climb, as they stopped at a mountain spring in a ravine at the base of the mountain to refresh themselves (they found no water on the top of Ararat), and later "at six in the evening" as they sought a place for the first night's stay, at 12,360 feet, approaching the region of snow. As soon as darkness gave way in the morning hours, the climbers continued upward, but failing to reach the summit on this first climb, they descended to pass the night in the region of grass, to which they set fire to warm themselves. On the third day they returned to the monastery from which they had started. When they finally reached the summit, upon their third try, they explored it in detail. (They were able to affirm that no frozen wood existed on the peak in evidence of the biblical ark once having rested there!) They camped just under the summit for the most satisfying night of their expedition; Parrot described the feelings it provoked:

> It was a delicious evening which I spent here, my eyes at one time set on my good humored companion, at another on the clear sky on which the summit of the mountain was projected with wondrous grandeur; and again, on the grey night, spreading in the distance and in the depth beneath me. Thus I become resigned to the single feeling of peace, tenderness, love, thankfulness, submission—the silent evoking of the past, the indulgent glimpse of the future; in short, that indescribably delightful sensation which never fails to affect travelers at great heights and under agreeable circumstances; and so, favored by the temperature of 40° Fahr—no slight warmth for the atmosphere at our elevation—I lay down to rest under a protecting rock of lava.[2]

A reading of Thoreau's description in his Journal of his "expedition" up Monadnock, his experiences with his camp sites, and his "exploration" of its summit will find ready contexts to parallel those of the climbers of Monadnock's more renowned counterpart.[3] Monadnock offered in June considerably less arctic summit than had Ararat in August, but Thoreau found upon it recurrent suggestions that "here was a small piece of arctic region." The sounds proved "a little strange . . . as if you were in Labrador," and we are reminded that added to Thoreau's vicarious experiences of mountain climbing in Arabia Petraea was an assortment of recent northern travels. His responses to Monadnock on this June expedition show a preoccupation with two alternating, recurring features: its parallels with arctic phenomena on the one hand and the color and terrain of Arabia Petraea on the other. These geographical extremes stressed the same quality for him: that of the mountain's "stern, gray, barren solitude," its hints of timelessness, the "Ararat-brown color of antiquity," that of earth's venerable brows, of nature still "peculiarly unhandseled and untracted," its natural terraces of rock "the steps of this temple . . . the same whether it rises above the desert or a New England village." "Even the inscribed rocks are as solemn as most ancient gravestones. . . . They reminded me of the grave and pass of Ben Waddi (?)." It is easy to imagine the biblical Ararat rising in Thoreau's memory with the sounds of the nighthawks that gave to his first night spent just below Monadnock's summit what he described as "fit expression to this rocky mountain solitude. . . . It was a thrumming of the mountain's rocky chords; strains from the music of Chaos, such as were heard when the earth was rent and these rocks heaved up."

As we noted at the very beginning of this study, the majority of Thoreau's formal compositions are in form travel works of one kind or another. It seemed appropriate to Emerson to gather together Thoreau's published essays into a posthumous book titled *Excursions*. Thoreau's other publications (excluding *Walden* for the moment) were all constructed and advertised in open bid for the market stemming from the travel genre's sure popularity. As we should expect, these works show more direct and open influences of his travel reading upon his structures and themes. Forthright as this influence proves to be, it is not primarily of that obvious pattern which we found in the "Excursion to Canada." As we observed when we spoke of his researches for that piece, his reading thereafter was used in both a more original and a more pervasive way—by combining aspects of different routes rather than imposing different accounts of the same one upon one another. This we can see with particular clarity if we look at those longer travel pieces which Thoreau himself saw through publication: *A Week on the Concord and Merrimack Rivers* (1849), the two portions of his Maine travels, "Ktaadn and the Maine Woods" (1848) and "Chesuncook" (1858), and "Cape Cod" (1855).

Never did his travel reading serve Thoreau more effectively than in the *Week*. Although the earliest of his travel accounts, it is, next to *Walden*, his best book. In it is much of his most vivid writing, if not his most artful, and though it offers fewer details of the route than "Cape Cod," for instance, it gives more of the experiences of the traveler. Written at the beginning of his career, it is paradoxically a voyage taken in "the afternoon of the year," [4] somewhat shaded by the pale cast of the memory of a joy and a companion lost, a voyage ending with only the enduring stars as reminders of "our fairest and most memorable experiences," and in the universal refuge of silence.[5] Only in the very last line, with its wild apple tree reminding him of spring freshets, does Thoreau tap that tone of renascence which the cycle of the seasons was to convey so deliberately in *Walden*.

While we speak of the *Week* as a travel book, we keep in mind that the forty-five asides which interrupt the account of travel proper take up by far the greater number of pages. They serve to remind us that the structure of the literal travel account is but framework in this case for a philosopher's log. There is nothing about travel in the title, in order to leave room for a different kind of voyaging which takes place upstream. The literal framework of the voyage itself constitutes approximately 131 of the book's 420 pages.

For all its somber autumn return, the voyage "out" sings of youthful spirits and high adventures. Only two years before he wrote up the log of this river voyage, Thoreau had read Henry Brackenridge's *Journal of a Voyage up the River Missouri, Performed in 1811,*[6] a day-by-day log of some 160 pages describing a voyage in a keelboat 1,300 miles up the Missouri from its mouth. The rowing up the Missouri took two months, the return on the descending current less than two weeks. The author, then a young man of twenty-five, explained in his Preface that "the voyage was undertaken in the spirit of adventure, which characterizes so many of our countrymen." He opened his account with a description of the Missouri and the history of its discovery, just as Thoreau does regarding the Musketaquid; he then set off from the village of St. Charles, "on Tuesday, the 2nd of April, 1811, with delightful weather." Thoreau's departure is "on Saturday, the last day of August, 1839 . . . a mild afternoon, as serene and fresh as if Nature were maturing some greater scheme of her own." There follows in parallel order in both accounts a description of the craft in which the adventurers have embarked (*Voyage,* p. 31,[7] *Week,* pp. 12–13) and the scenery along the river banks (*Voyage,* p. 34, *Week,* pp. 17–19); the voyagers feel that they have entered upon their voyages in earnest (*Voyage,* p. 34, *Week,* p. 20, reiterated on p. 81), describe with comparable awe the beauty of their first evening's camp by the river (*Voyage,* pp. 34–35, *Week,* pp. 38–39), pass their first fellow voyagers (*Voyage,* p. 38, *Week,* p. 48) and their first villages (*Voyage,* p. 38, *Week,* p. 49). Although Thoreau can not, like Brackenridge, be the first to discover the islands which he passes, he proceeds to humor himself with the discoverer's prerogative of naming them (*Week,* p. 43). Like Brackenridge, these Concord sailors take frequent land excursions to explore the territory bordering the river, and at night wrap themselves up in their buffalo robes and blankets (*Voyage*, p. 35, *Week*, pp. 119, 180, 249). And interestingly enough, both Missouri and Concord voyagers furnish Sunday diversion to churchgoers, although they differ significantly in their interpretations of the experience:

> Being Sunday, the good people were dressed out in their best clothes, and came in groups to the bank to gaze upon us, as we passed by under sail. The sight was no doubt agreeable to them, and we were no less pleased at catching another glimpse of civilization (*Voyage*, pp. 47–48).

> As we passed under the last bridge over the canal, just before reaching the Merrimack, the people coming out of church paused to look at us from above, and apparently, so strong is custom, indulged in some heathenish comparisons; but we were the truest observers of this sunny day (*Week*, pp. 63–64).

Even with this obvious a paralleling, it is not necessary to assume that Thoreau had Brackenridge's account beside him when he worked on his own book during his months at Walden Pond, nor even that he had it with him when he wrote up his Journal account of his trip six years earlier. Thoreau is not a devious borrower; what he takes deliberately he marks deliberately, and such literary ruses as he perpetrates upon his readers are done with splendid exposure of their "trickery." He lets us in completely on his method, since he expects us to measure it within the integrity of the product. In the *Week*, for instance, he is frank in telling us that he kept his log or "journal" of his voyage en route, writing it up each evening to keep abreast of the day's "events." While he takes some travel books along with him to read, he also confesses to having to make recourse to his favorite traveler, Alexander Henry, only through memory, even while he proceeds to quote accurately and at length whole pages from Henry's *Adventures*.[8] He makes attempt neither to explain nor to deceive us with the obvious fact that he is also rewriting his traveler's "journal" back at Concord, at his desk, probably by the light of his reading lamp, with either Henry's book or carefully copied excerpts from it (saved in some college notebook or early journal) immediately before him for accurate transcription. If Brackenridge's *Voyage* had also been on his desk, it too would probably have been there for such obvious purpose of direct reference. Apparently it was not. But this is no reason

SUMMER BOATING ON THE CONCORD RIVER,
A SKETCH BY MAY ALCOTT

BOATING ON THE ALTIN-KOOL IN THE ALTAI MOUNTAINS OF WESTERN SIBERIA

Sketched by Thomas Atkinson in his *Oriental and Western Siberia* to assume that it had any less intense or lasting effect upon its reader. In contrast with Thoreau's reading of Henry, we do not have to guess at his notebook preservation of Brackenridge's experiences, for an extant college notebook contains generous excerpts from Brackenridge's book taken in 1837 when Thoreau first read it. Brackenridge's experiences could lie just as close to the surface of the memory of the young Concord voyager, as he now made his own first river exploration, as did those quite different experiences of Alexander Henry's, experiences whose more open exploitation in the *Week* smell so much more of the lamp. The general pattern and structure of Brackenridge's account, stitched into a good memory through identification with what was once and could now, with reprovocation, be again a meaningful experience of river voyaging, would offer Thoreau an easy and natural frame for his own view. Nor was Brackenridge's account, although in many ways the closest parallel to his own, the only description of river voyaging with which Thoreau was familiar by the time he took his own trip. Other chronological, journalized narratives had offered him the usual stages and activities characterizing the river travels of Back, Lewis and Clark, Ross Cox, Volney, Humboldt, Charlevoix and Cartier (among other early French explorers), even those of Alexander Henry himself. The rather monotonous similarity of such accounts, familiar to anyone who has read more than two, lies in the uniform pattern into which the activity of such travel inevitably falls.[9] Thoreau transformed the ordinary ritual of river travel, not by tampering in any way with the basic structure of the travel account, but by adding to it the dimensions of a more imaginative response. In the *Week* he did this by turning the trip into a philosopher's holiday and making sure that his imaginative eye saw in the passing scene the visions to match his thoughts and reflections.

Although he thus transcended the ordinary pattern of the travel accounts he read, Thoreau carried over much of the immediacy of the travelers' experiences directly to his own. It would be inevitable for such an imaginative reader as Thoreau, having traveled for ten weeks on the Missouri, for sixteen up the St. Lawrence, for twenty-four on the Columbia, and for forty on the Great Fish River (to cite only a few of his previous trips, representing respectively his experiences with Brackenridge, Champlain, Lewis and Clark, and Back), to derive much of his current pleasure from imagining himself upon the upper reaches of a Missouri or a Columbia or a Coppermine River as he pushed his boat up the Merrimack. It is no surprise, therefore, to find him describing Concord's Ball's Hill at which he pauses as "the St. Anne's of Concord voyageurs," and a desolate islet as if it were only leagues from the "Icy Sea." [10] Since his previous river travel had been limited to no single continent, we find him describing misty trees in the distance as bordering an Amazon or an Orinoco, and cliffs overhanging the river as comparable to the ruins along the Nile.[11] He sees in Indian graves on the bank near Goff's Falls (between Manchester and Bedford, N.H.) parallels to the graves of the lost Atures on the upper Orinoco, and in the rapids of the Amoskeag Falls a match for the cataracts seen by Humboldt, even to the rainbow which hovered over them.[12]

Such mingling of the waters of many rivers which Thoreau's reading enabled him to perform is a paramount contribution to the *Week*. As James Russell Lowell recognized, in one of the best criticisms ever written of the book,[13] the piece is really about the river-gods, gods found in the Musketaquid and the Merrimack only because such journeying waters are allied, as are all rivers of the globe, with those streams which flow down from the Unknown, hinting of Paradisaical sources. The significance of this voyage of Thoreau's is that it is universalized; that which all rivers have in common becomes the key to the theme. The opening chapter, having first carefully released the Musketaquid from the limitations of time by comparing it with the Nile and the Euphrates, ends by freeing it as decisively from the boundaries of Massachusetts:

> The Mississippi, the Ganges, and the Nile, those journeying atoms from the Rocky Mountains, the Himmaleh, and Mountains of the Moon, have a kind of personal importance in the annals of the world. The heavens are not yet drained over their sources, but the Mountains of the Moon still send their annual tribute to the Pasha without fail, as they did to the Pharaohs. . . . Rivers must have been the guides which conducted the footsteps of the first travelers. They are the constant lure, when they flow by our doors, to distant enterprise and adventure; and, by a natural impulse, the dwellers on their banks will at length accompany their currents to the lowlands of the globe, or explore at their invitation the interior of continents.[14]

Only after so widening the scope of his route does Thoreau return to the Concord stream before him, wherein he sees "the lapse of the current, an emblem of all progress, following the same law with the system, with time, and all that is made," and resolves thereupon to launch himself upon its bosom "and float whither it would bear me."

The Maine Woods [15] is quite another kind of travel book, and the particular contribution which Thoreau's travel reading made to it is in turn somewhat different. Since only the first two sections of the work were published in Thoreau's lifetime, and since all three sections were more separate narratives than parts of a single finished work, we shall limit our observations to "Ktaadn" and "Chesuncook."

In these pieces Thoreau is the explorer of the wilderness. The voyages which take place are of no more significance in themselves than the land journeys; both are but the typical means and stages of an expedition of exploration boring into the interior of a continent. It matters little that the area is northern Maine rather than the Northwest or that the time is 1846 rather than 1606.[16] Thoreau does his best to invest his adventures with the excitement common to all explorations. He reminds us that explorations westward to the Pacific have left many a lesser Oregon and California behind them and that the howling wilderness up the Penobscot represents a country "virtually unmapped and unexplored . . . where still waves the virgin forest of the New World." [17] He depicts most feelingly those moments when he "most fully realized that this was primeval, untamed, and forever untamable Nature, or whatever else men call it."

> It is difficult to conceive of a region uninhabited by man. We habitually presume his presence and influence everywhere. And yet we have not seen pure Nature, unless we have seen her thus vast and drear and inhuman. . . . Nature here was something savage and awful, though beautiful. I looked with awe at the ground I trod on, to see what the Powers had made there, the form and fashion and material of their work. This was that Earth of which we have heard, made out of Chaos and Old Night. Here was no man's garden, but the unhandseled globe.[18]

No travel account which Thoreau read describing the primitive and uninhabited regions of the world improved on this picture of his own, and very few even approached it in vividness. Appropriately enough, primitive man as well as primitive nature dominates these accounts. Lying around the fire at an Indian camp on the Penobscot, listening to the Indians talking in a language which he can neither speak nor understand, Thoreau feels "as near to the primitive man of America . . . as any of its discoverers ever did." [19] As he describes the log houses on the shores of Chesuncook Lake, he explains his interest in seeing how a pioneer lives on this side of the country: "His life is in some respects more adventurous than that of his brother in the West; for he contends with winter as well as the wilderness, and there is a greater interval of time at least between him and the army which is to follow." [20]

Such interests and descriptions reflect the typical subject matter of the books of exploration which Thoreau was reading in such abundance. His preparation for the writing of "Ktaadn" was quite as much his reading of McKenney, Cochrane, Clapperton, Back, John Smith, Charlevoix, Henry, and Lescarbot as it was the actual trip which he undertook on August 31, 1846, the anniversary of his embarkation on the Concord eight years before. For "Chesuncook" he was prepared with the additional reading of some fifty-seven other accounts of exploration in addition to the *Jesuit Relations*. And all of this preparatory vicarious exploration, we must again remind ourselves, was of regions other than that which Thoreau now explored in Maine. It is this background of different but comparable routes which in the final analysis gives both accounts their unity of tone and theme. In "Ktaadn," the bateau in which Thoreau travels, "a fur trader's boat," reminds him of "Charlevoix and Canadian Voyageurs"; the wolfish-looking dogs in backwoods settlements are likened to the Indian dogs described by the first *voyageurs* as " 'their wolves' "; he finds the same plentifulness of fish on the St. John which the Sieur Champdoré found in 1608; and the longest rapids on his voyage, at the end of Ambejujis Lake, prompt him to note, "I suppose that it was like running the rapids of the Sault Saint Marie, at the outlet of Lake Superior, and our boatman probably displayed no less dexterity than the Indians there do." [21] In "Chesuncook" Thoreau accompanies "two explorers" for lumber, an object which helps to ally his expedition to those which penetrated other and remoter wildernesses. In the course of his narrative he specifically fuses his own travel experience upon particular occasions with that of the Jesuit missionaries, of Arnold's expedition, of Josselyn, of the Indians "very far north and northwest," of John Smith, and of the explorers in the Arctic.[22] In both Maine accounts Thoreau uses his experience with foreign travel to break the limits of time, place, and proportion, subtly and naturally, without distortion or artificiality. By the time the reader has completed these travels, he has been tellingly reminded of Balboa's first sight of the Pacific from the mountains of the Isthmus of Darien, of whales and elephants and giraffes in the same breath with moose, of the cannibals of Brazil, and of Humboldt's description of the primitive forests in the Southern Hemisphere.[23]

Thoreau's third travel work, *Cape Cod*,[24] has often been cited as a peculiarly "New England" book, perhaps because of the local histories so frequent in its pages. But this narrative, like the previous ones we have discussed, has a distinctive tone and theme which give it a unity sufficient to include considerable local history without real danger to the universality of its experience. Of all Thoreau's travel books, this one moves most richly into the past, is most conscious of human history,[25] even while it paints on the vastest canvas the immensities of sky, water, and horizon. The ocean pounds at the doors of men's houses, and Thoreau spends most of his hours walking the beach, that thin line between man and nature. The reader's introduction to the route is a handbill headed " 'Death! one hundred and forty-five lives lost at Cohasset,' " followed by the scene of a shipwreck and as grim a picture of man's struggle with the sea as the most objective reporter could wish. Man's relation to the ocean, "which, we are told, covers more than two thirds of the globe," is one side of Thoreau's theme; the other is man's attempts to conquer this barrier which, like the wildernesses stretching inland, has always challenged him with the urge to sail into the Unknown. In his Journal Thoreau exclaimed, "As I sail the unexplored sea of Concord, many a dell and swamp and wooded hill is my Cerum and Amboyna." [26] In "Cape Cod" he simply enlarged his microcosm. Whereas in the *Week* he was the river voyager, and in "Ktaadn" and "Chesuncook" the explorer of the wilderness, here he is the discoverer of oceans and continents, the explorer of seas, the first Columbus. Thus he does not mind moving back into the past, even a strictly historical past, for discovery is by its nature temporal. Of peculiar relevance is his continuous attention to what comes first: the first voyager, the first sight, the first landing, the first settlement, the first child, the whole cycle of human progress, and all of it stemming from the discoverer.

Once again travel literature contributed peculiarly to Thoreau's presentation of his theme. It furnished him illustrations of lives which the ocean sustained, the ways of life of those who lived on terms with it around the world: in the Netherlands, Greenland, the Falkland Islands, Brittany, the Hebrides, Nova Scotia, Kamchatka, even on the coast of Persia in 325 b.c.[27] It supplied him histories of those who crossed the ocean, accounts illustrating the rigors of the struggle between sea and settlers. It furnished him instances of those whom the ocean sometimes isolated, the Captain Cooks, Robinson Crusoes, the Rileys stranded on strange shores. It gave him other examples of those who lived on the ocean, whose business was sea-business, and who corresponded, in their relation to the sea, with the hunters and trappers of the West in relation to the wilderness: the fishermen off the Grand Banks or the coast of Labrador, in the Strait of Belle Isle or Chaleur Bay, whalers and sealers, and those who plied the seas in merchantmen, making the vast waters a highway for their global commerce.[28] But even more important than those who got their living from the ocean were those who explored it, who sailed it "in expectation," as Thoreau put it; these were the superior breed of men to whom *Cape Cod* was dedicated and whom all other features of Thoreau's route justified.

> The heroes and discoverers have found true more than was previously believed, only when they were expecting and dreaming of something more than their contemporaries dreamed of, or even themselves discovered, that is, when they were in a frame of mind to behold the truth. Referred to by the world's standard, they were always insane.[29]

Columbus, Champlain, Darwin, Anson, Cook, Poutrincourt, Gorges, Cabot, Verrazano, Gomez, Alphonse, Gosnold, Pring, Franklin, Nearchus, the Northmen, all these voyaging discoverers make direct contributions to this travel book; the list of those additional discoverers ancient and modern whom Thoreau had read and who indirectly affected his work would be longer yet.

What of the ocean itself in this sea book? At one moment Thoreau calls it "but a larger lake," holding on to his notion of the microcosm by mixing salt water with fresh. At another time, seeing how easy it is to lose all sense of perspective while watching either chip or spar floating on the waves, he begins to "doubt whether the Atlantic itself would bear a still closer inspection, and would not turn out to be but a small pond, if it should come ashore to us." Size becomes irrelevant to the Universe, just as it bore no necessary relation to universality.[30] But for the most part Thoreau takes the vast view and, through the geographical images which his far-flung travels furnish, emphasizes the universality of the scene by extending it globally. The reader is reminded that beaches which he walks stretch north to Greenland and line the west coast as well, from the Strait of Juan de Fuca to the Columbia River; the same clearness of water-view which he enjoys from Truro can be experienced from the base of the Andes or from Ramsgate; whether northeaster, sirocco, or simoon, the same storms whip the Sahara, the Bay of Biscay, and Cape Wrath.[31] So Thoreau hammers home the far view and the relativity of space. As to that of time, here, too, his reading supplied him with pictures of eternal seas, from the Arctic to the Indian, the untamable wilderness of the world, unchanging in man's lifetime. "We do not associate the idea of antiquity with the ocean, nor wonder how it looked a thousand years ago, as we do of the land, for it was equally wild and unfathomable always. . . . To go to sea! Why, it is to have the experience of Noah." [32]

No better summary could be found of the way in which Thoreau used his knowledge of geography to expand the horizons of a particular place than a passage from a portion of "Cape Cod" which he worked over carefully shortly before his death. He describes his walk northward along the outer rim of the Cape between the Highland Light and Truro as follows:

Again we took to the beach for another day . . . walking along the shore of the resounding sea, determined to get it into us. We wished to associate with the ocean until it lost the pond-like look which it wears to a countryman. We still thought that we could see the other side. Its surface was still more sparkling than the day before . . . the wind blew and the billows broke in foam along the beach. The nearest beach to us on the other side, whither we looked, due east, was on the coast of Galicia, in Spain, whose capital is Santiago, though by old poet's reckoning it should have been Atlantis or the Hesperides; but heaven is found to be farther west now. At first we were abreast of that part of Portugal *entre Duoro e Mino,* and then Galicia and the port of Montevedra opened to us as we walked along; but we did not enter, the breakers ran so high. The bold headland of Cape Finisterra, a little north of east, jutted toward us next, with its vain brag, for we flung back,—"Here is Cape Cod,—Cape Land's Beginning." A little indentation toward the north—for the land loomed to our imaginations by a common mirage—we knew was the Bay of Biscay, and we sang:—

> "There we lay, till next day,
> In the Bay of Biscay O!"

A little south of east was Palos, where Columbus weighed anchor, and farther yet the Pillars which Hercules set up; concerning which, when we inquired at the top of our voices, and could not see distinctly,— the inhabitants shouted *Ne plus ultra* (no more beyond), but the wind bore us the truth only, *plus ultra* (more beyond). We spoke to them through the surf about the Far West, the true Hesperia, or end of the day, the This Side Sundown, where the sun was extinguished in the Pacific, and we advised them to pull up stakes and plant those pillars of theirs on the shores of California, whither all our folk were gone,—the only *ne plus ultra* now. Whereat they looked crestfallen on their cliffs, for we had taken the wind out of all their sails.[33]

Under the guise of playful whimsey, Thoreau gradually extends the geographical borders of his walk to keep pace with the expansion of his spirits. A walk on Cape Cod sands fuses with one along the coast of Spain, then, having jumped an ocean, rejumps both ocean and continent to end up on the beach of California, and finally, on mythical stilts, encompasses the globe. At the same time and through the same means the boundaries of history are extended to reflect man's quests of discovery, for ancient Galicia, Cape Finisterre, and the fabled Atlantis, to the harbor where Columbus weighed anchor and to the Pillars of Hercules moved to the western limit of the New World. So Thoreau mirrors the infinite challenge to man to push beyond the limits of the Unknown, even while he can not resist the touch of irony which in this case compromises the challenge of heaven by placing the Hesperides in California, "whither all our folk were gone."

❧ CHAPTER XVII ❧

The Great Circle Sailed

The other side of the globe is but the home of our correspondent. Our voyaging is only a great-circle sailing.

"Conclusion," *Walden,* 1854

Nature supplied the universal archetypes, its natural facts symbols of spiritual facts, as Emerson maintained. "All perception of truth is the detection of an analogy," Thoreau declared in his Journal; "we reason from our hands to our heads." But man's experience with and knowledge of these natural facts was codified for his more or less systematic apprehension in two forms of reference that offered Thoreau further "vehicles of thought," both significant adjuncts to the universality suggested by nature. One was history and the other geography— geography as that inclusive subject which Thoreau's day knew. Of the two, the latter was for Thoreau probably the more significant. It was usually the geographical facts of man's life which Thoreau culled from history to emphasize the timelessness of man's universal experiences. The kind of history that most concerned him was not that of trends, evolutions or movements of peoples, not so much that of chronology of human events as the immediacy of man's way of life, the full and honest picture, with the details left in, of man's intimate struggle with matter and spirit. The past was only important for Thoreau as it was for Emerson, as it showed "how far the process has gone, of transmitting life into truth." [1] Thus the histories written by early travelers formed the largest bulk of Thoreau's history reading: works of such "historians" as Beverley, John Smith, Charlevoix, Crantz, Lawson, Lescarbot, Montanus, Tschudi, and Sagard. We come back to the preeminence of geography for him.

That the facts of geography should become for him symbols of abstract qualities and ideas, even of spiritual values, in addition to being illustrations of analogous physical phenomena, was to be expected of a metaphysician and a Transcendentalist. Over and over again his geographical knowledge contributed appropriate means for symbolizing the qualities of mind and spirit which were his ultimate subject matter. The river Platte became symbol for the shallow life "tinkling over its sands," versts and steppes stood for the impassable boundaries of intelligence and faith between peoples, the Sahara was the emptiness which a man sees anywhere as a result of the barrenness of his own experience.[2] Mountains the world over became "stepping-stones to heaven . . . by which we gradually take our departure from earth." [3] Such instances are familiar to readers of his works. We need only keep in mind how rife his pages are with them. Geographical data served, like Whitman's grass, as universal hieroglyphics of spiritual truth.

More important, Thoreau's travel reading gave him for symbols not only the substance of his global familiarity, its details, but the very concepts of travel itself: of voyaging, of exploration and discovery. The literal means of encompassing the physical world came to stand vividly for their figurative counterparts in the coverage of man's inner life, the theme of all Thoreau's works. The navigator's relation to undiscovered islands in the sea represented Thoreau's to the spiritual discoveries in his native fields.[4] The terra firma of geography became symbol for his concept of those solid grounds in society "whose port you make by dead reckoning to all weather. All the rest are but floating and fabulous Atlantides which sometimes skirt the western horizon of our intercourse. They impose only on seasick mariners who have put into some Canary Island on the frontiers of society." [5] When he wrote of the "great and glorious experience" which the ideal emancipation from ties of Past and Present could offer men, he couched it entirely in terms of voyaging, of winds and cargoes, reefs and Indiamen, and shipwrecked mariners on a desolate island.[6] The Concord River upon which he sailed took on metaphysical import: "This current allies me to all the world. . . . Its channel conducts our thought as well as our bodies to classic and famous ports, and allies us to all that is fair and great. . . . A river is superior to a lake in its liberating influence. It has motion and indefinite length." [7]

Rivers symbolized that meditative release necessary for metaphysical thinking, while the journeys on them symbolized the philosophic search itself. No reader could expect less from a week spent voyaging with Thoreau.

The concepts of exploration and discovery underwent similar transformations. Thoreau advanced upon the realms of the night as explorer and discoverer. A sixteenth-century exploring expedition stood for Thoreau's life, and the planning hand behind the venture became symbol for the inexplicable power which served him.

> No matter what imprudent haste in my career; I am permitted to be rash. Gulfs are bridged in a twinkling, as if some unseen baggage train carried pontoons for my convenience, and while from the heights I scan the tempting but unexplored Pacific Ocean of Futurity, the ship is being carried over the mountains piecemeal on the backs of mules and llamas, whose keel shall plow its waves, and bear me to the Indies.[8]

Geographic exploration became his most consistently used symbol for philosophic search. As early as 1840 he was declaring in his Journal that "to travel and 'descry new lands' is to think new thoughts and have new imaginings." [9] The unexplored became his own untried enterprises. "To an adventurous spirit any place—London, New York, Worcester, or his own yard—is 'unexplored land,' to seek which Fremont and Kane travel so far." [10] The concept of travel became the single most reiterated and conspicuous symbol in all of Thoreau's writings: the title "traveler" became "the best symbol" for all earnest living—"a going from—toward"; and life was best symbolized by a "journey." Man should enter his house as a khan or caravansary and make all his meals of journeycake and hasty pudding.[11]

And to what end all this symbolization through such a multitude of geographical analogies, and more particularly through this basic equation of life with travel? The analogies were sufficient to shoulder many truths, of course, and did. But one paramount message pulls them all together, even as Thoreau's very resources for such analogies help to confirm its truth: namely, that the only "provincialism" is of the mind. This conviction is more intelligibly central to the philosophy of Henry Thoreau than many of the more familiarly tapped Transcendental doctrines by which he is so often underexplained. It is as close to absolute as any value which Thoreau could bring himself to believe. Of all the opinions he expressed, this one was most consistently and persistently maintained, a "constant" in his life, a working premise, a usable truth. Henry James, together with all those who have charged Thoreau with parochialism, should have heeded it well, for one can not charge failure of the man in this regard without striking at the very core of his intent. "These continents and hemispheres are soon run over—but an always unexplored and infinite region makes off on every side from the mind, further than Cathay." [12] This was a truth to the proof of which Thoreau dedicated his life and art. He tried to show his own success in achieving such "cosmopolitanism" and thus his right to reassure others of its rewards. To miss this message is to read him without listening to him.

In the spaces of thought are the reaches of land and water over which men go and come. The landscape lies fair within. The deepest and most original thinker is the farthest travelled.

(Journal, August 13, 1840)

Go where we will on the *surface* of things, men have been there before us . . . and our boundaries have literally been run to the South Seas, on the old patents. . . . The frontiers are not east or west, north or south; but wherever a man fronts a fact.

(A *Week*, 1849)

The excursions of the imagination are so boundless, the limits of towns so petty.

(Journal, September 20, 1851)

I demand of my companion some evidence that he has traveled further than the sources of the Nile. . . . You call yourself a great traveler, perhaps, but can you get beyond the influence of a certain class of ideas?

(Journal, January 11, 1857)

We come in the end to *Walden*. We have of course been looking at it all along. Thoreau's first book, *A Week on the Concord and Merrimack Rivers*, had converted the obvious activity of travel and voyaging into a structural metaphor for self-exploration. Thoreau's account of his trip into the Maine woods offered the metaphor of the exploration of the primitive and the wilderness, which in turn stood for exploration of the will, of the self's freedom, of those qualities preserving the human race, the sources of one's fresh identity and renewed selfhood. "Cape Cod" converted the great human dramas of first discoveries (of seas and of continents) into the metaphor for perpetual renewal of man's questing spirit in its search for new Atlantises in discoverable worlds of thought. But no book that Thoreau wrote made more effective structural use of the analogy of travel— this time all phases of it—than *Walden*. To study nature; to know thyself: these were synonymous activities for Thoreau as for Emerson. To explore oneself through an exploration of the natural world —that total world of the geographer, its natural features and its human environmental phenomena together—this was a route so characteristically Thoreau's that its definition in the analogy which unified *Walden* already seemed familiar and unobtrusive by 1854. To write a travel book about a traveler who explores one place thoroughly, that he may thereby discover the resources of his own nature and spirit, is only the logical extension of the metaphor toward which all Thoreau's travel experience pointed. Thoreau had foreseen the implications of the metaphor from the very start of his Walden experience; as he wrote soberly in his first travel book, "True and sincere traveling is no pastime, but it is as serious as the grave, or any part of the human journey." [13] Matthiessen called *Walden* one of the firmest products in our literature of the "life-giving analogies" between the processes of art and daily living. [14] It also stands as Thoreau's best concrete expression of living at home "like a traveler." Seen in this light, the book is Thoreau's characteristic presentation of truth through paradox, an account of a traveler's stay in one place. We commenced our study of Thoreau with a paradox; it is fitting to conclude by looking at another. But it is not entirely another, as we can see, but only our original one removed to the tenth power, now translated to the conceptual level where its contradictions for Thoreau could be resolved under the shaping influences of his imagination.

Even on the literal level, of course, there is "travel" all the time in this book. Its author moves about more often than he sits still, and the greatest proportion of sitting which he talks about takes place in an object symbolic of motion, a boat. Without distorting the solidity of Thoreau's experiences *at* Walden Pond, it is worth while to remind ourselves at once of the constant presence of the traveler on the scene.

Thoreau presents his arguments in the first chapter as communications to his fellow townsmen from one who has "traveled a good deal in Concord." He would have them guide their lives as the sailor who keeps the polestar in his eye. His second chapter begins with an account of his own rejection of place, the Hollowell Farm; its real attraction for him was his recollection of a voyager's impressions of it. He would say to his fellows, "once for all, as long as possible live free and uncommitted." The only house he ever had before his present one, he reminds us, was either a boat or a tent. When he comes to speaking of exactly "What I Lived For," his analogies work further paradoxes. With as stolid and rooted an image as one could ask for, he describes his aim in the following exhortation: "Let us . . . work and wedge our feet downward through the mud and slush of opinion, and prejudice, and tradition, and delusion, and appearances, that alluvion which covers the globe . . . till we come to a hard bottom and rocks in place, which we call *reality*, and say, This is, and no mistake." But note the analogies with which he fills up the rest of the paragraph to illustrate his meaning.[15] The "work" he has in mind is forthwith likened to train travel, to boat travel (downstream and through rapids), to the climbing of mountains, to hikes downhill, and to the sailing over seas with Ulysses.

The next four chapters, concerned as they seem to be with experiences "on location" and with states of being, show similar tendencies to move with the traveler. Thoreau's reading finds him under the influence of books which circulate round the world; he does not wonder that Alexander carried the *Iliad* with him on his expeditions. The chapter "Sounds," although it expresses his respect for an Oriental contemplation, reflects primarily his fascination with the trains which link him to so much more than society. He crosses their tracks like a cart path in the wilderness; he is traveling, too, but his route goes another way. "Solitude" is filled with walks along the stony shore of the pond; the long rainstorms in the spring and fall which confine him to his house "for afternoon as well as forenoon" are unusual interruptions of regular excursions. Among his visitors is "many a traveler" coming out of his way to see his house and, as an "excuse for calling," asking for a drink of water.

Chapters VII through X are organized geographically, moving the reader outward from Walden as Thoreau himself moves from his beanfield to his woods, to the village, "still further westward . . . 'to fresh woods and pastures new' "; [16] to Goose Pond, Flint's Pond, White Pond, Fair Haven, and Baker Farm. In chapters XI and XII we are reminded of Thoreau's theories on travel: just as one journeying on the prairie is naturally a hunter, and on the headwaters of the Missouri and Columbia a trapper, the author describes how he, too, was once a hunter, how now he fishes, and so like the best travelers makes closest acquaintance with nature. Chapter XIII sees him going "a-graping to the river meadows" and, as the pond freezes over, skating, wood gathering, and walking (walks on which for many weeks he meets no one at all). "No weather interfered fatally with my walks, or rather my going abroad, for I frequently tramped eight or ten miles through the deepest snow to keep an appointment with a beech tree." [17] So he continues moving, taking his trips "abroad" to all the cellar holes in the region, back to Flint's Pond and Goose Pond, to the Lincoln Hills, to Lincoln; and then, with the chapter "The Pond in Winter," he brings the reader full circle back with him to Walden Pond and the concrete minutiae that characterize this central eye of water, now with its white eyelid shut, this cynosure, the place he started from in the second chapter. Even the cycle of the seasons, which in the chapter "Spring" serves to universalize time (making the day an epitome of a year, the year symbolic of a life), is finally fused with Thoreau's own walks that keep pace with all migrations to new pastures of life: "And so the seasons went rolling on into summer, as we ramble into higher and higher grass." [18]

Thus in this "Journal" of Everyman's life the groundwork is laid on a literal level for the role which travel is to play symbolically in the final chapter. The "Conclusion" to *Walden*, significantly enough, is not the universalizing of time (already achieved in the preceding chapter) but the universalizing of place. "The universe is wider than our views of it," the author reminds us. "The other side of the globe is but the home of our correspondent. Our voyaging is only a great-circle sailing." The final justification for Thoreau's whole philosophy of life is presented to us as but the other side of the traveler's coin:

> If you would learn to speak all tongues and conform to the customs of all nations, if you would travel farther than all travelers, be naturalized

in all climes, and cause the Sphinx to dash her head against a stone, even obey the precept of the old philosopher, and Explore thyself.[19]

The "thousand regions" which lie at hand "yet undiscovered" challenge one to be expert in "home-cosmography." All Thoreau's experiences at Walden Pond have led to the paramount recognition that life is exploration and discovery and that any place where a universal truth is experienced is a microcosm of the world. This realization he now makes the climactic theme of his book.

The effectiveness of such a theme depended peculiarly upon the skill with which its author employed the resources furnished by his travel reading. Thoreau availed himself in *Walden* of all the ingredients of place we have hitherto seen him using—the local and the global, the small and the large, the near and the remote, the voyaging, the exploring, the discovering. While grounding his philosophic search at Walden Pond, he took care to hook the particularities of this place with their geographical counterparts around the globe, to harmonize his most local experience with the most far-reaching. He turned the Musketaquid Valley into "the Oriental Asiatic valley of my world," the seat of life. The opposite shore of Walden Pond stretched away toward the prairies of the West and the steppes of Tartary without demarcation.[20] The extraordinary expansion which closes Chapter XVI mingled the pure Walden water with the sacred water of the Ganges; Thoreau's well symbolized all the wells of the world at which men drink, even as its waters flowed to the farthest ends of the earth. The pond at his doorstep became a Mediterranean Sea, a small ocean. In the final chapter of the book he drove home his theme by equating the most concentrated living with the most expansive travel. The exploration of one's own being became no less than the exploration of new "streams" and "oceans" and "higher latitudes," leading to the discovery of "whole new continents and worlds." [21] The mind's adventure was symbolized by means of as rich an assortment of travelers, travels, and foreign places as Thoreau ever presented in one place in his writings. And the reader was finally urged to be nothing less than a perpetual voyager and explorer, to "start now on that farthest western way, which does not pause at the Mississippi or the Pacific, nor conduct toward a worn-out China or Japan, but leads on direct, a tangent to the sphere, summer and winter, day and night, sun down, moon down, and at last earth down too." [22]

So traveler and philosopher were made one. The view from Thoreau's cabin door, as that from any man's, though physically contracted, offered ample vision of those continents and hemispheres of the mind to which all the phenomena of the physical globe but pointed. As Thoreau had said many years before, "The universe is a sphere whose center is wherever there is intelligence. The sun is not so central as a man." [23]

Notes

The following abbreviated forms of reference are used in the notes:

Canby, *Thoreau*	Henry Seidel Canby, *Thoreau* (Boston, 1939)
Correspondence	Carl Bode and Walter Harding, eds., *The Correspondence of Henry David Thoreau* (New York, 1958)
Journal	Bradford Torrey and Francis H. Allen, eds., *The Journal of Henry D. Thoreau* (Walden Edition; Boston and New York, 1906). Vols. I–XIV
Miller, *Consciousness*	Perry Miller, *Consciousness in Concord: The Text of Thoreau's Hitherto Lost Journal (1840–1841)* (Boston, 1958)
Walden	Vol. II of *The Writings of Henry David Thoreau* (Walden Edition; Boston and New York, 1906)
Week	*A Week on the Concord and Merrimack Rivers.* Vol. I of *The Writings of Henry David Thoreau* (Walden Edition; Boston and New York, 1906)
Writings	*The Writings of Henry David Thoreau* (Walden Edition; Boston and New York, 1906). Vols. III–VI

Notes

Chapter I: Departure and Return

1. *Journal*, I, 471. 2. *Ibid.*, IX, 104.
3. *Ibid.*, III, 255. 4. *Ibid.*, V, 496.
5. "Henry David Thoreau," *Atlantic Monthly*, X (Aug., 1862), 239–49.
6. Review of *Letters to Various Persons, Atlantic Monthly*, XVI (Oct., 1865), 504–5.
7. Review of W. E. Channing's *Thoreau, the Poet-Naturalist, Atlantic Monthly*, XXXIII (Feb., 1874), 230–31.
8. Quoted from *Birds and Poets* and *Signs and Seasons* by John Burroughs, *Atlantic Monthly*, XL (July, 1877), 113, and *Century*, XXV (March, 1883), 673.
9. Review of "April Days," *Nation*, XXVI (March 28, 1878), 214.
10. Henry James, *Hawthorne* (London, 1879), pp. 96–97. This did not represent James's whole or final view of Thoreau, of course; cf. *The American Scene* (New York, 1907), p. 264: "We may smile a little as we 'drag in' Weimar, but I confess myself, for my part, much more satisfied than not by our happy equivalent, 'in American money,' for Goethe and Schiller. The money is a potful in the second case as in the first, and if Goethe, in the one, represents the gold and Schiller the silver, I find (and quite putting aside any bimetallic prejudice) the same good relation in the other between Emerson and Thoreau. I open Emerson for the same benefit for which I open Goethe, the sense of moving in large intellectual space, and that of the gush, here and there, out of the rock, of the crystalline cupful, in wisdom and poetry, in Wahrheit and Dichtung; and whatever I open Thoreau for (I needn't take space here for the good reasons) I open him oftener than I open Schiller."

11. Review of "Summer," *Atlantic Monthly,* LIV (Aug., 1884), 286.
12. F. B. Sanborn, "The Maintenance of a Poet," *Atlantic Monthly,* LXXXVI (Dec., 1900), 820.
13. The remark is attributed to Elizabeth Hoar by Channing in his *Thoreau, the Poet-Naturalist* (Boston, 1873), p. 341.
14. See F. B. Sanborn, *The First and Last Journeys of Thoreau* (Boston, 1905), Vol. II, for Thoreau's record of the trip. The original MS is in the Huntington Library, "Note on a Journey from Concord, Mass., to Minnesota and Return" (HM13192), and should be consulted to correct liberties taken by the editor. See also R. L. Straker, "Thoreau's Journey to Minnesota," *New England Quarterly,* XIV (Sept., 1932), 549–55.
15. See Walter Harding's "A Check List of Thoreau's Lectures," *Bulletin of the New York Public Library,* LII (Feb., 1948), 78–87.
16. *Correspondence,* p. 24. Three years later Thoreau was still inquiring about the West but this time receiving quite different reassurance from his former schoolteaching friend and Concord neighbor Isaiah Williams, who had been to Ohio: "You are ready to ask—how I like the West. I must answer—not very well—I love New England so much that the West is comparatively odious to me. . . . If I were in New England again I would never leave her" (*Correspondence,* p. 49).
17. Sanborn, *First and Last Journeys of Thoreau,* I, 2–3.
18. *Correspondence,* p. 112.   19. *Ibid.,* pp. 102, 116.
20. Nathaniel Hawthorne, *American Notebooks,* ed. Randall Stewart (New Haven, 1932), p. 175.
21. *Ibid.,* pp. 166–68.   22. *Ibid.,* p. 320, n. 410.
23. *Walden,* pp. 5, 91–93, 352. "The nearest that I came to actual possession was when I bought the Hollowell place . . . but before the owner gave me a deed to it, his wife . . . changed her mind and wished to keep it, and he offered me ten dollars to release him. . . . However, I let him keep the ten dollars and the farm too, for I had carried it far enough" (p. 91).
24. Letter to Horatio Bridge, Concord, May 3, 1843: *The Portable Hawthorne,* ed. Malcolm Cowley (New York, 1948), pp. 618–19.
25. Canby, *Thoreau,* p. 144: "On May 1 he was off." J. W. Krutch, *Henry David Thoreau* ("American Men of Letters Series"; New York, 1948), p. 63: "When on May 1, 1843, Thoreau set off. . . ."
26. *Correspondence,* pp. 98–99.
27. Thoreau's music box, in these particular weeks of his life, is like the proverbial pea under the shell. Upon the arrival of the Hawthornes in Concord, Thoreau came at least twice to listen to their music box (*American Notebooks,* p. 145); later he went for the express purpose of borrowing it, only to have Mrs. Hawthorne lend it to him volun-

tarily (*Correspondence*, p. 76). It furnished particular comfort to him in his own home (according to Edward Emerson, *Henry Thoreau* [Boston and New York, 1917], p. 88). In January of 1843 Richard Fuller sent him one of his own as a present (*Correspondence*, p. 76), which he loaned Hawthorne on his April 7 visit ("left in my keeping," Hawthorne says, *American Notebooks*, p. 175) but which Hawthorne seems to have appreciated less than its owner (perhaps in contrast to his wife's music box?): "Many times I wound and rewound Mr. Thoreau's little musical box; but certainly its peculiar sweetness has evaporated, and I am pretty sure that I should throw it out of the window, were I doomed to hear it long and often. It has not an infinite soul." It must have been returned shortly to Thoreau, for on Sept. 28 on Staten Island he was listening to it (see text, p. 19). (Cf. Van Wyck Brooks, *The Flowering of New England* [New York, 1937], p. 282: "The music-box at the Manse belonged to Thoreau, Henry David Thoreau, the pencil-maker, Emerson's protege, who had gone to Staten Island for a visit, to tutor the children of Emerson's brother William.")

28. *Correspondence*, pp. 98–99.
29. *Ibid.*, p. 99.   30. *Ibid.*, p. 141.
31. *Ibid.*, p. 100.   32. *Ibid.*, p. 107.
33. Letter to Lidian Emerson, *ibid.*, pp. 119–20.
34. *Week*, p. 253.
35. *Correspondence*, pp. 143 and 124.   36. *Ibid.*, p. 131.
37. Cf. Thoreau's letter to Lidian Emerson from Staten Island, June 30: "My actual life is unspeakably mean, compared with what I know and see that it might be—Yet the ground from which I see and say this is some part of it" (*ibid.*, p. 120).
38. *Ibid.*, p. 125.   39. *Ibid.*, pp. 99–100.
40. Huntington Journal Fragments (HM13182): Journal fragments of the 1840s including personal comments on love and friendship and a fifty-page journal of the Staten Island episode, a holograph MS now in the Henry E. Huntington Library, San Marino, California. It was printed in part and inaccurately by Sanborn, *First and Last Journeys of Thoreau*, I, 64–117.
41. *Correspondence*, pp. 141 and 142.
42. Huntington Journal Fragments.

Chapter II: The Substitute Route

1. In the "Working Index" to the geographical references in Thoreau's published and unpublished writings which it was necessary to make for this study, there appear some 500 proper names of "foreign" places (i.e., those outside the United States), in addition to over 100

places within Thoreau's own country but beyond the boundaries of his firsthand knowledge. The "Index" as a whole runs to 108 pages and identifies some 2,200 separate geographical references.

2. For anyone interested in pursuing the specific foreign references cited in this paragraph, their sources follow in the order cited in the text: *Journal*, II, 368; *ibid.*, III, 161; *ibid.*, II, 209; *ibid.*, II, 388, 296; *ibid.*, I, 434–35, 147–48; *Week*, p. 246; *Journal*, II, 233; *ibid.*, I, 40, 305, 422, 308; *Week*, p. 279; *Journal*, I, 343, 346; *Week*, p. 113; *Journal*, I, 308, 38, 368; *Week*, p. 54; *Journal*, I, 309, and *Week*, p. 96; *Journal*, I, 23; *Week*, p. 243; *Journal*, II, 5, 261; *Week*, pp. 345–46.

Except for occasional trips to Provincetown, Nantucket, and around Long Island, Thoreau indulged his interests in sea voyages only at second hand. His library contained books on navigation that had belonged to his grandfather, the immigrant John Thoreau, who traded in Boston up to 1776 and privateered during the American Revolution.

3. Letter to Parker Pillsbury, April 10, 1861; *Correspondence*, p. 611. Cf. Channing's well-known apologia for Thoreau, that "usually all the popular books were sealed volumes to him" (*Thoreau, the Poet-Naturalist* [Boston, 1873], p. 58).

4. Thoreau had withdrawn Sir George Back's *Narrative of the Arctic Land Expedition* (London and Philadelphia, 1836) from the Harvard Library in 1837; see Kenneth W. Cameron's record of Thoreau's withdrawals from Harvard between 1833 and 1860, *Emerson the Essayist* (Raleigh, N.C., 1945), II, 191–208.

5. For the full titles of travel works read by Thoreau, the reader is referred to the Bibliography. Except where fuller description seems relevant, references in the text and the notes are shortened. Since this "Bibliography of Travel Works Read by Thoreau" also lists the references in Thoreau's writings to each individual travel work, such sources are not necessarily repeated in the notes.

6. Aside from general statements about the role of the Journal in Thoreau's routine (Canby, *Thoreau*, pp. 307–9) and Torrey's introductory remarks in the published edition of 1906 (*Journal*, I, v–viii), little specific study of the manuscript Journal has been reflected in discussions of it. Perry Miller's Introduction to his edition of the heretofore missing third volume (*Consciousness*), offers some orientation in the early Journal.

7. *Journal*, I, 207.

8. References are frequent in the Journal to Thoreau's laborious and exacting pruning, as in this December 27, 1853, entry: "I wish that I could buy at the shop some kind of india-rubber that would rub out at once all that in my writing which it now cost me so many

perusals, so many months if not years, and so much reluctance, to erase."

9. See Perry Miller, *Consciousness*, pp. 19–27, for discussions of these pre-Journal versions—the "Ur-Journal" as Miller termed them—and their correlation with the Journal itself of the early forties.

10. Thoreau's withdrawals from the library of the Society of Natural History in Boston are reported by Kenneth W. Cameron, "Emerson, Thoreau, and the Society of Natural History," *American Literature*, XXIV (March, 1952), 21–30.

11. Widener Extract Book, p. 190. See note 20 below.

12. Parts I and II of Herndon's *Exploration* appear on Thoreau's inventory of his own library (Index Rerum, in the Huntington Library, reprinted with some inaccuracies of transcription by F. P. Sanborn, *Henry David Thoreau* [Boston, 1917], pp. 505–17). See also Walter Harding, *Thoreau's Library* (Charottesville, Va., 1957), p. 58.

13. *Journal*, I, 413.

14. Arthur Christy, *The Orient in American Transcendentalism* (New York, 1932), p. 281.

15. *Journal*, VII, 480.

16. The ten holograph notebooks containing references to Thoreau's travel reading are the following: in the Huntington Library, the Index Rerum for 1836–60 (HM945), a Commonplace Book for 1836–41 (HM13201), and the Notes of the Minnesota Trip, May 4–July 10, 1862 (HM13192), printed by F. P. Sanborn for the Bibliophile Society, *The First and Last Journeys of Thoreau* (Boston, 1905); in the Library of Congress, a Literary Notebook for 1840–48, printed in facsimile by Kenneth W. Cameron (Hartford: Transcendental Books, n.d.); in the Widener Collection of the Harvard Library, the first volume of an Extract Book upon natural history for 1851–58 (labeled in catalogue "1853–1858"); in the Berg Collection of the New York Public Library, the second volume of the Extract Book for 1858–60 (173768B); in the Morgan Library, the Canadian Notebook of extracts relating to Canada, dated "1850" (MA595), a College Notebook of miscellaneous extracts and notes of the 1830s (MA594), edited by Kenneth Cameron, *The Transcendentalists and Minerva* (Hartford, 1958), I, 130–358, a Notebook of Reflections concerning for the most part the contrast between modes of thought of East and West, dated approximately 1846–47 (MA608), and the Indian Notebook, 11 volumes of extracts from 1851 to 1860 (MA596–606). Although manuscripts are formally identified in the documentation, I have sometimes used Thoreau's more descriptive titles for them in the text.

17. See Widener Extract Book, pp. 5–9; Indian Notebook 3 (MA598).

18. *Journal*, XIV, 86. See Albert Keiser, "Thoreau's Manuscripts on the

Indians," *Journal of English and Germanic Philology*, XXVII (Second Quarter, 1928), 183–99.

19. *Journal*, IX, 74.

20. The two notebooks are undated and unsigned; the volume in the Widener Collection has 358 pages, that in the Berg has 280. Arthur Christy discussed the larger volume rather cursorily in "A Thoreau Fact-Book," *Colophon*, Vol. IV, Part XVI (March, 1934), but he made no mention of the companion volume. That the latter is a continuation of the earlier notebook is clear from the chronology of the contents of the two (the Widener volume contains excerpts from reading done between 1851 and 1858, the Berg volume covers that done from 1858 through 1860) and from the similarity in content and in the titles given them by Thoreau ("Extracts, Mostly from Natural History" for the Widener volume, "Extracts mostly upon Natural History" for the Berg volume).

21. Thoreau frequently stressed the subjective character of his Journal: "In a journal it is important in a few words to describe the weather, or character of the day, as it affects our feelings. That which is so important at the time cannot be unimportant to remember" (*Journal*, VII, 171). Cf. also his fuller statements on the value of his Journal as the place where he could "set down such choice experiences that my own writing may inspire me and at last I may make whole parts. . . . Each thought that is welcomed and recorded is a nest egg, by the side of which more will be laid. Thoughts accidentally thrown together become a frame in which more may be developed and exhibited. Perhaps this is the main value of a habit of writing, of keeping a journal" (*Journal*, III, 217). Or earlier still: "My Journal should be the record of my love. I would write in it only of the things I love, my affection for any aspect of the world, what I love to think of. I have no more distinctness or pointedness in my yearnings than an expanding bud, which does indeed point to flower and fruit, to summer and autumn, but is aware of the warm sun and spring influences only. I feel ripe for something, yet do nothing, can't discover what that thing is. I feel fertile merely. It is seedtime with me. I have lain fallow long enough" (*Journal*, II, 101).

22. See below, p. 301, note 11, for graphic evidence of the precipitousness with which Thoreau sometimes made his transcriptions.

23. Widener Extract Book, pp. 81, 19, 302, 119, 28; Berg Extract Book, pp. 4, 236.

24. *Journal*, XIV, 211.

25. Emerson, "The American Scholar," *Complete Works* (Boston and New York, 1903), I, 85.

Chapter III: The Summing Up

1. The total figures cited in this chapter represent the minimum number of works read by Thoreau; my bibliography of his travel reading must not be considered definitive.
2. Excerpts from both Andersson and Swan appear in Indian Notebook 9 (MA604).
3. Berg Extract Book (173768B), pp. 244–47.
4. Kenneth W. Cameron (*Emerson the Essayist* [Raleigh, N.C., 1945], II, 191–208) finds no withdrawals by Thoreau from the Harvard Library between 1837 and 1849 except for the year 1841, when he took out considerable Elizabethan literature. There is no record of book withdrawals by him after 1860.
5. Of 34 works borrowed by Thoreau from the Society of Natural History in Boston during the years 1851, 1852, 1853, 1854, 1858, and 1859 (Kenneth W. Cameron, "Emerson, Thoreau, and the Society of Natural History," *American Literature*, XXIV [March, 1952], 21–30), 4 were travel books.
6. For Thoreau's own inventory of his library, see Index Rerum (HM945), the large commonplace book in the Huntington Library. F. P. Sanborn prints (with some inaccuracies) Thoreau's listing in his *Henry David Thoreau* (Boston, 1917), "Appendix A," pp. 505–17. See also Walter Harding, *Thoreau's Library* (Charlottesville, Va., 1957).

   Thoreau often listed the "spine" title of a work in listing his own books, a practice which has led at times to errors in identification. The reader is referred to the annotated Bibliography of Travel Works Read by Thoreau for some instances in which I have differed with Professor Harding's identifications (see bibliographical entries under Hunter, Perry, Richardson, Rivero, Sitgreaves, and Tytler). Professor Harding assumed that the "Colorado Exploring Expedition 1 v." listed in Sophia Thoreau's hand was a duplicate listing of Thoreau's own earlier entry of "Sitgreaves' Exped. Zuni & Colorado Rs. 1 v." While I have not been able to make a positive identification, the "spine" title of Sitgreaves' 1853 edition from which Thoreau copied his excerpts does not match Sophia's title; I have therefore included this second entry as an additional but as yet unidentified work.

   "Locations" cited for books in *Thoreau's Library* need to be corrected for a number of books which are in the Berg Collection of the New York Public Library (the two autographed Pietro Bachi editions, the autographed 1856 edition of Gray's *Manual of Botany*, and the autographed Harlan's *Fauna Americana*, for instance).

7. "Have you met with the letter of a Turkish cadi at the end of Layard's 'Ancient Babylon'? That also is refreshing, and a capital comment on the whole book which precedes it,—the Oriental genius speaking through him" (Letter to Harrison Blake, Dec. 22, 1853, *Correspondence*, p. 313). A copy of the cadi's letter appears in the Berg Extract Book; see also text, pp. 140–41.

8. *The Travels and Researches of Alexander von Humboldt*, by William Macgillivray (New York, 1842), No. LIX in Harper's Family Library.

9. *Journal*, III, 248–51.

10. HM934: a manuscript in the Huntington Library containing seven of Thoreau's early essays; also in Sanborn, *Thoreau*.

11. A record of the the minimum number of new travel books read during the decade of the 1850s, totaled by year, runs as follows: 1850, 5; 1851, 13; 1852, 19; 1853, 7; 1854, 17; 1855, 17; 1856, 14; 1857, 11; 1858, 12; 1859, 7; 1860, 10. The profile represents Thoreau's usual well-balanced coverage of varied areas of the world. Although he read more travel works on his own country than on any other single region of the world, he read more books on voyages of circumnavigation and foreign discovery than he did accounts of America. Such special interests at special times in Thoreau's life as his interest in Mexico stirred by the Mexican War or his early interest in Eastern thought do not make obvious grooves in the pattern of his travel reading. During the former period he read more travel books on Africa than on Mexico; during the latter, more on South America than on Asia.

12. *Correspondence*, p. 613.

13. Victor von Hagen, *South America Called Them* (New York, 1945), p. 160.

14. Solon J. Buck, *Travel and Description, 1765–1865,* in *Collections of the Illinois State Historical Library* (Springfield, Ill., 1914); Ralph Rusk, *The Literature of the Middle Western Frontier* (New York, 1925).

15. Even without endeavoring any systematic coverage of Thoreau's reading of travel accounts in the periodicals of his day, one can not avoid entering a labryinth of footpaths through a wide assortment of both popular and specialized journals, as well as in current newspapers, indicating an unexplored corollary to Thoreau's reading in travel books.

Thoreau acknowledges a "reviewer" as specific source for his quotation from Ross's *Voyage of Discovery* (*Week*, pp. 390–91), as he also does with the Botta references (*Journal*, I, 343; *Week*, pp. 107, 130). Arthur Christy (*The Orient in American Transcendentalism* [New York, 1932] p. 306), ascribed Thoreau's quotations by mistake to Botta's original article, therefore including it in his bibliography of works on the East read by the Transcendentalists; but there appears to be no direct evidence that Thoreau read Botta's original piece.

The first appearance of the Botta reference in Thoreau's recently published Journal for 1840–41 (Miller, *Consciousness*, pp. 133–34) a full year before Thoreau read the Botta review to which it refers, emphasizes once again the necessity for distinguishing carefully between the actual body of Thoreau's chronological Journal record and that material recorded momentarily and "out of order" in margins, flyleaves, or front cover linings (where this reference actually appears; see Miller's note, p. 134). We must conclude that these "momentary impulses," as Miller identifies them, were not only recorded in pencil (as Miller noted) but were apparently jotted down at any time. The flyleaves were available for marginalia at any time; in this instance, both entries (on the flyleaf and in the 1842 Journal) are at the most no further than a few weeks apart, both recorded after Thoreau's reading of the *Athenaeum* review.

Chapter IV: The Voyageur Sublimed

1. Letter to Harrison Blake, Jan. 1, 1859, *Correspondence*, p. 538.
2. *Journal*, I, 424.
3. *Collected Poems of Henry Thoreau*, ed. Carl Bode (Chicago, 1943), p. 239.
4. *Journal*, IV, 80, 249; V, 74, 342; VI, 271.
5. "A Winter Walk," *Writings*, V, 177; *Journal*, III, 178.
6. *Journal*, I, 305–6; V, 211–12.
7. In the *Journal* (V, 242–43) Thoreau records the following about his grandfather: "I remember Helen's telling me that John Marston of Taunton told her that he was on board a vessel, during the Revolution, which met another vessel,—and, as I think, one hailed the other,—and a French name being given could not be understood, whereupon a sailor, probably aboard his vessel, ran out on the bowsprit and shouted 'La Sensible,' and that sailor's name was Thoreau. My father tells me that, when the war was on, my grandfather, being thrown out of business and being a young man, went a-privateering." For Thoreau's references to his Scandinavian origins, see *Journal*, III, 304–5, and IX, 352.

For Thoreau's effectiveness as a teller of the "tales of Norsemen of adventure by sea and land," see Walter Harding, *Thoreau: Man of Concord* (New York, 1960), pp. 178–79. Thoreau left vivid responses to the seamen he encounterd on land, as in the following description in the *Week* (p.257): "Sometimes there sits the brother who follows the sea, their representative man, who knows only how far it is to the nearest port, no more distances, all the rest is sea and distant capes,—patting the dog, or dangling the kitten in arms that were stretched by the cable and the oar, pulling against Boreas or the trade winds."

8. Canby, *Thoreau*, p. 377.
9. *Journal*, VI, 299; IV, 261; III, 73; V, 404. Cf. Melville's viewpoint expressed a year earlier (*Moby-Dick*, ed. Luther S. Mansfield and Howard P. Vincent [New York, 1952], pp. 3–4).
10. *Journal*, VII, 450; VIII, 389–90.
11. "Cape Cod," *Writings*, IV, 178–79.
12. *Walden*, pp. 132–34. A New England cellar reminded Thoreau "of travelers' stories of the London docks, of rows of hogsheads, of bonded liquors" (*Journal*, XIII, 249).
13. *Week*, pp. 222–25.
14. *Journal*, VI, 25–26.
15. *Journals of Ralph Waldo Emerson*, ed. E. W. Emerson and W. E. Forbes (Boston and New York, 1912), VII, 386. For samples of Thoreau's own self-titling, see *Journal*, III, 51, 308; IV, 29, 106, 114, 131, 132, 135, etc.
16. See *Correspondence*, pp. 155–56, 489–90.
17. *Journal*, XI, 55, 226.
18. *Ibid.*, I, 11.   19. *Ibid.*, IX, 225–26.
20. Evariste Huc, *Recollections of a Journey through Tartary, Thibet, and China* (New York, 1852), II, 93–95. Thoreau also read in another travel account (Joseph Wolff's *A Narrative of a Mission to Bokhara* [New York, 1845], p. 114) that "the stables in Turkey have elevations made on purpose for travellers, where they are not exposed to the danger of being kicked by the horses, and these elevated places are pretty clean."
21. "Chesuncook," *Writings*, III, 97.
22. Cf. Emerson's familiar reminder in his funeral eulogy of Thoreau: "He . . . could have been competent to lead a Pacific Exploring Expedition." See also "A Yankee in Canada," *Writings*, V, 31–32.
23. See Huntington Notes of Trip to Minnesota (HM13192): "Notes on a Journey from Concord, Mass., to Minnesota and Return," partially reprinted in F. B. Sanborn, *The First and Last Journeys of Thoreau* (Boston, 1905), Vol. II. A general inventory listed "Best pants, 3 pr socks, Flannel short, 1 pr drawers, cotton bathing, 5 handchks +2, Towel & soap, medicine, compass & microscope, spy glass, insect boxes, clothes brush, 1 slippers, 3 shirts, 5 (+1) bosoms"; further items are broken down by location: included in "carpet bag" are a "Half-thick coat, waist coat, smoke cap, Botony

Time & card—pencil, buttons, scissors, Thin coat, Trochees, Envelopes, Tape"; "In pocket," "candies, pins needles thread, stamps & *money*, 2 handchks—matches, Jacknife—watch, Ticket—guidebook etc., shoestring—map of U.S., notebook, letters"; and one item further defined with respect to location: "Left pocket $78.10, Right, $60, Bosom, $40," with an addendum noting "Send home smoke cap, pair drawers."

24. *Journal*, I, 95–96.
25. W. E. Channing, *Thoreau, the Poet-Naturalist* (Boston, 1873), pp. 65–66.

Chapter V: Part of the Human Journey

1. See *Journal*, Nov. to April, I, 9–10, 11, 15, 19, 30, 39, 40.
2. Cf. *ibid.*, I, 347.
3. *Week*, p. 347.
4. *Journal*, IV, 97.   5. *Ibid.*, VII, 59.
6. "Ich lebe nun hier mit einer Klarheit und Ruhe, von der ich lange kein Gefühl hatte. Meine Übung, alle Dinge wie sie sind zu sehen und abzulesen, meine Treue, das Auge licht sein zu lassen, meine völlige Entäusserung von aller Prätention kommen mir einmal wieder recht zu stratten und machen mich im Stillen höchst glücklich" (*Goethes Werke* [Weimar, 1903], XXX, 212).
7. *Week*, p. 347; cf. *Goethes Werke*, XXX, 11.
8. *Week*, pp. 347–48.
9. "Ich halte die Augen nur immer offen und drüke mir die Gegenstände recht ein. Urteilen möchte ich gar nicht, wenn es nur möglich wäre" (*Goethes Werke*, XXX, 190).
10. *Journal*, I, 247–48.
11. *Week*, p. 348.
12. Cf. *Goethes Werke*, XXX, 22.
13. Thoreau praised particularly Goethe's "description of Venice and her environs as seen from the Marcrusthurm" (*Journal*, I, 15). Thereafter, at one time it was the spires of the city that reared before his mind's eye as he paddled up "a narrow, winding canal" in the forests of Maine, "tall dark spruce and arborvitae towered on both sides in the moonlight, forming a perpendicular forest-edge of great height. like the spires of a Venice in the forest" ("Chesuncook," *Writings*, III, 114); at another it was the Venetian harbor that floated before him as he looked out across Gloucester Bay and "saw the moonlight reflected from the smooth harbor and lighting up the fishing vessels, as if it had been the harbor of Venice" (*Journal*, XI, 187–88), or even as he scanned the field-grass protruding above the sur-

face of the flooded Concord meadows, like "masts of vessels in a crowded Venice harbor" (early in MS draft of *Walden* [HM924] in the Huntington Library; also in J. L. Shanley, *The Making of Walden* [Chicago, 1957]).

14. *Week*, p. 352; *Journal*, IV, 114–15.

15. "Autumnal Tints," *Writings*, V, 289; *Journal*, II, 373. For other statements expressing reservations with regard to "scientific" observation, see *Week*, p. 100; "Walking," *Writings*, V, 231; *Journal*, IV, 470–71; XIII, 141, 168–69, 181; XIV, 117–18; etc.

16. *Journal*, X, 164. Cf. for example, *Goethes Werke*, XXI, 89.

17. *Goethes Werke*, XXX, 213. "Und so lasst mich aufraffen, wie es kommen will, die Ordnung wird sich geben."

18. *Walden*, p. 104.

19. *Goethes Werke*, XXX, 67. "Ich mache diese wunderbare Reise nicht, um mich selbst zu betriegen, sondern um mich an den Gegenständen kennen zu lernen."

20. *Journal*, XIV, 274.   21. *Ibid.*, XIII, 160.

22. *Week*, p. 348.

23. *Journal*, III, 185. Cf. also XI, 286.

24. *Week*, p. 100.

25. *Ibid.*, pp. 348–49. See *Goethes Werke*, XXX, 132. Cf. Thoreau's similar criticism of a favorite author: "Have just finished reading Gilpin's 'Lakes of Cumberland.' An elegant writer of English prose. I wish he would look at scenery sometimes with the eye not of the artist. It is all side screens and fore screens and near distances and broken grounds with him" (*Journal*, IV, 283).

26. *Week*, pp. 230–31.

27. *Ibid.*, p. 111.   28. *Ibid.*, p. 107.

29. *Ibid.*, p. 109. Cf. *Journal*, VII, 108: "What a strong and hearty but reckless hit-or-miss style had some of the early writers of New England, like Josselyn and William Wood and others elsewhere in those days; as if they spoke with a relish, smacking their lips like a coachwhip, caring more to speak heartily than scientifically true."

30. *Week*, pp. 230–31.

31. See *ibid.*, pp. 291–92. See also *ibid.*, p. 228, and *Journal*, IV, 136, for reminders of Thoreau's reading in Henry. One might cite any number of passages from the *Travels* illustrative of Henry's style, such as the long account of a bear hunt (pp. 142–44) or the following account for its characteristic formal directness and understatement:

"From Cumberland House, I pursued a westerly course, on the ice, following the southern bank of Sturgeon Lake, till I crossed the neck of land by which alone it is separated from the great river Pasquayah, or Sascatchiwaine. In the evening, I encamped on the north bank of the river, at the distance of ten leagues from Cumberland House. The depth of the snow, and the intenseness of the cold, rendered my progress so much slower than I reckoned upon that I soon began to fear the want of provisions. The sun did not rise til half past nine o'clock in the morning, and it set at half past two in the afternoon; it is, however, at no time wholly dark in these climates; the northern lights, and the reflections of the snow, affording always sufficient light for the traveler. Add to this, that the river [the Saskatchewan], the course of which I was ascending, was a guide with the aid of which I could not lose my way. Every day's journey was commenced at three in the morning.

"I was not far advanced, before the country betrayed some approaches to the characteristic nakedness of the Plains. The wood dwindled away, both in size and quantity, so that it was with difficulty we could collect sufficient for making a fire, and without fire we could not drink; for melted snow was our only resource, the ice from the river being too thick to be penetrated by the axe" (*Travels and Adventures in Canada* [New York, 1809], pp. 226–27).

32. *Walden*, pp. 80, 336.
33. *Ibid.*, p. 74; *Week*, pp. 324–25.
34. *Correspondence*, pp. 538, 558–59.
35. *Journal*, XIV, 111. Thoreau referred to railroad car luxuries, "divans, ottomans, etc.," as "oriental things . . . invented for the ladies of the harem and the effeminate natives of the Celestial Empire, which Jonathan should be ashamed to know the names of. . . . I would rather ride on the earth in an ox cart." In the same vein he warned that the traveler who stopped at the "best house" would discover that "the publicans presume him to be a Sardanapalus, and if he resigned himself to their tender mercies, he would soon be completely emasculated" (*Walden*, pp. 40–41).
36. *Journal*, X, 456. "You should travel as a common man. . . . [Otherwise] you would not see the natives at all" (*ibid.*, IX, 400–402). The specific work Thoreau referred to seems to have been William Emory's *Report of the United States and Mexican Boundary Survey, Made under the Direction of the Secretary of the Interior* (Washington, 1857), which Thoreau was reading at the time he made his Journal comment. He owned Emory's earlier travel report on New Mexico and California (*Notes of a Military Reconnaissance* [Washington, 1848]).
37. "Herald of Freedom," *Writings*, IV, 307.
38. See *Journal*, II, 240–48, 261–64; see also text, pp. 25, 46.
39. Thoreau withdrew Michaux from the Harvard Library on June 2 (he was reading Darwin on June 7, 11, and 14). There are some indications that Thoreau might have read Humboldt's *Personal Narrative* as early as 1843 ("A Walk to Wachusett," *Writings*, V, 132), but there appears no proof of such reading until 1852 (Widener Extract Book, p. 110). He *had* read by this time (June, 1851) the transla-

tion of Humboldt's *Aspects of Nature* (Philadelphia, 1849 and 1850); evidence of his debts to it appears throughout his writings (*Journal*, II, 11; "Walking," *Writings*, V, 220, 231, 233; "Yankee in Canada," *ibid.*, V, 92; "Cape Cod," *ibid.*, IV, 121, 191; "Chesuncook," *ibid.*, III, 167).

The quotation from Michaux in *Walden* (p. 277) which Walter Harding (*The Variorum Walden* [New York, 1962], p. 307, n. 25) could not find in Michaux's *North American Sylva* comes from his *Voyage*.

40. Berg Extract Book (173768B), pp. 167–72.
41. For some of Thoreau's uses of his reading of Darwin's *Voyage*, see *Journal*, II, 228, 240–48; "Walking," *Writings*, V, 226; *Walden*, p. 14; "Cape Cod," *Writings*, IV, 40, 122.
42. *Journal*, IX, 252.
43. See *ibid.*, XIV, 228–29.
44. Charles Darwin, *Voyage of a Naturalist round the World* (New York, 1846), II, 499–500, 503.
45. "But this habit of close observation,—in Humboldt, Darwin, and others. Is it to be kept up long, this science? Do not tread on the heels of your experience. Be impressed without making a minute of it. Poetry puts an interval between the impression and the expression,—waits till the seed germinates naturally" (*Journal*, II, 341).
46. *Journal*, II, 377; IX, 57–58. Cf. Darwin, *Voyage*, II, 501.
47. Darwin, *Voyage*, II, 502–3.
48. *Journal*, II, 263; "Cape Cod," *Writings*, IV, 127.

Chapter VI: More Than the Count of Cats

1. "The truth, the quite incredible truth about Thoreau, the truth that we resist in spite of his own repeated witness, is that he spent a quarter of a century in a quest for transcendent reality, in an attempt to discover the secret of the universe. It is, after all, a matter only of belief. . . . Thoreau believed; he accepted the conditions, he claimed the promises. He had the map to the hidden treasure, and his whole life was spent in the search. Only when we see him and his life in this light do the pieces of the puzzle fall into place; his divergent interests are reconciled and all his paradoxes are resolved by the simple fact of his transcendentalism" (Ethel Seybold, *Thoreau: The Quest and the Classics* [New Haven, 1951], p. 7).
2. *Walden*, pp. 107–8; Miller, *Consciousness*, p. 34.
3. *Journal*, XIV, 330.   4. *Ibid.*, II, 376–77. Cf. also IV, 248.
5. "Ktaadn," *Writings*, III, 24, 16.
6. *Journal*, III, 9–10, 25–27, 32.   7. *Ibid.*, VI, 83.
8. Letters to Harrison Blake, *Correspondence*, pp. 558, 214.

9. Thoreau expressed a similar pleasure when speaking of voyaging: "We move now with a certain pomp and circumstance, with planetary dignity. The pleasure of sailing is akin to that which a planet feels. It seems a more complete adventure than a walk. . . . We are further from the earth than the rider" (*Journal*, IV, 325).

10. Walter Harding (*The Variorum Walden* [New York, 1962], p. 316, n. 14) attributes Thoreau's reference to the cats of Zanzibar to Charles Pickering's *The Races of Man* (London, 1851), a book which Thoreau read in the summer of 1853, which reports on the number of domestic cats to be seen in Zanzibar (but offers no "count").

Chapter VII: The Route Taken

1. W. E. Channing, *Thoreau, the Poet-Naturalist* (Boston, 1873), p. 41.

2. Lescarbot's *Histoire* gave summaries of voyages by Cartier, Champlain, Roberval, Monts, and Poitrincourt.

3. Thoreau studied both the 1613 and the 1632 editions of Champlain's *Les Voyages*, deciding quite soundly that the latter was "a very incorrect reprint." The accounts of Cartier and Roberval were in the single volume *Voyages de découverte au Canada* (Quebec, 1843).

4. Only two additions were made to this Canadian Notebook after 1852: excerpts on the Amazon and on the Yangtze River, from Herndon's *Exploration of the Amazon* and Huc's *Journey through the Chinese Empire*; made in 1854 and 1855 respectively, the additions were obviously for comparison with the account of the St. Lawrence. For admirably careful and scholarly treatment of this notebook, see Lawrence Willson's "Thoreau's Canadian Notebook," *Huntington Library Quarterly*, XXII (May, 1959), 179–200; Professor Willson views portions of this notebook as constituting a "first step" in Thoreau's collection of materials on the Indians of North America.

5. See "Yankee in Canada," *Writings*, V, 98.

6. Indian Notebook 3 (MA598); John Long, *Voyages and Travels of an Indian Interpreter and Trader* (London, 1791).

7. Thoreau read both accounts in the *Maine Historical Society Collections*, 1st ser., I (1831), 341–416.

8. Kenneth W. Cameron, *Emerson the Essayist* (Raleigh, N.C., 1945), II, 196–98.

9. *Journal*, II, 335–36. Cf. also III, 40–41.

10. *Ibid.*, II, 336–37. Cf. Thoreau's repetition in the "Excursion to Canada" (*Writings*, V, 85) of this last sentence: whereas in the

Journal the comment clearly refers to his reading, in the context of the travel account it is made to apply to the physical scene before him.

11. Cf. Canadian Notebook (MA595), pp. 12, 26.
12. *Journal*, XIII, 68.   13. See *ibid.*, II, 74.
14. *Writings*, V, 21, 30.
15. See *ibid.*, V, 39, 79–80, 95–96, etc.   16. *Ibid.*, V, 37–39.
17. *Correspondence*, p. 299.   18. *Ibid.*, p. 506.
19. *Journal*, IX, 232.
20. *Writings*, V, 67–68.
21. *Journal*, IX, 390.
22. Huntington Journal Fragments (HM13182).

Chapter VIII: The Western Impulse

1. Index Rerum (HM945).
2. "Walking," *Writings*, V, 221.
3. *The Writings of Thomas Paine*, ed. M. D. Conway (New York, 1894), II, 402.
4. James Russell Lowell, "Thoreau," *My Study Windows* (Boston, 1888), p. 206.
5. Canby, *Thoreau*, p. 180.
6. *Journal*, I, 131.
7. Miller, *Consciousness*, p. 159.
8. Huntington Journal Fragments (HM13182) and F. E. Sanborn, *The First and Last Journeys of Thoreau* (Boston, 1905), I, 85–86. Thoreau quotes excerpts from the court speech of a miner in Wisconsin to illustrate the West's contribution to the English language; he finds there "good Greekish words" in abundance—"good because necessary and expressive; 'diggings,' for instance. If you analyze a Greek word you will not get anything simpler, truer, more poetical; and many others, also, which now look so ram-slang-like and colloquial when printed, another generation will cherish and affect as genuine American and standard. Read some western stump speech, and though it be untoward and crude enough, there will not fail to be some traits of genuine eloquence, and some original and forcible statement, which will remind you of the great orators of antiquity. I am inclined to read stump-speeches of the West rather than the Beauties of our Atlantic orators."
9. *Writings*, IV, 346.
10. *Journal*, II, 144.
11. "Walking," *Writings*, V, 218.
12. The essay has recently received more attention; see Lawrence Willson, "The Transcendentalist View of the West," *Western Humanities Review*, XIV (1960), 181–85, and C. A. Tillinghast, "The

West of Thoreau's Imagination: The Development of a Symbol,"
Thoth, VI (1965), 42–50.

13. *Writings*, V, 205–48.

14. Thoreau applied his view with startling aim at his country neighbors:
"If I were to look for a narrow, uninformed and countrified mind, as
opposed to the intelligence and refinement which is supposed to
emanate from cities, it would be among the rusty inhabitants of an
old-settled country" ("Ktaadn," *Writings*, III, 24).

15. *Journal*, X, 89, "Chesuncook," *Writings*, III, 112.

16. *Writings*, III, 132 ff.

17. See "Life Without Principle," *Writings*, IV, 465–66; *Journal*, III,
265–66; VII, 491, 500.

18. *Correspondence*, p. 296.   19. *Ibid.*, p. 436.

20. *Writings*, IV, 227–52.

21. Thoreau read Theodore Irving's account of De Soto's *Conquest of
Florida* (New York, 1851). Probably because of his particular interest in the Mississippi, he owned Beltrami's *La Découverte des
Sources du Mississippi* (New Orleans, 1824); he also borrowed in
1855 from the Society of Natural History in Boston Beltrami's
anonymous defense of his account (*To the Public of New York and
of the United States* [New York, 1825]). He read in 1858 J. G. Shea's
"History of the Discovery of the Mississippi River" in the *Historical
Collections of Louisiana*, ed. B. F. French, Part IV (1853), pp. vii-
xxxix.

22. See the whole passage in "Ktaadn," *Writings*, III, 90–92.

23. Thoreau's reading of western travel books is distributed as follows:
before 1840, 4; 1850, 1; 1851, 2; 1852, 6; 1853, 1; 1854, 4; 1855, 1;
1856, 3; 1857, 4; 1858, 2; 1859, 3; 1860, 3. For the remaining six we
have no sure dates of his reading; they were added to his personal
library sometime after 1840.

24. See *Walden*, p. 4, also *Journal*, I, 395, XI, 326, and Huntington
Journal Fragments for Oct. 16, 1843: "Do you hear it ye [Malnoffs?]
—ye Patagonians—ye Tartars—ye Nez Pirces—the world's going to
be reformed, going to change."

25. See *Collected Poems of Henry Thoreau*, ed. Carl Bode (Chicago,
1943), p. 134.

26. *Correspondence*, p. 485.

27. *Writings*, V, 217, 224.

28. Berg Extract Book (173768B).

29. Canby, *Thoreau*, p. 335.

Chapter IX: The Voyage Out

1. "Cape Cod," *Writings*, IV, 188; *Journal*, V, 28.

2. *Walden*, p. 97; *Journal*, III, 360.

3. "For my own part, but for the geographers, I should hardly have known how large a portion of our globe is water, my life is chiefly passed within so deep a cove" (*Week*, p. 253). Thoreau read in collections of voyages by E. C. Drake, Ramusio, Brosses, Bry, Hakluyt, Purchas, Nevins, Irving (*Voyages of the Companions of Columbus*), and in *Voyages de découverte au Canada* (Quebec, 1843). John Nevins' *New Collection of Voyages and Travels* seems to be the unidentified "Collection of Travels" listed by Kenneth W. Cameron (*Emerson the Essayist* [Raleigh, N.C., 1945], II, 197) among Thoreau's Harvard Library withdrawals for Dec.22, 1856; see Indian Notebook 9 (MA604).

4. See text, pp. 240–41.

5. *Journal*, VI, 74.

6. "Cape Cod," *Writings*, IV, 123.

7. "Yankee in Canada," *Writings*, V, 67.

8. The Harvard Library withdrawal simply lists "Morrell, Narrative," which could refer to Mrs. Abby Jane Morrell's *Narrative of a Voyage to the Ethiopic and South Atlantic Ocean* (New York, 1833) covering the same route and experiences.

9. The only evidence for Thoreau's reading of *Typee* is a reference to "a custom in Typee" (the agility of young savages in climbing lofty trees) in an early draft of *Walden* (Huntington Drafts of *Walden* [HM924]).

10. See *Week*, p. 278, *Journal*, IV, 421, and VI, 369.

11. "Cape Cod," *Writings*, IV, 269.

12. *Voyage of a Naturalist round the World* (New York, 1846), I, 11.

13. *Journal*, II, 228, 244–48, and Indian Notebook 3 (MA586). Thoreau's reference to the New Hollander who "goes naked with impunity" in the opening pages of *Walden* (p. 14) is derived from his reading in Darwin (*Voyage*, I, 220–21), not in the *Voyages of Capain James Cook round the World* as suggested by Professor Harding (*The Variorum Walden* [New York, 1962], p. 269, n. 36).

   With reference to the young Darwin sheltered beneath his tree from the tropical shower, compare Concord's Darwin: "When compelled by a shower to take shelter under a tree, we may improve that opportunity for a more minute inspection of some of Nature's works. I have stood under a tree in the woods half a day at a time, during a heavy rain in the summer, and yet employed myself happily and profitably there prying with microscopic eye into the crevices of the bark or the leaves of the fungi at my feet" (*Week*, p. 319).

14. *Journal*, II, 244.

15. "Cape Cod," *Writings*, IV, 40, 122.

16. Washington Irving, *Life and Voyages of Columbus* (London, 1831), I, 175.

17. Widener Extract Book, p. 110.
18. Juliette Bauer, *Lives of the Brothers Humboldt* (New York, 1853); see Widener Extract Book, p. 164.
19. *Journal*, III, 264.
20. Alexander von Humboldt, *Aspects of Nature* (Philadelphia, 1849 and 1850), p. 156.
21. See *Journal*, II, 262.
22. Part I of the *Exploration* by Herndon was published by Congress in 1853, Gibbon's Part II the following year. It appears, from the order of his inventory of his own library, that Thoreau may have owned Gibbon's account before Horace Mann gave him Herndon's Part I (Walter Harding, *Thoreau's Library* [Charlottesville, 1957], p. 58).
23. *Journal*, VI, 323–49.
24. See Indian Notebook 7 (MA602).
25. Cf. *Journal*, II, 146–47.
26. Widener Extract Book, p. 279.
27. *Journal*, VIII, 99–100.
28. *Walden*, p. 22.

Chapter X: Eastward over the World

1. Joseph Wolff, *Narrative of a Mission to Bokhara* (New York, 1845), p. 71.
2. *Ibid.*, p. 76.   3. *Ibid.*, pp. 69–70.
4. *Week*, p. 60.
5. Huntington Journal Fragments (HM13182).
6. Wolff, *Narrative*, p. 94.
7. *Ibid.*, p. 74.   8. *Ibid.*, pp. 104, 211–19.
9. *Ibid.*, p. 188.   10. *Ibid.*, pp. 135–36.
11. *Writings*, VI, 312.
12. *Journal*, II, 35, and "Cape Cod," *Writings*, IV, 54; cf. Austen Layard, *Ninevah and Its Remains* (New York, 1849), I, 245 ff., 140, and 145.
13. *Journal*, II, 35; Layard, *Ninevah*, I, 248.
14. Layard, *Ninevah*, I, 26.
15. *Ibid.*, I, 87.   16. *Ibid.*, I, 81–82.
17. *Journal*, II, 21.
18. Layard, *Ninevah*, I, 82–83.
19. *Walden*, pp. 137–43.
20. Widener Extract Book, pp. 170–73; Berg Extract Book (173768B), p. 14; and *Journal* (see Bibliography).
21. Austen Layard, *Discoveries among the Ruins of Nineveh and Babylon* (New York, 1853), p. 408; *Journal*, IV, 11.
22. Widener Extract Book, p. 172.

23. *Journal*, IV, 15.   24. *Ibid.*, IX, 246.
25. *Correspondence*, p. 313; Layard, *Discoveries*, pp. 663–64.
26. *Journal*, I, 167.   27. See *ibid.*, IX, 258–61.
28. Widener Extract Book, pp. 19–20.
29. *Ibid.*, pp. 111–19. It was in Sleeman that Thoreau read of the Kohinoor diamond, to which he contrasted a seed (*Journal*, XIV, 334).
30. Widener Extract Book, p. 12; Frederick Parrot, *A Journey to Mount Ararat* (New York, 1846), p. 26.
31. Widener Extract Book, p. 13. See Walter Harding, "Thoreau and the Kalmucks: A Newly Discovered Manuscript," *New England Quarterly*, XXXII (March, 1959), 91–92, for a brief practiced response on Thoreau's part to this quotation from Parrot.
32. Berg Extract Book, p. 4; see text, p. 39. It is interesting to note what Thoreau did not choose to record as well as that which he did. In this instance, he copied only the first half of the experience which Mme Pfeiffer described (as one episode) in her account; he stopped copying precisely at the following portion, an addition which at the least illuminates the hardiness of Mme Pfeiffer's narrative: "But the pleasure I had in contemplating this scene met with a sudden shock.
   "A short distance before we reached the plateau, we noticed, at several places on the ground, spots of blood, to which we paid very little attention, as a horse or a mule might have scratched themselves [*sic*] against the rocks and left those traces behind. But soon we came to a spot that left no doubt of the origin of these stains—it was covered with a complete pool of blood—and looking down into the abyss below, we saw two human bodies, one hanging scarcely a hundred feet below the ledge on which we were—the other, which had rolled further, half hidden by the projecting craig. This told its own tale, and we hastened away from the hateful scene of murder. I could not get it out of my mind for days together" (Ida Pfeiffer, *A Lady's Voyage round the World* [New York, 1852], p. 232).
33. *Walden*, p. 25.
34. Pfeiffer, *A Lady's Voyage*, pp. ix–x.
35. *Journal*, III, 200, 205; see *A Lady's Voyage*, p. 77.
36. Widener Extract Book, pp. 28–29.
37. See *A Lady's Voyage*, pp. 104–5, 128–30, 186–87. Cf. *Journal*, IV 461; V, 349; VI, 46. Thoreau's reading in Pfeiffer offers another small piece of evidence suggesting the peculiar scrupulousness with which he recorded his recollections. He read on p. 171 of her *A Lady's Voyage* of the custom in Persia of placing shallow vessels containing water outside their doorsteps at night to make the ice which they deemed such a luxury for their tables; he noted over a year later in his Journal, in July, "There is a great contrast between night and

day now, reminding me that even in Hindostan they freeze ice in shallow vessels at night in summer (?)." The question mark flags the uncertainty. A careful review of Mme Pfeiffer's report reveals that the days were indeed too warm for freezing ice in the region of the world she described; the actual month of the year was February!

38. *Journal*, III, 194–95; Pfeiffer, *A Lady's Voyage*, pp. 93, 182.
39. Pfeiffer, *A Lady's Voyage*, pp. 148–49.
40. *Journal*, III, 304.
41. *Journal*, IX, 251–52.
42. Evariste Huc, *Recollections of a Journey through Tartary, Thibet, and China, during the Years 1844, 1845, and 1846* (New York, 1852) II, 23.
43. See text, p. 23; and Huc, *Tartary*, I, 14.
44. Widener Extract Book, pp. 81–82.
45. Huc, *Tartary*, I, 39; cf. *Journal*, III, 485.
46. Widner Extract Book, p. 85; Huc, *Tartary*, I, 152.
47. Widener Extract Book, p. 83; Huc, *Tartary*, I, 94; *Writings*, V, 228.
48. Widener Extract Book, p. 82, Huc, *Tartary*, I, 62.
49. Widener Extract Book, pp. 82, 85.
50. *Journal*, IV, 15.
51. Widener Extract Book, pp. 84, 86.
52. Huc, *Tartary*, II, 41.
53. *Ibid.*, II, 51.   54. *Ibid.*, II, 125, 126–27.
55. *Ibid.*, II, 134.   56. *Ibid.*, II. 144.
57. Widener Extract Book, p. 86. By reading the Appleton's Popular Library Edition of Huc's narrative, Thoreau missed a portion of Huc's account of the return trip to the Chinese border, for the American edition did not include the last two chapters appearing in William Hazlitt's translation of the work (*Travels in Tartary, Thibet, and China during the Years 1844–5–6* [London, n.d.]), and not repeated in Huc's second book, *A Journey through the Chinese Empire* (New York, 1855), which Thoreau read. Lawrence Willson ("Thoreau's Canadian Notebook," *Huntington Library Quarterly*, XXII [May, 1959], 189, n. 40) mistakenly refers to the second work as a later edition of Huc's first book.
58. Huc, *Tartary*, II, 37–38.
59. *Ibid.*, II, 65.   60. *Ibid.*, II, 210–12; Widener Extract Book, p. 86.
61. Richard Burton, *The Lake Regions of Central Africa* (New York, 1860); see text, pp. 185–86.
62. "His [Burton's] journey to Mecca in the disguise of a Moslem made him famous, but he merely confirmed what his predecessor [J. L. Burckhardt, *Travels in Arabia* (London, 1829)] had so ably described, and added little to geographical knowledge" (Sir Percy Sykes, *A History of Exploration* [New York, 1934], p. 281). See

also Byron Farwell's *Burton: A Biography of Sir Richard Francis Burton* (New York, 1963).

63. Richard Burton, *Personal Narrative of a Pilgrimage to Al-Madinah and Meccah*, I, 22–23. (Page references to Burton are to the London, 1889, two-volume edition, since I have not been able to secure the 1856 American edition which Thoreau read.)

64. Burton, *Pilgrimage*, I, 23–26.

65. *Ibid.*, I, 148–49; *Journal*, IX, 251–52.

66. See Indian Notebook 9 (MA604): "Burton, Personal Narrative, 1st. Ed., N.Y. 1856 not the complete work." Thoreau proceeds to copy excerpts from pp. 65, 97, 279, 318, 321, 337, 338, 339, 340, 341, 343, and 344 of Burton's book.

67. *Journal*, IX, 236.

68. See "Cape Cod," *Writings*, IV, 178. Although the immediate context for Thoreau's singing performance would appear to be the walking tour taken with Channing in 1855, the narrative of the trip published posthumously would have been revised and rewritten following his subsequent trip (his fourth, also a walking tour but this time by himself) in the summer of 1857 immediately following his reading of Burton. In fact, this last walk on Cape Cod was not only along the same shore of the previous visit but was, until the last minute, to have been made with the same companion (see Thoreau's letter to Blake, *Correspondence*, p. 484).

69. See Indian Notebooks 10 and 11 (MA605, MA606).

70. Thomas W. Atkinson, *Oriental and Western Siberia* (New York, 1858), pp. 46–47.

71. *Ibid.*, p. 49.

72. "Chesuncook," *Writings*, III, 142. Thoreau was reading Atkinson's accounts of the lumber activities in Siberia sometime between February and May of 1858, as indicated by his note-taking from the book which occurs sometime after his note-taking from Mrs. Traill's *Backwoods of Canada*, which he withdrew from the Harvard Library on Feb. 15, and before his subsequent note-taking from Hennepin's *Description de la Louisiane*, withdrawn from the Library on May 27. During this period he would have been revising "Chesuncook" for its appearance in the *Atlantic Monthly* in June.

Chapter XI: Young Africa

1. *Journal*, VII, 99–100.

2. Although the only direct reference to Mungo Park appears in *Walden* (p. 353), the absence of references in the Journal or notebooks simply suggests an earlier reading, to be expected in light of the fame of Park's travels, even as it would be rather unnatural to suppose Tho-

reau's ignorance of an account every schoolboy must have read. An early reading would also suggest the readily available 1840 New York edition.

3. James Riley, *An Authentic Narrative* (Hartford, 1836).

4. I am indebted to Sir Percy Sykes's standard *History of Exploration* (New York, 1934) for this reminder and for that bird's-eye view of a continent's exploration which enables one to see the forest in spite of the trees.

5. Mungo Park, *The Life and Travels of Mungo Park* (New York, 1840 and 1842), p. 98.

6. *Ibid.*, p. 115.

7. See *ibid.*, pp. 125–26 and note; the editor's reference in the *Travels* is to William Keating's account of the prairie fires set by the Indians. Thoreau also noted in Henry Youle Hind's *Northwest Territory* (pp. 52–53) similar references to the Indians' habits of burning the prairies (Berg Extract Book [173768B], p. 193). In his notebook, under a heading which he designates "Fire on the Prairies," he gathers from Hind's book a series of excerpts relating to this phenomenon which so interests him (Berg Extract Book, pp. 190–92). In the Indian Notebook 11 (MA606), there is still further relevant material from Hind.

8. Park, *Travels*, p. 211.

9. Thoreau withdrew only Volume I of Clapperton's two-volume edition containing Denham's Journal (London, 1826) from the Harvard Library in 1834, when he was in his second year at Harvard College. He read in 1860 Barth's *Travels and Discoveries in North and Central Africa . . . and a Sketch of Denham and Clapperton's Expedition* (Philadelphia, 1860), which questioned Denham's accuracy.

10. *Journal*, V, 302; *Week*, pp. 209–10.

11. Hugh Clapperton, *Narrative of Travels and Discoveries in Northern and Central Africa* (London, 1826), I, xlvii, 10, 12.

12. "The story [in such fabulous books of wisdom as the Veeshnoo Sarma] which winds between and around these sentences, these barrows in the desert, these oases, is as indistinct as a camel track between Mourzuk and Darfur" (*Journal*, I, 346); cf. also *Week*, p. 153.

13. Clapperton, *Narrative*, I, 22, liv.

14. *Journal*, V, 306.

15. Bayle St. John, *Adventures in the Libyan Desert* (New York, 1849), pp. 27–28. Thoreau took note of St. John's later observations on the comment of those "waterless wastes" referred to in his first response; the author, contemplating a ruin in the desert, found man's imprint speaking of a civilization "as extinct as the mammoth or the mastodon" (Berg Extract Book, p. 240).

16. Clapperton, *Narrative*, I, 35.

17. *Ibid.*, I, 36, 41, 67, 219, 40, 42, 39, 209.
18. Indian Notebook 11.
19. *Week*, p. 127.
20. Barth, *Travels and Discoveries*, pp. 447–48.   21. *Ibid.*, pp. 537–38.
22. Indian Notebook 9 (MA604).
23. Karl Johan Andersson, *Lake Ngami* (New York, 1856), pp. 13–14.
24. *Ibid.*, p. iv. See Widener Extract Book, pp. 296–300, and Indian
    Notebook 9; between them these notebooks contain very long ex-
    cerpts copied from twenty-three pages of the Andersson book.
25. Andersson, *Lake Ngami*, pp. 431–32.
26. David Livingstone, *Travels, and Researches in South Africa* (New
    York, 1858), pp. 75–76. Thoreau copies excerpts from pp. 12, 80,
    92, 104, 137, 149, 157, 164, 189, 211, 213, 289, 420, 434, 590, 593,
    640, 641, 642, 643, 653, 670 (in Berg Extract Book, pp. 23–24, and
    Indian Notebook 9).
27. Thoreau appears to have been particularly attracted by Livingstone's
    blunt reliability, his truthful inclusion of a fact at no matter what
    expense to the conventional potentials for exploiting an experience.
    Many of his excerpts from Livingstone deal with factual challenges
    to popular views. For example: "There are comparatively few tropical
    birds in South Africa with gaudy plumage. . . . The majority have
    decidedly a sober dress, though collectors, having generally selected
    the gaudiest as the most valuable, have conveyed the idea that the
    birds of the tropics for the most part possess gorgeous plumage"; or,
    "To talk of the majestic roar of the lion is mere majestic twad-
    dle. . . . Only a native pretends to distinguish between the roar of
    a lion and that of an ostrich" (Berg Extract Book, p. 23).
28. Livingstone, *Travels*, pp. 104, 105.
29. Indian Notebook 9.
30. Berg Extract Book, p. 23.
31. Livingstone, *Travels*, pp. 559–63. Cf. Thoreau (*Journal*, III, 155–56):
    "I, standing twenty miles off, see a crimson cloud on the horizon.
    You tell me it is a mass of vapor which absorbs all other rays and
    reflects the red, but that is nothing to the purpose, for this red vision
    excites me, stirs my blood, makes my thoughts flow, and I have new
    and indescribable fancies. . . . If there is nothing [in your descrip-
    tion] which speaks to my imagination, what boots it? What sort of
    science is that which enriches the understanding but robs the imagi-
    nation? "
32. Livingstone, *Travels*, pp. 188, 194.
33. Clapperton, *Narrative*, I, 46.
34. "Is not the midnight like central Africa to most? Are we not tempted
    to explore it, to penetrate to the shores of its Lake Tchad, to discover
    the course of its Nile, perchance in the Mountains of the

Moon? . . . In the mountains of the Moon, in the Central Africa of the night—there is where all Niles hide their heads. The expedition up the Niles extend but to the Cataracts, past the ruins of Thebes, or perchance to the mouth of the White Nile; but it is the Black Nile that concerns us. Of some of the great rivers, like the Nile and the Orinoco (?), men still only conjecture the sources" (*Journal*, III, 264). Cf. "Night and Moonlight," *Writings*, V, 323.

35. Ptolemy was of course finally justified, with H. M. Stanley's discovery of the *Montes Lunae* in 1885 (*In Darkest Africa* [New York, 1890], p. 405), completing proof that Lake Victoria shared honors with the Ruwenzori (as the "Mountains of the Moon" were known locally) as the Nile's source.

36. J. Ludwig Krapf, *Travels and Researches in Eastern Africa* (Boston, 1860), p. 444.

37. *Ibid.*, Appendix, pp. 448–53.

38. See *Journal*, XIV, 297.

39. Richard Burton, *The Lake Regions of Central Africa* (New York, 1860), pp. 307–8.

40. *Correspondence*, p. 613.

Chapter XII: Winters to Rival Concord's

1. For this background of arctic exploration I am indebted to Jeanette Mirsky's *To the Arctic: The Story of Northern Exploration from Earliest Time to the Present* (New York, 1948).

2. Thoreau copied excerpts from Franklin's *Narrative* into his Extract Book (Widener Extract Book, pp. 261–69) and Indian Notebook 8 (MA603) early in 1855; see also the reference in "Cape Cod" (*Writings*, IV, 173–74). There is no evidence that Thoreau read Franklin's work earlier than this date, even though he refers to him frequently by name (in 1843 in "A Winter Walk," for instance, *Writings*, V, 177). Such references are derived from other accounts; Back, for example, defers repeatedly to Franklin's *Narrative* (see Sir George Back, *Narrative of the Arctic Land Expedition* [London and Philadelphia, 1836], pp. 63, 306–7). A secondhand reference to a feature of "Franklin's Journey" in his Journal for March 9, 1854, suggests that Thoreau had not yet read the *Narrative* for himself.

3. Later in the same year (1860) Thoreau read McClintock's book (*The Voyage of the "Fox" in the Arctic Seas* [Boston, 1860]), probably after June 10; see the Berg Extract Book (173768B), p. 304.

4. Agassiz and Maury were not travel writers, of course, but Thoreau read their reports (Agassiz's in Josiah C. Nott and George R. Gliddon, *Types of Mankind* [Philadelphia, 1856–57], and Maury's in an article in *Revue des Deux Mondes* for March, 1850) in connection with

his arctic travels. Maury also reviewed, in the same issue of the *Revue*, Frederick de Tschudi's *Das Thierleben der Oppenwelt* (Leipzig, 1850), and Thoreau, after noting that this latter book "would be worth seeing," translates Maury's extensive quotations from pp. 121, 122, 125, 126, 130, 132, 136, 137, 139, 140, 141, 142, 143, 145 (Berg Extract Book, pp. 10 ff.).

5. "Sir James Clark Ross's *A Voyage of Discovery and Research in the Southern and Antarctic Regions During the Years 1839–1843* (London, 1846, 2 vols.)," *North British Review*, VIII (November, 1847), 94–116. See Thoreau's *Week*, pp. 390–91. I find no sure evidence that Thoreau read more of Ross than this review.

6. Sir W. Edward Parry, *Three Voyages for the Discovery of a Northwest Passage* (New York, 1845), II, 79; Sherard Osborn, *Stray Leaves from an Arctic Journal* (New York, 1852), pp. 123–24.

7. Widener Extract Book, p. 301; Elisha Kane, *Arctic Exploration* (Philadelphia, 1856), I, 44. Kane refers to his earlier disappointing sight of the cliffs which Thoreau read of in Kane's first book on the first Grinnell Expedition, p. 135.

   Walter Harding (*Thoreau's Library*) appears to be mistaken in identifying the 1856 edition of Kane's *Grinnell Expedition* as the "Arctic Searching Expedition" listed by Thoreau in his personal library. There is no such "spine title" to Kane's first book, and the evidence indicates that Thoreau did his reading of and copying from the 1853 edition (see Harding's citation of borrowings from Kane's book in *The Variorum Walden* [New York, 1962], p. 316). Thoreau's listed title fits accurately John Richardson's *Arctic Searching Expedition*, which Thoreau had at hand for continuous Journal use from at least March, 1852, through January, 1853, suggesting ownership rather than library borrowing.

8. Parry, *Three Voyages*, II, 43. Thoreau even adopts Parry's asbestos simile when he confirms Parry's observation through an experience of his own in Concord: "From the under side of the ice in the brooks, where there was a thicker ice below, depended a mass of crystallization, for five inches deep, in the form of prisms. . . . The very mud in the road, where the ice has melted, was crystallized with deep rectilinear fissures, and the crystalline masses in the sides of the ruts resembled exactly asbestos in the disposition of their needles" ("Natural History of Massachusetts," *Writings*, V, 128). Thoreau appears to have read Parry sometime before 1842; cf. "A Winter Walk," *Writings*, V, 177, and *Journal*, I, 470.

9. Parry, *Three Voyages*, II, 130–31.

10. Osborn, *Arctic Journal*, pp. 52–53: "I do not think anything could excel the alacrity with which the floe was suddenly peopled by about five hundred men, triangles rigged, and the long saw (called icesaws)

used for cutting the ice was manned. A hundred songs from hoarse throats resounded through the gale; the sharp chipping of the saws told that the work was flying." Cf. *Walden*, pp. 328, 324: "In the winter of '46–7 there came a hundred men of Hyperborean extraction swooped down on to our pond one morning, with many carloads of ungainly looking farming tools,—sleds, plows, drillborrows, turf-knives, spades, saws, rakes, and each was armed with a double-pointed pike-staff, such as is not described in the New England Farmers or the Cultivator."

It is interesting to recall Thoreau's interest in the uses to which the Walden ice so harvested was put—packed in the clipper ships for transport not only to "Charleston and New Orleans" but "with favoring winds . . . wafted past the sight of the fabulous islands of Atlantis and the Hebrides . . . floating by Ternate and Tidore and the mouth of the Persian Gulf, melting in the Tropic gales of the Indian seas, and landed in ports of which Alexander only heard the names." Such reference to the literal shipping of ice to the Orient in Thoreau's day makes less eccentric the following excerpt which Thoreau copied into his Extract Book (Widener Extract Book, p. 55) from Sir Francis Head's *The Emigrant*, pp. 21–22: "*Temperature of ice:* 'In Lower Canada it occasionally sinks to forty degrees below zero, or to seventy-two degrees below the temperature of ice just congealed. It is evident, therefore, that if two ice-houses were to be filled, the one with the former, say Canada ice, the difference between the quantity of cold stored up in each would be as appreciable as the difference between a cellar full of gold and a cellar full of copper; in short the intrinsic value of ice, like that of metals, depends upon the investigation of the assayer—that is to say, a cubic foot of Lower Canada ice is definitely more valuable, or in other words, it contains infinitely more cold than a cubic foot of Upper Canada ice, which again contains more cold than a cubic foot of Wenham ice, which again contains infinitely more cold than a cubic foot of English ice; and thus, although each of these four cubic feet of ice has precisely the same shape, they each, as summer approaches, diminish in value, that is to say, they each lose a portion of their cold, until, long before the Lower Canada ice has melted, the English ice has been converted into luke-warm water."

11. Osborn, *Arctic Journal*, p. 43. Osborn's prose was at times too florid for Thoreau, whose taste in style remained incorruptible even under overexposure to travel writing. An instance of this also offers insight into the precipitous manner in which Thoreau made his transcriptions from his reading. Quick to record descriptions of recurrent phenomena which he himself might witness, he commenced to copy as he read the following passage by Osborn describing the arctic night (*Arctic*

Journal, pp. 122–23): "For some time after the sun had ceased
to visit our heavens, the southern side of the horizon, for a few
hours at noon, was strongly illumined, the sky being shaded, from
deep and rosy red through all the most delicate tints of pink and
blue, until, in the north, a cold bluish-black scowled angrily over the
pale mountains, who, in widowed loneliness, had drawn their cowls
of snow around, and uncheered by the roseate kiss of the bridegroom
sun, seemed to mourn over the silence and darkness at their feet."
In one of his rare instances of incompleted recording, Thoreau copied
no further than "widowed loneliness," then scratched out the entire
entry!

12. Osborn, *Arctic Journal,* p. 115, and Widener Extract Book, p. 67.
13. Elisha Kane, *Grinnell Expedition in Search of Sir John Franklin*
    (New York, 1853), pp. 275, 305, 343, 350, 390.
14. Parry, *Three Voyages,* I, 84. Cf. *Journal,* VI, 98, and "Chesuncook,"
    Writings, III, 172.
15. See *Journal,* VI, 22–23, 32–34, 38, 48–49, 104, 139–41, 177, 210.
16. *Ibid.,* IX, 167, 192–95, 203, 227–28, 229.
17. See *ibid.,* IX, 152; X, 303; XIII, 176.
18. *Ibid.,* X, 317; I, 470. Parry, *Three Voyages,* II, 132; cf. also Vol. II,
    pp. 49, 309, and Vol. I, p. 230.
19. See *Journal,* V, 394.
20. "Natural History of Massachusetts," *Writings,* V, 125.

Chapter XIII: The Physical Macrocosm

1. J. W. Krutch, *Henry David Thoreau* (New York, 1948), p. 51.
2. Emerson, "Nature," *Complete Works* (Boston and New York,
   1903), I, 43.
3. Cf. *Journal,* I, 307: "For to the sick, nature is sick, but to the well, a
   fountain of health." See also Walter Harding, *Thoreau: Man of
   Concord* (New York, 1960), p. 162 (from Bronson Alcott's *Journals*
   [Boston, 1938], p. 201): "June 9, 1859. Sanborn, Henry Thoreau,
   and Allen take tea and pass the evening with us. We discuss questions of philosophy and the Ideal Theory as applied to education.
   Thoreau is large always and masterly in his own wild ways. With a
   firmer grasp of the shows of Nature, he has a subtler sense of the
   essence and personality of the flowing life of things than most men,
   and he defends the Ideal Theory and Personal Identity to my great
   delight."
4. Canby, *Thoreau,* p. 334.
5. *Journal,* X, 306.   6. *Ibid.,* VIII, 205.
7. *Writings,* V, 107.
8. *Journal,* XI, 438.

9. *Ibid.*, XIII, 180–81.   10. *Ibid.*, IX, 281; *Week*, p. 158.

11. Berg Extract Book (173768B), p. 195; Widener Extract Book, p. 268.

12. *Journal*, II, 225. Cf. "I was just aroused from my writing by the engine's whistle, and, looking out, saw shooting through the town two enormous pine sticks, stripped of their bark, just from the Northwest. . . . They suggest what a country we have got to back us up that way" (*ibid.*, V, 298–99).

13. Widener Extract Book, p. 119.

14. Berg Extract Book, p. 200.

15. Widener Extract Book, pp. 304, 296.

16. Berg Extract Book, p. 245. See also "A Winter Walk," *Writings*, V, 166. "The withdrawn and tense sky seems groined like the aisles of a cathedral, and the polished air sparkles as if there were crystals of ice floating in it. As they who have resided in Greenland tell us . . . the 'cutting smoke [frost smoke] frequently raises blisters on the face and hands, and is very pernicious to the health.' But this pure, stinging cold is an elixer to the lungs, and not so much a frozen mist as a crystallized midsummer haze, refined and purified by cold."

17. Berg Extract Book, pp. 198–208.

18. *Journal*, II, 11.

19. Widener Extract Book, pp. 296–97; Karl Johan Andersson, *Lake Ngami* (New York, 1856), pp. 180–83.

20. Berg Extract Book, p. 24.   21. *Ibid.*, p. 195.

22. *Journal*, VI, 139–40. See also *ibid.*, II, 352, 355; XII, 344–45.

23. *Ibid.*, III, 27.   24. *Ibid.*, III, 290–91; IV, 270.

25. *Ibid.*, V, 410; IX, 147; XIV, 298.

26. Isaac Holton, *New Granada: Twenty Months in the Andes* (New York, 1857), p. 150.

27. "Almost every night, we heard some trees crack and fall whilst we lay here in the woods, though the air was so calm that not a leaf stirred. The reason of this breaking I am totally unacquainted with. Perhaps the dew loosens the roots of the trees at night; or, perhaps there are too many branches on one side of the tree" (Peter Kalm, *Travels into North America* [London, 1770–71], II, 140; Widener Extract Book, p. 6). Cf. Thoreau: "Once, when Joe had called again, and we were listening for moose, we heard, come faintly echoing, or creeping from far through the moss-clad aisles, a dull, dry, rushing sound with a solid core to it, yet as if half smothered under the grasp of the luxuriant and fungus-like forest, like the shutting of a door in some distant entry of the damp and shaggy wilderness. If we had not been there, no mortal had heard it. When we asked Joe in a whisper what it was, he answered, "Tree fall." There is something singularly grand and impressive in the sound of a tree falling in a perfectly calm night

like this, as if the agencies which overthrow it did not need to be excited, but worked with a subtle, deliberate, and conscious force, like a boa-constrictor, and more effectively then than even in a windy day. If there is any such difference, perhaps it is because trees with the dews of the night on them are heavier than by day" ("Chesuncook," *Writings*, III, 115). Thoreau had reviewed his reading notes from Kalm (taken in the fall of 1851 when he withdrew the *Travels* from the Harvard Library) in the fall of 1852 in connection with the composition of his "Excursion to Canada," where he used material from Kalm. He took his second trip to Maine (described in "Chesuncook") the following September.

28. *Journal*, V, 292. Cf. Volney's description of "El Shan" (*Travels through Syria and Egypt* [London, 1787; New York, 1798], II, 270).
29. Widener Extract Book, p. 300; Berg Extract Book, p. 200.
30. Widener Extract Book, p. 298; Berg Extract Book, pp. 220, 51, 247.
31. "Walking," *Writings*, V, 225.
32. "In the account of Lewis' and Clark's Expedition. It is stated that . . . the mosquitos prevented Clark's killing the bighorn though they needed them for food—for they were in such multitudes that he could not keep them from the barrel of his rifle long enough to take aim" (note among MS Fragments [AM278.5] in Harvard's Houghton Library). Alexander Henry described a similar situation (*Travels and Adventures in Canada* [New York, 1809], p. 246). The explorer Sir John Franklin would not kill a mosquito, an idiosyncrasy which Thoreau found impressing other travelers (see Sir George Back, *Narrative of the Arctic Land Expedition* [London and Philadelphia, 1836], p. 180).
33. *Journal*, IX, 100–101: Thoreau acknowledges his reading in periodicals (articles on the alligator and "The Lion and His Kind" in *Harper's Magazine* for December, 1854, and May, 1855, respectively) with which he is supplementing his knowledge from travel books.
34. "I went to a menagerie the other day, advertised by a flaming showbill as big as a barn door. The proprietors had taken wonderful pains to collect rare and interesting animals from all parts of the world, and then placed them by a few stupid and ignorant fellows. . . . You catch a rare creature, interesting to all mankind, and then place the first biped that comes along, with but a grain more reason in him, to exhibit and describe the former" (*Journal*, II, 367–68; cf. also II, 271ff.).
35. *Journal*, VII, 421.
36. *Ibid.*, VII, 288, 290; cf. also VII, 240, 367. The slaughter of buffalo by the Cree Indians (described by Henry Youle Hind, *Northwest Territory* [Toronto, 1859], p. 55) disturbed Thoreau as much as that of the moose of Maine ("Chesuncook," *Writings*, III, 134–35); he

approved of the Chinese custom of carrying fish ova in hollow reeds from one province to another, to preserve life (*Week*, p. 23).

37. *Writings*, V, 89.
38. *Journal*, XII, 334. Thoreau read, for instance, in Parry (*Three Voyages for the Discovery of a North-west Passage* [New York, 1845], II, 124) the following description of the northern portion of the continent: "Here, once the earth is covered, all is dreary, monotonous whiteness; not merely for days or weeks, but for more than a full year together. Whichever way the eye is turned, it meets a picture calculated to impress upon the mind an idea of inanimate stillness, of that motionless torpor with which our feelings have nothing congenial; of anything, in short, but life. In the very silence there is a deadness with which a human spectator appears *out of keeping*. The presence of a man seems an intrusion on the dreary solitude of this wintry desert, which even its native animals have for a while forsaken."
39. *Walden*, pp. 87–88.

Chapter XIV: Natives to the World

1. *Walden*, p. 171.
2. "Walking," *Writings*, V, 230; cf. also *Journal*, I, 446.
3. *Journal*, I, 398; *Walden*, p. 12.
4. Albert Keiser, "Thoreau's Manuscript on the Indians," *Journal of English and Germanic Philology*, XXVII (Second Quarter, 1928), 193–99.
5. *Writings*, IV, 202.
6. *Journal*, II, 131; VI, 158.
7. Widener Extract Book, p. 187.
8. Staten Island Journal, "Thurs. Nov. 9th" (Huntington Journal Fragments [HM13182]).
9. For references to the civilized man's clothing in relation to the savage's, see *Walden*, pp. 14, 28, 29–30; *Journal*, I, 198; XII, 331–32.
10. *Writings*, V, 325.
11. Widener Extract Book, p. 82.
12. *Writings*, III, 167.
13. *Week*, p. 127.
14. *Journal*, XII, 331, and Thomas W. Atkinson, *Oriental and Western Siberia* (New York, 1858), pp. 242–45 (copied into Indian Notebook 10 [MA605]). In Burton and Parrot, Thoreau read detailed descriptions of desert homes, particularly the "kibitka" (Frederick Parrot, *Journey to Mount Ararat* [New York, 1846], pp. 27–28). Cf. also *Journal*, I, 253: "The charm of the Indian to me is that he stands free and unconstrained in Nature, is her inhabitant and not her guest,

and wears her easily and gracefully. But the civilized man has the habits of the house. His house is a prison. . . . He walks as if he sustained the roof; he carries his arms as if the walls would fall in and crush him, and his feet remember the cellar beneath."

15. "Paradise (to be) Regained," *Writings*, IV, 294.
16. Cf. especially Richard Burton, *The Lake Regions of Central Africa* (New York, 1860), p. 461; Josiah Gregg, *Commerce of the Prairies* (New York, 1844), p. 264 ff.; Alexander von Humboldt, *Personal Narrative* (London, 1852–53), III, 73–75. Thoreau showed particular interest in the Caribs (see Indian Notebooks 10 and 11 (MA605, MA606).
17. *Walden*, pp. 38–39. Cf. also *Journal*, IV, 201–2.
18. *Journal*, IV, 82; *Writings*, IV, 473.
19. Charles Darwin, *Voyage of a Naturalist round the World* (New York, 1846), I, 213.
20. Henry Youle Hind, *Northwest Territory* (Toronto, 1859), p. 81.
21. Insert in Indian Notebook 7 (MA602). Cf. Walter M. Gibson, *The Prisoner of Weltevredep* (New York, 1856), pp. 120–22. We are reminded that Whitman also used these people as examples of the lowest order of humanity, the "Koboos" in *Leaves of Grass*.
22. *Walden*, p. 242; *Journal*, II, 124.
23. *Journal*, I, 335.
24. *Ibid.*, V, 410, 411–12.   25. *Ibid.*, VI, 11; IX, 340.
26. *Ibid.*, I, 446.
27. See *ibid.*, III, 146. Inserted into Indian Notebook 7 is a clipping from the New York *Tribune* entitled "Strange Inhabitants of the Great Basin" which concludes, "The question of the existence of these people, and the evidence of a superior civilization once existing in the Great Basin, is one which will be settled before many years."
28. *Writings*, V, 290.   29. *Ibid.*, V, 234.
30. *Journal*, XI, 437–38.   31. *Ibid.*, XII, 369.
32. Walter Colton, *Land of Gold* (New York, 1850), p. 307.
33. *Writings*, V, 218. For further views of Thoreau's on the gold diggers, see especially "Life Without Principle," *Writings*, IV, 464–68.
34. *Journal*, III, 194–95.
35. *Ibid.*, III, 176; *Writings*, IV, 373.
36. *Journal*, II, 400.   37. *Ibid.*, IV, 15.
38. Huntington Journal Fragments.
39. *Journal*, IV, 250; Widener Extract Book, p. 115.
40. Widener Extract Book, pp. 84, 86.
41. *Journal*, I, 341; *Writings*, IV, 54.
42. Berg Extract Book (173768B), p. 239.
43. Literary Notebook, Library of Congress.

44. *Journal*, XII, 405; III, 194, 265–67.
45. *Week*, pp. 65–66.
46. *Ibid.*, pp. 77–78; cf. also "Natural History of Massachusetts," *Writings*, V, 105. The moral bigotry and cowardice of New Englanders which Thoreau inveighed against so frequently he attributed to the fact that "like the Hindus and Russians [?] and Sandwich Islanders (that were), they are the creatures of an institution" (*Journal*, XI, 326).
47. Huntington Journal Fragments; *Journal*, IX, 252.
48. *Journal*, III, 20–21.
49. *Writings*, V, 12–14; *Walden*, pp. 85–86.
50. *Journal*, III, 263; II, 4.
51. *Writings*, IV, 473, 387.
52. *Week*, pp. 131–32.
53. *Walden*, p. 86.
54. Notebook of Reflections (MA608). See also *Journal*, III, 197.
55. *Writings*, V, 174.

Chapter XV: The Poetic Translation

1. Cf. *Week*, p. 347.
2. By February, 1852, Thoreau had the following five notebooks available for recording from his reading: the Canadian Notebook (MA595), a Commonplace Book (HM957), the Widener Extract Book, a Notebook of Reflections (MA608), Indian Notebook 1 (MA596).
3. F. O. Matthiessen, *American Renaissance* (New York, 1941), p. 91.
4. *Journal*, II, 131.
5. *Ibid.*, II, 161.   6. *Ibid.*, II, 171.
7. "Walking," *Writings*, V, 225.
8. Thoreau's early essay on Columbus appears in MS in the Huntington Library (HM934), written at the same time that Thoreau withdrew from the Harvard Library Irving's *Voyages of Columbus*, January 8, 1834.
9. *Writings*, IV, 292.
10. *Journal*, II, 11.
11. Alexander von Humboldt, *Personal Narrative* (London, 1852–53), I, 30. Cf. *ibid.*, I, 28–29, and Washington Irving, *Voyages of Columbus* (London, 1831), I, 169.
12. *Journal*, IV, 21.   13. *Ibid.*, IV, 402–3.
14. Irving, *Voyages of Columbus*, I, 242, 248.   15. *Ibid.*, I, 200.
16. *Journal*, II, 6; III, 485; VII, 38; III, 443; X, 160.
17. *Walden*, p. 37; *Journal*, II, 228.

18. *Journal*, XII, 234.
19. *Writings*, V, 163–83.
20. *Journal*, II, 96.
21. *Week*, p. 253; *Journal*, III, 112; IV, 146.
22. *Journal*, VIII, 358; *Week*, p. 258.
23. *Journal*, XII, 278; XIII, 386, etc.   24. *Ibid.*, XI, 304.
25. "A Walk to Wachusett," *Writings*, V, 172. Cf. also *Journal*, IX, 214, 261.
26. *Writings*, IV, 121.
27. *Week*, p. 52.
28. *Ibid.*, pp. 62–63.   29. *Ibid.*, p. 130.
30. *Ibid.*, p. 152.   31. *Ibid.*, pp. 160, 380.
32. *Ibid.*, p. 245.   33. *Ibid.*, pp. 265–66.
34. Cf. *ibid.*, p. 121.   35. *Ibid.*, pp. 164–65.
36. *Ibid.*, pp. 59–61.

Chapter XVI: Models and Analogies

1. *Journal*, X, 452–53.
2. Frederick Parrot, *Journey to Mount Ararat* (New York, 1846), p. 176.
3. *Journal*, X, 452–80.
4. *Week*, p. 17.   5. *Ibid.*, p. 418.
6. Thoreau withdrew Brackenridge from Harvard Library, January 16, 1837; he recorded his note-taking from it on the following day (see College Note-Book [MA594]).
7. References in the text to Brackenridge's *Voyage* are to the reprint of the second edition published in Baltimore, 1816, which appears in R. G. Thwaites's *Early Western Travels*, *1748–1846* (Cleveland, 1904), Vol. VI.
8. See *Week*, p. 230; cf. *ibid.*, pp. 228, 291.
9. ". . . we sat up to read the Gazetteer, to learn our latitude and longitude, and write the journal of the voyage" (*ibid.*, p. 119).
10. *Ibid.*, pp. 19, 113.   11. *Ibid.*, pp. 198, 266–67.
12. Cf. *ibid.*, pp. 251, 260, with Humboldt, *Aspects of Nature* (Philadelphia, 1849), pp. 170–72, 167. Thoreau was fascinated, as was Humboldt, with the color of the rivers he sailed. Cf. the "Nile-like blackness" which he finds characterizing the Concord with Humboldt's similar description of the Orinoco (*Week*, p. 91; *Aspects*, p. 163).
13. Review of *A Week on the Concord and Merrimack Rivers* (*Massachusetts Quarterly Review*, III [December, 1849], 40–51), reprinted in *Thoreau Society Bulletin*, XXXV (April, 1951), 1–3.
14. *Week*, pp. 3, 10–11.

15. The title is Channing's for the 1864 book, which comprised the two accounts previously published separately in 1848 and 1858, plus "The Allegash and East Branch," Thoreau's Journal account of his last Maine trip.

16. Cf. Thoreau's descriptive instructions for following one of his Maine routes (letter to Thomas Wentworth Higginson, Jan., 1858, *Corrrespondence*, pp. 507–8). "If you go to the Madawaska in a leisurely manner, supposing no delay on account of rain or the violence of the wind, you may reach Mt. Kineo by noon, & have the afternoon to explore it. The next day you may get to the head of the Lake before noon, make the portage of 2½ miles over a wooden R R & drop down the Penobscot half a dozen miles. The 3rd morning you will perhaps walk half a mile about Pine Stream Falls, while the Indian runs down, cross the head of Chesuncook, & reach the junction of the Caucomgomock & Umbazookskus by noon, and ascend the latter to Umbazookskus Lake that night. If it is lowwater, you may have to walk & carry a little on the Umbazookskus before entering the lake. The 4th morning you will make the carry of 2 miles to Mud Pond (Allegash water) & a very wet carry it is, & reach Chamberlain Lake by noon, & Heron Lake perhaps that night, after a couple of very short carries at the outlet of Chamberlain. At the end of 2 days more, you will probably be at Madawaska."

17. *Writings*, III, 91–92.

18. *Ibid.*, III, 77–78.   19. *Ibid.*, III, 150–51.

20. *Ibid.*, III, 138.

21. *Ibid.*, III, 9, 10, 60, 85. Thoreau read his first and most extensive account of the rapids of Sault Ste Marie in 1833 in Thomas McKenney's *Sketches of a Tour to the Lakes* (Baltimore, 1827).

22. *Writings*, III, 106, 116, 145, 147, 157, 158, 170, 172.

23. *Ibid.*, III, 80, 128, 134, 149, 167–68.

24. Like *The Maine Woods, Cape Cod* was a posthumous publication edited by Channing in 1864; but although Thoreau had seen only the first four chapters in print, in 1855, he had worked upon some of the remaining sections up to the time of his death and seems to have considered all sections as constituting a whole.

25. "I do not see why I may not make a book on Cape Cod, as well as my neighbor on 'Human Culture.' It is but another name for the same thing, and hardly a sandier phase of it" (*Writings*, IV, 3).

26. *Journal*, XIV, 262.

27. See *Writings*, IV, 34, 60, 68, 144, 201, 214, 215.

28. *Ibid.*, IV, 181, 25, 104, 162.   29. *Ibid.*, IV, 121.

30. *Ibid.*, IV, 124, 68.   31. *Ibid.*, IV, 192, 270, 122, 205, 262.

32. *Ibid.*, IV, 188–89.   33. *Ibid.*, IV, 178–79.

Chapter XVII: The Great Circle Sailed

1. Emerson, "The American Scholar," *Complete Works* (Boston and New York, 1903), I, 88. Thoreau remarked (*Week*, p. 310) that "the history which we read is only a fainter memory of events which have happened in our own experience."
2. *Journal*, VI, 417; *Writings*, IV, 420–21; *Journal*, VI, 237.
3. *Journal*, V, 141.
4. *Ibid.*, XIV, 261.   5. *Ibid.*, I, 77.
6. *Writings*, VI, 197.
7. *Journal*, XI, 4–5.
8. *Week*, pp. 312–13.
9. Miller, *Consciousness*, p. 153.
10. *Writings*, VI, 362.
11. *Journal*, II, 286. "Men have written travels in journal form, but perhaps no man's daily life has been rich enough to be journalized" (*ibid.*, III, 239–40).
12. Miller, *Consciousness*, p. 153. Cf. also *Week*, p. 383.
13. *Week*, p. 326.
14. F. O. Matthiessen, *American Renaissance* (New York, 1941), p. 173.
15. *Walden*, p. 108: "Let us spend one day as deliberately as Nature, and not be thrown off the track by every nutshell and mosquito's wing that falls on the rails. Let us rise early and fast, or break fast, gently and without perturbation; let company come and let company go, let the bells ring and the children cry,—determined to make a day of it. Why should we knock under and go with the stream? Let us not be upset and overwhelmed in that terrible rapid and whirlpool called a dinner, situated in the meridian shallows. Weather this danger and you are safe, for the rest of the way is down hill. With unrelaxed nerves, with morning vigor, sail by it, looking another way, tied to the mast like Ulysses. If the engine whistles, let it whistle till it is hoarse for its pains."
16. *Walden*, p. 192.
17. *Ibid.*, p. 292.   18. *Ibid.*, p. 351.
19. *Ibid.*, p. 354.   20. *Ibid.*, p. 97.
21. *Ibid.*, p. 353.   22. *Ibid.*, pp. 354–55.
23. *Week*, p. 373.

A Bibliography of Travel Works
Read by Thoreau

This bibliography only contains books describing travels outside New England. All bibliographical data are taken from the title pages of the works. Original spelling and punctuation have been preserved, but capitalization I have made uniform according to standard bibliographical practice. Special notation has been made where unessential descriptive material has been omitted from titles. An asterisk before a title indicates the edition which Thoreau read.

Each bibliographical description is followed by references to the evidence in Thoreau's writings or elsewhere which explicitly identify his reading of the work. These references are dated as exactly as possible and are arranged chronologically. Roman numerals refer to volumes of *The Writings of Henry David Thoreau* (Boston and New York, 1906); when preceded by "J" they refer to the separately numbered *Journal* volumes of the *Writings* (ed. Bradford Torrey). I have also used the following abbreviations in designating sources:

C	Carl Bode and Walter Harding, eds., *The Correspondence of Henry David Thoreau* (New York, 1958)
CC	"Cape Cod"
LW:Har	Library withdrawal from Harvard: Kenneth W. Cameron, *Emerson the Essayist* (Raleigh, N.C., 1945), II, 191–208
LW:BSNH	Library withdrawal from Boston Society of Natural History: Kenneth W. Cameron, "Emerson, Thoreau, and the Society of Natural History," *American Literature*, XXIV (March, 1952), 21–30
MS.173768B	Berg Extract Book
MS.HM13201	Huntington Commonplace Book, 1836–41
MS.HM13182	Huntington Journal Fragments (Staten Island Journal)
MS.HM13192	Huntington Notes of Trip to Minnesota
MS.HM924	Huntington drafts of *Walden*
MS.HM934	Seven essays by Thoreau (Huntington MS)
MS.HM957	Huntington Commonplace Book, 1841–73
MS.LC	Library of Congress Literary Notebook
MS.MA594	Morgan College Note-Book
MS.MA595	Morgan Canadian Notebook
MS.MA596–606	Morgan Indian Notebooks 1–11
MS.MA608	Morgan Notebook of Reflections
MS.Wid	Widener Extract Book
MW	"The Maine Woods"
PL:MS.HM945	Thoreau's personal library, listed in Huntington Index Rerum, and in *Thoreau's Library*, ed. Harding (Charlottesville, Va., 1957)
W	*Walden*
Wk	*A Week on the Concord and Merrimack Rivers*

A Bibliography of Travel Works
Read by Thoreau

About, Edmond François V. *Greece and the Greeks of the Present Day.
Trans. by Authority. New York, 1857.
J:X, 234–35 (Jan. 3, 1858).

[Adams, James Capen.] Hittell, Theodore Henry. *The Adventures of
James Capen Adams, Mountaineer and Grizzly Bear Hunter of California. San Francisco, 1860. [Adams' adventures first appeared under
his name in the New York Weekly from 1859 to 1860.]
MS.173768B (1860–); MS.MA606 (1860).

Andersson, Karl Johan. *Lake Ngami: or, Explorations and Discoveries
during Four Years' Wanderings in the Wilds of South-western
Africa. . . . New York, 1856.
MS.Wid (1856); MS.MA604 (1856).

Arnold, Benedict. *"Arnold's Letters on his Expedition to Canada in
1775," Maine Historical Society Collections, 3d ser., I (1831) 341–
416. [Arnold's letters were preceded by Col. Montresor's Journal of a
reconnoitering expedition from the Chandiere River to the Kennebec,
1761.]
J:III, 238 (Jan. 27, 1852); C:506 (Jan. 28, 1858); MW:III, 147
(June, 1858); MW:III, 226, 272 (pub. 1864).

Atkinson, Thomas W. *Oriental and Western Siberia: A Narrative of
Seven Years' Explorations and Adventures in Siberia, Mongolia, the
Kirghis Steppes, Chinese Tartary, and Part of Central Asia. New York,
1858.
J:VII, 480 (Oct. 3, 1855); MS.MA605 (1858).

—— *Travels in the Regions of the Upper and Lower Amoor, and the

Russian Acquisitions on the Confines of India and China. . . . With Map and Numerous Illustrations. New York, 1860.
MS.MA606 (1860).

Back, Sir George. **Narrative of the Arctic Land Expedition to the Mouth of the Great Fish River and along the Shores of the Arctic Ocean, in the years 1833, 1834, and 1835.* London, Paris, and Philadelphia, 1836.
LW:Har (April 24, 1837).

Bard, Samuel A. *See* Squier, E.G.

Barrow, Sir John. **A Voyage to Cochinchina in the Years 1792 and 1793, with an Account of a Journey Made in 1801–1802 to the Chief of the Booshanna Nation.* London, 1806.
LW:Har (Sept. 30, 1834).

Barth, Heinrich. *Travels and Discoveries in North and Central Africa. From the Journal of an Expedition Undertaken under the Auspices of H.B.M.'s Government in the Years 1849–1855, etc. . . . and a Sketch of Denham and Clapperton's Expedition, by the American Editor.* Philadelphia, 1860. [An abridged edition.]
MS.MA606 (1859).

Bartram, John. **Observations on the Inhabitants, Climate, Soil, Rivers, Productions, Animals and Other Matters Worthy of Notice, Made by Mr. John Bartram. In His Travels from Penn. to Onondago, Onego, and the Lake Ontario in Canada. To which Is Annexed a Curious Account of the Cataracts at Niagara. By Mr. Peter Kalm, a Swedish Gentleman Who Travelled There.* London, 1751. ["With Bartram is bound a Tract on 'The Advantages of a Settlement upon the Prairie in N. America. . . .' Lon. 1763. Also Post's Journals." (Thoreau's note.)]
MS.MA604 (1856).

Bartram, William. **Travels through North and South Carolina. . . . Containing an Account of the Soil and Natural Productions of Those Regions, Together with Observations on the Manners of the Indians. Maps & Plates.* Philadelphia, 1791.
W:II, 75–76 (1845–54); J:II, 376–77, 378 (Aug. 6, 1851); MS.MA 598 (1851); MS.Wid (March 26, 1856); "Succession of Forest Trees":V, 199 (1860).

Beckwourth, James P. **The Life and Adventures of James P. Beckwourth, Mountaineer, Scout, and Pioneer, and Chief of the Crow Nation of Indians. With Illustrations. Written from His Own Dictation, by T. D. Banner.* New York, 1856.
MS.MA604 (1856).

Beltrami, Giacomo Constantino. *La Découverte des Sources du Mississippi.* New Orleans, 1824.
PL:MS.HM945; LW:BSNH (Oct. 23–Nov. 11, 1852).

Best, George. *A True Discourse of the Late Voyages of Discoveries for the Finding of a Passage to Cathaya by the North-West under the Conduct of Martin Frobisher, Generall. . . .* London, 1578.

W:II, 352–55 (1845–54).

Biddle, Richard. **A Memoir of Sebastian Cabot: With a Review of the History of Maritime Discovery.* Philadelphia, 1831.

MS.MA595 (Nov., 1850–Dec., 1855); LW:Har (Sept. 17, 1855); MS.MA603 (1855); CC:IV, 233 (June, 1855).

Bossu, Jean Bernard. **Nouveaux Voyages aux Indes Occidentales, Contenant une Relation des differens Peuples qui habitent les environs du . . . Mississippi.* 2 vols. Paris, 1768.

LW:Har (April 26, 1859); MS.MA606 (1859).

—— **Nouveaux Voyages dans l'Amerique Septentrionale, Contenant une collection de lettres ecrites sur les lieux, par l'auteur; a son ami, M. Douin . . . ci devant son camarade dans le Nouveau Monde.* Amsterdam, 1777.

LW:Har (April 26, 1859); MS.173768B (April 26, 1859); MS.MA606 (1859).

Brackenridge, Henry Marie. **Journal of a Voyage up the River Missouri, Performed in 1811.* Baltimore, 1815.

LW:Har (Jan. 16, 1837); MS.MA594 (Jan. 17, 1837).

Brereton, John. **A Briefe and True Relation of the Discoverie of the North Part of Virginia . . . Made This Present Yeare, 1602, by Captaine Bartholomew Gosnold. . . .* London, 1602. [Reprinted in *Massachusetts Historical Society Collections*, 3d ser., VIII (1843), 83–123.]

CC:IV, 242–47 (June, 1855).

Brosses, Charles de. **Terra australis cognita: or Voyages to the Terra Australis, or Southern Hemisphere during the 16th, 17th and 18th Centuries.* Trans. with additions by John Callander. 3 vols. Edinburgh and London, 1766–68.

Vol. I, LW:Har (Jan. 19, 1837).

Bry, Théodore de. *Collectiones Peregrinationum in Indiam Orientalem et Indiam Occidentalem, XXV Partibus comprehensas a Theodoro, Joan-Theodoro de Bry, et a Matheo Merian publicatae.* 3 vols. Frankfurt-am-Main, 1590–1634.

LW:Har (Feb. 9, 1853); MS.MA602 (1853); MS.MA604 (1857).

Bryant, William Cullen. **Letters of a Traveller; or, Notes of Things Seen in Europe and America.* New York, 1850.

MS. Wid (1853); MS.MA602 (1853).

Buffon, Count Georges-L. de. *Lettres a un Ameriquain sur l'histoire naturelle generale et particuliere de monsieur de Buffon, troisieme partie.* Hamburg, 1751.

"Walking": V, 222 (pub. June, 1862).

Bullock, William. *Six Months' Residence and Travels in Mexico, Con-*

taining Remarks on the Present State of New Spain, etc. 2 vols. London, 1825.

Vol. II, LW:Har (March 19, 1834).

Burton, Richard F. *The Lake Regions of Central Africa, a Picture of Exploration.* New York, 1860.

J:XIV, 297 (Dec. 30, 1860); MS.MA606 (1860).

—— *Personal Narrative of a Pilgrimage to Al-Madinah and Meccah.* New York, 1856.

J:IX, 251–52 (Feb. 10, 1857); MS.MA604 (1857); MS.Wid (1857).

Cabot, Sebastian, *Navigatione di Sebastiano Cabota.* In *Secondo Volume delle Navigatione et Viaggi racolto gia da M. Gio. Battista Ramusio* . . . , pp. 211–19. Venice, 1583.

MS.MA605 (1858).

—— See also Biddle, Richard; Hakluyt, Richard; Purchas, Samuel; Ramusio, Giovanni Battista.

Cartier, Jacques. See *Voyages de découverte au Canada.*

Carver, Jonathan. *Three Years' Travels throughout the Interior Parts of North America. . . . Together with a Concise History of the Genius of the Indians.* 5th or 6th American ed. Charlestown, 1802.

PL:MS.HM945; J:IV, 97 (June 13, 1852).

Champlain Samuel de. *Les Voyages de la Nouvelle France occidentale . . . et toutes les découvertes qu'il a faites en ce païs depuis l'an 1603. iusques en l'an 1629. . . .* Paris, 1632.

LW:Har (Oct. 28, 1850); MS.MA595 (Nov., 1850–Dec., 1855); MS.MA598 (1851); C:524 (Nov. 6, 1858).

—— *Les Voyages du sieur de Champlain.* Paris, 1613. [This edition Thoreau declared to be the best; see MS.MA595.]

LW:Har (Nov. 18, 1850); MS.MA595 (Nov., 1850–Dec., 1855); CC:IV, 85, 227, 257 (June, 1855); MS.MA606 (1859).

Charlevoix, R. P. François-X. de. *Histoire et description generale de la Nouvelle France, avec le Journal Historique d'un Voyage fait par ordre de Roi dans Amerique Septentrionale. . . .* 3 vols. Paris, 1744.

MW:III, 6 (Jan., 1848); MS.MA595 (Nov., 1850–Dec., 1855); LW:Har (Nov. 5, 1851); J:III, 350 (March 14, 1852); MS.MA599 (1852); "Yankee in Canada" V, 52, 81 (Jan., 1853); CC:IV, 227–42 (June, 1855).

Cholmondeley, Charles. *Ultima Thule: Thoughts in New Zealand.* London, 1854.

PL:MS.HM945; C:376–77 (June 27, 1855).

Clapperton, Hugh. *Narrative of Travels and Discoveries in Northern and Central Africa, in the Years 1822, and 1824, by Major Denham, f.r.s., Capt. Clapperton, and the Late Dr. Oudney. . . .* 2 vols. London, 1826.

Vol. I, LW:Har (April 23, 1834).

Clark, William. *See* Lewis, Meriwether.

Cochrane, Charles Stuart. *A Journal of a Residence and Travels in Co-lombia during the Years 1823 and 1824.* 2 vols. London, 1825.
Vol. I, LW:Har (March 5, 1834).

Colton, Walter. *Land of Gold; or, Three Years in California.* New York, 1850.
J:II, 73 (Oct. 17 [?], 1850).

Cook, James. *The Voyages of Capt. James Cook round the World.* 7 vols. London, 1821.
J:II, 343 (July 25, 1851); CC:IV, 215 (June, 1855); MS.Wid (1857); MS.MA606 (1860).

Cox, Ross. *Adventures on the Columbia River, Including the Narrative of a Residence of Six Years on the Western Side of the Rocky Moun-tains among Various Tribes of Indians Hitherto Unknown.* New York, 1832.
LW:Har (Sept. 25, 1833); MS.HM13182 (Oct. 16, 1843 [dated by Sanborn]).

Crantz, David. *The History of Greenland: Containing a Description of the Country, and Its Inhabitants. . . . Trans. from the High-Dutch, and Illustrated with Maps and Other Copper-plates.* 2 vols. London, 1767.
CC:IV, 149 (June, 1855); CC:IV, 60–61 (1855); J:XIII, 395 (July 7, 1860); LW:Har (Nov. 7, 1860); MS.MA606 (1860); MS.173768B (1860–).

Culbertson, Thaddeus A. *"Journal of an Expedition to the Mauvaises Terres and the Upper Missouri in 1850," in *Smithsonian Institution: Fifth Annual Report*, 1850, pp. 84–145. Washington, 1851.
MS.MA600 (1852); MS.Wid (1852).

Dablon, Claude. *"Relation of the Voyages, Discoveries, and Death of Father James Marquette and the Subsequent Voyages of Father Claud-ius Alloney," *Historical Collections of Louisiana*, ed. B. F. French, IV (1846), 1–77.
LW:Har (Dec. 7, 1858).

Dana, Richard Henry, Jr. *Two Years before the Mast: A Personal Narrative of Life at Sea.* New York, 1840.
J:VII, 452 (Aug. 9, 1855).

[Darwin, Charles.] King, P. B., Robert Fitzroy, and Charles Darwin. *Nar-rative of the Surveying Voyages of His Majesty's Ships "Adventure" and "Beagle," between the Years 1826 and 1836, Describing Their Exam-ination of the Southern Shores of South America, and the Beagle's Circumnavigation of the Globe.* 3 vols. London, 1839.
W:II, 22–23 (1845–54).

Darwin, Charles. *Voyage of a Naturalist round the World.* 2 vols. New York, 1846.

W:II, 14 (1845–54); J:II, 228 (June 7, 1851); J:II, 240–48 (June 11, 1851); J:II, 261–64 (June 14, 1851); MS.MA598 (1851); CC:IV, 40, 122 (June, 1855); "Walking":V, 226 (pub. June, 1862).

[De Soto, Hernando.] Irving, Theodore. *The Conquest of Florida, by Hernando de Soto. New York, 1851.
    MS.MA602 (1854).

Donck, Adriaen van der. *"Description of the New Netherlands. Trans. from the Original Dutch by Hon. Jeremiah Johnson," *New York Historical Society Collections*, 2d ser., I (1841), [125]–242.
    W:II, 43 (1845–54); MS.Wid (1851); MS.MA599 (1852).

Drake, E. C. A *New and Universal Collection of Authentic and Entertaining Voyages and Travels, from the Earliest Accounts to the Present Time. . . .* London, 1768.
    J:IV, 226 (July 14, 1852); "Night and Moonlight":V, 325 (Feb. 28, 1859).

Druilletes, Father Gabriel. *"Narrative of a Voyage Made for the Abuaquios Missions . . . ,"* trans. J. G. Shea, *New York Historical Society Collections*, 2d ser., Part I, III (1857), 309–22.
    MS.MA605 (1858).

Dwight, Timothy. *Travels in New England and New York.* 4 vols. New Haven, 1821–22; London, 1823.
    CC:IV, 207, 212, 226 (pub. 1865).

Edwards, Frank S. *Doniphan's Campaign. A Campaign in New Mexico with Col. Doniphan.* Philadelphia, 1847.
    MS.MA597 (1851).

Ellis, Rev. William. *Three Visits to Madagascar during the Years 1853–1854–1856. . . . Illus. by Woodcuts from Photographs.* New York, 1859.
    MS.173768B (1859).

Emory, Lieut. Col. William Hensley. *Notes of a Military Reconnaissance, from Fort Leavenworth, in Missouri, to San Diego, in California, Including Part of the Arkansas, Del Norte, and Gila Rivers. By Lieut. Col. W. H. Emory. Made in 1846–1847. . . .* Washington, 1848. [Contents: Report of J. W. Albert of his Examination of New Mexico in 1846, 1847; Report of Lieut. Col. P. St. George Cooke on his march from Sante Fe, N.M., to San Diego; Journal of Capt. A. R. Johnston.]
    PL:MS.HM945.

—— *Report of the United States and Mexican Boundary Survey, Made under the Direction of the Secretary of the Interior.* 2 vols. Washington, 1857.
    MS.MA606 (1858); J:XI, 456 (Feb. 25, 1859).

Ewbank, Thomas. *Life in Brazil; or, A Journal of a Visit to the Land of the Cocoa and the Palm. With an Appendix Containing Illustrations of Ancient South American Arts.* New York, 1856.
    MS.MA604 (1856).

Ferris, Benjamin G. *Utah and the Mormons. The History, Government, Doctrines, Customs, and Prospects of the Latter-day Saints from Personal Observation during a Six Months' Residence at Great Salt Lake City.* New York, 1854.
J:VI, 490 (Aug. 31, 1854).

Forbes, James David. *Travels through the Alps of Savoy and Other Parts of the Pennine Chain, with Observations on the Phenomena of Glaciers.* Edinburgh, 1843.
LW:BSNH (March 14–May 9, 1854); MS.Wid (1854); J:VI, 226 (April 27, 1854).

Franchère, Gabriel. *Narrative of a Voyage to the North West Coast of America, in the Years 1811, 1813, and 1814; or, The First American Settlement on the Pacific. . . .*Trans. and ed. J. V. Huntington. New York, 1854.
PL:MS.HM945 [inaccurately transcribed as "Franchore" by F. P. Sanborn, *Henry David Thoreau* (Boston, 1917), p. 514].

Franklin, Sir John. *Narrative of a Journey to the Shores of the Polar Seas, 1819–1822.* Philadelphia, 1824.
"Winter Walk":V, 177 (Sept., 1843); CC:IV, 173–74 (June, 1855); MS.Wid (1855); MS.MA603 (1855).
—— See also Kane, Elisha K., and McClintock, Sir Francis Leopold.

Frobisher, Martin, See Best, George.

Gerard, Cecile Jules Basile. *The Adventures of Gerard, the Lion Killer, Comprising a History of His Ten Years' Campaign among the Wild Animals of Northern Africa.* Trans. Chas. E. Whitehead. New York, 1856.
J:VIII, 403–4 (July 8, 1856); J:VIII, 421 (July 21, 1856).

Gerstaecker, Frederick. *Wild Sports in the Far West.* Trans. Harrison Weir. Boston, 1859.
MS.MA606 (1860).

Gibson, Walter M. *The Prison of Weltevreden; and a Glance at the East Indian Archipelago. Illustrated from Original Sketches.* New York, 1856.
MS.MA604 (1857).

Goethe, Johann Wolfgang von. *Italienische Reise.* In *Goethes Werke.* Stuttgart and Tubingen, 1828–33. Vols. 30–31.
J:I, 9–10 (Nov. 15, 1837); J:I, 11 (Nov. 16, 1837); J:I, 15 (Dec. 8, 1837); J:I, 19 (Dec. 18, 1837); J:I, 30 (Feb. 27, 1838); J:I, 39, 40 (March 14, 1838); J:I, 123 (Feb. 24, 1840); Wk:I, 347, 351 (1845–49); "Life Without Principle":IV, 481 (pub. Oct., 1863).

Gordon-Cumming, Roualeyn George. *Five Years of a Hunter's Life in the Far Interior of South Africa.* 2 vols. New York, 1850.
J:II, 130–32 (Dec. 30, 1850); J:II, 161 (Feb. 14, 1851); J:II, 171 (between Feb. 27 and March 14, 1851); "Walking":V, 225 (pub. June, 1862).

Gorges, Sir Ferdinando. *"A Briefe Narration of the Originall Under-takings of the Advancement of Plantations into the Parts of America, Especially Shewing the Beginning, Progress, and Continuance of That of New England," *Maine Historical Society Collections*, II (1847), 13–65.
CC:IV, 227–42 (June, 1855).

Gregg, Josiah. *Commerce of the Prairies: or, The Journal of a Santa Fe Trader, during Eight Expeditions across the Great Western Prairies, and a Residence of Nearly Nine Years in Northern Mexico.* 2 vols. New York, 1844.
MS.MA600 (1852).

Grinnell Expeditions. *See* Kane, Elisha K.

Hakluyt, Richard. *Divers Voyages Touching the Discovery of America and the Islands Adjacent.* Ed. J. W. Jones. Printed for the Hakluyt Society. London, 1850.
CC:IV, 227–42 (June, 1855); MS.MA603 (1855); MS.MA605 (1858).

Hall, Col. Francis. *Travels in Canada and the United States in 1816 and 1817.* Boston, 1818.
LW:Har (Sept. 11, 1833).

Hammond, Samuel H. *Hunting Adventures in the Northern Wilds; or, A Tramp in the Chataugay Woods, over Hills, Lakes, and Forest Streams.* New York, 1856.
MS.Wid (1856).

Hayes, Isaac I. *An Arctic Boat Journey, in the Autumn of 1854.* Boston, 1860.
MS.MA606 (1860).

Head, Sir Francis B. *The Emigrant.* London, 1847.
MS.MA595 (Nov., 1850–Dec., 1855); J:III, 279 (Feb. 5, 1852); MS.Wid (1852); MS.MA599 (1852); "Walking": V, 221 (pub. June, 1862).

Hearne, Samuel. *A Journey from Prince of Wale's Fort in Hudson's Bay, to the North Ocean. . . . In the Years 1769, 1770, 1771, and 1772.* London, 1795.
"Yankee in Canada":V, 100–101 (Jan., 1853).

Heckewelder, John Gottlieb Ernestus. *A Narrative of the Mission of the United Brethren among the Delaware and Mohegan Indians, from Its Commencement, in the Year 1740, to the Close of the Year 1808. . . .* Philadelphia, 1820.
MS.MA599 (1852); LW:Har (May 9, 1854); MS.MA602 (1854).

Hennepin, R. P. Louis. * *Description de la Louisiane, nouvellement découverte au Sud'Ouest de la Nouvelle France par order du roy. Avec la Carte du Pays: Les Moeurs et la Maniere de vivre des Sauvages. . . .* Paris, 1683.

LW:Har (May 27, 1858).

—— *Voyages curieux et nouveaux de Messieurs Hennepin et De la Borde, Ou l'on voit Une Description tres Particuliere, d'un Grand Pays dans L'Amerique, entre le Nouveau Mexique, et la Mer Glaciale.* . . . Amsterdam, 1711.

LW:Har (Dec. 7, 1858); MS.MA605 (1858).

Henry, Alexander. *Travels and Adventures in Canada and the Indian Territories between the Years 1760 and 1776.* New York, 1809.

Wk:I, 228, 291 (1845–49); J:IV, 136 (June 23, 1852).

Herndon, Lieut. William L., and Lardner Gibbon. *Exploration of the Valley of the Amazon.* Maps and plates. 2 vols. Washington, 1853–54.

PL:MS.HM945; MS.MA595 (Nov., 1850–Dec., 1855); J:VI, 335–36 (June 8, 1854); MS.MA602 (1854); "Life Without Principle":IV, 479 (pub. 1863).

Hind, Henry Youle. *Northwest Territory. Reports of Progress; Together with a Preliminary and General Report on the Assiniboine and Saskatchewan Exploration Expedition. . . . Printed by Order of the Legislative Assembly.* Toronto, 1859.

MS.173768B (1859); J:XIII, 305 (May 20, 1860); MS.MA606 (1860).

—— See also *Report on the Exploration.*

Holton, Isaac Farwell. *New Granada: Twenty Months in the Andes.* New York, 1857.

MS.Wid (1857); MS.MA604 (1857).

Howitt, William. *A Boy's Adventures in Australia; or, Herbert's Note Book.* Boston, 1855.

J:IX, 291 (March 13, 1857); MS.MA603 (1857).

—— *Land, Labor and Gold; or, Two Years in Victoria: with Visits to Sidney and Van Diemen's Land.* 2 vols. Boston, 1855.

"Life Without Principle":IV, 465–67 (1854); J:VII, 491, 492, 496 (Oct. 18, 1855); J:VII, 500–501 (Oct. 19, 1855); MS.Wid (1855); MS.MA603 (1855).

Huc, Evariste Regis. *A Journey through the Chinese Empire.* 2 vols. New York, 1855.

MS.MA595 (Nov., 1850–Dec., 1855); MS. 173768B (1855).

—— *Recollections of a Journey through Tartary, Thibet, and China, during the Years 1844, 1845, and 1846.* 2 vols. New York, 1852. (Half-title: Appleton's Popular Library of the Best Authors.)

J:III, 474 (April 28, 1852); J:III, 485 (April 30, 1852); J:IV, 15 (May 3, 1852); MS:Wid (1852); "Walking":V, 228 (pub. June, 1862).

[Hudson, Henry.] *"Extract from the Journal of the Voyages of the Half-Moon, Henry Hudson, Master, from the Netherlands to the

Coast of North-America, in the Year 1609," *New York Historical Society Collections*, 2d ser., I (1841), 317–22.
MS.MA598 (1851).

Humboldt, Alexander von. **Personal Narrative of Travels to the Equinoctial Regions of the New Continent during the Years 1799–1804.* Trans. Thomasina Ross. 3 vols. London, 1852–53.
J:IV, 21 (May 5, 1852); MS:Wid (1852); J:V, 117 (May 1, 1853); J:XII, 278 (Aug. 4, 1859); J:XIII, 386 (July 4, 1860).

Hunter, John. **Memoirs of a Captivity among the Indians of North America.* . . . London, 1823.
PL:MS.HM945 [Harding lists the American ed., Philadelphia, 1823, which Thoreau must have owned *after* 1856, since his excerpts are all taken from the London ed.]; LW:Har (Dec. 7, 1854); MS.Wid (Dec. 7, 1854); MS.Wid (1856).

Irving, Theodore. *See* De Soto, Hermando.

Irving, Washington. **A History of the Life and Voyages of Christopher Columbus.* 4 vols. London, 1831.
LW:Har (Jan. 8, 1834); MS:HM934 (1836–37); "Paradise (to be) Regained":IV, 292 (Nov., 1843); MW:III, 90 (March, 1848); Wk:I, 279, 418 (1845–49); W:II, 352–55 (1845–54); J:IV, 21 (May 5, 1852); J:IV, 402–3 (Oct. 28, 1852); "Yankee in Canda":V, 67–68 (Jan., 1853); CC:IV, 121, 178–79 (June, 1855); J:XII, 278 (Aug. 4, 1859); J:XIII, 386 (July 4, 1860).

―――― **Voyages and Discoveries of the Companions of Columbus.* Philadelphia, 1831.
LW:Har (Jan. 22, 1834).

Josselyn, John. **An Account of Two Voyages to New England.* . . . A *Large Chronological Table of the Most Remarkable Passages, from the First Discovering of the Continent of America, to the Year 1673.* London, 1764. [Thoreau also read the reprint of the above in *Massachusetts Historical Society Collections*, 3d ser., III (1833), 211–354.]
MS.MA598 (1851); LW:Har (Jan. 19, 1854); MS.Wid (Jan. 19, 1854); J:VI, 76 (Jan. 23, 1854); J:VI, 108 (Feb. 8, 1854); MS.MA 602 (1854); J:VII, 108 (Jan. 9, 1855).

Kalm, Peter. **Travels into North America; Containing Its Natural History; and a Circumstancial Account of Its Plantations and Agriculture in General.* . . . Trans. John Rheinhold Forster. 3 vols. London, 1770–71.
MS.MA595 (Nov., 1850–Dec., 1860); LW:Har (Aug. 11, 1851); MS. Wid (Aug. 11, 1851); J:II, 463 (Sept. 5, 1851); J:II, 466 (Sept. 6, 1851); MS.MA598 (1851); "Yankee in Canada":V, 21, 30, 38–39, 65 (Jan., 1853); CC:IV, 126, 201 (June, 1855).

Kane, Elisha K. **Arctic Exploration, the Second Grinnell Expedition in Search of Sir John Franklin, 1853–1854–1855.* 2 vols. Philadelphia, 1856.

J:IX, 192–95 (Dec. 19–24, 1856); J:IX, 200 (Dec. 28, 1856); MS.
Wid (1856); MS.MA604 (1856); J:XI, 17, 31, 36 (July 8, 10, 1858);
C:580 (May 20, 1860).

—— *Grinnell Expedition in Search of Sir John Franklin, a Personal
Narrative.* New York, 1853.
W:II, 352–55 (1845–54); J:VI, 139, 140 (Feb. 26, 1854); MS.Wid
(1854); MS.MA602 (1854); "Forest Trees":V, 197 (Oct. 6,
1860).

Keating, William H. *Narrative of an Expedition to the Source of St.
Peter's River, Lake Winnipeg, Lake of the Woods, etc. Performed in
the Year 1823, by Order of the Hon. J. C. Calhoun, Sec. of War,
under the Command of Stephen H. Long, Major U.S.T.E.* 2 vols.
Philadelphia, 1824.
MS.MA599 (1852).

Krapf, J. Ludwig. *Travels, Researches, and Missionary Labours, during
an Eighteen Years' Residence in Eastern Africa. . . . With an Ap-
pendix Respecting the Snow-capped Mountains of Eastern Africa; the
Sources of the Nile; the Languages and Literature of Abessinia and
Eastern Africa, etc. . . .* Boston, 1860.
MS.173768B (1860).

Laet, Joannes de. *Novis orbis, seu Descriptionis Indiae Occidentalis libri
XVII.* Batavia, 1633. (Half-title: Americae utrinsque descriptio.)
[Thoreau also read the excerpts from Laet in *New York Historical
Society Collections,* 2d ser., I (1841), 281–84.]
LW:Har (Jan. 14, 1851).

[Lahontan, Louis Armand.] *Voyages du baron de La Hontan dans l'A-
merique Septentrionale, qui contiennent une Relation des differens
Peuples qui y habitent. . . .* Amsterdam, 1705.
LW:Har (Feb. 2, 1852); MS:Wid (Feb. 2, 1852); J:III, 287 (Feb. 7,
1852); J:III, 337 (March 6, 1852); MS.MA599 (1852); V, 67 (Jan.,
1853); C:621 (June 25, 1861).

Laing, Samuel. *Journal of a Residence in Norway.* London, 1837.
W:II, 29–30 (1845–54).

Lane, Edward William. *An Account of the Manners and Customs of
the Modern Egyptians, Written in Egypt during the Years 1833, 1834,
and 1835, Partly from Notes Made during a Former Visit to That
Country in the Years 1825, 1826, 1827, and 1828.* 2 vols. London,
1842.
MS.MA606 (1860); MS.173768B (1860).

Lawson, John. *The History of Carolina.* London, 1718. [Thoreau also
read this account in *A New Collection of Voyages and Travels,* ed.
John Nevins, London, 1711, where it was titled "A New Account of
Carolina by Mr. Lawson."]
MS.MA600 (1852); MS.MA604 (1856); MS.Wid (1856); J:IX,
451 (June 21, 1857).

Layard, Austen Henry. *Discoveries among the Ruins of Nineveh and Babylon, with Travels in Armenia, Kurdistan, and the Desert; Being the Results of a Second Expedition Undertaken for the Trustees of the British Museum*. New York, 1853.
J:VI, 9 (Dec. 3, 1853); J:VI, 11 (Dec. 5, 1853); J:VI, 15 (Dec. 9, 1853); C:313 (Dec. 22, 1853); MS.173768B (Dec., 1853); MS.Wid (1854); J:IX, 214 (Jan. 11, 1857); J:IX, 261 (Feb. 15, 1857); J:XII, 92–93 (March 28, 1859); J:XII, 340 (Sept. 22, 1859).

—— *Nineveh and Its Remains; with an Account of a Visit to the Chaldaean Christians of Kuridistan, and the Yezidis, or Devil-Worshippers; and an Inquiry into the Manner of Arts of the Ancient Assyrians*. 2 vols. New York, 1849.
J:II, 35 (between June 9 and 20, 1850); CC:IV, 54 (1855).

Le Jeune, Vimont, et al. *Relation de ce qui s'est passe en la Nouvelle France*. . . . Paris, 1632–72. [Thoreau withdrew from Harvard Library the volume for each year except 1646.]
LW:Har (Oct. 5, 1852); J:IV, 388 (Oct. 15, 1852); LW:Har (Nov. 11, Dec. 30, 1852); MS.MA595 (1852); MS.Wid (1852–58); MS. MA599–605 (1852–58); J:IV, 456 (Jan. 2, 7, 1853); LW:Har (Feb. 9, Nov. 28, 1853); J:VI, 42, 45–46 (Jan. 1, 1854); LW:Har (Dec. 7, 1854); LW:Har (March 26, 1856); LW:Har (Jan. 13, May 27, 1858); MS.173768B (1858).

Lescarbot, Marc. *Histoire de la Nouvelle-France*. Paris, 1612.
MW:III, 60 (Jan., 1848); LW:Har (Nov. 18, 1850); MS.MA595 (Nov., 1850–Dec., 1855); MS.MA598 (1851); CC:IV, 227–42, 247–51 (June, 1855).

[Lewis, Meriwether, and William Clark.] *History of the Expedition under the Command of Captains Lewis and Clark to the Sources of the Missouri, Thence across the Rocky Mountains, and down the Columbia to the Pacific Ocean. Performed during the Years 1804, 1805, and 1806, by Order of the Government of the United States. Prepared for the Press by Paul Allen, Esq.* 2 vols. Philadelphia, 1814.
PL:MS.HM945; W:II, 352–55 (1845–54).

Livingstone, David. *Livingstone's Travels and Researches in South Africa. . . . With Portrait; Maps by Arrowsmith; and Numerous Illustrations*. New York, 1858.
MS.MA604 (1857); MS.173768B (1858).

Long, Major Stephen H. *See* Keating, William H.

Loskiel, G. H. *History of the Mission of the United Brethren among the Indians in North America. In Three Parts*. . . . Trans. Christian Ignatius Latrobe. London, 1794.
J:VIII, 34 (Nov. 27, 1855); LW:Har (Dec. 10, 1855); MS.Wid (Dec. 10, 1855); MS.MA603–604 (1855–56).

Lyell, Charles. *A Second Visit to the United States of North America.
2 vols. New York, 1849.
MS.MA604 (1857).

Lyon, Capt. G. F. *The Private Journal of Capt. G. G. Lyon, of H.M.S.
"Hecla," during the Recent Voyage of Discovery under Captain Parry.
Boston, 1824.
PL:MS.HM945.

McClintock, Sir Francis Leopold. *The Voyage of the "Fox" in the Arctic Seas. A Narrative of the Discovery of the Fate of Sir John Franklin
and His Companions. Boston, 1860.
MS.MA606 (1860); MS.173768B (after June, 1860).

McKenney, Thomas L. *Memoirs, Official and Personal, with Sketches
of Travels among the Northern and Southern Indians. 2 vols. in 1.
New York, 1846.
PL:MS.HM945.

—— *Sketches of a Tour to the Lakes, of the Character and Customs of
the Chippeway Indians, and of the Incidents Connected with the
Treaty of Fond du Lac. Baltimore, 1827.
LW:Har (Sept. 25, 1833); MW:III, 85 (Jan., 1848); MS.MA602
(1853).

Mackenzie, Alexander. *Voyages from Montreal, on the River St. Law-
rence, through the Continent of North America, to the Frozen and
Pacific Oceans; in the Years 1789 and 1793. . . . With Original
Notes by Bougainville and Volney. 2 vols. London and Edinburgh, 1802.
Wk:I, 91–92 (1845–49); "Yankee in Canada":V, 100–101 (Jan.,
1853); LW:Har (Feb. 28, 1859); MS.173768B (Feb. 28, 1859);
MS.MA606 (1859).

[McLellan, H. B.] McLellan, Isaac. *Journal of a Residence in Scotland,
and a Tour through England, France, etc. Compiled from the Manuscripts of H. B. McLellan. Boston, 1834.
PL:MS.HM945 (–1840).

MacTaggard, John. *Three Years in Canada: An Account of the Actual
State of the Country in 1826–1827–1828. . . . London, 1829.
MS.MA595 (Nov., 1850–Dec., 1855); J:II, 225 (June 3, 1851); MS.
MA598 (1851); "Yankee in Canada":V, 94 (Jan., 1853).

Marcy, Randolph Barnes. Exploration of the Red River of Louisiana, in
the Year 1852 . . . Assisted by George B. McClellan. With Reports
on the Natural History of the Country, and Numerous Illustrations.
Washington, 1853.
PL:MS.HM945; MS.MA602 (1854); MS.Wid (1854).

Maximilian [Alexander Philipp]. * Travels in the Interior of North Amer-
ica. By Maximilian, Prince of Wied. . . . Trans. H. Evans Lloyd.
London, 1843.
MS.MA600 (1852).

Melville, Herman. *Typee, a Peep at Polynesian Life.* New York, 1846.
MS.HM924.

Michaux, François André. **Voyage a l'ouest des monts Alleghanys dans les etats de l'Ohio, du Kentucky et du Tennessee, et retour a Charleston par les hautes-Carolines, etc.* Paris, 1808.
W:II, 277 (1845–54); "Walking":V, 221 (pub. June, 1862);
LW:Har (June 2, 1851); J:II, 230–32 (June 8, 1851); MS.MA598
(1851); J:V, 399 (Aug. 24, 1853); J:IX, 137 (Nov. 2, 1856); J:IX,
397, 414 (June 12, 1857).

Montanus, Arnoldus. *See* Ogilby, John.

Montresor, John. *See* Arnold, Benedict.

Moodie, Susanna S. *Life in the Clearings versus the Bush.* Philadelphia,
1856.
MS.MA604 (1856).

—— **Roughing It in the Bush; or, Life in Canada.* 2 vols. London,
1852. MS.MA602 (1853).

Morrell, Benjamin. *A Narrative of Four Voyages to the South Sea,
North and South Pacific Ocean, Chinese Sea, Ethiopic and Southern
Atlantic Ocean, etc.* (1822–1831). New York, 1832.
LW:Har (Nov. 11, 1834). [Thoreau might have withdrawn Mrs.
Abby Jane Morrell's work (*Narrative of a Voyage to the Ethiopic and
South Atlantic Ocean, etc.,* 1829–1831, New York, 1833) rather than
Benjamin Morrell's.]

Nearchus. *See* Vincent, William.

Nevins, John. *A New Collection of Voyages and Travels.* London, 1711.
MS.MA604 (1856).

——*See also* Lawson, John.

[Nicollet, Joseph N.] **Reports of Exploration and Surveys to Ascertain
the Most Practical and Economical Route for a Railroad from the
Mississippi River to the Pacific Ocean, Made under the Direction of
the Secretary of War, in 1853–1854* [1853–1856]. . . . 12 vols. Washington, 1855–60. [Thoreau read Vols. I and II (pub. 1855).]
MS.MA604 (1856); MS.MA604 (1857).

Ogilby, John. *America: Being the Latest, and Most Accurate Description
of the New World; Containing the Original of the Inhabitants and
the Remarkable Voyages Thither, etc.* . . . London, 1671. [This is
a translation of Montanus' original work in Dutch, Amsterdam,
1671.] J:VI, 136 (Feb. 21, 1854); CC:IV, 227–42 (June, 1855).

Olmsted, Frederick Law. **A Journey through Texas; or, A Saddle-Trip
on the Southwestern Frontier, with a Statistical Appendix.* New York,
1857.
MS.Wid (1857); MS.MA604 (1857).

Osborn, Lieut. Sherard. **Stray Leaves from an Arctic Journal; or, Eight-*

een Months in Search of Sir John Franklin's Expedition, in the Years 1850–1851. New York, 1852.

J:IV, 320 (Aug. 27, 1852); MS.Wid (1852).

[Park, Mungo.] *The Life and Travels of Mungo Park; with an Account of His Death from the Journal of Isaaco, the Substance of Later Discoveries Relative to His Lamented Fate, and the Termination of the Niger.* New York, 1840 and 1842. (Half-title: Harper's Family Library, No. LV.)

W:II, 352–55 (Aug. 9, 1854).

Parrot, Frederick. *A Journey to Mount Ararat. . . .* Trans. W. D. Dooley. New York, 1846.

J:III, 27 (Sept. 27, 1851); MS.Wid (1851); J:X, 452–53 (June 2, 1858); J:X, 466, 469 (June 3, 1858).

Parry, Sir William Edward. *Three Voyages for the Discovery of a Northwest Passage from the Atlantic to the Pacific, and Narrative of an Attempt to Reach the North Pole.* 2 vols. New York, 1845.

J:I, 470 (1837–47); "Winter Walk":V, 177 (Sept., 1843); J:IX, 232 (Jan. 26, 1857).

Perry, Matthew Galbraith. *Narrative of an Expedition of an American Squadron to the China Seas and Japan in 1852, 1853 and 1854. Compiled from the Original Notes and Journals of Com. Perry by Rev. Francis Hawks.* New York, 1857.

PL:MS.HM945 [Harding lists the Philadelphia ed, 1856].

Peters, DeWitt C., M.D. *The Life and Adventures of Kit Carson, the Nestor of the Rocky Mountains; from Facts Narrated by Himself.* New York, 1858.

MS.MA606 (1859).

Pfeiffer, Ida. *A Lady's Voyage round the World: A Selected Trans. from the German by Mrs. Percy Sinnett.* New York, 1852.

W:II, 25, 124 (1845–54); J:III, 194 (Jan. 15, 1852); J:III, 194–95 (Jan. 16, 1852); J:III, 200 (Jan. 17, 1852); J:III, 205 (Jan. 18, 1852); J:III, 304 (Feb. 14, 1852); MS.173768B (1852); MS.Wid (1852).

Pike, Major Zebulon M. *An Account of Expeditions to the Sources of the Mississippi, and through the Western Parts of Louisiana to the Sources of the Arkansas, Kansas, LaPlatte, and Pierre Juane Rivers, Performed by Order of the Government of the United States, in the Years 1805–1806–1807. . . .* Philadelphia and Baltimore, 1810.

PL:MS.HM945; MS.MA600 (1852); MS.HM13192 (June 1, 1861).

Post, Christian Frederich. *Second Journal of Christian Frederich Post, on a Mission from the Governor of Pennsylvania to the Indians on the Ohio.* London, 1759.

LW:Har (Dec. 10, 1855); MS.MA604 (1856).

Purchas, Samuel. *Purchas His Pilgrimes. . . .* 4 vols. London, 1624–25.

[Thoreau made particular note of certain contents of Purchas in Indian Notebook 8: "In Purchas's Pilgrims, V: Columbus' first voyage, Drake's voyage and voyages round the world by other, Hudson's voyages p. 507 3rd. v., Barkley's Travels p. 625, Greenland pp. 651 and 707, Aerreva on W. Indies p. 855, Acosta on W. Indies, DeSoto in Florida in 1532, Champlains 1st voyage in 1601, 25 pp. of Lescarbot; Also Purchas's 'Relations of the World and the Religions,' etc. a separate volume."]

J:III, 352 (March 16, 1852); CC:IV, 242–47 (June, 1855); MS.MA603–604 (1855–56); MS.MA605–606 (1858–59).

Rafn, Carl Christian. *Antiquitates Americanae;* . . . Copenhagen, 1845. [Contains "America Discovered by the Scandinavians in the Tenth Century." Identified under "Six Tracts" withdrawn by Thoreau from Harvard Library; see Cameron, *Emerson the Essayist*, II, 195, 206.]

MW:III, 90–92 (March, 1848); LW:Har (Nov. 5, 1849); MS.Wid (1852); CC:IV, 140, 187–88, 191–92, 247–51 (June, 1855).

Ramusio, Giovanni Battista. *Navigationi et Viaggi.* Venice, 1550–1606. [Editions of Ramusio's collection appeared in irregular succession and title pages vary according to volume and edition. Thoreau referred to all three volumes of the work at various times, using the particular editions of each volume available to him in the Harvard Library, namely, the 4th ed. of Vol. I (1588), the 3d ed. of Vol. II (1583), the 2d ed. of Vol. III (1565).]

CC:IV, 227–42 (June, 1855); MS.MA605 (1858).

Reid, Mayne. *The Boy Hunters; or, Adventures in Search of a White Buffalo.* Boston, 1853.

MS.MA604 (1857); MS.Wid (1857).

—— *Desert Home; or, The Adventures of a Lost Family in the Wilderness.* Boston, 1852.

MS.Wid (1856).

—— *The Forest Exiles; or, The Perils of a Peruvian Family amid the Wilds of the Amazon.* Boston, 1855.

MS.Wid (1856).

—— *Young Voyagers; or, The Boy Hunters in the North.* Boston, 1854.

J:VI, 158 (March 9, 1854); MS.Wid (1854); MS.MA602 (1854); MS.Wid (1856); MS.MA604 (1857).

Report on the Exploration of the Country between Lake Superior and the Red River Settlement. Printed by Order of the Legislative Assembly. Toronto, 1858. [Reports are by G. Gladman, H. Y. Hind, and others. Thoreau read "A French trans." of this work, as he indicated in his notebook.]

MS.MA606 (1860); MS.173768B (1860).

Richardson, John. *Arctic Searching Expedition: Journal of a Boat*

Voyage in Search of Ships under Command of Sir John Franklin. New York, 1852.

PL:MS.HM945 [not listed by Harding]; MS.MA595 (Nov., 1850–Dec., 1855); J:III, 358 (March 23, 1852); J:III, 360 (March 29, 1852); J:III, 363 (March 30, 1852); J:III, 365 (March 31, 1852); J:III, 372 (April 1, 1852); J:IV, 82 (June 5, 1852); MS.Wid (1852); MS.MA600 (1852); "Yankee in Canada"; V, 48 (Jan., 1853); MW:III, 296 (1857).

Riley, James. *An Authentic Narrative of the Loss of the American Brig "Commerce," Wrecked on the Western Coast of Africa, in the Month of August, 1815. . . . Revised, and His Life Continued, by the Author, in January, 1828.* Hartford, 1836.

C:319 (Jan. 21, 1854); CC:IV, 200 (June, 1855).

Rivero, M. E., and J. J. von Tschudi. **Peruvian Antiquities.* Trans. F. Hawks. New York, 1853.

PL:MS.HM945 [Harding lists the 1855 ed.].

Roberval, François de la Roch, sieur de. See *Voyages de découverte.*

Sagard, Theodat. **Le Grand Voyage du Pays des Hurons avec un dictionaire de la langue Huronie. . . . Par Fr. Gabriel Sagard Theoadt, Recollet de S. Francois, de la Province de S. Denys en France.* Paris, 1632.

MS.Wid (1855); MS.MA603 (1855).

—— *Histoire du Canada et Voyages que Les Freres Mineurs Recollects y ont faicts pour la Conversion des Infidelles.* 4 vols. Paris, 1636.

J:VII, 126 (Jan. 20, 1855); J:VII, 143 (Jan. 25, 1855); MS.MA603 (1855).

St. John, Bayle. **Adventures in the Libyan Desert and the Oasis of Jupiter Ammon.* New York, 1849.

MS.173768B (1860–).

Schoolcraft, Henry R. *Narrative of an Expedition through the Upper Mississippi to Itasco Lake, the Actual Source of the River; Embracing an Exploratory Trip through the St. Croix and Burntwood (or Broule) Rivers: in 1832.* New York, 1834.

MS.MA595 (Nov., 1850–Dec., 1855); MS.MA596 (1851); MS.MA600 (1852); MS.MA602 (1854).

Shea, J. G. "History of the Discovery of the Mississippi River," *Historical Collections of Louisiana,* ed. B. F. French, Part IV (1853), pp. vii–xxxix.

MS.MA605 (1858).

Silliman, Benjamin. **Remarks Made on a Short Tour between Hartford and Quebec in the Autumn of 1819.* 2d ed. New Haven, 1824.

MS.MA595 (Nov., 1850–Dec., 1855); LW:Har (Feb. 10, 1851); "Yankee in Canada":V, 79, 98 (Jan., 1853).

Sitgreaves, L. *Report of an Expedition down the Zuni and Colorado Rivers by Captain L. Sitgreaves, Corps Topographical Engineers. . . .* Washington, 1853.
PL:MS.HM945 [Harding lists the 1854 ed., but Thoreau identifies the 1853 ed. as the source of his excerpts]; MS.MA602 (1854); MS.Wid (1854).

Sleeman, W. H. *Rambles and Recollections of an Indian Official.* 2 vols. London, 1844.
J:IV, 209 (July 9, 1852); MS.Wid (1852); J:XIV, 334 (1861).

Smet, Father P. J. de. *Oregon Missions and Travels over the Rocky Mountains, in 1845–1846.* New York, 1847.
MS.MA597 (1851).

Smith, Edmond Reuel. *The Araucanians; or, Notes of a Tour among the Indian Tribes of Southern Chile.* New York, 1855.
MS.MA604 (1856).

Smith, John. *Historie of Virginia, New England, and the Summer Isles . . . from the Beginning in 1584 to 1626.* London, 1632.
MW:III, 90–92 (March, 1848); MS.MA595 (Nov., 1850–Dec., 1855); J:IV, 494 (Feb. 23, 1853); J:V, 21 (March 15, 1853); J:VII, 267 (March 23, 1853); MS.MA602 (1853); CC:IV, 180–81, 226–27, 266 (June, 1855); J:XII, 397 (Oct. 17, 1859).

Smyth, C. P. *Astronomical Experiments at Teneriffe, 1856.* London, 1858. [Thoreau may have read of Smyth's experiences, summarized in this work, as they appeared in periodicals.]
J:XI, 48, 49 (July 15, 1858).

Squier, E. G. [Samuel A. Bard, pseud.] *Waikna; or, Adventures on the Mosquito Shore.* New York, 1855.
MS.MA604 (1857).

Sterne, Lawrence. A *Sentimental Journey.* London, 1786.
PL:MS.HM945 (–1840).

Strachey, William. *"The Second Book of the First Decade of the Historie of Travaile into Virginia Brittannia . . . 1607," Massachusetts Historical Society Collections,* 4th ser., I (1852), 219–47.
MS.MA603 (1855).

Swan, James G. *The Northwest Coast; or, Three Years' Residence in Washington Territory.* New York, 1857.
MS.MA604 (1857).

Talbot, Edward Allen. *Five Years' Residence in the Canadas: Including a Tour through Part of the United States of America, in the Year, 1823. . . .* 2 vols. London, 1824.
LW:Har (March 16, 1852); MS.Wid (March 16, 1852).

Tanner, John. *Narrative of the Captivity and Adventures of John Tanner (U.S. Interpreter at the Sault de Ste. Marie) during Thirty Years' Residence among the Indians, in the Interior of North America.*

Prepared for the Press by Edwin James, M.D. New York, 1830.
LW:Har (May 9, 1854): MS.Wid (May 9, 1854); J:VI, 373–74
(June 21, 1854); MS.MA602 (1854); J:IX, 299 (March 20, 1857).

Taylor, Bayard. *Eldorado, or, Adventures in the Path of Empire: Comprising a Voyage to California, via Panama, Life in San Francisco and Monterey; Pictures of the Gold Region, and Experiences of Mexican Travel.* New York, 1850.
MS.MA603 (1854); MS.MA603 (1855).

Tonti, Henri de, chevalier de [supposed author]. *Relation de la Louisiane et du Mississippi.* [Reprint of 1697 ed., *Dernières Découvertes dans l'Amérique Septentrionale de M. De La Sale, etc.*] In J. F. Bernard's *Recueil de Voiages du Nord*, Amsterdam, 1715–26, V, 35–195. [Tonti's account was translated by Thomas Falconer, "On Discovery of the Mississippi," *Historical Collections of Louisiana*, ed. B. F. French, I (1846), 52–83.]
LW:Har (Dec. 7, 1858).

Traill, Mrs. Catherine Parr (Strickland). *The Backwoods of Canada: Being Letters from the Wife of an Emigrant Officer, Illustrative of the Domestic Economy of British America.* London, 1838.
LW:Har (Feb. 15, 1858).

Tschudi, J. J. von. *Travels in Peru, on the Coast, in the Sierra, across the Cordilleras and the Andes, into the Primeval Forests.* Trans. Thomasina Ross. London and New York, 1847.
PL:MS.HM945.
—— *See also* Rivero, M. E.

Tytler, Patrick Fraser. *Historical View of the Progress of Discovery on the More Northern Coasts of America, from the Earliest Period to the Present Time. . . . With Descriptive Sketches of the Natural History of the North American Regions. By James Wilson . . . to Which Is Added an Appendix, Containing Remarks on a Late Memoir of Sebastian Cabot, with a Vindication of Richard Hakluyt. . . .* (Halftitle: Harpers Family Library, No. LIII.) New York, 1855.
PL:MS.HM945. [Not listed by Harding. Thoreau's inscribed and annotated copy is in the Baker Library, Hanover, N.H., and appears to be the "Discovery on the N. Coast of America. I v" listed by Thoreau and ascribed by Harding to a book with a somewhat different title by Thomas Simpson.]

[Verrazano, Giovanni da.] *"The Voyages of John de Verazzano along the Coast of North America from Carolina to Newfoundland, A. D. 1524,"* tran. Jos. G. Cogwell, *New York Historical Society Collection,* 2d ser., I (1841) 37–69.
MS.MA599 (1852).

Vincent, William. *The Voyage of Nearchus from the Indus to the Euphrates, Collected from the Original Journal Preserved by Arrian,*

and Illustrated by Authorities Ancient and Modern. London, 1797.
CC:IV, 215 (June, 1855); MS.MA604 (1856); MS.Wid (1856).

Volney, Constantin François de Chasseboeuf, Comte de. *Travels through Syria and Egypt, in the Years 1783, 1784, and 1785.* 2 vols. London, 1787; New York, 1798. [In this instance, Thoreau read the translation.]
MS.LC (1841–).

Voyages de découverte au Canada, entre l'annee 1534 et 1542, par Jacques Quartier, le sieur de Roberval, Jean Alphonse de Xanctioque, etc. Quebec, 1843.
LW:HAR (Nov. 18, 1850); MS. MA595 (Nov., 1850–Dec., 1855); MS.MA598 (1851); "Yankee in Canada":V. 7, 38–39, 88, 89, 90–91, 95–96, 98 (Jan., 1853); CC:IV, 227–42 (June, 1855).

[Vries, David P. de.] *"Short Historical and Journal Notes of Several Voyages Made in the Four Parts of the World, Namely, Europe Africa, Asia, and America, by David Pieterzen de Vries . . . ,"* trans. Henry C. Murphy, *New York Historical Society Collections*, 2d ser., Part I, III (1857), 9–137.
MS.MA599 (1852); MS.MA605 (1858).

Waddington, George, and Barnard Hanbury. *Journal of a Visit to Some Parts of Ethiopia.* London, 1822.
LW:Har (Sept. 30, 1834).

Wafer, Lionel. *A New Voyage and Description of the Isthmus of America, Giving an Account of the Author's Abode There.* London, 1699.
LW:Har (Feb. 28, 1859); MS.173768B (Feb. 28, 1859); "Night and Moonlight":V, 325 (Feb. 28, 1859); MS.MA606 (1859).

Warburton, George D. [Cover erroneously ascribes authorship to Eliot Warburton.] *The Conquest of Canada.* 2 vols. New York, 1852.
"Yankee in Canada": V, 30 (Jan., 1853).

——Hochelaga; or England in the New World. 2 vols. in 1. New York, 1846. (Half-title: Library of Choice Reading, Vols. CXVII–CXVIII.)
MS.MA595 (Nov., 1850–Dec., 1855); MS.MA598 (1851).

West, John. *The Substance of a Journal during a Residence at the Red River Colony, British North America; and Frequent Excursions among the North-west American Indians, in the Years 1820–1823.* London, 1824.
LW:Har (Oct. 6, 1859); MS.MA606 (1859).

Wilkes, Charles. *Voyage round the World; Embracing the Principal Events of the Narration of the United States Exploring Expedition* [to South Pacific and Antarctic]. New York, 1851.
W:II, 352–55 (1845–54).

Wines, Enoch Cobb. *Two Years and a Half in the Navy: or, Journal of a Cruise in the Mediterranean and Levant, on Board of the U.S.

Frigate "Constellation," in the Years 1820, 1830, and 1831. 2 vols. Philadelphia, 1832.

Vol. I, LW:Har (Nov. 11, 1834).

Wolff, Rev. Joseph. *A Narrative of a Mission to Bokhara in the Years 1843–1845 to Ascertain the Fate of Col. Stoddard and Capt. Conolly*. New York, 1845.

Wk:I, 60, 131–32 (1845–49); MS.HM13182 (1850[?]).

Wrangel, Ferdinand Petrovich. *Narrative of an Expedition to the Polar Sea, in the Years 1820, 1821, 1822, and 1823. Commanded by Lieut., now Admiral Ferdinand Wrangel*. Ed. Major Edward Sabine. London, 1840; New York, 1841.

MW:III, 211 (1857); MS.Wid (1857); MS.MA604 (1857).

Index

THOREAU'S
MICROCOSM
AND
MACROCOSM